D0903972

At War with the Church

GEORG BERNHARD MICHELS 🐾

At War with *the Church*

Religious Dissent in Seventeenth-Century Russia

STANFORD UNIVERSITY PRESS

STANFORD, CALIFORNIA

1999

Stanford University Press
Stanford, California
© 1999 by the Board of Trustees of the
Leland Stanford Junior University

Printed in the United States of America
CIP data appear at the end of the book

COVER: The dust jacket illustration includes an excerpt from a
1683 investigation of schismatics conducted by Novgorod church
agents, juxtaposed with a modified version of an early eighteenth-
century engraving of the Novospasskii Monastery, one of the
citadels of Muscovite church power. The jacket illustration was
designed by Deborah Lefkowitz.

For Deborah

CONTENTS 🐚

TABLES

ACKNOWLEDGMENTS 🪶

Access to much of the source material used in this book was made possible by the support of the Deutsche Forschungsgemeinschaft of the Federal Republic of Germany, which enabled me to spend the academic year 1988–89 at the Academy of Sciences in Moscow, Leningrad, Novosibirsk, and Petrozavodsk of the former Soviet Union. The Mrs. Giles Whiting Foundation of New York and the Russian Research Center of Harvard University greatly assisted my work by providing fellowships during the academic years 1990–91 and 1991–92 respectively.

This study would not have been possible without the unremitting support of my teacher and adviser, Edward Keenan. I am very grateful for his helpful suggestions, criticisms, and insights during our many years of working together. I also wish to acknowledge the thoughtful comments of Steve Ozment, with whom I discussed my work on numerous occasions and shared ideas on parallels between the Russian Schism and the Reformation.

I have learned much from discussions on seventeenth-century religious culture with Nikolai Iurevich Bubnov, James Cracraft, Natalia Sergeevna Demkova, Natal'ia Sergeevna Gur'ianova, Peter Hauptmann, Frank Kämpfer, Aleksandr Il'ich Klibanov, Robert Nichols, Nikolai Nikolaevich Pokrovskii, Irina Vasilevna Pozdeeva, Vladimir Sergeevich Shul'gin, and George H. Williams.

Viktor Ivanovich Buganov, my *nauchnyi rukovoditel'* while I was in the Soviet Union, gave me the opportunity to present parts of my work to a critical audience of scholars at the Institute of History in Moscow. My friend and colleague, Andrei Ivanovich Pliguzov, has been a challenging and provocative critic of my ideas for the past ten years; his shared enthusiasm for early modern Russian church studies continues to be an inspiration.

Nancy Kollmann read the entire manuscript with critical attention and generously shared her insights. Dan Kaiser read portions of the manuscript and provided much encouragement. I am also indebted to Robert Crummey for his astute observations about my work as it has been presented in other forms, and for his continually thought-provoking questions.

I received helpful bibliographic references from Vladimir Nikolaevich Alekseev, Anna Arthur, Irina Aleksandrovna Cherniakova, Edward Kasinec, Hugh Olmsted, Vera Stepanovna Rumiantseva, and Tat'iana Vladimirovna Starostina.

I am extremely grateful to my friend and teacher, Dean S. Worth, of the University of California at Los Angeles. Without his early guidance and inspiration, my academic career in the United States would never have taken place.

My special thanks go to Madelyn and Irving Lefkowitz, for their moral support and encouragement, and to my wife, Deborah Lefkowitz, for her loving presence in my life during the past sixteen years and in particular, for sharing both the stresses and joys of writing this book.

G.B.M.

At War with the Church

The Orthodox Church and
the Russian Schism

This study probes the lives of religious dissenters in Russia during the second half of the seventeenth century, when the Russian Orthodox Church was confronted by widespread disobedience for the first time in its history. My purpose is to shed light on the behavior and thought that inspired this unprecedented outbreak of dissent. Most of the individuals whose lives this book illuminates were brutally oppressed and subsequently forgotten by later generations of dissenters as well as by historians. What were the sentiments and aspirations of these men and women who dared to oppose the church?

To a large extent, the method used here is to reconstruct what historians such as Carlo Ginzburg have called the "culture of the lower classes" or simply "popular culture." Like Ginzburg, I define popular culture in the ethnographic sense as a complex web of attitudes, beliefs, and forms of behavior found among the lower reaches of society.[1] I understand my work in analogy to anthropological fieldwork: I intend to learn about the intentions and aspirations of the "common man" without distorting viewpoints and intermediaries. The term common man signifies here anyone who was excluded from the power structure of the Muscovite social and political system: peasants, artisans, women, simple monks and priests, and the many men and women—both clerics and laymen—who roamed the roads of Russia as beggars, vagabonds, and brigands. In short, I intend to reconstruct submerged religious and social realities that for centuries have been passed over by most historians.[2]

I

It is not surprising that the Russian Orthodox Church became a significant target of popular hostility during the second half of the seventeenth century. The church was then one of the most vigorous institutions of Muscovite power under the new Romanov dynasty, for it had emerged from the Time of Troubles with its power base intact, while other Muscovite institutions had been weakened. Filaret, the father of the first Romanov tsar, became the leader of the church in 1619, and under his leadership the Orthodox Church developed into a powerful bureaucracy. By the 1630s numerous territories had been directly subordinated to the control of the Patriarch's Office, which began to compete for power with other government departments. Indeed, this period saw the beginning of efforts to expand ecclesiastical power into local areas, a process that would reach its culmination under Peter I. and Catherine II.[3]

Filaret's powerful successor, Patriarch Nikon of Muscovy and All Rus' (1652–58), initiated the crisis that is the focus of this study. Soon after becoming patriarch, Nikon undertook an ambitious reform project: under the influence of high-ranking clerics from Constantinople and the Greek diaspora he entrusted Jesuit-trained scholars from Ukraine and White Russia with a critical review of the forms of Russian worship.

By comparing Greek and Russian Church Slavonic liturgical manuscripts, these scholars quickly came to the conclusion that Russian liturgies and rituals had degenerated over the centuries from their original Greek source. Nikon's solution was simple: the purity of Russian religion was to be restored by conforming to the practices of the Greek Orthodox Church. By decree he altered the sign of the cross, the design of liturgical vestments, the wording of prayers, and most importantly, the contents of the liturgical books that regulated the details of church ceremonies.[4] Throughout the rest of the seventeenth century these changes provided the touchstone for numerous conflicts between Russian society and the church, leading to a split in religious practice commonly known as the Russian Schism or Raskol.

What was the nature of the seventeenth-century Russian Schism? What were the underlying causes of the divisions between church and society? What happened in Russian society during the five decades following the implementation of Nikon's reforms? Who were the opponents of the Nikonian changes, and why did they resist the changes? These are the questions on which my analysis of religious dissent in early modern Russia focuses.

I argue against the more or less firmly entrenched interpretation, according to which Nikon's interference with familiar forms of worship stirred protests by preachers and polemicists who became known as the defenders of the old Muscovite religion, or simply Old Believers.[5] According to this view, Old Believers expressed widely held societal discontent with the new Nikonian religion and quickly became the leaders of a broad popular movement against the church; the ensuing struggle between this movement and the church resulted in the Russian Schism.[6]

Historians have traditionally viewed the conflict between Old Belief and the Orthodox Church as occurring in three principal stages. During the initial stage, 1653–66, the movement was led by the "zealots-of-piety" (*revniteli blagochestiia*), a group of reformers who wanted to restore the purity of Muscovite piety and fought against corruption in the Russian church and popular religion. The "zealots" are sometimes compared to Western Protestant reformers and are assumed to have enjoyed a similar level of support in Russian society. The principal leaders of this early period were archpriests Avvakum and Neronov.[7]

The trial of the "zealots" by a church council in 1666 is generally considered as the beginning of the second phase of the Russian Schism. All members of the Old Believer movement were excommunicated and their most important leaders exiled beyond the Arctic Circle to the prison camp of Pustoozero on the Pechora River. These exiled men—foremost among them the enigmatic Avvakum—became known as the "Pustoozero prisoners" (*Pustoozerskie souzniki*). They wrote numerous treatises and letters that aggressively attacked the official church as schismatic.

Historians have maintained that these texts were widely disseminated during the next fifteen years (1667–82), further spreading the message of Old Belief. The texts were well received, it is claimed, because they were written in "democratic" language that formulated widely held grievances, and most importantly, they expressed popular opposition to the forces of change unleashed by Russian officialdom—secularization, modernization, and growing socioeconomic exploitation. In short, the religious language, logic, and political theology of the Pustoozero exiles are thought to have been the catalysts that brought existing popular grievances into the open.[8]

The third, and final, phase of the Old Believer movement, according to the traditional view, began after the execution of the "Pustoozero prisoners" in 1682, by which time Old Belief had gained support in virtually all the lower segments of Muscovite society. But with the martyrdom of its leadership and increased persecution, it is claimed that the movement also experienced a serious crisis, and a second generation of Old Believers began to develop its own interpretations of the writings inherited from the Pustoozero founding fathers.[9]

Not surprisingly, theological unity was quickly lost, and the Old Believer movement split into two principal camps during the 1690s: the Priestist and the Priestless camps. The former assumed that Avvakum and other founding fathers had condoned the role of priests; the latter not only rejected priests, describing them as agents of the Antichrist, but also called on believers to dispense with all sacraments except marriage. During the eighteenth century both Priestist and Priestless movements underwent further subdivisions. While greatly weakened by continuing struggles, Old Belief continued to exist well into the twentieth century. Indeed, the remnants of the movement are beginning to make a comeback today in post-Soviet Russia.[10]

What is common to the three phases traditionally distinguished by historians is the dominant role attributed to a handful of Old Belief leaders. Opposition to Nikon's reforms was largely seen through the prism of texts written by these Old Believers. In other words, the theological or ideological teachings (depending on one's viewpoint) contained in Old Believer texts were held responsible for the outbreak of the Russian Schism.

However, scholars have not distinguished between Old Believers and other little-known dissenters who had no relations or contacts with Old Believers, but who also rejected Nikon's liturgical reforms. Indeed, we must ask whether Old Believer texts can be seen as reliable windows into the minds of ordinary Russian dissenters, who were for the most part illiterate.

My central argument is that much about the Russian Schism has remained a riddle precisely because historians have drawn primarily on the narrative texts, polemic writings, letters, and panegyric *Vitae* of the Old Believers. In fact, the leaders of this movement were quite atypical dissenters. Not only had they all once enjoyed powerful positions within the church, but the ideas they developed to reject Nikon's reforms were almost all based in written culture. For example, polemics comparing Nikon to the Roman pope and calling him the Antichrist had their roots in anti-Catholic treatises that circulated widely in the Russian church. Calculations about the coming end of times were largely derived from apocalyptic manuscripts compiled in Ukraine at the end of the sixteenth century, when the Catholic Church attempted to annex the Orthodox Church. The detailed critique of Nikon's liturgical changes in Old Believer manuscripts demonstrates familiarity not only with Russia's principal monastic libraries, but also with written traditions of other Orthodox cultures such as Serbian and Ukrainian.[11]

The archival documents reflecting the actual impact of Nikon's liturgical reforms on seventeenth-century Russian society have not yet been assessed by a focused study. Only the tip of the iceberg is known, and from the surface, submerged areas appear to be of the same quality as visible areas. But what did the men and women who did not identify themselves as Old Believers, or who left nothing in writing, have to say about the church? What were their motives for rejecting Nikon's liturgical reforms? Were their attitudes similar to those expressed in the Old Believer texts traditionally studied by historians? Indeed, were they as deeply concerned about Nikon's reforms as the Old Belief writers? How frequent were conflicts over the new liturgies, and how did such conflicts relate to non-liturgical conflicts between the church and society? By focusing on such questions, this study seeks to probe more deeply into the social realities of the Russian Schism.

It is helpful to draw an analogy to studies of Western religious history: in the past, historians paid attention only to the main protagonists of religious movements, but during the last two decades scholars such as Ginzburg and Le Roy Ladurie have called attention to the social ambiance of dissent. No longer are we limited to heresiarchs such as Waldes, Wiclif, and Hus, who were subjected to official polemics, extraordinary investigations, and show trials; now we also can read about ordinary men and women, such as the miller Menocchio of Friuli or the Albigensian peasants of the remote Pyraenean village of Montaillou.[12]

My study, influenced by scholars of the French Annales School, explores the popular dimensions of religious dissent, although it is not exclusively concerned with popular culture.[13] Among the dissenters were former members of the Muscovite power structure, including archimandrites, archpriests, merchants, discharged officials, and exiled boyars—troublemakers who, through their personal ambitions, rejected the accepted code of elite behavior. These Muscovite renegades will be studied along with the common man.

In short, I seek to include information about *all* Russians—from peasant to boyar, from simple monk to hierarch—who renounced loyalty to the accepted religious culture of their society. Does their fate help us to understand the historical processes that led to the emergence of the modern Russian state church? If the acts of non-conformity that these fearless men and women committed had been successful, would the Russian church have developed differently? In fact, the Russian Orthodox Church was one of the great victors of the seventeenth century, and served as a pillar of the imperial regime until the February Revolution of 1917. But, as will become clear in this study, a high price was paid for this ascendancy of the church: the destruction of an unknown number of dissenters.[14]

The story told here is one of violence and oppression. The confrontations between church and dissenters followed a pattern: at the beginning, an act of defiance or disobedience attracted attention in Moscow; at the end, military detachments descended on local communities and hunted down the suspects. Even if one lived in impenetrable forests or swamps or, as in the case of the Solovki monks, on a remote windswept island in the White Sea, one was not safe. Denunciations always reached Moscow and no matter how heroic the resistance, leaders of local revolts were executed or exiled to the far north and Siberia. Rank-and-file rebels became fugitives and roamed the roads of Russia, desperately searching for food and means of sustenance. The seventeenth century is filled with dramatic stories of resistance, persecution, and defeat.

PRIMARY SOURCES

This book departs from the traditional research focus on Old Believer writings found in the manuscript divisions of Russian libraries, museums, and institutes. Instead, my focus is on the little-known archives of seventeenth-century bishoprics, monasteries, and central church and state offices (*prikazy*) that investigated manifestations of religious dissent. The interrogations, protocols, reports, notes (*otpiski*), memoranda (*pamiati*), and other records produced by these institutions allow us to resurrect the voices of the vast majority of Russian dissenters.

The neglect of this documentary evidence by traditional interpreters of seventeenth-century religious dissent is somewhat surprising, considering that the archives were explored before the October Revolution. Documentary sources about the Russian Schism have been published by scholars such as E. V. Barsov, N. I. Subbotin, V. G. Druzhinin, and I. I. Rumiantsev.[15] In addition, published documents can be found in rare nineteenth-century journals and monographs edited by obscure local archival and church societies.[16] During the 1920s and 1930s the Soviet scholar V. K. Nikol'skii and his French colleague P. Pascal obtained new information from the Siberian Office (*Sibirskii prikaz*) about Archpriest Avvakum.[17] Recently, V. S. Rumiantseva delved into the archives of several Muscovite agencies such as the tsar's Secret Chancellery and edited two collections of documents, most of which previously had been identified—and partially published—by the nineteenth-century scholar Ia. L. Barskov.[18]

This study draws on substantial new information from records that have never before been studied. For example, I use here, for the first time, documents from the diocesan archives that have been stacked away and virtually forgotten since the seventeenth century.[19] Among these archives are the repositories of the bishoprics of Vologda, Riazan', Kholmogory, Novgorod, and Viatka.[20]

The best maintained and most comprehensive of these is the repository of the northern Vologda archbishopric, which has been described and inventoried by the nineteenth-century local historians (*kraevedy*) P. I. Savva-itov and N. I. Suvorov.[21] The archive of the Solovki Monastery, with widely scattered holdings in St. Petersburg, Moscow, and Petrozavodsk, is another important and almost untapped resource on seventeenth-century religious history.[22] Most important, however, is the information gathered by central agencies. Documents from the Patriarch's Office, the tsar's Secret Chancellery, the Service Chancellery, the Foreign Office, the Novgorod Office, and other similar institutions—most of them located in the Russian State Archive of Ancient Acts (RGADA) in Moscow—provide the backbone of this study.[23]

The historian who delves into this paperwork is immediately confronted by an unexpected difficulty: documents attesting to the occurrence of liturgical dissent in Russian society are submerged among a huge number of diverse documents that, furthermore, are dispersed among many repositories. The scholar E. V. Barsov, for example, had to sift through thousands of archival items in the repositories of the imperial ministries of Justice and Foreign Affairs before he found the documents on liturgical dissent that he was seeking. He compiled a collection of ten seventeenth-century cases, which he organized into a new archival fond called "schismatic affairs."[24] Similarly, the documents pertaining to liturgical dissent used in this work represent only a small fraction of the enormous bureaucratic record that was searched.

In contrast to the relative ease with which rhetorical texts can be accessed, great patience is required to locate archival documents because of a complicated process used to transmit historical data: diverse investigating agencies deposited their information in different places. Adding to the difficulties, the abolition of seventeenth-century institutions by Peter I. led to the further dispersal of archives. The problem applies particularly to church institutions because Peter I. transformed the church into a state agency.

The fate of the Patriarch's Office, one of the principal investigating agencies, illustrates this problem. A Petrine decree (*ukaz*) issued in December 1700, two months after the death of Patriarch Adrian, declared the Patriarch's Office defunct and specified that from then on "heresy and Raskol matters" were to be conducted in person by Adrian's successor, Stefan Iavorskii.[25] Soon afterwards, the archival holdings of the Patriarch's Office were distributed to other offices.[26] Almost no information about the seventeenth century made its way into the archive of the Holy Synod, which became the successor of the Patriarch's Office.[27] But I have located such data in the archive of the Armory and other fonds of the Russian State Archive of Ancient Acts.

The work of the historian of the seventeenth-century Russian Schism is akin to that of an archeologist who has to excavate material from a nearly obliterated past. By contrast, the scholar venturing into the history of Petrine and post-Petrine religious dissent can draw on the well organized archives of just a few investigating institutions.[28] Notable also is the remarkable quantity of archival documents available to historians of the two great Western schisms.[29]

Several observations are necessary about the nature of the historical information used in this study. Most important, the records kept by Muscovite agencies are not as complete as the voluminous records kept, for instance, by the Roman Inquisition.[30] Although Muscovite investigations produced quite a bit of paperwork, much of the information focuses on legal procedures and instructions—as opposed to the mindset of Russian dissenters—and appears deceptively extensive due to the numerous repetitions in memoranda, notes, instructions (*nakazy*), and other similar documents.

In spite of itself, the bureaucracy procured useful information because individual cases were usually investigated by several agencies, each contributing different kinds of data. This allows us to reconstruct a larger composite picture. For example, the dissenter Sila, a tailor from Rostov, was initially under scrutiny by the metropolitan of Rostov. For several months episcopal officials searched the town of Rostov for Sila's supporters and interrogated them. At some point during the investigation emissaries of both the patriarch and the tsar got involved; they asked their own questions, and letters were exchanged between various Kremlin offices and Rostov. Finally, Sila was taken to Moscow, where he was investigated by agencies that specialized in diverse offenses including crime (*vorovstvo*) and lèse-majesté (*slovo i delo*). Torture was applied to compel Sila to verify aspects of his previous testimony.

This rather lengthy process of examination was by no means exceptional. It was even more elaborate in cases such as the revolt of the Solovki monks, where at least three local and seven central agencies claimed authority. Clearly, the involvement of competing institutions that studied cases from different angles not only increased the amount of relevant historical data, but also enhanced its reliability.[31]

This inquisitorial method also led to another peculiarity that distinguished Russian heresy investigations from those in the West: there were no systematic efforts to edit the protocols of interrogations. In Western heresy trials, documents were often written in three stages. First, a scribe took notes at the hearing. Then, from this draft the same scribe (or another one) would compile minutes. Finally, several scribes would copy these minutes onto parchment. Completion of this final version could take more than a year, after which the confessions would be deposited in the inquisitional archive.[32] In Russian heresy trials, the process was much shorter: investigators sent notes and reports to the Kremlin immediately after the interrogation of suspects, apparently because the tsar and the patriarch wanted to root out disobedience as soon as possible.

This rather hasty operation had an interesting effect. Untrained in Western methods of religious investigation, and unfamiliar with inquisitorial handbooks, the Russian officials did not develop any standard procedures for heresy investigations.[33] They were much less inclined to ask leading questions than their Western counterparts. They certainly did not make any systematic efforts to adjust deviant belief and behavior to well-known heretical ideas, or make the confessions of their victims conform to their own expectations.[34] Thus, the information culled from Russian documents, far from merely reflecting the biases of the investigators, provides considerable insight into the motives for dissent.

The only distortion that has to be taken into account in this study is that investigators often paid extraordinary attention to what they considered the central act of disobedience: failure to assimilate the new liturgies introduced by Patriarch Nikon. Adherence to the new liturgies was a convenient and unambiguous litmus test for measuring loyalty and obedience. Failure to accept the new liturgies was considered sufficient evidence for expulsion from the church and execution. As a result, it is sometimes difficult to piece together the fragments of reality that reflect the motives of individual dissenters. Yet, the investigators inadvertently recorded many facets of belief that were important to those interrogated. I have studied these matters for insight into possible motives for dissent.

HISTORIOGRAPHY

Ever since Russians discovered their history in the early eighteenth century, the Russian Schism has engaged the minds of Russia's leading intellectuals and scholars.[35] It has become one of the most popular topics of Russian historiography, resulting in a large number of essays and monographs.[36] This monograph could not have been written without the groundbreaking contributions of several generations of scholars. It is not the quality of research, but rather the grandiose interpretive schemes derived from a fairly limited focus on Old Believer texts that this study seeks to address.

For example, nineteenth-century church historians such as N. F. Kapterev and P. S. Smirnov contributed crucially to our knowledge of both the liturgical reforms and the ideology of seventeenth-century Old Believers. Indeed, Kapterev's work remains unsurpassed as a reference work for the patriarchate of Nikon, and Smirnov's substantial monograph is, to this day, the unmatched bibliography for lesser-known Old Believer texts. However, without probing into the societal attitudes of the times, both scholars saw the personal concerns of a few Old Believers as characterizing widely held popular sentiments. The apocalyptic agony of Archpriest Avvakum's letters and petitions, the anti-Western sentiments of Abbot Spiridon's manuscript book, or the polemic attacks on the most minute liturgical changes by the priests Lazar' and Nikita Dobrynin were seen to correspond to general societal moods. In their view, the Russian Schism was a massive refusal of the ignorant and xenophobic Russian nation to accept modernity. Clinging stubbornly to what they perceived as the "holy ancient heritage" (*sviataia starina*) of Old Muscovy, seventeenth-century Russians were thought to be highly susceptible to the ideas of Old Believer writings.[37]

This biography-centered approach also characterized the work of nineteenth-century populist historians who, unlike church historians, had great sympathy for the Old Believers. The earliest populist study, written by A. P. Shchapov during the 1850s, relied heavily on Old Belief manuscript miscellanies from the library of the Solovki Monastery and the hagiographic biographies of a few seventeenth-century figures written by the early eighteenth-century Old Belief intellectual Semen Denisov. Shchapov agreed with the church historians that the "masses" were ignorant and that their understanding of religion was limited to a primitive ritualism. However, he maintained that the leaders of the revolt against Nikon's reforms—that is, men like Avvakum and other Old Believers—had a "completely spiritual and democratic approach" (*chisto-dukhovno-demokraticheskoe nachalo*). Indeed, he thought their preaching and writing fulfilled a very progressive function: it encouraged the "popular masses" (*massy naroda*) to rebel against the existing institutional order.[38]

Shchapov established several important historical contexts that help to elucidate the genesis of seventeenth-century popular dissent. For example, he described the underdevelopment of local church institutions and the existence of local anti-church traditions. He was also the first to point to the merger of Christian and pre-Christian forms of belief in certain manifestations of Russian dissent. At the same time, however, he postulated that there was not much difference between popular superstition (*sueverie*) and Old Belief thinking. In fact, he saw Old Believers as the literate mouthpieces of the simple folk. However, Shchapov's observations are based on very limited sources. Without access to seventeenth-century archives, he relied on historical information from the eighteenth century in addition to Old Believer texts. Indeed, he assumed that seventeenth- and eighteenth-century Russian dissent were basically indistinguishable.[39]

Shchapov popularized his views about the Old Believers as mobilizers of the "masses" in a number of journalistic essays and monographs, but again he drew on very little documentary evidence.[40] Other populists followed in his footsteps. Widely read works by authors such as V. V. Andreev and I. I. Kablits were journalistic masterpieces, but not based on solid archival explorations.[41]

The broad interpretive models of the nineteenth century have held enormous sway over twentieth-century thinking. Scholars still focus on Old Believer texts and tend to view the Russian Schism as a major historical conflict over fundamental questions of Muscovite identity, involving large sections of Russian society under the leadership of a few Old Believers. The American historian F. Conybeare asserted that the schism was the logical result of the "exclusive nationalism" and "intellectual anemia" of the Russian "masses," which for centuries had refused to accept any form of innovation.[42] Similarly, Sergei Zenkovsky, whose study presents a valuable synopsis of a vast array of Old Believer writings, pointed out that Old Believer sentiments were reflections of deeply rooted and centuries-old popular convictions about Russian Orthodox purity and religious superiority. In particular, he asserted that Nikon's reforms had a disastrous psychological effect on Russian society because they seemed to confirm eschatological fears and resentments of non-Orthodox foreigners.[43]

M. Cherniavsky maintained that "the founding fathers of the Raskol," in fighting against Nikon's random "condemnation of the Russian historical past" and in trying to preserve Russia's sacred mission as the Third Rome, spread their message "rapidly over large parts of the Russian state." His evidence was drawn almost exclusively from Old Believer writings about the tsar, legends about Patriarch Nikon, and apocalyptic treatises.[44] The influential survey written by James Billington also relied on important Old Believer texts and maintained that "changes in church practices led directly to the 'eschatological psychosis' of the mid-seventeenth century," and that "in the popular imagination . . . history was at or near its end."[45] Other similar views could be cited.[46]

Although most Western scholars have tended toward broad assertions about the significance of Old Belief during the seventeenth century, a few have provided both data and hypotheses suggesting a more differentiated assessment. The best example is the masterful study of Archpriest Avvakum by French historian P. Pascal. Pascal presents an original interpretive scheme, according to which Avvakum is viewed as the principal Old Believer, as well as the head of a new alternative church that stood for genuine religious sentiment and spirituality. Avvakum's church was viewed as engaged in constant struggle with Nikon's church, which used religion only as a means to bolster political and administrative power. To Pascal, the Old Believers under Avvakum were "the more serious Christians." Similar to the Jansenists in France, Old Believers were thought to be highly successful in their missionary activities because they translated the Christian message from the bookish language of Church Slavonic into the Russian vernacular. Pascal concludes that the schism was a profound spiritual rift that never healed because it permanently deprived the church of its best religious elements.[47]

There can be no doubt that Pascal wrote this study with great enthusiasm for his subject, and this may have led him to attribute too much importance to Avvakum. Still, Pascal's study remains unsurpassed in at least two respects. First, almost no other monograph, (with perhaps the exception of V. S. Rumiantseva's recent book discussed below), has utilized so much historical information about lesser-known dissenters. For example, Pascal's observations about local outbreaks of the schism—say in Karelia or the Pomor'e district—should be standard reading for those who assume the Old Believer movement extended into remote provinces. According to Pascal, local leaders such as monks who had escaped from the rebellious Solovki Monastery, acted on their own; they had their own followings and became founders of communities that had no contact with Avvakum and his circle.

Second, Pascal drew on substantial new archival information about well-known Old Believers. He meticulously reconstructed Avvakum's activities during his exile in Siberia, even including information that appears to contradict his own principal finding. Clearly, the Siberian files Pascal consulted demonstrate that Avvakum had not yet broken with the church during the 1650s, and that he willingly acted as the executor of official policies in the cathedral church of the archbishopric of Tobol'sk. Thus, Pascal's work is a gold mine for scholars studying seventeenth-century dissent.[48]

Two other Western scholars also have presented careful and differentiated assessments of the relations between Old Belief and Muscovite society. P. Hauptmann's remarkable study of Avvakum points to contradictions in the archpriest's behavior that made it unlikely that he became a popular hero before his excommunication in 1667. For example, Hauptmann demonstrates that Avvakum obtained money from the tsar and other high-ranking officials and aspired to be employed by the Kremlin. Only when refused such privileges did Avvakum turn fully against the official church.[49]

Particularly noteworthy are recent essays by Robert Crummey. He has distanced himself from what he calls "a broad definition of Old Belief," making a number of important distinctions between the terms "Old Belief" and "Raskol." According to Crummey, Old Belief comprises "the groups of Eastern Orthodox Christians who have defined and identified themselves by their rejection of certain liturgical practices . . . such as the three-finger sign of the cross"; Raskol, by contrast, "encompasses all who reject[ed] their historical allegiance to the official Russian Orthodox Church."[50]

But at the same time, Crummey argues that "Old Believer culture was varied and complex," and includes both literary and popular manifestations of dissent under the same rubric.[51] For example, he analyzes the highly learned works of Avvakum's student, the monk Avraamii, as one cultural system within Old Belief.[52] At the other end of the spectrum, he describes illiterate peasant sectarians as "the most radical elements within the [Old Belief] coalition of opposition to church and state."[53]

I agree with Crummey that it is important to differentiate between Raskol and Old Belief. My definition of Raskol is based on the term *raskol* as it appears in church polemics, and includes only those dissenters who rejected the liturgical reforms of Patriarch Nikon but failed to identify themselves as Old Believers. Crummey does not study opposition to Nikon's reforms from the perspective of ordinary Russians, and my approach differs in this respect. I question whether illiterate peasants and other non-elite Muscovites indeed knew about the Old Believers. Had they ever met men such as the monk Avraamii, listened to his preaching, or read any portion of his work? Or were there reasons for rejecting Nikon's reforms that had nothing to do with Old Belief teachings?

Crummey points out that the first generation of Old Believers created "a canon of sacred texts" which "formed the cultural backbone of the movement." These texts were accessible to men and women "of various social backgrounds" and influenced popular culture by "osmosis." Thus, Crummey appears to follow Zenkovsky and Cherniavsky by postulating a significant influence of Old Belief high culture or book culture on ordinary

Russians. Certainly, he expresses the dominant view of the Russian Schism by stating that all manifestations of protest against the official liturgies shared Old Belief's "devotion of pre-Nikonian Orthodoxy" as "the only authentic expression of the Christian faith left in the world."[54] In short, Crummey's valuable observations about the complexity of seventeenth-century dissent apply primarily to the ideas and beliefs formulated in Old Believer texts.

The focus of much Soviet and post-Soviet Russian scholarship also has been on the analysis of Old Believer texts. The works of V. I. Malyshev, N. S. Demkova, N. Iu. Bubnov, and I. V. Pozdeeva, to name some of the most prominent scholars, have contributed significantly to our knowledge of the transmission of seventeenth-century Old Believer texts and indeed support Crummey's finding that early Old Belief was by no means a monolithic movement. However, the studies of these eminent philologists shed little light on the social realities of the Russian Schism.[55]

In another manifestation of the tendency among Soviet scholars to draw broad conclusions about dissent and society on the basis of Old Believer texts, A. N. Robinson assumed that the names of the leading Old Believer writers "had become commonly known" to ordinary Russians and that their texts provided the ideology for mobilizing the disenfranchised and oppressed against the exploitative social order. A. S. Eleonskaia also emphasized the agitational character of Old Believer writings. The "enormous popularity" (*ogromnaia populiarnost'*) of the Old Believers was attributed to their use of the vernacular and their remarkable ability to articulate commonly held grievances. For example, comparisons of the tsar and the patriarch to the Antichrist generated anger with the existing secular and ecclesiastical order.[56] Other similar examples could be cited.[57]

It appears that these and other Russian scholars were strongly influenced by their nineteenth-century populist predecessors, whose views were assimilated early in the Soviet period by scholars such as S. P. Mel'gunov.[58] The standard Soviet work by V. G. Kartsov, which was published in 1971 as a special textbook for students and historians, codified Melgunov's interpretation that Old Believers such as Avvakum assumed leadership of a broad movement of protest against the prevailing socioeconomic order. In particular, Kartsov defended the thesis that there were intricate connections between Old Belief and mass rebellions such as the Peasant War under Stepan Razin.[59]

The best Soviet studies on religious dissent are those devoted to specific geographic regions.[60] Towering above all other works is the monograph by N. N. Pokrovskii on Old Belief (*staroobriadchestvo*) in eighteenth-century Siberia. Even though Pokrovskii paid little attention to seventeenth-century developments, his study set an important precedent that might well be applied to the earlier period. Most importantly, he attempted to capture the "genuine voice" (*podlinnyi golos*) of Siberian peasants by reconstructing information about obscure individuals from church and state archives. Pokrovskii noticed the "colorfulness" (*pestrota*) and "multi-facetedness of the Raskol" (*mnogolikost' raskola*), and emphasized the social and ideological distances separating well-established Old Belief communities in the Urals from simple peasant households and hermitages in the vast hinterlands of Siberia.[61]

In its scope and erudition, Pokrovskii's work recalls Druzhinin's nineteenth-century masterpiece on the schism and the Don Cossacks.[62] Both works de-emphasize the leadership role of Old Believers such as Avvakum, and both have greatly influenced my study.

The remarkable studies of L. E. Ankudinova and V. S. Rumiantseva must also be mentioned. These studies of seventeenth-century dissent were based on documentary evidence such as government reports and investigations.[63] Although both scholars attribute crucial leadership roles to figures such as Avvakum and claim Old Believer texts provided the ideology for a mass movement, their data do not support these conclusions. For example, the obscure peasant monks and artisans studied by Rumiantseva certainly never heard of Avvakum or read Old Believer texts. Rumiantseva also shows that local preachers and lay prophets acted on their own initiatives. In similar fashion, Ankudinova documents that certain artisans and merchants made their own decisions in refusing to accept the new sign of the cross. Her a priori claim that these "town dwellers" (*zhiteli posada*) were active followers of Avvakum is not supported by any evidence. Nevertheless, both scholars assembled new documentation that suggests the complex and multi-faceted origins of protests against Nikon's reforms.[64]

While it appears that Russian historians are now distancing themselves from the interpretation of Old Believers as anti-feudal ideologists, the tendency to attribute pivotal historical roles to a handful of Old Believers is still widespread. Viktor Zhivov, for example, observes that texts written by Avvakum and his friends represented "the voice of the seventeenth century" and that "the entire great stream of Russian history relates to the problems [they] raised."[65] An essay by another Russian historian asserts that Avvakum fought desperately during this "time of national catastrophe" to "stop Ancient Rus' from fading away into eternity." Since the archpriest wrote in simple Russian, his ideas were said to be commonly accessible to the common folk (*prostetsy*). Or as one famous scholar, A. I. Klibanov, put it recently, "[Avvakum] was a new phenomenon in the history of popular spiritual culture (*narodnaia dukhovnaia kultura*)." Thus, Russian historians continue to claim that the seventeenth century experienced a deep struggle—if not social, then spiritual—over Russia's future, and the Old Believers were at the center of this controversy.[66]

I strongly disagree with historians who have approached seventeenth-century dissent as one "great movement" called Old Belief.[67] Inspired by the studies of scholars such as P. Pascal and N. N. Pokrovskii, I have found the historical evidence about Old Belief and dissent to be fragmentary and contradictory, hardly allowing any broad generalizations. I view the Russian Schism as a series of specific conflicts resulting from particular historical conditions and contexts. I show through careful analysis of the documentary evidence that the sum total of these conflicts does not amount to a great movement comparable in scope to the Reformation or the Great Western Schism of the fourteenth century. Moreover, my analysis calls into question whether the causes of the conflicts studied here can be considered truly great.

TERMINOLOGY

Considerable difficulties of definition and terminology arise when addressing the issue of what to call the religious dissenters of the seventeenth century. Unlike many Western heretics, the vast majority of these dissenters did not have a name for themselves.[68] Only a small minority of Russians identified themselves as defenders of the "old belief" (*staraia vera*) or "old Orthodoxy" (*staroe pravoslavie*), or as "seekers of the old [religion]" (*staroliubtsy*) or adherents of "old piety" (*staroe blagochestie*). They include well-known writers such as Archpriest Avvakum and deacon Fedor Ivanov, and they have justifiably been categorized as Old Believers (*starovertsy*)—even though this particular designation gained wide currency only during the eighteenth century.[69] By contrast, the vast majority of other dissenters never applied these or similar labels to themselves. In fact, most dissenters were illiterate and probably did not understand the connotations of the term Old Belief, since the concept had developed in the written culture.

This book will distinguish therefore between Old Belief and other forms of dissent. The term Old Belief is meant here in the strictest sense, that is, describing only men and women who identified themselves as Old Believers. These Old Believers had in common that they openly professed a special mission to reestablish the old religious order in Muscovy.

In this sense, the Old Believers of the seventeenth century were not different from their epigones of the eighteenth century. As Zenkovsky put it, the eighteenth-century Old Believers were "missionaries" who tried to diffuse "the ancient Russian beliefs and traditions" in their writings as well as in their preaching.[70] Seventeenth-century Old Believers envisioned a similar reconquest of Russia for the old rites. The principal heroes of early Old Belief saw themselves as the founders of a new church called "the Church of God" (*tserkov' Bozhiia*) or "Church of Christ" (*tserkov' Khristova*), which they hoped would compete with the official church. Members of this new church became known as the "elect" (*izbrannye*), "true brethren" (*vernye brat'ia*), "Children of Zion" (*sionskie chady*), or simply "the Christians" (*khristiane*).[71] One also finds the self-designations "zealots" (*revniteli*) or "zealots-of-piety" (*revniteli blagochestiia*); these are terms that the influential historian Kapterev singled out to describe the collective identity of early Old Belief.[72]

Again, similar to their eighteenth century epigones, seventeenth-century Old Believers were determined to build new congregations of Christians entirely based on "the holy Orthodox dogma, the laws of the church, the traditions of many generations, and the order and rules of Christianity." Or as Sergei Zenkovsky put it, Old Belief sought "the spiritual union of the Russian people with Christ."[73] Indeed, Old Belief might be called a "spiritual church" (*ecclesia spiritualis*) that tried to rejuvenate and purify the ancient spiritual and monastic traditions of the Russian Orthodox past.[74]

Let me add one important caveat: a potential source of confusion in using Old Belief as a designation for this seventeenth-century "spiritual church" is that early Old Believers themselves apparently never used the term to define their community. Russian designations for Old Belief appear not to have been introduced into Old Believer texts until the 1720s. Only then did Old Believers begin to define their movement with a common designation. The preferred Russian terms became *staroobriadchestvo* or *staroobriadstvo*. However, *staroverie*, *staroverstvo*, and *staroverchestvo* are frequently found as well. Old Believers used these newly created terms to describe a well-organized church or an alternative system of religious doctrines. For example, Pavel Liubopytnyi, an eminent *staroverchestvo* writer of the first half of the nineteenth century, considered himself and his co-religionists "joint members of the Old Belief Church" (*so-chleny starovercheskoi tserkvi*). Similarly, Mikhail Karlovich, a Moscow Old Believer who wrote a book about the *staroobriadtsy*, spoke of a struggle between "two orthodoxies hostile to each other." This means that during later centuries the Russian variants of the term Old Belief were well defined.[75]

During the seventeenth century, Old Belief did not yet have the connotations found in the works of later writers such as Liubopytnyi or Karlovich. No Old Believer thinker had yet defined the term, and no theological treatise had yet been written about it.[76] In this book, Old Belief stands for a much less-developed and less-organized community, both theologically and socially. It can hardly be seen as an umbrella term that gave geographically separated communities a common definition as one church. Only a common group of teachers and a body of canonical texts gave Old Belief a distinctive identity during the seventeenth century.

Opponents of the Nikonian reforms, who did not define themselves as Old Believers or did not profess allegiance to Old Belief texts or teachers, will be described here with neutral terms such as "dissenters" or "dissidents." Because all of their activities were principally investigated as transgressions against Nikon's new liturgical order, I also speak of "liturgical dissenters." In order to capture the language of exclusion used by the Russian church and state, I sometimes have left official labels intact: to investigators, all opponents of Nikon's liturgical reforms eventually became known as "schismatics" (*raskol'niki*). Even though official texts also applied the term schismatic to Old Believers, I have decided to limit its use to opponents of Nikon's reforms who were not visibly influenced by Old Believer teaching and preaching.

STRUCTURE

The first half of this book critically examines the formative period of the Russian Schism (1652–66). The purpose is to distinguish between the foundation of Old Belief by legendary figures such as Avvakum, and the emergence of unrelated phenomena of liturgical dissent.

Chapter One focuses on the patriarchate of Nikon (1652–58) and the immediate societal impact of his liturgical reforms. I examine the assumption contained in Old Believer texts that Nikon was the most important instigator of the Russian Schism, and that his reforms immediately provoked shock and outrage among ordinary Russians. In doing so, I present new information about the first protests against Nikon's revisions, as well as a detailed assessment of their social significance.

Chapter Two is devoted to manifestations of dissent during the "interpatriarchal period" (*mezhpatriarshe vremia*), that is, the period between Patriarch Nikon's abdication in 1658 and the arrests and trial of the principal Old Believers in 1666. My intention again is to elucidate prevailing societal attitudes toward the liturgical reforms, but the principal focus is on the emergence of what might be called the first Old Belief community. I discuss the composition of this community and the stories of its principal leaders, as well as some of the texts and ideas generated by its members. In particular, I examine the first library of Old Believer texts assembled by Bishop Aleksandr of Viatka. This library provided blueprints for the production and dissemination of most later Old Believer texts.

Chapter Three shows that the polemic language of the seventeenth-century church strongly contributed to the frequent identification of Old Believers as the main perpetrators of the Russian Schism. Perceived as the organizers of a dangerous conspiracy against the Muscovite church called *raskol* ("schism"), they were officially demonized. The idea that a schism had been created by a handful of Old Believers held remarkable sway over the Russian church elite. In particular, the term schism was applied indiscriminately to diverse manifestations of religious nonconformity, and this led to a confusion in church texts of Old Believers with other dissenters. Once the term schism is understood as a broad mental category that provided churchmen with a simple description of Russian dissent, it can be seen how Old Belief and diverse other phenomena of dissent could be classified in a misleadingly uniform way.

The second half of this book attempts to reconstruct the little-known world of dissent that existed independently of what I have defined here as Old Belief. I de-emphasize the study of Old Believer communities and texts and instead, concentrate on the largely submerged lives of ordinary dissenters during the remainder of the seventeenth century (1666–1700).

Chapter Four establishes the thesis that monastic environments produced a large proportion of the so-called schism cases (*raskol'nye dela*) recorded in seventeenth-century archives. Clearly, liturgical dissent had more adherents among nuns and monks than among any other social group. To understand this phenomenon, I explore the behavior of these clerics within the larger context of seventeenth-century monasticism. Why were monks and nuns prone to dissident behavior? Answers are sought in new church policies that disrupted the traditional patterns of monastic life.

Chapter Five examines the role of priests in spreading opposition to the liturgical reforms among seventeenth-century Muscovites. Why did priests become dissenters, and to what degree did they have a mobilizing influence on their parishioners? To address these questions, I look at the changing relationship between church authority and priests, and how the liturgical reforms interfered with this relationship. I first reconstruct church efforts to reeducate the parish clergy in the new liturgical books, and then assess the success of these efforts. This is the best way to gauge the actual role played by priests in the social dissemination of dissent.

Chapter Six explores the behavior and religious attitudes of lay dissenters. Who were they and why would they choose to confront church authority? In my analysis I look critically at the assertion of Soviet scholarship that peasants mobilized by Old Belief propaganda rose in revolt against both church and state. Were peasants really an audience for Old Believer teachings? Were they involved in such large numbers that entire regions of Muscovy rejected the new liturgical order? Also, did craftsmen and merchants oppose Nikon's reforms because, as Soviet historians have argued, Old Believer preaching unleashed growing anti-feudal sentiments in urban milieux? Or were they motivated by purely religious considerations of their own? Such questions guide this analysis of the social significance of religious dissent in rural and urban environments.

The findings of this study contrast with much of the historiography of seventeenth-century religious dissent: my conclusion is that the Russian Schism did not result from Old Belief preaching and writing. While Old Believers played significant roles, the schism emerged largely from disparate conflicts that pitted local communities and ordinary Russians against official church authority. These conflicts were almost always unrelated to Old Belief and can be understood only by looking at the religious and social dynamics of the milieux in which they occurred. By investigating the factors that contributed to specific manifestations of seventeenth-century dissent, I seek to replace a homogeneous picture with a mosaic reflecting individual social realities and nuances.

CHAPTER ONE 🙰

Patriarch Nikon and the Emergence of Dissent, 1652-58

On July 25, 1652, Nikon, the powerful and ambitious metropolitan of Novgorod, was enthroned as the new patriarch of Russia in the Uspenskii Cathedral in the Kremlin. The ceremony was attended by the tsar and all the leading personalities of the Muscovite state and society. They expected Nikon's rule to introduce a period of harmony between the Russian Orthodox Church and rank-and-file believers. Indeed, Nikon had just enjoyed two major successes that seemed to guarantee stability and popularity: in April, he had initiated the return of the relics of Iov, the first patriarch of Russia (1589–1605), from the small town of Staritsa to the Kremlin; and in early July, he had entered the capital triumphantly at the head of a procession that carried the bones of Metropolitan Filipp, a prestigious church leader of the sixteenth century.[1]

Soon after his ascension to the patriarchal throne, Nikon embarked on a reform project that had been contemplated by his predecessors, but never realized: the revision of Russia's ancient liturgies to bring them into agreement with the practices of the rest of the Eastern Orthodox world. It is widely believed that the printing and dissemination of revised liturgical books aroused apocalyptic fear among Muscovites and led to significant outbreaks of hostility against the church. This standard view, which is based on the study of Old Believer texts, also holds that this revolt spread quickly and, during the few short years of Nikon's patriarchate (1652–58), succeeded in destroying the unity of the Muscovite church.[2]

Before embarking on my own analysis, a brief recapitulation of the catastrophic scenarios conjured up in seventeenth-century Old Believer texts might be helpful. Arguing that nothing less than Russia's religious destiny was at stake, these texts spoke about a deep division (*razdelenie*) or dualism (*razdvoenie*) in Russian society.[3] The first Old Believers continuously evoked images of a dramatic struggle between the supporters of Nikon, whom they labeled "Nikonians" (*Nikoniane*), and themselves, whom they saw as defenders of the true Muscovite religion. Patriarch Nikon was seen as the precursor of the Antichrist, or as the Antichrist himself. Russian clerics and laymen had to decide between the forces of good and evil; if they made the right choice, they would become part of God's "chosen flock" (*izbrannoe stado*) and ascend to Heaven; if they made the wrong choice and stayed on Nikon's side, they would suffer eternal damnation. No Russian could afford to ignore Nikon's reforms, or refuse to take sides.[4]

De-emphasizing the polemic interpretation reiterated in Old Believer texts, I investigate contemporary societal attitudes toward Nikon's liturgical reforms.[5] First, I examine the religious and secular issues that routinely occupied church investigators during the Nikon patriarchate. Was the issue of the new liturgies significant to large numbers of Russians? Second, I examine the contexts in which conflicts over Nikon's new liturgies were recorded. Who were the first opponents of the reforms? What factors motivated their opposition? And, most importantly, how popular were these early dissenters among their contemporaries?

On the basis of new documentary evidence presented in this chapter, I challenge the scenario presented by traditional historiography. First, the actual response to Nikon's revisions in his own time was quite insignificant and left very few, if any, traces in documentary records and other sources. Second, the few isolated protests that did occur were often preceded, or accompanied, by conflicts that had little to do with the liturgical revisions. These conflicts that pitted church authority against Russians, and Russians against one another, were largely ignored by seventeenth-century Old Believer texts.

Later in this chapter I introduce three figures of almost mythological proportions whom eighteenth-century Old Belief historians identified as the founding fathers (*ottsy*) of their movement. I demonstrate that these founding fathers were only peripherally involved in a great struggle over the new liturgies. Most of their preaching was against what they considered abominable popular vices, such as drunkenness, sexual promiscuity, and religious indifference. Precisely because they were religious zealots and unwilling to compromise, these first Old Believers remained unpopular and

largely isolated. If their opposition to the new liturgies had any social influence at all, it was limited to very small audiences.

THE PATRIARCHATE OF NIKON

Nikon introduced several liturgical changes: a new way of making the sign
of the cross, new liturgical vestments for the clergy, and—most importantly—revised liturgical books. Although protests against Nikon were
attributed to popular anger over these changes, archival evidence shows
that ordinary Russians were protesting issues of more immediate concern
in their everyday lives.

During 1653–54 Nikon repeatedly ordered that the three-finger sign of
the cross (*troeperstie*) was to supersede the ancient Russian custom of using
two fingers.[6] Memoranda and articles (*stat'i*) distributed by the Kremlin to
hierarchs and parish priests demanded immediate compliance and did not
bother to explain that the new sign of the cross was the norm in Greece and
other parts of the Orthodox world.[7] In October 1655, provisions for the
three-finger sign of the cross were included in a Russian translation of *The
Tablet* (*Skrizhal'*), an important Greek commentary on Orthodox liturgy,
originally published in Venice in 1574.[8]

The Tablet began by threatening Russians who persisted in the two-
finger sign of the cross (*dvoeperstie*) with anathema:

> We have accepted this tradition since the beginning of faith from the
> Holy Apostles, the Holy Fathers, and the Holy Seven Councils. [They
> instructed] us to make the sign of the Honorable Cross with the three
> first fingers of the right hand. Any Orthodox Christian who does not
> make the sign of the cross according to this Eastern church tradition
> . . . is a heretic and imitator of the Armenians. He will be damned and
> severed from the Father, the Son, and the Holy Spirit.[9]

This threat was repeated by a church council edict of April 1656.[10]

Russian church historians, such as E. Golubinskii, believed that
Nikon's actions provoked the hostility of ordinary Muscovites and thus
prepared the way for the Russian Schism.[11] However, there seems to be
little documentary evidence to support Golubinskii's claim. To begin with,
church services in the Uspenskii Sobor (the patriarchal cathedral in the
Kremlin), remained packed with people even after the new sign of the cross
had become the official norm. An eyewitness of these services, a Greek
visitor named Pavel of Aleppo, did not record any evidence of outrage or
distress on the part of the crowd.[12]

Furthermore, church records from the patriarchal archive are silent about any negative popular reactions to the three-finger sign of the cross. Nikon's contemporaries appear to have been concerned about other issues. For example, a list of popular grievances that was used to justify the deposition and exile of Nikon in 1666 noted that the patriarch had destroyed stone churches in order to acquire building materials for new monastic institutions. The list focused, in particular, on the building of the Voskresenskii and Iverskii monasteries—gigantic construction projects that Nikon had developed on his own initiative. Complaints by both laymen and clerics also centered on the arbitrary subordination of parishes to these monasteries. The Iverskii Monastery, for example, which Nikon had built on the Valdai Heights, imposed new taxes on many parishes that had traditionally belonged to the Novgorod eparchy.[13]

The archive of the Iverskii Monastery, which contains the richest surviving information about Nikon's activities during the 1650s, provides no information on protests against the new sign of the cross. Peasants and priests living in the vicinity of the Iverskii Monastery were among the first Muscovites to be exposed to the change. They were not only directly subject to Nikon's will, but also lived under the supervision of Ukrainian monks who are known to have used the three-finger sign of the cross.[14] Contrary to what one might expect, records dealing with matters of discipline in the monastery and its hinterlands give no indication that local peasants and priests were disturbed by the liturgical preferences of their masters. Rather, they appear to have been concerned with issues such as land distribution and taxation.[15]

There were occasions when conflicts over the sign of the cross could have erupted into the open, if indeed this had been an important issue. For example, in October 1653, emissaries from Novgorod came to villages in the Valdai area where the Iverskii Monastery was being built. They proceeded to consecrate new churches, a process that required using the new form of the blessing. Again, there is no evidence that anyone expressed anger or protest.[16] The typical reaction to the introduction of the three-finger sign of the cross was indifference.

Soon afterwards, Nikon introduced another change: Greek liturgical vestments for the clergy. From Nikon's perspective, this particular change was the most important, and we may therefore assume that he would have had any form of dissent recorded and investigated. However, there is little evidence of investigation, which suggests that such dissent, if it occurred, was short-lived and without larger social impact.

In 1655, Nikon instructed scribes of the patriarchal court to keep detailed records of liturgical services that he conducted in the Uspenskii

Cathedral and other Moscow churches. The result was a thick book titled *Book Registering the Vestments and Liturgies of the Great Lord and Holiest [Patriarch] Nikon*. The scribes who compiled the book paid minute attention to Nikon's liturgical ceremonies, as well as to the roles of other participating clerics. The information they gathered suggests not only that Nikon was obsessed with the details of Greek liturgical vestments, but also that substantial numbers of clerics, both high- and low-ranking, went along with his new dress code.[17]

One might expect Nikon to have reacted with violence against anyone who refused to go along with his demands. But there is no indication that he resorted to force when he introduced the new vestments. For example, when he ordered the clergy to wear new Greek headgear, many of them were initially upset and grumbled about him behind his back. However, it seems that they changed their attitudes in a matter of days. Pavel of Aleppo relates that monks no longer wanted to wear their old Russian cowls (*klobuki*) because they were afraid of appearing ridiculous: "They threw off their old cowls and spat on them before our eyes. They said if Greek vestments were not of divine origin, our patriarch would not have been the first to put them on. . . . " In the end, Moscow priests and monks rushed to the Kremlin to acquire new headgear and the available supply was quickly depleted. Pavel of Aleppo laconically commented: "If any of [our] monks from Mount Athos had brought along whole loads of skullcaps and cowls, he could have sold them for the highest price."[18]

The introduction of new headgear for priests and monks greatly disturbed seventeenth-century Old Believers, as indicated by repeated references in tracts that were written during the 1670s.[19] However, there is no indication that this reform bothered significant numbers of Muscovites.[20]

According to Soviet historians such as V. G. Kartsov and V. S. Rumiantseva, who apparently relied on the findings of nineteenth-century church historians, the first large-scale expression of discontent against Nikon's reforms occurred in the summer of 1654, soon after a church council had developed blueprints for the revision of liturgical books.[21] In August 1654, Prince Mikhail Petrovich Pronskii, administrator for the city of Moscow during the tsar's absence, reported that inhabitants of various Moscow quarters (*slobody*) had complained about Patriarch Nikon. One complaint referred to the ongoing revision of liturgical books:

> The patriarch maintains a known heretic, the monk Arsenii, in his household. He has given him free rein in every respect and ordered him to participate in the revision of printed books. This monk corrupted (*pereportil*) many books, and he and Nikon are leading us to

our final perdition. This monk had been exiled to the Solovki Monastery for his many heresies, instead of being punished by death.[22]

Does this passage prove there was a broad movement of discontent with Nikon's revised books? Assuming that Pronskii's report is correct (even though no other evidence documents the event), in order to understand its social significance we need to place it in the context of other grievances expressed by the petitioners.

The petitioners indicated to Pronskii that they were suffering from the plague that had struck Moscow with great force, and felt bitter that Patriarch Nikon and his friends—among them the monk Arsenii—had left the capital to live in the relative security of the suburban Troitsa Monastery. They demanded that Nikon return immediately to the capital; otherwise, their parish priests would follow the patriarch's example and run away, leaving the parishioners to die without access to blessings and sacraments.[23] The call for Nikon's return clearly indicates that the patriarch was the recognized leader of the Russian church even after he had embarked on the revision of liturgical books. Later Old Believer tracts, in marked contrast, create the impression that Muscovite contemporaries perceived Nikon as their mortal enemy.[24]

Clearly, the profound spiritual confusion of the Muscovites who confronted Pronskii had not been caused by Nikon's revisions. While facing the imminent danger of death, they saw themselves left without pastoral supervision and access to salvation and their anxiety was compounded by the fact that Nikon had conducted a massive campaign against icons that lay individuals had purchased. According to contemporary observers, these so-called "community icons" (*mirskie ikony*) had been one of the most important focal points of Russian popular religion.[25] When the petitioners approached Pronskii, they carried with them " . . . icon boards (*ikonnye tski*) and said that the images on these boards had been scraped off." They perceived a direct connection between the destruction of their icons and the pestilence that had ravaged Moscow.[26] As an example, they presented an icon depicting Christ that Nikon had ordered to be confiscated:

> This icon of the Savior was seized from Sofron Fedorov, of the Novgorod merchant guild, and taken to the patriarchal court. . . . Its face had been scraped off and the image scratched out by patriarchal order. Sofron claimed that he had had a vision in front of this icon which instructed him to show it to the laity and to warn them that they should oppose this act of desecration. But they responded that the wrath of God has now come upon all of them for this, that this is what the iconoclasts did, and the people now all blame the patriarch. . . .[27]

It may be concluded that the reference to the revision of liturgical books was of only minor concern to the discontented population of Moscow.[28] The principal source of grievance was the patriarch's insensitivity to popular religious needs during the plague.[29]

The attitudes of Muscovites toward icons became the subject of a substantial investigation (*delo*) in June 1657 involving hundreds—if not thousands—of men and women living in various parts of the capital.[30] The immediate cause of the investigation was a strange occurrence: in early June, a large number of parishioners had walked into their churches and removed their "community icons." Not listening to their priests or to anyone else who tried to interfere, they took the icons home with them. The alarmed authorities spoke of "rebellion" (*miatezh*) and "confusion in churches" (*smiatenie v tserkvakh*).[31]

Why did Muscovites remove their icons? It appears they wanted to prevent Nikon from destroying them. For example, Ivan Chernousov, who was accused of taking three icons from his parish church, reported to the investigative commission that he had acted as soon as he heard Nikon "had given the order to seize all icons from parish churches [and] to take them to the patriarchal court."[32] Others had heard rumors that the patriarch was about to seal off all churches in the capital.[33] Much of the fear may have been exaggerated, because the commission could confirm only that Nikon had ordered two icons taken from the Church of St. Anastasiia, and that they were returned the same day.[34]

It is important to note that the icons confiscated by Nikon were not old Russian icons, but so-called "Latin" or "Frankish" (*friazhskie*) icons. They showed Western influences in style and painting and often resembled the realistic images on Protestant woodcuts and broadsheets that were circulating then in some western-Russian towns. Many were on cheap paper and cost very little. Thus, Nikon's actions against icons were clearly not directed at symbols of the old Russian religion, whereas his liturgical changes definitely were.[35]

The same Muscovites who were concerned about the fate of their icons showed no apparent hostility toward the on-going revision of liturgical books, although there were many reasons why they might have done so. The revisions introduced by Nikon followed no apparent pattern and were carelessly done, a fact later emphasized by Old Believers.[36] Even the editors (*spravshchiki*) aware of the poor quality of their work, and they apparently anticipated hostile reactions. The editors of the Triodion, for example, apologetically explained that the book had been revised on the basis of "ancient Greek, Slavic, and Serbian manuscripts" and emphasized that not one change was due to their own arbitrariness (*ot sebe zhe nichtozhe sovnesosha*).[37] The revisers of the Heirmologion issued in May 1656 were more honest. They explained that they had been so rushed that mistakes inevitably had occurred.[38] Similar disclaimers can be found in the prefaces of other liturgical books of the Nikon period.[39]

However, the editors' apprehension was not justified. Sales records of the patriarchal printing press reveal a large popular demand for the revised books, with good sales not only in Moscow, but in the provinces as well. Clearly, Nikon did not have to use force to impose his new books on the populace.[40]

Among the first to buy the new Service Book in September 1655 were two priests from the parish churches of St. Nicholas at the Stone Bridge (*u Kamennogo mostu*) and St. George Beyond the Nikitskie Gates (*izza Nikitskikh vorot*).[41] The purchase by the St. Nicholas priest is of interest because this church was one of the first to be stormed two years later by Muscovites rescuing their icons. Clearly the priest and his parishioners had held no grudge against Nikon when they eagerly accepted his new liturgies. There is also no reason to believe that two years later, when they claimed to have been exclusively concerned with the well-being of their icons, their favorable attitude toward the new books had changed.[42]

Other sources confirm that the introduction of revised liturgical books had nothing to do with later disturbances over icons in June 1657. The parish priest Ivan of the Spasskii Church in the Basketmaker Quarter (*Koshel'naia sloboda*) bought the new Service Book nearly two years before he came to the attention of church investigators in connection with the removal of icons, and relations between Ivan and his parishioners had clearly not deteriorated due to his purchase.[43] When Ivan's "spiritual children" were investigated for taking home their icons, he protected them by corroborating their testimonies with his signature: there were only three troublemakers, one of whom had to "take his icons home because he was sick and wanted to say his prayers at home." All other parishioners were fishing at the Moscow River on the day of the disturbances.[44]

By March 1656, six months after its release by the printing press, parish priests from all over Moscow (including areas where disturbances over icons would occur a year later) had bought the new Service Book. Priest Aleksandr of the St. Dmitrii Church in the Arbat district was so eager to own a new Service Book that he bought a second copy after his first copy was recalled by the printing press for revisions.[45] Priests from the Kadashevo settlement and Tver' Street also appear in the register as frequent purchasers; others came from the districts of Luzhniki, Sadovniki, and Kitaigorod.[46] Of the two hundred Service Books sold, at least fifty-five went to different parishes in Moscow.[47]

Not much is known about the distribution of new liturgical books outside Moscow; this was the responsibility of local bishops, and diocesan archives do not contain this information. Several clerics who were in Moscow on business took advantage of the opportunity to acquire the new books directly from the printing press. For example, on January 15, 1656, Abbot Ivan from the distant Pechenskii Monastery on the Kola Peninsula, and the priest Sergei from the northern Kirillov Monastery each bought a copy. Among purchasers at the printing press we also find parish priests from the Viaz'ma, Kostroma, and Tula areas, and a deacon from Mezen' on the White Sea littoral.[48] Considering that the book cost one ruble ten altyn—a formidable sum for a rural parish priest—we must assume these clerics would have thought twice before spending their money had there been any doubt in their minds as to the correctness of the new liturgical books.

These new books were also in demand among non-clerics, as indicated by the fact that residents of many Russian towns such as Nizhnii Novgorod, Galich, and Kholmogory were among the first purchasers.[49] Book traders, who had their stands in the Moscow market, bought large quantities of the books from the patriarchal press and apparently had no difficulty reselling them at a profit. For example, the trader Maksim Galakhtionov acquired ten copies of the first edition and thirty copies of the fifth edition of the Service Book, and trader Leontii Ivanov acquired twenty copies to sell at the vegetable market (*ovoshchnoi riad*). The largest buyer was Ivan Fokin, who acquired at least seventy copies to sell.[50] Demand for the new books clearly contradicts the assumption that Nikon's liturgical reforms led to widespread societal discontent. In fact, it appears that many Muscovites were favorably disposed toward the new books.

Even those with good reason to be dissatisfied with the church bought the new books. The merchant (*gost'*) Vasilii Shorin, for example, who was annoyed by the rude business practices of Patriarch Nikon, bought four Service Books immediately after they had been issued and sent a client (*chelovek*), a certain Kalistrat, to procure one of the first copies of the Horologion. Other merchants followed his example.[51] The inhabitants of the Kadashevo settlement, who were often in conflict with church authority over a variety of secular issues, apparently saw no reason for rejecting the new books.[52] Even individuals from the town of Viaz'ma, a notorious trouble spot for the church, and the towns of Ustiug and Kostroma, both of which had witnessed violent uprisings against state and church only a few years earlier, acquired the new liturgical books.[53] Thus, it is clear that preexisting societal discontent did not automatically lead to popular protests against Nikon's reforms.

Traditional scholarship has not accurately distinguished between preexisting social discontent and the immediate impact of Nikon's liturgical reforms. This applies particularly to the parish clergy, often identified as the earliest inciters of liturgical dissent. For example, it has been assumed that Nikon had to use "his whole enormous police power to enforce them [liturgical revisions] against the opposition of the lower clergy."[54] However, the documentary evidence does not support such an interpretation. While there is no question that many priests were unhappy with Nikon, there are also good indications that most of this discontent was not due to the liturgical reforms.

We know, for example, by the time of Nikon's departure from the patriarchal throne in July 1658, numerous parish churches had fallen into disuse because their priests had fled. Examples are found in the tax registers of the Patriarchal Treasury Office (*Patriarshii kazennyi prikaz*).[55] The reasons local priests fled can be reconstructed on the basis of their surviving petitions, which complain about overtaxation and violence perpetrated by church officials—not about the introduction of new liturgical books.[56] Other petitions request the replacement of dilapidated churches, illustrating some priests' miserable living conditions.[57] In summary, the lot of priests seems to have worsened during the Nikon era.

Some evidence indicating that a few priests may have found the liturgical revisions distressing is contained in a petition that circulated among Kremlin priests during the 1650s. Found among the papers of the tsar's Secret Chancellery, the petition had been hidden in the vestibule of the Blagoveshchenskii Cathedral at the Kremlin in 1657 and discovered by accident some ten years later. It appears to be the only surviving document from Nikon's patriarchate that addresses the revision of books in any detail, and it has unique historical value because it places the revision within the larger context of Nikon's church policies.[58]

The unknown author of this petition was among the first Muscovites of record to openly criticize Nikon's revision of liturgical books. He apparently had good connections with the patriarchal court and had access to information that other Muscovites could not obtain.[59] He learned that manuscripts from Muscovite monastic libraries had not been used in the revision process and that the editors had drawn on manuscripts of questionable value sent by the "patriarchs of Palestine." The author strongly disliked the influence of Greek clergymen on the revision process, insisting that they were unscrupulous careerists who had come to Muscovy only to enrich themselves, for example, by distributing indulgences (*razreshatel'nye gramoty*) to the Muscovite population. The author was particularly upset by the presence of the aforementioned monk Arsenii the Greek, blaming him for the introduction of the three-finger sign of the cross and the new Service Book of 1655.[60]

How important was this criticism of Nikon's revisions to the author? It turns out that he devoted only about three folio pages out of thirty-three to the liturgical reform and the incompetence of its perpetrators; most of the petition was about other matters. This is in sharp contrast to later Old Believer petitions that criticized the new liturgies in great detail.[61]

The author primarily was concerned with the hardships of parish priests resulting from new ecclesiastical controls. He emphasized that under Nikon, parish priests could no longer seek appointments from local bishops, but had to negotiate directly with the patriarchal court in Moscow. This served the purpose of filling the patriarch's treasury and enriching patriarchal officials (especially Nikon's favorite, the powerful secretary Ivan Kokoshilov) and resulted in the massive dislocation and impoverishment of parish priests, as discussed above.[62]

One example given by the author is that priests who had, for one reason or another, lost their parish positions needed to obtain special transit papers (*perekhozhie*) before they could establish themselves in new parishes. Many priests were exposed to great hardships because of this rule:

> A transit paper costs a priest who has no protection (*bezzastupnomu popu*) up to four, seven, ten, and even fifteen rubles. . . . Many priests without such papers travel two or three times to Moscow to procure them. The children of these poor priests wander about homeless. . . . Even if such a priest submits a petition . . . he will hardly receive his right because the guards do not allow him into the [Patriarchal] Treasury Office without charge; not to mention letting him see a clerk or secretary. When Ivan Kokoshilov was appointed to the Treasury Office and they introduced the transit papers, they distributed them to whomever they saw fit . . . many [then] paid only one ruble. . . . [63]

The petition indicates that Muscovite priests had good reason to be dissatisfied with Nikon. But there is no evidence of protest by these priests against Nikon's liturgical revisions.[64]

The most comprehensive source on Nikon's patriarchate, the tax income books (*prikhodnye okladnye knigi*) of the Patriarchal Treasury Office, indicate that the tax average parish priests had to pay dramatically increased under Nikon. For example, during 1656 a patriarchal emissary, Semen

Izvol'skii, visited the parishes of the Suzdal' eparchy and told priests they would have to collect considerably higher taxes from their parishes.[65] Semen's entries in the tax books indicate assessments at least twice that levied in 1628 under Patriarch Filaret (and what priests had been paying for twenty-eight years). In some cases, the tax jumped to extraordinary heights for no apparent reason. For example, the parish priest of the village of Eltesunov, located in the patrimony of Orina Nikitichna, had paid only five altyns five den'gi in 1628 and in 1656 paid two rubles more. The priest of the village Ust', which belonged to the Troitsa Monastery, had his tax increased by four rubles.[66] The Suzdal' tax registers contain other data showing that the financial burden of virtually every priest had increased.[67]

Thus, the anonymous petition of 1657 places the issue of liturgical reform in its societal context and is more accurate than the Old Believer texts customarily studied by historians. It is interesting to note that Old Believers who wrote several decades after the end of Nikon's patriarchate did not deal with the misery of the priests, or other unpopular developments, such as Nikon's attack on "Latin" icons or the destruction of parish churches. Instead, Old Believers wrote almost exclusively about Nikon's liturgical revisions and their religious implications.[68] Thus, the societal impact of Nikon's revisions cannot be distilled from Old Believer texts.

Still, historians usually have assumed a priori that such literary texts reflected widely held sentiments. For example, in their references to one of the earliest Old Believer tracts, the *Book* of Abbot Spiridon Potemkin, scholars V. S. Rumiantseva and J. H. Billington asserted that Spiridon's polemic against the Nikonian reforms expressed the attitudes of many Muscovite contemporaries.[69] Rumiantseva uses Spiridon's highly theological text to illustrate the thinking of "the camp of opposition" (*lager' oppositsii*) against the official church.[70] According to Billington, Spiridon's ideas had become so deeply "fixed in popular imagination" that "his own death in 1664 [sic] was seen as a sign that history itself was drawing to a close."[71]

In contrast to such historical interpretations, the documents cited here do not indicate that Nikon's liturgical reforms caused any great anxiety among Muscovites. I conclude that these reforms did not enter into the larger societal and religious conflicts of the 1650s, but remained the concern of only a handful of individuals. However, other policies instituted by Nikon *did* occasion widespread fear and discontent; these policies include the arbitrary confiscation of "Latin" or "Frankish" icons and new regulations that imposed great hardships on priests.

ATTITUDES TOWARD BOOK REVISIONS IN THE EPARCHIES OF ROSTOV AND SUZDAL'

Most of the information cited thus far regarding societal attitudes toward Nikon's liturgical reforms sheds light on only a limited geographic area: the capital of Moscow. The question naturally arises how inhabitants of other areas of Muscovy reacted toward the new books. Could it be that there were widespread protest movements against the new liturgies elsewhere?

Contrary to what might be expected, I did not find evidence in church archives. It seems impossible to establish, on the basis of reliable historical data, that the Muscovite hinterlands reacted negatively to the liturgical changes during the Nikon period. The affairs of the vast Vologda eparchy, for example, which are better documented than those of any other Russian diocese, appear to have been completely silent on the subject after Archbishop Markell introduced the new liturgical books in February 1656.[72] We do know, however, that inhabitants of Vologda—both clerics and non-clerics—were frequent purchasers of the new liturgical books, as their names appear repeatedly in the sale registers of the patriarchal printing press.[73] The town of Murom, which is similarly well documented in church records, did not register a single incident of protest after the archbishop of Riazan' introduced the new books, and Murom inhabitants also appear as voluntary purchasers of the new books.[74] Similar observations can be made about the town of Novgorod and its hinterlands based on the archive of the St. Sophia Cathedral, which contains information about many religious issues of interest to seventeenth-century Novgorodians.[75]

There were apparently only three exceptions to this general pattern: the refusal of the archimandrite of the Solovki Monastery to accept the new liturgical books, the loud protest of three preachers in Rostov, and the critical attitudes of some clerics living in and around Suzdal'. I will focus on the attitudes of the Rostovians and Suzdalians toward the new liturgies; the Solovki case will be discussed in the next chapter because it was analogous to an incident at the Troitsa Monastery that occurred a few years later.

The largest protest against the liturgical revisions that has been documented in church records of the Nikon period occurred in the town of Rostov. In January 1657, Metropolitan Iona wrote to Moscow that he had arrested Sila Bogdanov, a tailor from the Rostov trading colony. According to Iona's letter, which survives in records of the Foreign Office, Sila and his "disciples" (*ucheniki*) had stopped attending church services, and had also begun to encourage fellow Rostovians to stay away from church. Puzzled, the metropolitan had Sila arrested and interrogated. The protocol of this interrogation was sent to Moscow, and served as the basis of further investigations conducted by Kremlin officials.[76]

There is no question that Sila actively preached against the liturgical changes introduced under Nikon. He was particularly opposed to the new three-finger sign of the cross.[77] Just as disturbing to him was the appearance of "papal crosses" (*kryzhi papezhskie*) on hosts (four-ended crosses that replaced the traditional eight-ended ones).[78] He was also deeply disconcerted by changes in the consecration of holy water that had been introduced in 1655.[79] Sila did not keep his discontent to himself; he stood at the entrances to local churches preaching, that the Muscovite church had become heretical and Rostovians should refuse to take communion because those who introduced the new crosses had lost their Orthodox faith.[80]

How much support did Sila find among the population of Rostov? Did he manage to keep Rostovians from attending church services? According to the Soviet historian V. S. Rumiantseva, Sila represented a mass movement of discontent with the official church.[81] However, existing historical records do not support her contention.

My research shows that Sila's protests against Nikon's liturgical changes remained isolated outbursts of anger and did not reflect widely held sentiments. A search by church officials for adherents of similar ideas led only to the capture of two of Sila's friends, Fedor and Aleksei. These captives, described as market-gardeners (*ogorodniki*), had taken up preaching and like Sila, stood at church entrances saying "many insulting words" (*mnogie ponosnye slova*) about Patriarch Nikon. No other supporters of Sila could be found even though the bishop's officials searched with great care (*s velikim radeniem*).[82]

There is other evidence that the behavior of the three captured dissenters was unusual for the town of Rostov. The testimonies of Fedor's and Aleksei's parish priests, for example, make no mention of other parishioners who rejected the liturgical changes. These priests, Khariton Semenov and his son Ivan, admitted that they themselves had previously used the two-finger sign of the cross, but had been in full compliance with the new liturgical norms ever since learning about them.[83] Although the church investigators remained skeptical, they could find no evidence that the two-finger sign of the cross was being used in Rostov. The two priests were soon released from custody and given three rubles each from the tsar's personal treasury to compensate for the "unnecessary red tape" (*naprasnaia volokita*).[84]

Since the three-finger sign of the cross and the new Service Book had apparently been accepted without visible resistance by the parishes to which Fedor and Aleksei belonged, why did these two—and not other parishioners—dissent? One possible explanation is that both Fedor and Aleksei were extraordinarily fervent and therefore much more sensitive to religious change than the average Muscovite. Fedor, for example, was so opposed to the three-finger sign of the cross that he was "ready to die" (*khochet umeret'*) for the old sign he had learned in his youth. Aleksei complained with similar conviction about the new crosses on hosts.[85] Both apparently meant what they said: they did not recant their beliefs even under torture, demonstrating a steadfastness rarely found among seventeenth-century opponents of the new liturgical books.[86]

Although the reasons for such religious conviction are hard to determine, in the case of Fedor and Aleksei we can reconstruct them at least in part.[87] According to the testimonies of their parish priests, neither had attended church services for some time *before* the new Service Books arrived in Rostov.[88] The last time their priests remembered seeing them was when they came to confession during the pestilence of 1654. It is possible that some of Fedor's and Aleksei's relatives, perhaps even their intended brides (both said they never married), perished in the plague. It appears that they never returned to church following the plague.[89]

There is evidence that the fear of death, whether occasioned by the pestilence or other circumstances, motivated many religious radicals during the 1650s.[90] Two examples are given here. Fedor Shilovtsov from the Moscow Kadashevo suburb began to destroy crosses and icons after the death of his best friend. The record of Shilovtsov's interrogation described the origins of his behavior as follows:

> His doubt and thinking about icons began in the following way: On January 1 of the current year 1651, Abram Alekseevich Ragozin from the Kadashevo settlement died. Abram was his close friend and he grieved over him and cried bitterly for a long time. From this sorrow he lost his mind. He began to wonder whether it was proper to prostrate oneself before holy icons because simple and drunken men paint them carelessly, handle them, and simply sell them in the market place. . . .[91]

The peasant Kondrat from the Voronezh area experienced a similar religious conversion when he fell ill while visiting Moscow during the pestilence in early 1654:

> He was lying sick when St. Nicholas appeared to him in his dream, ordering him to go out and . . . tell everyone to repent their evil ways and that their religious authorities should teach them not to fornicate on Mondays, for that is the Day of the Archangel. They also were not

to work before lunchtime on Wednesdays; and on Fridays, Sundays, and Holidays of the Lord, they were not to work all day. Those days were to be strictly honored, and they were to refrain from revelry, pride, sodomy, fornication, swearing, and envy. Instead they should love one another. . . . [92]

To return to the Rostovians Fedor and Aleksei, their behavior can be understood in the context of the religious conversions and preaching that existed in Russia during these years. It is unclear how many self-proclaimed preachers there were altogether, but the number may have been significant. Still, it is important to remember that this kind of extremism was not generated by Nikon's liturgical reforms; it existed independently and only on exceptional occasions led to discontent with the reforms. Sila and his friends represent such exceptions.

While we have only indirect clues about the genesis of Fedor's and Aleksei's attitudes toward the new liturgies, we are better informed about Sila. The origins of his protest lie in a traumatic experience that occurred during the transfer of the relics of the Muscovite saint Filipp from the Solovki Monastery to Moscow in July 1652.[93] Sila associated the transfer with the sudden death of Iona's predecessor, Metropolitan Varlaam. Varlaam, according to the Chronicle of the Rostov eparchy, had been called to Moscow by Nikon to witness the arrival of the relics. While inspecting them, he had suddenly and, for no apparent reason, collapsed and died.[94] Sila was very affected by this story and spent much time contemplating Varlaam's fate. He concluded that God had intervened to save Varlaam's soul from the evil intentions of the "swindlers" (*plutniki*) who were responsible for transferring the relics.[95]

There are indications that Sila venerated Varlaam, who had been metropolitan of Rostov since 1619. During interrogations, Sila mentioned Varlaam as the most important source of his beliefs.[96] This is surprising considering that Varlaam was one of the first Russian hierarchs to introduce liturgical reforms into the churches of his eparchy. In 1651, before the period of Nikon, scribes of the metropolitan see copied a decree demanding the abolition of "polyphonic" singing (*mnogoglasie*), and copies were disseminated to all parishes and monasteries of the Rostov eparchy.[97] In this decree, Varlaam instructed local church representatives to oversee the immediate introduction of this liturgical change and to provide information on dissenters.[98] Thus, Sila must have supported church power at least as late as 1651, even though this power stood for the imposition of significant liturgical changes.[99]

Varlaam's sudden death was, in all likelihood, the catalyst for Sila's radically changed attitudes toward the church. He was further angered when he discovered that Filipp's relics no longer worked miracles and that his favorite local saint, Ignatii, had also ceased to answer his prayers.[100] Sila's outrage may have reflected an important religious change: Nikon devalued local saints, emphasizing all-Muscovite saints such as Filipp instead.[101] Ceremonial records indicate that the number of Rostov saints, traditionally very large, was significantly reduced. In the month of May alone, Rostovians had celebrated the Feasts of Isidor (May 14th), Isaiah (May 15th), Leontii (May 23), and Ignatii (May 28). Under Nikon, the names of saints Isaiah and Leontii disappeared from the records; Isidor and Ignatii were soon to lose their status as well.[102]

The evidence cited above indicates that the relationship between Sila and Iona was tense before the new liturgical books were introduced in late 1655. It is clear that Sila did not like the metropolitan and accused him of many other wrongdoings such as bribery, greed, and deceit.[103] Despite Sila's expressed opposition to liturgical changes, his preaching is more likely a result of prior conflicts with Metropolitan Iona. Such an interpretation is also supported by the vagueness with which Sila referred to specific liturgical changes. When church investigators pressed him to give examples, he always responded with confusion.[104] Unable to pin down exactly what had been changed in church services, Sila was repeatedly reprimanded by the interrogators for his ignorance.[105]

However, Sila's behavior has similarities to the religious radicalism of other craftsmen and artisans living in Muscovy's trading colonies during this period. In addition to the aforementioned examples, the tailor Timofei Gavrilov was accused of preparing a poisonous mixture to kill Patriarch Nikon in 1660. It is probably no coincidence that his case was investigated by the same officials who had interrogated Sila and his students.[106] In 1650, a butcher was arrested in Pskov for disseminating "blasphemous magical books" (*bogomerskie volshebnye knigi*). In 1658, Kir'iashka Zav'ialov from the commercial center of Kholmogory was arrested for calling himself tsarevich.[107] Other cases could be cited, but suffice it to say that the milieu in which the three Rostovians lived produced a number of religious dissenters. The feature distinguishing their religious fervor from that of other preachers was their opposition to the new liturgical books.

Thus, Sila and his two friends stand out in the history of early Russian religious dissent. These sectarians were exceptionally inspired, and there is no doubt that their preaching against the new liturgical books presaged the religious fervor of later preachers. This may explain why eighteenth-century Old Believers claimed them as members of their movement.[108] But there is no evidence that these isolated Rostov preachers found support for their concerns in contemporary society.

Other towns of Muscovy reacted with similar apathy toward Nikon's liturgical reforms, as demonstrated by historical data on religious protests in the town of Suzdal'. Stefan, the archbishop of Suzdal' and Nikon's close friend, was more fiercely hated than Iona of Rostov.[109] Whereas Iona's power was not threatened by the activities of a few radical preachers, Stefan was overthrown by a mass movement of popular discontent. However, there is no indication he was unseated for having introduced the new liturgical books; historical evidence suggests he was toppled for other reasons.

In 1659, Archimandrite Avraamii of the powerful Spaso-Evfimiev Monastery in Suzdal' complained to the tsar that Stefan and his relatives had ruined him. He claimed that the main church of the monastery stood empty because "all have fled from the archbishop" (*ot arkhiepiskopa vse rozbrelisia*). Avraamii's discontent was echoed in numerous other petitions that reached the tsar's court from Suzdal' and its hinterlands.[110]

Why were the inhabitants of the Suzdal' eparchy so dissatisfied with Stefan? One factor that certainly contributed to their anger was that Stefan succeeded the popular Archbishop Iosif, who had been removed by Nikon under questionable circumstances.[111] There is no reason to believe that Iosif's replacement by Stefan had anything to do with the issue of liturgical reform. In fact, there is no substantial evidence that Iosif was opposed to Nikon's reforms. It is true, as A. A. Titov has pointed out, that Iosif's signature is missing from the acts of the Church Council of 1656 calling for the revision and distribution of the new Books of Needs (*potrebniki*). However, it is also true that he bought the new liturgical books at the patriarchal printing press.[112] And even if we allow for the possibility that Stefan was the first to implement the liturgical reforms in Suzdal', there is no proof that this is what made him unpopular.

In 1660, a church council was convened in Moscow to investigate complaints against Stefan. However, he was deeply offended when summoned to Moscow, and answered questions only reluctantly. He denied almost all the accusations, refusing even to sign the protocol of his interrogation.[113]

The proceedings of this church council are unusually comprehensive. Surviving records include not only Stefan's answers to his interrogators, but also the collective and individual responses of hundreds of Suzdal' clerics and laymen providing us with the most important historical evidence about the conflict at Suzdal'. Their testimonies tell us a great deal about popular attitudes toward the church during Nikon's patriarchate, and in particular, how Suzdalians regarded the revised books and liturgies.[114]

The Church Council of 1660 investigated fifty-one different complaints submitted by Suzdal' petitioners. To simplify analysis, these have been divided into three categories: category I comprises complaints referring to liturgical changes; category II, grievances resulting from Archbishop Stefan's abusive behavior in secular matters; and category III, complaints about Stefan's interference with traditional modes of popular piety.[115]

An analysis of the distribution of grievances in category I reveals that the revision of liturgical books was merely a minor source of discontent among Suzdalians. Only one deacon belonging to the clerical staff of the cathedral complained about the bishop's use of the new Service Books. And even this cleric was not so much disturbed by the use of the new Service Book per se, but rather how it was used. He observed that the archbishop celebrated the new liturgy "according to his personal whim" (*samochinno*), and that "he distorted (*prevrashchal*) it by changing ceremonies from one day to the next (*segodnia tak, a zavtra inako*)."[116]

A small number of clerics resented Stefan's efforts to regulate the use of the Lamb of God; this included the archimandrite of a Suzdal' monastery, an archpriest, and several priests and monks who complained that the bishop had spoken about the Lamb in derogatory terms.[117] The replacement of the Ceremonial Books (*ustavy*), which are compendia regulating the liturgical conduct of clerics, was also not widely resented among the population of Suzdal'.[118] It was mostly nuns and clerics affiliated with the Nikol'skii Monastery who expressed resentment, possibly because this particular liturgical book had been given to them by the popular Patriarch Filaret, father of the first Romanov tsar.[119]

Table 1. Complaints about liturgical matters,
submitted by Suzdal' petitioners (Category I)

TYPE OF COMPLAINT	NUMBER OF OCCURRENCES
Using the new Service Books	1
Regulating use of the Lamb of God *(agnets Bozhii)*	24
Confiscation and burning of Ceremonial Books *(ustavy)*	64
Facing west, not east, while saying prayer for tsar	140
Holding cross in left hand	179
Arbitrary acts affecting celebration of the Mass	354

Source: Author's compilation, based on *Prilozheniia*, pp. 45-61.

A significantly larger number of complaints concerned the bishop's holding the cross in his left rather than right hand when blessing his flock. Those who complained were equally divided between clerics (94) and laymen (85). It is possible that this particular ritual was not hated because it was an innovation, but because it was accompanied by the humiliating demand that everyone kiss Stefan's hand.[120] Such an interpretation seems confirmed by the fact that nobody complained about the new shape of the cross, as did later Old Believers and the above-mentioned Rostov radicals.

Thus, it appears that no one in Suzdal' opposed two of the principal liturgical changes that later inspired Avvakum and other Old Believers to write polemic tracts, namely the introduction of the three-finger sign of the cross and the new Service Book.[121] Most upsetting to those who complained about liturgical practices were digressions attributed to Archbishop Stefan's personal whim. For example, 248 monks and nuns complained that Stefan had ordered the abbot of the Borisoglebskii Monastery to enter the altar area through the royal doors (*tsarskie dveri*) against his will.[122] Another abbot testified that he had been wearing only a stole (*patrakhel'*) when Stefan pulled him by the hand into the altar area.[123] Stefan had also ignored the failure of priests to fast properly before performing the liturgy. Finally, he had given alcoholic beverages to priests during the Lenten period, apparently attempting to console them after having beaten them nearly to death.[124]

It is interesting to note that the vast majority of complaints about Stefan's liturgical practices came from clerics.[125] This indicates that liturgical changes were of concern, if at all, to clerics rather than to laymen. This may not be surprising if we consider that clerics were more exposed to Stefan's arbitrariness and violence than were laymen.

Table 2. Complaints about Archbishop Stefan's abusiveness in secular matters, submitted by Suzdal' petitioners (Category II)

TYPE OF COMPLAINT	NUMBER OF OCCURRENCES
Patronage and nepotism	250
Failure to pray for the tsar and his family	553
Self-glorification in processions and speeches	567
Random violence	604

Source: Author's compilation, based on *Prilozheniia*, pp. 45-61.

Both the clergy and laity of Suzdal' were much more concerned about the non-liturgical aspects of Stefan's behavior, as clearly demonstrated by the grievances in category II of our typology.[126]

Category II contains a substantially larger number of total complaints than category I, indicating that the abuses listed here were perceived as more serious than the liturgical changes. Most frightening to the petitioners appears to have been the total lack of protection against the violent whims of the bishop and his relatives, as for example in the brutal treatment of priests:

> On orders of the archbishop, his brother, (who is the treasurer and monk Khristofor), cruelly beat the protodeacon Grigorii and two deacons ... from these blows they lay sick and suffered from infections (*gnili*) for a long time. The archbishop also gave orders to tonsure widowed priests by force, and so many of them actually became monks. A priest of the Pokrovskii Convent was removed from his church, and his wife and children are now being fed by their relatives.[127]

Further, monks, priests, and laymen alike were appalled by the arbitrary replacement of a local abbot by Stefan's personal confessor.[128]

One of the strongest outcries occurred after Stefan's failure to observe the requiem (*panikhida*) commemorating deceased members of the tsar's family. He had also refused to say Mass for the health of the tsar's wife and daughter. There are other documented cases of high-ranking hierarchs refusing to say Mass for members of the tsar's family, but apparently none of them resulted in the same level of popular protest.[129] Such Masses were among the oldest institutions of Russian Christianity, and priests were usually severely disciplined if they failed to pray for living and deceased members of the royal family.[130] During the 1640s, for example, the priest Iakov was defrocked for refusing to say a prayer for "the tsar's health" (*gosudarevo zdorov'e*). Another priest, Kirill, had failed to enter the names of Tsar Mikhail and his wife Evdokiia into necrologies (*sinodiki*) and was punished.[131]

It appears that, while the bishop's arbitrariness was resented more than liturgical changes, the greatest anxiety was caused by Stefan's random interference with important aspects of popular religiosity, i.e., icons, altars, and relics. The Church Council of 1660 registered the following category III complaints against Stefan:

Table 3. Complaints about Archbishop Stefan's
interference with traditional modes of piety,
submitted by Suzdal' petitioners (Category III)

TYPE OF COMPLAINT	NUMBER OF OCCURRENCES
Tampering with the gravesite of the patron saint of the Rizpolozhenskii Monastery	37
Destruction of altars in parish churches and removal of parish icons *(prikhodskie ikony)*	41
Lack of reverence for the Mother of God	88
Tampering with the altar in the cathedral	103
Tampering with local icons *(mestnye ikony)*	169
Removal of private icons *(osobnye obrazy)* from the cathedral	317
Removal of the remains of the Suzdal' patrons and bishops from the cathedral	409
Tampering with miracle-working icons of the Mother of God	504
Destruction of the graves of the Great Princes of Suzdal'	626
Prohibition against exchanging Easter eggs	1178
Destruction of altars in monastery and parish churches	1612

Source: Author's compilation, based on *Prilozheniia*, pp. 45-61.

This list of grievances demonstrates that Stefan's interference with traditional liturgical practices was harmless compared with his efforts to reshape, if not destroy, popular piety. Stefan's attacks on icons were a significant source of discontent among the Suzdal' populace, analogous to the protests generated by Nikon's behavior in Moscow a few years earlier.

Hundreds of people, ranging from archimandrites to ordinary laymen, were outraged by Stefan's interference with the veneration of Marian icons. First, he took away the candles that had always burned in front of the Mother of God miracle-working icons in the cathedral. Then, he had gold and other precious pieces of ornamentation removed, arguing "that Mary never walked around with gold and precious stones." Processions in honor of the Virgin and special feast days celebrating particular Marian icons, such as those of the Kazan' Virgin, were reduced to a bare minimum.[132] Each of these measures was vehemently protested.

Stefan's policy toward icons may have reflected the rhetorical effort of the Muscovite patriarchate to give a genuine Christian meaning to the veneration of icons. The following passage on icon worship, for example, is in the acts of the Church Council of 1667: " . . . ignorant people call these icons their gods. They simply seem not to know about the oneness of God and engage in pantheism (*mnogobozhie*)."[133] There is, however, no direct evidence that any bishop besides Stefan acted according to this rhetoric. By contrast, Stefan condemned the veneration of private icons as a "swinish heresy" (*svinaia eres'*), possibly under the influence of his protector Nikon who had acted in a similar fashion in Moscow. He also did not hesitate to call a popular local icon "a swinish God substitute" (*svinoi bog*).[134]

Even more upsetting to Suzdalians was Stefan's tampering with altars. The emissaries sent by the Church Council of 1660 to inspect all altars in the town of Suzdal' and surrounding villages confirmed the massive accusations against Stefan. Some altars had been totally destroyed, others had been disassembled and remodeled, and still others had been moved to new locations.[135] They also found that Stefan had had great difficulty finding willing executors of this much-hated policy and had promised positions in the priesthood, or ownership of homesteads, to those who helped him destroy the altars.[136] The Council of 1660 strongly condemned Stefan's actions, ordering that the altars were to be rebuilt "and arranged exactly as they had been before (*ustroit' po prezhnemu*)."[137]

Why did Stefan provoke the Suzdal' populace by actions apparently unparalleled elsewhere in Muscovy?[138] There are indications that his targets were not random, but rather, carefully selected. In the town of Suzdal', for example, only the altars of five monasteries and four parishes were affected. One of the hardest hit was the Spaso-Evfimiev Monastery under Archimandrite Avraamii, who had fallen victim to Stefan's violence on prior occasions.[139] Other devastated churches, including that of the popular Rizpolozhenskii Monastery, were located in the middle of the Suzdal' trading colony, where some of Stefan's most outspoken critics lived.[140] The brothers Likhopin, for example, had complained bitterly to the tsar about having been excommunicated for refusing to let their nephew Ivan serve in the bishop's bureaucracy. There was also conflict between the archbishop and local residents over the ownership of real estate and access to pastures for cattle.[141]

The intensity of reactions provoked by the destruction of altars was comparable to that provoked by the removal of remains of Suzdal' patrons' from the cathedral. No one took seriously Stefan's shallow excuse that he needed "more space inside the church building" (*dlia radi prostranstva tserkovnogo*).[142] The defilement of the great princely tombs gave rise to anxiety among Suzdalians and several laymen had nightmares; a *guba* elder and a minor official saw horrifying apparitions of the dead princes in their dreams.[143]

Such anxious reactions confirm that the average layman in Suzdal' was not focused on the issue of liturgical reforms. For most of these people it was more important to keep peace with the patrons of Suzdal', the princely families of Shuiskii and Skopin, whose tombs as well as the altars they had endowed, had to be restored. The dead princes were perceived as the providers of health and it was therefore wise not to irritate them. The bishop's actions radically violated these basic religious beliefs.

Finally, Suzdalians responded with great anger to Stefan's suppression of the popular custom of bringing eggs to church during Easter services. Several parish priests claimed Stefan had told them "if one approaches the cross or an icon and greets them with an egg saying 'Christ has risen', and if one responds 'Truly,' one is selling Christ." Elders and sworn officials (*tseloval'niki*) throughout the Suzdal' eparchy complained that "on Easter Sunday the archbishop ordered the priests of his eparchy to prevent greetings with eggs inside church buildings and not to allow parishioners [with eggs] into their churches." Almost twelve hundred Suzdalians expressed unhappiness with this change. Again, this measure was apparently not part of Nikon's liturgical reform policies, but rather the result of Stefan's personal whim, as indicated by the fact that the archbishop made every effort to downplay what he had done.[144]

The revolt of the Suzdal' populace against Nikon's favorite is revealing. While some of Stefan's measures may have been copied from Nikon, his arbitrary and violent behavior cannot be explained in this way. Most of Stefan's measures were strongly condemned by the Church Council of 1660, and there are indications that he himself admitted he had gone too far. In any case, Stefan would not have been able to return to Suzdal' in 1667 if he had continued his unpopular policies.[145]

The apathy toward the introduction of liturgical books in Suzdal' mirrors the scenario of general indifference found in Rostov. The Rostov preachers' personal crusade against the new liturgical books would be taken up a few years later by the Suzdal' priest Nikita Dobrynin.[146] During the 1650s and early 1660s, however, there is no indication that any Suzdal' clerics preached against Stefan's liturgical policies.

Thus, I conclude that conflicts between Stefan and the population of Suzdal' had little to do with the introduction of new liturgical books. A few clerics may have had negative attitudes toward the new liturgies. However, many more Suzdalians were upset by Stefan's random use of violence and by his attacks on icons and altars. I find further, contrary to traditional assumptions, that the introduction of new liturgical books in the archbishoprics of Rostov and Suzdal' did not trigger widespread reactions of fear or resentment among the general population.

THE FIRST OLD BELIEVERS

The patriarchate of Nikon is usually associated with the dramatic struggles of a handful of figures whom the eighteenth-century Old Belief Church (*staroobriadchestvo*) perceived as its founding fathers (*ottsy*).[147] This scholarly focus is based on a number of literary texts that were written fifteen to thirty years after the actual events. The authors, who identified themselves as Old Believers, focused on the stories of a few men while remaining silent about the other scenarios of dissent that I have discussed above.

A Kremlin deacon named Fedor Ivanov, who began writing during the late 1660s, can be considered the first Old Belief historian of the Nikon period. He expressed great admiration for the courage and heroic achievements of archpriests Avvakum, Loggin, and Daniil, and emphasized the historical importance of their struggle.[148] Should Russia become part of the "Latin" West with its "Roman rhetoric, grammar, and philosophy?" Or should its native religious past be maintained? Despairing about the Old Believers' inability to win the upper hand during the Nikon period, Ivanov prophesied that the "last Rus' is here" (*posledniaia Rus' zde*).[149]

During the 1670s, Ivanov and a handful of other Old Believers began to compile historical miscellanies featuring Avvakum's *Vita* and letters.[150] The works attributed to the archpriest have since become the principal sources for reconstructing the earliest manifestations of the Russian Schism.[151] Claiming to speak in the name of the "Russian people" (*russkii narod*), these polemicists identified themselves as the true Russian Orthodoxy and denounced the Nikonian innovations as manifestations of faithlessness (*bezverie*), unbelief (*neverie*), or outright paganism. Some recalled the Time of Troubles, conjuring up images of a new Polish invasion designed to establish the Catholic Church (*kostel*) in Russia.[152] Others spoke of a struggle similar to the great split in Western Christianity during the sixteenth century. An influential letter by Archpriest Avvakum, for example, compared the "Nikonians" not only to the Roman Catholics, but also to the Lutherans and Calvinists. Like these Western "heretics," Nikon and his friends were dividing the Christian world and "creating a schism" (*raskol tvoriat*) in Russian Orthodox religion.[153]

I propose to look beyond Old Belief's own interpretation of the Nikon period, and to provide a careful analysis of the founding fathers' actual social influence. Were they indeed the leaders of a large-scale movement of protest? How successful were they in attracting followers?

Few Russian historical figures have received as much attention as the founding father Archpriest Avvakum. Indeed, the first scholarly publications on the origins of the schism featured Avvakum's *Vita*. The Russian reading public learned about seventeenth-century religious dissent in articles about the archpriest in journals and literary encyclopedias. N. S. Leskov and other well-known writers further popularized the image of Avvakum in their fiction.[154]

This focus on Avvakum is still a dominant feature of schism studies, and has led some modern historians to equate the emergence of the Russian Schism with the work of Avvakum. M. Cherniavsky, for example, called the opponents of Nikon's reforms "Avvakumians," and P. Pascal assigned to Avvakum the role of a new "church leader" (*chef d'église*).[155]

There is little doubt the story of Avvakum was known to ordinary Russians during the modern era of Russian history. For example, peasant dissenters in Siberia stated in mid-eighteenth century that they had heard about the archpriest's sojourn there. A hundred years later, peasants took pride in claiming they were directly descended from the archpriest. And even during the 1930s, after Stalin's collectivization had destroyed much of Russian peasant culture, they still recalled stories about the heroism of Avvakum. Thus, he was considered a popular hero by ordinary Russians.[156]

But when and how did information about Avvakum reach the Russian "masses"? Did they already know about him before his works and *Vita* began their wide circulation during the eighteenth century?[157] More specifically, how did Avvakum relate to ordinary Russians when he began to fight Patriarch Nikon? Did he already enjoy popular sympathy and disseminate his teachings during Nikon's patriarchate?

There is evidence that Avvakum began to formulate his protest against Nikon's reforms soon after the patriarch changed the sign of the cross in July 1653. Avvakum's *Vita*, written about twenty years after the actual events, recalls that:

> Daniil and I wrote down excerpts from books about the sign of the cross and about the prostrations, and we gave them to the tsar; much had been written. I don't know where he hid the excerpts, but it seems that he gave them to Nikon. Soon afterward . . . Nikon seized Daniil, defrocked him in the presence of the tsar, and after much torture, exiled him to Astrakhan'. . . . Then they seized me during a vigil . . . and put me in a prison cell, and at the patriarchal court they put me on a chain for the night.[158]

Other writings attributed to Avvakum and written during the 1670s elaborate on this first clash with official church authority. In all of these accounts, Avvakum asserted that the patriarch perceived him as a major threat and that his subsequent arrest and exile to Siberia were entirely due to his opposition to Nikon's reforms.[159]

We don't know what became of Avvakum's excerpts from books because there is no indication they were ever deposited in the patriarchal archive.[160] Did the tsar or the patriarch ever consider these excerpts important enough to read? Indeed, why should the patriarch have paid any attention to them? Was Avvakum an influential person? To answer these questions, we must briefly consider Avvakum's social position at the time Nikon introduced his first liturgical reform.

Evidence demonstrates that Avvakum had good reason to address a petition to the tsar rather than issue an appeal to a larger public audience. During 1653 Avvakum found himself at the low point of his career. He had just been expelled by the populace of his parish in the Volga town of Iurevets. He later complained to the tsar that "these evil people had beaten [him] with a cudgel, crushed [him] with their feet, and pulled [his] hair with their hands." Thanks to God's intercession, he had "barely escaped with his life" (*ele zhiv*). This brutal mob attack had involved, according to one version of Avvakum's *Vita*, a crowd of more than fifteen hundred people, and had left him without income or position. In short, he was at the mercy of the Kremlin.[161]

Avvakum would hardly have broken his ties with the church. In fact, his own statements suggest that he was immensely proud of serving the church. At Iurevets, for example, he saw himself as the loyal ally of the Patriarch's Office (*patriarkhov prikaz*) and enjoyed holding the rank of archpriest. This ecclesiastical rank gave him ultimate authority in the supervision of local religious affairs, and Avvakum had immediately set out to reform local morals "for the sake of the Church of God." He drastically interfered with popular customs such as gambling and the carnivalesque performances of minstrels. He also tried to stop rampant drunkenness, random violence, and fornication (*bludnia*). One source suggests that he may even have been too zealous in gathering the church tithe. Thus, in 1653 Avvakum was closely identified with official church policies, and clearly opposed to widespread popular customs.[162]

This assessment is confirmed by the sense of duty which characterized Avvakum's behavior after his expulsion: he rescued the patriarchal treasury box from an angry mob and immediately reported back to the Kremlin.[163] Apparently, the humiliated archpriest expected he would be given another position, or at least recognized for his heroism. This was not an unreasonable expectation since his religious reform efforts had won the sympathies of some high-ranking members of the Kremlin elite such as Fedor M. Rtishchev, Vasilii P. Sheremetev, and the brothers Boris and Gleb I. Morozov. In fact, it was due to their influence during the late 1640s that the obscure village priest had apparently been promoted to the office of archpriest as a reward for the many sufferings endured while trying to reform parishioners in one of the Morozov estates.[164]

Still, in 1653 his high-placed protectors were not able—or not willing—to help Avvakum, possibly because they did not want to spoil relations with the tsar, who was known as Nikon's protector and had just appointed him patriarch. As a result, Avvakum was simply left to his own devices. When Nikon introduced the first of his reforms, Avvakum was unemployed and living in Moscow. Scant evidence from the archive of the patriarchal printing press suggests that he was interested in the ongoing liturgical reforms, and that he had bought at least two liturgical books.[165]

What efforts did the unemployed archpriest make to oppose the patriarch's reforms? A letter, dated September 14, 1653 and addressed to another Old Believer, Ivan Neronov, is the only surviving text in Avvakum's handwriting from this period, predating all his other known letters by at least ten years.[166] Curiously enough, this letter makes no explicit reference to Nikon's revision of the liturgies. Rather, it focuses on a dramatic encounter between the angry Avvakum and the clerical staff of the Kazan' Cathedral on Red Square, an event that occurred in August 1653. It appears that Avvakum came into conflict with these clerics because he wanted to take over the vacant post of his mentor, Neronov, who had been exiled a few weeks earlier. The disagreement erupted into a confrontation over questions of precedence in liturgical performances and had nothing to do with the contents of the liturgies per se, but rather with the question of who had the right to perform specific ceremonies—an issue that often arose in churches during the seventeenth century.

On August 13, 1653, the priest Peter was reading from the Book of Sermons (*poucheniia*), a task that had traditionally been performed by Neronov. To an informant who denounced Avvakum to the patriarch, there were good reasons for Peter to take over Neronov's part. First, he had done so before when Neronov had traveled to his native Vologda. Second, Peter was a proficient reader and singer. The informant continued with a detailed description of the ensuing events:

> Peter took the book and proceeded [to preach]. . . . [Suddenly]
> Avvakum entered the altar area, apparently in great anger, and said:

"It is my turn! And now you keep me from taking my place of honor (*mne-de i zhrebiia i chesti nest' nyne*)!" And I responded: "When your turn comes, . . . you may read even ten pages if you like." He retorted: "You forgot the love of our father [Neronov]! During his previous trips and absences this did not happen and you did not dare to take away my place of precedence (*pervenstvo*). Father gave me the order, and that is how it should be because I am, after all, the archpriest!" And I told him that he might be archpriest in Iurevets, but not for us: "We never heard from Ivan Neronovich that you were to be our superior (*chto tebe byt' u nas bol'shomu*); and even if he had said so, it was not his business: He tells you something, and we count for nothing." And this is what the archdeacon also said to us: "Are you really not able to read the sermons? Why do you let Avvakum read them? Preach yourselves!"[167]

Avvakum angrily departed, only to return in even greater fury later in the day. He placed himself at the entrance of the church and delivered an angry sermon against the patriarch, using words that the informant deemed too indecent to repeat in his letter.[168]

Was this sermon about the new liturgies? Or did Avvakum denounce the patriarch for other reasons? No contemporary source provides answers to these questions. However, a later remark by Avvakum, which explicitly recalls the events of 1653, suggests that the angry archpriest may have delivered quite a different speech about the patriarch:

I saw through this son-of-a-bitch before the pestilence [of 1654]. This great deceiver and son of a whore (*bliadin syn*)! When in the presence of the [tsar's] confessor, Stefan, he sighs and cries like a wolf in sheep's clothing. From the window of his palace he throws money to beggars, and riding along the road he flings gold coins at them! And this blind world praises him: such a dear lord! There was none like him in ages! However, young women—forgive me for God's sake—and nuns are living as favorites (*vremennitsy*) in his chambers. They gratify His Most Lecherous Great Majesty, and he deflowers them through fornication. . . . The wife of the priest Maksim, who was living with me, . . . was in this prelate's bedroom and drank vodka with him. . . . I know other trifling details of this kind. One must spit on them all. Word for word, such will be the Antichrist.[169]

Thus, it is possible Avvakum made a scandal by publicly exposing the patriarch's weaknesses that were noted also by less emotional observers.[170] In any case, there is no documentary evidence that Avvakum was arrested for opposing the new liturgies. Rather, he may have fallen victim again to his own reform zeal, which he no longer directed against the common people but against the patriarch himself.[171]

It is unlikely that Avvakum received much support after his sermon against Nikon, especially if we consider that Nikon—not only according to Avvakum's own recollection—was popular among ordinary Muscovites for distributing alms.[172] We do know, however, that the archpriest marched away demonstratively, telling everybody that "the [Kazan'] priests had taken away his Book [of Sermons] and chased him out of the church." The following day he attempted to force his way into a church building of another Moscow parish. When this attempt failed, he proceeded to perform Mass in Neronov's abandoned home, gathering a small group of supporters around him whom he called "the brethren in God" (*brat'ia o Gospode*).[173] While Avvakum was reading to them about the expulsion of John Chrysostomos, agents of the patriarch broke in and arrested them, and shortly afterwards Avvakum was exiled to Siberia.[174] The official document ordering his exile does not make a single reference to his opposition to the new liturgies, but rather condemns him for "unruly behavior" (*bezchinstvo*).[175]

Thus, the surviving archival evidence does not allow a clear-cut evaluation of the early Avvakum. New liturgies were probably not yet his primary concern; he considered himself a religious "zealot" (*revnitel'*) and took great pride in refusing to make any compromise with religious corruption.[176]

Even though we don't know much about Avvakum's priorities in 1653, we can be certain about one thing: in late 1653 Avvakum was hardly in a position to launch a major preaching campaign against the ongoing liturgical reforms. Like countless other parish priests and archpriests during the patriarchate of Nikon, he had become a victim of the patriarch's arbitrary violence.[177] All attempts to reclaim what he considered his rightful position were in vain, and he arrived in Tobol'sk in Siberia—far removed from the heartlands of Muscovy—a few months later.[178]

Did Avvakum have any support in 1653? As we have seen, his former boyar supporters did not intervene on his behalf. It is likely, however, that he maintained some contact with them, as indicated by his visits to their homes ten years later. Also, Gleb I. Morozov's wife, Feodosiia, would eventually become one of Avvakum's most important allies, probably during his brief sojourn in Moscow during the summer of 1664.[179] If Avvakum had any non-elite support during this period, it was limited to the few "brethren in God" supporters. These "brethren" will be carefully examined later, when I discuss the circles that formed around the first Old Believers.

Archpriest Daniil was one of the most visible of these "brethren in God," and he is often mentioned in seventeenth-century Old Believer texts as a close ally of Avvakum. For example, Avvakum's *Vita*, as we have seen above, refers to Daniil as the co-author of Avvakum's petition against the new liturgies. He is also repeatedly mentioned in texts written by the "Pustoozero prisoners" during the 1670s. Not surprisingly, the first historian of the eighteenth-century Old Belief Church, Semen Denisov of the Vyg Community, elevated him to the rank of founding father.[180]

A look at Daniil's tragic fate sheds more light on the nature of Avvakum's confrontation with ordinary Muscovites. Indeed, Daniil's story—even more than Avvakum's—suggests that the first Old Believers failed to attract a substantial following. Like Avvakum, Daniil had held the office of archpriest with a mandate from the Kremlin to introduce proper Christian morals in the town of Kostroma, and he too suffered the fate of expulsion. In May 1652, the inhabitants of Kostroma physically attacked him with the support, or at least connivance, of the voevoda. Factual information about this event survives in records of the investigation conducted by emissaries from Moscow. Daniil gave the following account during his interrogation:

> The parish priests told us that their parishioners come to church services armed with knives. They stand at the church doors and thresholds, scream into the buildings at their spiritual fathers, and intend to stab them. Others who see me, the archpriest, and other good folk, bring them into agitation (*zador*) and do all kinds of nasty things in both the town and its districts: they provoke rebellion and lawlessness. And in this rebellion several people have been beaten to death, others have almost died from their blows. The voevoda . . . and his officials . . . did not help [us], and despite orders by the tsar, they took no action against these lawbreakers and disobedient people. When we seized lawbreakers by our own force and took them to the voevoda, his officials would not imprison them, but instead took bribes and let them go.[181]

Daniil concluded his testimony with the following story:

> During the night of May 25th . . . the peasant Koz'ma Vasil'ev and his companions began to sing songs on the banks of the Volga river. I went out to stop them, but they beat me almost to death. One blow was so severe that it threw off my skullcap and I fell unconscious. Then, Vasil'ev and his men went to the cathedral, and at the court of the voevoda they beat me again with a cudgel. At half-past midnight I ordered one of the guards to ring the church bell. The voevoda came out, but he did not defend me, and the peasants ran away. . . . [182]

The investigators from Moscow discovered that Daniil had forbidden minstrels (*skomorokhi*) to sing their songs, and that he had also preached against drunkenness.[183] This finding indicates that Daniil had, in all likelihood, been attacked for meddling with common popular practices.

The passage quoted above and a brief mention of Daniil by Avvakum in September 1653 are the last reports we have of Daniil before he vanished into historical obscurity. No evidence of Daniil's having protested the revision of books has come down to us, and later Old Belief assertions that Daniil was a cofounder of their movement cannot be further clarified. However, the evidence suggests that Daniil was hardly a popular figure; he could more justly be remembered as a victim of local violence.

Another of Avvakum's friends and supporters was Archpriest Loggin of Murom, also considered a founding father by later generations of Old Believers.[184] Authentic information about Loggin survives in a handful of documents that were ignored by later Old Believers as well as by historians of the Old Belief. Among these documents are the proceedings that led to Loggin's expulsion from the church in September 1653. The proceedings can be reconstructed on the basis of a report that was in all likelihood dictated by Neronov to his son soon after the events.[185] This is the account that Neronov addressed to the tsar:

> Sire, in July of this year [1653] there was a meeting with our chief of fathers (*otsenachal'nik*), [Nikon], in the patriarchal palace. At that time they read a note by the voevoda of Murom that Archpriest Loggin had defamed the images of Our Lord Jesus Christ, of the Mother of God, and of All the Saints. The archpriest said in his defense: "Far be it from me to profane these images either verbally, or in my thoughts. I bow to them and venerate them with fear. But once at the voevoda's home, the voevoda's wife came to [me] for a blessing and [I] said to her: 'Are you not wearing white make-up?' (*ne belena li ty*). These words were picked up by Afanasii Otiaev, who said: 'Why do you complain about white paint (*belila*)? Without white paint the icons of the Savior, the Mother of God, and All the Saints cannot be painted.' The voevoda intervened and . . . said: 'Afanasii is quite right.' And [I], Loggin, responded: 'For each instrument there is a proper use and the compounds with which icons should be painted are made by the icon painter. And you wouldn't want to put those compounds [i.e., icon paint] on your face. The Savior, purest Mother of God, and the Saints must be honored much more than their images. . . .'" [Nikon] did not deliberate much, and gave orders to hand Loggin over to a stern bailiff.[186]

Thus, Loggin's expulsion from the church was apparently the result of his religious zeal. Rather than condoning what he considered unacceptable secular and religious behavior—in this case the wearing of make-up and the profanation of icons—he got involved in a dangerous quarrel with the voevoda, the most powerful official in Murom.[187]

Further evidence suggests that Loggin's clash with the voevoda was the end result of a long confrontation with the local populace. A petition by a handful of local friends, which survives in the archive of the Riazan' eparchy, described Loggin's dilemma: "[The inhabitants of Murom] love damned drunkenness more than divine mercy and have united to expel their pastor and teacher." They were led in this endeavor by Ivan Sergiev, who "was an enemy of God and a second Judas" and wanted to "steal the office of archpriest for himself." Loggin's supporters felt that they were surrounded by "evil witnesses who were plotting the expulsion of their father," and that they were powerless because all of this happened at the connivance of the voevoda.[188]

Thus, again we see the tragic isolation of an early Old Believer in a hostile social environment. Loggin's fate was sealed from the beginning because he dared to preach openly against religious indifference and popular practices such as drinking and gambling. This remarkable courage brought him the admiration of a foreign observer, the German Protestant Olearius, who heard about Loggin's efforts "to teach the word of God to the people, and to admonish and punish." Olearius also knew about the arrest and punishment of the preacher. Recalling the tragic fate of earlier religious reformers in Muscovy, he commented laconically that "the Russians are equally hostile to criticism today, and anyone who proposes anything of the kind [i.e., reform] fares no better than ... Log[g]in of Murom, who began to preach."[189]

Later Old Believer writings hardly refer to Neronov, whose name we have already mentioned in connection with Avvakum, Daniil, and Loggin. Unlike these three figures, Neronov never became identified as a founding father and his writings were not copied by later generations of Old Believers.[190] This silence is due largely to Neronov's recantation of Old Belief at the 1666 Church Council, but it belies his importance during the patriarchate of Nikon. Avvakum, for example, considered Neronov his "spiritual father" (*otets dukhovnyi*).[191] As we have seen, Avvakum wrote letters seeking his advice and sought refuge at his home after his eviction from the Kazan' Cathedral. Indeed, if Old Belief had a leader during the 1650s it was not Avvakum, but Neronov.

Neronov had even better connections with members of the Kremlin elite than Avvakum—not surprising since he was about thirty years older. In fact, Neronov's career had been launched during the 1620s by the founders of the Romanov dynasty, Tsar Mikhail Fedorovich and his father Patriarch Filaret. Both had been impressed when this obscure deacon from the hinterlands of Vologda started a preaching campaign in the capital against the cutting of beards and the trimming of hair as harmful foreign customs.

They had rescued the preacher from violent beatings triggered by his sermons and made him a guest of honor in the Kremlin.[192] Since then, Neronov had been a regular visitor at the Kremlin, a tradition that continued until the end of his life in 1670. Indeed, Neronov was intimately acquainted with the entire Romanov clan as well as their chief advisors such as Fedor M. Rtishchev and Ilia D. Miloslavskii. The younger Romanov tsar, Aleksei Mikhailovich (1645–76), and his wife, Mariia Miloslavskaia, were particularly fond of the preacher, and so it is not surprising that he appealed to them for help in several letters after his arrest by Patriarch Nikon in August 1653.[193]

These letters—and letters addressed to the tsar's personal confessor—not only provide insights into Neronov's attitudes toward the new liturgies, but also his day-to-day struggles during the early 1650s. Since they predate all other Old Believer letters by at least ten years, they are an unparalleled source of information about the genesis of Old Belief under Patriarch Nikon.[194]

Neronov's letters might be seen as a preliminary attempt to formulate an Old Belief ideology. The archpriest was indeed concerned about Nikon's effort to change the liturgical rites: he asserted that "great confusion" (*velikoe nesoglasie*) had been caused by the introduction of the new sign of the cross. He considered this along with a few other minor changes to be an attack on the ancient Christian tradition in Russia which had not been altered since the days of St. Vladimir of Kiev. In a style that became typical of later Old Believer writings, he spoke of a great "catastrophe" (*pogibel'*) and a great "turmoil" (*miatezh*) that had befallen Russia: "Don't you understand the present misfortunes of all of Russia? All of piety has ceased to exist and the children of the church cry everywhere." At one point, Neronov even insisted that Russia was about to be annexed by the Roman Catholic Church and that the end of times was near. Indeed, he was the first Old Believer to use the word "schism" (*raskol*) to describe the consequence of Nikon's reforms.[195]

Despite the shared feature of polemic hyperbole, Neronov's letters differ considerably from the letters of other seventeenth-century Old Believers. His primary concern was not the correction of books, and he was not against liturgical reform per se. Indeed, he proudly affirmed his role as sponsor and principal executor of one of these reforms: the introduction of single-voiced singing (*edinoglasie*). What he found unacceptable was the new atmosphere in the patriarchal court since Nikon had assumed power in 1652. Neronov considered the new liturgical rites to be only one factor amidst the general chaos that had descended upon Muscovy under Nikon.

The real danger that threatened the future of Russian piety, he felt, was the political conspiracy of the patriarch against forces in the Kremlin that had favored genuine church reform.[196]

Neronov further argued that Nikon's liturgical reforms were not connected with any reform of Christian morals: the patriarch had entrusted the work to men who did not themselves lead Christian lives. Most importantly, he had eliminated the influence of the tsar's confessor, Stefan Vonifat'ev, whom Neronov considered the principal reformer in Muscovy. In short, the "men of God" (*liudi Bozhie*) whom Vonifat'ev had protected in the past were now systematically being replaced by "slanderers" (*klevetniki*) and ruthless careerists.[197]

Neronov observed a dramatic policy shift within the Russian Orthodox Church. According to Neronov, the Christian reform policies sponsored by the previous patriarchs ever since the elder Romanov, Filaret, had authorized them in the 1620s, were now superseded by the power politics of Patriarch Nikon.[198] The tsar should know the truth about Nikon: he had not the least regard for religious matters, and sought only to increase his personal power. He not only ignored the reform agenda of the Romanov family, but was also openly hostile to the tsar. Nikon had once even boasted that "the tsar's assistance was good for nothing and of no use to [him]. In fact, [he] would spit and blow his nose (*pliuiu i smorkaiu*) on it." The young tsar should recall the example of his father, Mikhail Romanov, who had urged reformers to "denounce all who behave scandalously."[199]

According to Neronov, the very people whom the reformers had found guilty of religious wrongdoings in the past were now being given elevated positions by Nikon. At the same time, all the friends (*druzi*) of the tsar's confessor were denounced and "destroyed." "In their place [Nikon] installed others about whom nothing good is to be heard." Nikon even took a personal delight in torturing those "who love God . . . and had not feared humiliation and death to suffer for the true [faith]. . . ."[200] In a letter of May 1654, Neronov elaborated further on the same theme:

> I obeyed the order of Archpriest Stefan Nifantevich [the tsar's confessor], and showed submission and love toward Patriarch Nikon in every way as long as he was archimandrite and metropolitan. I never lied to him and always spoke the truth, asking him not to listen to slanderers. And now those who are criminals, whom he imprisoned and rightly called enemies when he was archimandrite and metropolitan, have become his friends and advisers. He gives powerful positions to those who execute his will, not the will of God. Sire, what good has ever come from those who were selected by the patriarch to hold offices? . . . [201]

Documents describing the circumstances preceding Neronov's arrest confirm that, in all likelihood, his fate was determined not by his opposition to the Nikonian reforms, but by clerical intrigues against him. In July 1653, the priests and deacons of the Kazan' Cathedral submitted a collective petition against the archpriest to the patriarch. The petition itself has not survived, but its contents can be reconstructed from the ensuing proceedings against Neronov.[202] During these proceedings Neronov had to endure probing questions about the moral conduct of his wife. His son was accused of common thievery—breaking into a locked church building.[203] Some witnesses against Neronov had obviously been bribed. For example, one priest was freed from prison in exchange for giving false testimony against Neronov, and another priest, Ivan Danilov, procured for his son a position in the church administration.[204] Other witnesses also found their denunciation of Neronov rewarding. For example, protodeacon Grigorii, who had been passed over in assignments to ecclesiastical posts under Nikon's predecessor, now saw his chance to regain official favor.[205]

Thus, the reasons Neronov lost his position are similar to those for the other early Old Believers discussed above. He fell victim to his own reform zeal—a fact that is further corroborated by the German traveler Olearius, who attributed Neronov's removal entirely to his preaching campaigns against religious corruption.[206] Or, as the author of Neronov's *Vita* put it:

> Certain people of high ecclesiastical rank conspired against him because they hated his teaching for its zealous emphasis on proper Christian conduct (*blagochinie*): with great courage he denounced all whom he saw behaving in an ungodly fashion, especially those powerful clerics who did not behave according to their station. This explains why they plotted against him with the result that he was deprived of his priestly rank, bound in iron chains, and broken down in jails.[207]

Neronov's *Vita*, the first version of which was written as early as 1659, is probably the most important non-documentary source on the earliest manifestations of Old Belief. Unlike the *Vita* of Avvakum, it was not written to glorify the heroic days of Nikon's patriarchate, but rather for the simple purpose of recording all major events in Neronov's career.[208] This *Vita* contradicts another important aspect of our current perception of Old Belief's origins: the attitudes of the first Old Believers toward the new liturgies could be quite flexible. For example, in January 1657 Neronov accepted the *Tablet* (*Skrizhal'*) which, as mentioned above, codified the new three-finger sign of the cross.[209] Shortly afterwards, he repeatedly participated in new church services at the Uspenskii Cathedral in the Kremlin. Neronov also visited Patriarch Nikon in the Kremlin on a daily basis until early 1658, and had long discussions with him about the necessity of spiritual reform—not about liturgical questions.[210]

It is unclear why Neronov made peace with Nikon after enduring nearly four years of exile and persecution. He probably became more friendly with the patriarch because he was restored to his former position of influence at the Kremlin and was given money from the patriarchal treasury.[211] When he finally left Moscow in early 1658 for his native Vologda, the patriarch gave him a special endowment of books and vestments. This endowment allowed Neronov to withdraw from preaching and retire to a small monastic community.[212]

Later Old Believer writings have obscured any indication that the first Old Believers were unsure about continuing their fight against the new liturgies. Neronov's story helps to explain rarely cited documentary evidence about Avvakum which indicates that Avvakum was not a typical exile deprived of his clerical rank and position; he was, in fact, restored as archpriest and served at the cathedral church of Tobol'sk. Indeed, under the protection of Nikon's friend, Archbishop Simeon, Avvakum became one of the most powerful church officials in Siberia from 1654–55.[213]

Ample evidence shows that Avvakum organized and headed church campaigns against drunkenness and sexual promiscuity during these years. On at least one occasion he was also in charge of a major investigation concerning the flight of serfs who had sought refuge in a small hermitage not far from Tobol'sk.[214] Later, Avvakum was assigned to an expeditionary force that was given the task of bringing Christianity to remote tribes in northern Siberia. A letter by Archbishop Simeon, dated January 1658 and related to the expedition, documents that Avvakum had been assigned all priestly functions. A short dispatch sent to the archbishop from Moscow in February 1658 indicates that Avvakum was to receive a "stipend of money, bread, and salt" for his services to the church. Thus, even Avvakum, whom later generations of Old Believers portrayed as the most important opponent of Patriarch Nikon, may not yet have been ready to sever his ties with the official church in order to fight for the old liturgies. In any case, he did little to disseminate the cause of Old Belief during his exile in Siberia. In fact, during 1654–58 Avvakum collaborated with church agents—the same men he later demonized as "precursors of the Antichrist."[215]

Thus, the evidence is puzzling and contradictory. On the one hand, it appears that the four individuals discussed here were the first to raise doubts about the ongoing liturgical reforms—which they did in 1653, a few years before the previously mentioned Rostov tailor Sila Bogdanov and other opponents of Nikon's reforms came on the scene. On the other hand, their conflict with church authority over the new liturgies did not seem to dominate their lives in 1653. In particular, documentary evidence suggests that opposing the new liturgies was not the cause for their arrests and exiles. Avvakum and Neronov, their bitter personal conflicts with Patriarch Nikon notwithstanding, did not yet perceive themselves as permanent outcasts from the church. Despite—or possibly because of—their experience of exile, they did not yet insist on the falsity of the new liturgies and, when given an opportunity, even accepted official church assignments for which they received money from the treasury. It therefore appears that the first Old Believers were more concerned with regaining their former positions within the church than with organizing a popular movement against the church.

There is evidence indicating that the preachers discussed here had friends and supporters. For example, Daniil could hardly have escaped Kostroma if a handful of "good folk" (*dobrye liudi*) had not supported him. Loggin had a few courageous supporters who did not fear local violence and wrote a petition on his behalf. Avvakum was arrested in Moscow with a handful of supporters, and Neronov made general references in his letters to men and women—in his words "God's elect" (*izbrannye Bozhie*) and "brethren in Christ" (*o Khriste brat'ia*)—who were arrested for supporting his mission.[216]

What is known about the men and women who became associated with the archpriests? Loggin's and Daniil's supporters probably will never be identified since neither of these "zealots" were of great interest to church authorities. Daniil may not have survived the ordeal of exile because he disappeared without a trace. Loggin, who was confined to his native village outside Murom, escaped and somehow managed to visit the exiled Neronov in June or July of 1654. Neronov viewed Loggin as a loyal executor of his own wishes and ordered (*povelel*) him to write at least one secret letter to the tsar's confessor. It appears that Loggin may have lost his own community of supporters after his expulsion from Murom and chose to promulgate Neronov's cause instead. Unfortunately, his other contacts are not known and we therefore cannot reconstruct to what degree, if at all, he contributed to the dissemination of Old Belief.[217]

We are better informed about Avvakum. One of his most fervent supporters was the learned Moscow resident Semen Bebekhov who wrote the clean copy of Avvakum's petition to the tsar. Semen, whose social identity and status are unknown, somehow managed to break out of his prison cell in the Kremlin and go into hiding. He may have been helped by a handful of Avvakum's other associates in Moscow. Of these, three appear to have been particularly important: Avvakum's brother Gerasim, the priest Semen Trofimov, and the secretary (*d'iak*) Fedor Zinov'ev. In addition, Avvakum enjoyed the support of Neronov's wife and sons, who had welcomed him to their home and helped him establish contact with some of Neronov's parishioners at the Kazan' Cathedral. When Avvakum was locked out of the church, one of these parishioners remarked that "a stable is better than that church" (*koniushnia-de inye tserkvi luchshe*). According to an observer, who later informed Neronov, thirty-three parishioners were arrested with Avvakum. Even assuming that several others escaped, it is unlikely that Avvakum had more than forty or fifty supporters in Moscow, and most of these belonged to the Kazan' parish on Red Square which had been under Neronov's leadership since the late 1640s.[218]

Hardly a popular hero, the archpriest's influence had spread among a very limited group of people. A further look at Avvakum's adventures in Siberia confirms this impression. The residents of Tobol'sk hated him: they sent appeals to the tsar to relieve them of the archpriest no fewer than five times. In particular, they resented Avvakum's preaching campaigns against drunkenness, adultery, fornication, and incest. When the tsar failed to intervene, they plotted to murder the troublemaker. Avvakum later recalled that a mob had assembled to drown him in the Tobol' River. He desperately sought refuge in the home of the voevoda, begging to be locked in a prison cell for protection. Afraid that the mob would break into his palace, the voevoda refused. Avvakum escaped because he had a handful of dedicated supporters who, with the tacit support of the voevoda's wife, hid the endangered archpriest in a baggage crate and carried him to safety.[219]

Again, we know nothing about these anonymous supporters—only that as in Moscow, Avvakum was not entirely isolated in Tobol'sk and enjoyed at least some sympathy among local residents. In order to probe more deeply into the composition, and possibly the religious beliefs, of the circles that formed around these early Old Believers, we must look at our best source of information: the correspondence and biography of the little-studied Neronov.

Neronov's *Vita* confirms that ordinary Russians probably had little sympathy for the early Old Believers. When Neronov was arrested by Nikon in July 1653, he looked back on a long career of suffering "for the sake of Christ." He had no less than ten times narrowly escaped with his life after raising his voice in public against popular practices. At the beginning of his career, probably around 1620, the following incident occurred; it can be seen as the first in a pattern that repeated itself many times throughout his life:

[Neronov] went to the town of Vologda . . . and it was there that he suffered for the first time. During these days the irrational people used to gather for demonic spectacles . . . and put terrifying masks on their faces imitating demons and ghosts. Ivan happened to pass such a spectacle . . . , and nearby he saw a large house from which came a multitude of young and old people. . . . He asked them: "Whose house is this and who are these people?" They told him: "This is the episcopal palace and we are ordained clerics and the bishop's servants." This [response] inflamed [Ivan's] spirit and he began to denounce them audaciously: "This cannot possibly be the bishop's home because bishops are appointed by God to be the shepherds of Christ's flock. They are supposed to teach God's people to refrain from all evil and to stay away from demonic festivals. . . . " They became furious, rushed upon him like wild beasts, and began to beat him mercilessly. While they were beating him, he continued to denounce them. When they were done with him, they left him barely alive. In fact, they thought he was dead.[220]

There is no indication that Neronov was any more popular during the 1650s. For example, in June 1654 he was assaulted by monks, priests, novices, and laymen living in the Vologda monastery where he had been confined after his arrest. The reason for this outbreak of violence was simply that the inhabitants of the monastery no longer could endure Neronov's sermons. For months he had continually berated them for laziness, too much sleeping, drinking, greediness, and a general failure to understand the true meaning of Orthodox religion. Priests hardly knew how to read liturgical books; peasants did not attend church services on Sundays; when monks visited local villages they did not care for the souls of the population, but got drunk instead; and finally, those in charge of the monastery laughed about illiterate priests and only too gladly exploited the general religious ignorance of their flock by having peasants cut wood during Holy Week.[221]

It finally dawned on Neronov that his admonitions were not welcome, but it was too late. He was locked into a monastic cell "like an evil criminal" (*zlyi razboinik*) and he feared he would be killed at any moment. After five weeks of solitary confinement, orders arrived from Moscow to transfer Neronov to another monastery.[222]

Despite such hostility, Neronov managed to win some supporters. He established a small community of "seekers of God" (*bogoliubtsy*) in Nizhnii Novgorod during the 1630s and early 1640s. One of the most influential members of this community was the wealthy merchant Ivan Zadorin, who entrusted Neronov with the construction and decoration of a stone church. Zadorin's money allowed Neronov to achieve some popularity among the urban poor: he welcomed them to his home, fed them, and dressed them. In addition, he taught basic literacy skills, cared for the sick and mentally deranged (*strannye*), counseled possessed and hysterical women (*besnye i klichushchie*), and attempted to teach his visitors about Jesus Christ, the Apostles, and the Bible.[223] Nevertheless, Neronov and members of his community suffered regular beatings and "many wounds" in mob attacks led by a "multitude of minstrels" (*mnozhestvo skomrakhov*). Given such a hostile social environment, Neronov's efforts to create an alternative Christian community appear to have been doomed.[224]

After Neronov left Nizhnii Novgorod in 1645 to serve as archpriest at the Kazan' Cathedral in Moscow, it is likely that a small core of his community continued to exist well into the 1650s, and that at least one of its members—Neronov's favorite, the priest Gavriil—became a fervent Old Believer. Possibly another few of Neronov's former "spiritual children" adopted Old Belief during the 1650s, but neither archives nor Old Believer writings provide any evidence.[225]

The community that formed around Neronov in Moscow underwent a similar development. During the late 1640s his sermons created a sensation in Moscow. Large crowds came to the Kazan' Cathedral out of curiosity, especially when the tsar and his family were present. Many poor and sick stayed in a shelter and hospital maintained by Neronov, and word got around that he offered help to everyone in need. However, few of his former parishioners sided with him after his arrest and his popularity quickly diminished.[226]

Neronov soon found new associates in two other clerics who had sought refuge in Moscow: the Archpriest Ermil of Iaroslavl'—probably a close kinsman of Neronov's, and the priest Lazar' from Romanov.[227] Neronov also was supported by four adult male members of the Pleshcheev clan, who belonged to the Kremlin elite and who were sympathetic toward both Avvakum and Neronov. They were the only boyars who openly gave their support to Neronov, even daring to write him two letters in prison. These letters are moving examples of the deep emotions that Neronov evoked in some of his supporters.[228]

Despite such fervent devotees, Neronov's activities in Moscow may not have left a permanent imprint on the development of Old Belief. Ermil eventually made peace with Nikon and apparently visited him in the patriarchal chambers. Even the Pleshcheevs, who were perhaps Neronov's most important supporters in Moscow, appear to have abandoned his cause not long after his arrest.[229] Whether Neronov's community could have continued to exist without such influential protectors is questionable. Avvakum, who was acquainted with Neronov's "spiritual children," saw little future for the community after Neronov's arrest. Commenting on those who lived in Neronov's house, he said: "Your house is topsy-turvy (*ni to ni se*). After I left, things have greatly deteriorated. They tell stories, drink heavily, and quarrel with each other. My wife could no longer endure it and walked out. Indeed, all brethren have dispersed."[230]

Further indication that Neronov's Moscow community probably disintegrated soon after his arrest is provided by a former supporter, who wrote to Neronov that he had to abandon the cause in order to find his son ecclesiastical employment. The dismayed archpriest also learned that his own family had expelled some of his favorites from their home. Neronov's son Feofilakt no longer participated in community celebrations of the liturgy and had recently disappeared. Even Avvakum's brother Gerasim, who appears to have been the crucial linchpin of the remaining community after the arrests of both Neronov and Avvakum, ended his resistance and accepted a lucrative parish position in Moscow.[231]

Still, a handful of supporters must have remained, because Neronov was able to secretly come to Moscow after he escaped from exile in late 1655. The identity of these supporters is unclear, but it seems they were not rank-and-file Muscovites. Indeed, there are clues that Neronov was hiding directly under the nose of the patriarch in the Kremlin during his brief stay. It is also likely that the intervention of a powerful personality near Nikon's Kremlin court, possibly Metropolitan Pitirim of Krutitsa, brought about Neronov's temporary reconciliation with the patriarch in early 1657. Thus, if Neronov had any influence during this period it was not because of local community support, but because he could still count on some political support in the Kremlin.[232]

Neronov was, at heart, a man of the church, with little tolerance for the religious practices of ordinary Russians. As one final example, after Neronov had completely recanted his belief in the superiority of the old liturgies in 1666, he was elevated to the rank of archimandrite of a monastery not far from Moscow. Again, he used his official position to discipline monks, parish priests, and peasants for their negligence in religious matters. In fact, his *Vita* claimed successes such as the complete eradication of drunkenness in the monastery. The inevitable happened: Neronov again fell victim to a popular revolt. Angry peasants "cursed him with all kinds of indecent swearwords and beat him out (*vybili*) of the Church of God."[233]

There was, however, an important difference between this attack and the many previous ones. This time the tsar intervened immediately on Neronov's behalf. Special emissaries of boyar rank were sent to the monastery to arrest Neronov's enemies. It appears that Neronov became more popular as a result of this drastic intervention on his behalf. The chronicler of his life noticed this dramatic turn of fortune: "those who had been his enemies and chased him took shame . . . because they did not want to make the tsar angry. . . . They sought to make peace with him out of fear of the tsar." Towards the end of his life, no one dared to challenge his authority and he was the indisputable ruler over his monastery and the surrounding parishes. As Neronov's biographer put it laconically, "he punished those [priests] who were disobedient . . . and was a generous and merciful father to those who obeyed him."[234]

The life of Neronov demonstrates the social isolation of the Old Belief founding fathers. Neronov gained popularity only by winning the support of the tsar and invoking his name to intimidate opponents, or by having enough money—from merchants or other sponsors—to distribute food and medicine to the poor. There is little evidence that his popularity was due to preaching against the new liturgies. Once he lost his protection, as happened on numerous occasions, his support dissipated fairly quickly.[235]

And there is no evidence that any other founding father came close to enjoying the same popularity as Neronov. One can only speculate what would have become of, say, Avvakum, if he had been willing to make long-term peace with the church. He could easily have risen to a high church position with real disciplinary authority.[236] As it happened, Avvakum's authority remained elusive after 1666, limited to the writing of pastoral letters from prison.[237] Ordinary Russians' later veneration of Avvakum was not due to his missionary activities, but to other factors that will be discussed in the next chapter.

SEVERAL CONCLUSIONS can be drawn from the observations in this chapter. Most importantly, Nikon's liturgical reforms did not unleash widespread societal protest. In fact, only a small number of individuals defended the old liturgies; Russian society remained largely indifferent.

Archival documents and neglected literary sources such as the *Vita* of Ivan Neronov suggest that those who protested were isolated and unpopular figures. The so-called founding fathers of Old Belief, among them Avvakum, were also unsuccessful in attracting followers. By their preaching campaigns against religious indifference and ignorance, they alienated many ordinary Russians. Neither the first Old Believers nor other early opponents of Nikon's reforms had sufficient clout to organize resistance against the official church, and by the end of Nikon's tenure as patriarch, all of them had in some way been neutralized.

If the first Old Believers wielded any influence, it was only over a few religious zealots. Evidence shows that small circles of friends formed around the archpriests Loggin, Avvakum, and Neronov, and it appears that elite members of society, such as the boyars Pleshcheev or the merchant Zadorin, rather than rank-and-file Muscovites played the most significant roles in these circles. Once deprived of their religious mentors, even some of the most inspired disciples appear to have accepted the new liturgies. By the end of the Nikon period, only remnants of these circles remained.

There is even insufficient evidence to demonstrate that the early Old Believers were totally committed to a struggle against Nikon's reforms. Indeed, they were often willing to renounce their opposition when offered the opportunity to resume formerly held church positions. They made significant compromises with official authority and, at least temporarily, helped to promote the church's cause by disciplining and punishing ordinary believers. Later Old Believer writings, such as the Pustoozero letters of Avvakum, paid little attention to the uncertainties of these first years.

If there was a massive struggle over religious issues during this period, it certainly was not over the introduction of the new liturgies. As we have seen, the Muscovite "masses" remained indifferent toward changes in church services. They were very sensitive, however, to changes affecting the more vital aspects of their religious world. The common man—cleric and layman alike—was upset about the confiscation of "Latin" and privately owned icons, the prohibition against bringing Easter eggs to church, and having to face death without pastoral guidance during the pestilence. None of the first Old Believers participated in these truly large-scale conflicts that, at least temporarily, challenged the power of the official church.

CHAPTER TWO

Protests Against the New Liturgies Following Nikon's Abdication, 1658-66

The absence of significant conflicts over the revision of liturgical books under Nikon might be explained by the fact that Nikon himself had no interest in bringing opponents of the new books to trial. In notes addressed to the tsar, Nikon explicitly distanced himself from the reforms, insisting that he had only carried out the will of visiting Greek hierarchs. Indeed, the letters he wrote during his tenure as patriarch and after his abdication in July 1658 maintain a strange silence about individuals who opposed the new books.[1]

But if Nikon was willing to overlook opposition to the liturgical reforms, others—powerful officials working for the tsar's court and high-ranking clergymen such as metropolitans Iona of Rostov and Pitirim of Krutitsa—were not. Several investigations of liturgical dissent during the years 1658–66 provide insights into societal attitudes toward the reforms following Nikon's withdrawal from Kremlin politics.

OFFICIAL INVESTIGATIONS OF DISSENT

During the eight-year period without a patriarch, investigating officials were mostly involved in proceedings against Nikon himself. Perceiving only one significant threat to the stability of the church—the intrigues launched by the former patriarch for the purpose of reclaiming the patriarchal throne—they paid little attention to liturgical dissent. The seeming indifference of these officials and hierarchs sharply distinguishes them from their successors, who viewed persecution of dissenters as the church's primary task. As I discuss in the next chapter, the well-known 1666 Church Council marked the start of a radically new attitude toward dissenters.

Metropolitan Iona, an ambitious man who apparently tried to succeed Nikon, was the most important instigator of dissent investigations during this earlier period. In August 1660, he played a leading role at a Moscow church council calling for Nikon's permanent replacement by a new patriarch.[2] During the following years, he gathered information to justify exiling Nikon and, for a short while, even managed to become the *locum tenens* (*mestobliustitel'*) of the patriarchal see.[3]

The same officials who had helped Iona to eliminate the Rostov dissenter Sila a few years earlier, Boyar Aleksei Nikitich Trubetskoi and the secretary Almaz Ivanov, again collaborated to discredit Nikon. On July 16, 1658, just six days after Nikon's abdication, Trubetskoi inspected Nikon's belongings in the abandoned patriarchal court. In April 1659, Ivanov was sent to the Voskresenskii Monastery to question Nikon regarding a derogatory remark about Metropolitan Pitirim, who was then acting as *locum tenens* of the patriarchal see.[4] And in February 1660, Trubetskoi headed the commission that interrogated Nikon about his reasons for leaving Moscow. Both officials appear in records of the patriarchal archive in crucial investigative roles on many other occasions as well. It is probably no overstatement to say that Nikon could not have been deposed in 1666 without the information they gathered.[5]

Why these and other investigators deviated from their overriding concern with the removal of Patriarch Nikon to address liturgical dissent remains unclear. Under orders from Nikon's main opponents, metropolitans Iona and Pitirim, they perhaps discerned opportunities to enhance their patrons' political clout. All of the five cases discussed in this chapter were principally investigated during the years 1660–62, when proceedings against Nikon reached their first culmination. They include: cases against Muscovy's most powerful monastic leaders, the archimandrites of the Troitsa and Solovki monasteries; a case against priest Terentii for calling Pitirim the Antichrist; a case against priest Nikon, whose ignorance about ongoing liturgical reforms annoyed Kremlin authorities; and finally, a case against the Chudov monk Savvatii, whose accusations of incompetence against the post-Nikonian church leadership were deemed intolerable.

At least one of these five cases was directly linked to political conflicts that emerged in the wake of Nikon's abdication. Dated spring 1661, it targeted one of the most powerful churchmen of Muscovy, Archimandrite Ioasaf of the Troitsa Monastery.[6] Ioasaf was an important player in church politics who eventually succeeded Nikon as patriarch in 1667. But in 1661, Ioasaf's power must have been considerably weakened by investigations into his support of the old liturgical rites. This allowed his ambitious competitors, Iona and Pitirim, to control the affairs of the Muscovite patriarchate for a few years.[7]

Ioasaf was the highest-ranking churchman ever officially accused of rejecting the Nikonian reforms, but he may not have been alone. The historian P. Mel'nikov once speculated that other Russian hierarchs, including the powerful bishops Makarii of Novgorod and Markell of Vologda, refused to accept the new liturgical books.[8] There is no documentary evidence to prove Mel'nikov's claim, and available records appear to contradict it. For example, Makarii and Markell spent large sums of money to buy hundreds of the new books from the patriarchal printing press.[9] The same holds true for other Russian bishops.[10] Thus, one cannot determine to what degree Ioasaf's behavior was copied by other hierarchs.

We know that Ioasaf at first supported Nikon's reform work and later turned against it. Priests of the Troitsa Monastery, following Ioasaf's orders, began to say Mass with the new books and discarded the old ones.[11] There is evidence that Ioasaf punished some priests for not singing according to the new liturgical norms.[12] The general impression is that Nikon's reforms had been successfully introduced into the monastery and its territory, and that most of its population—certainly the priests and monks— had freely accepted them.

When Ioasaf later contradicted his orders to use the new liturgy, he encountered difficulties with priests and monks. At one point, Ioasaf supported two protégés when they attacked the clergy of the monastery for using the new books. One of these protégés, his right-hand man Cellarer Averkii, interrupted services in the main church and scolded the psalm singers for chanting according to the new Psalter. The priests and monks also had other gripes: the elder Vavila, who was in charge of the hospital building, collected high taxes (*nalogi bol'shie*) in a random manner.[13] Under the leadership of the priest Tikhon, Troitsa monks complained in a petition to Ioasaf about Vavila's using the old liturgy:

> That wicked and damned hospital monk[. . . .]The monks find it hard to endure his evil abuses[. . . .]He acts as if he has [lost] his mind[. . .] interrupts the singing of the liturgy in our main church, says the litany, and always performs his priestly office according to the old Service Books.[14]

Ioasaf reacted angrily to these complaints: most of the petitioners were imprisoned, put in irons (*sazhali na chep'*), and subsequently exiled. Only a few aged clerics escaped this punishment by paying bribes.[15]

We can observe that the vast majority of monks and priests was in favor of the liturgical reforms; only a small number of powerful men around Ioasaf vehemently opposed them. There was indeed massive discontent, but it was caused by entirely different factors. One factor was the priests', monks', and peasants' resentment of the influence of Ioasaf's relatives. His brother-in-law, Archpriest Aleksandr of the Spasskii Cathedral in Moscow, had been granted numerous privileges that allowed him to exploit peasant households and parts of the monastery's forest.[16] Ioasaf's nephews Ioakim and Boris also had free access to the monastic hinterlands and took ruthless advantage of their uncle's protection for personal gain.[17] Thus, Ioasaf had already provoked great anger before he was attacked for protecting a handful of radicals who were preaching against the new liturgical books.

Another factor in Ioasaf's unpopularity was that he condoned the brutal practices of a few monastic elders. Most notorious among them was Deonisii Biriagin, who personally beat the inmates of the monastery and collected bribes from those who wanted to be left alone.[18] On other occasions Biriagin and his friends, the elders Makarii Siltsov, Kirill Zhukov, Anton Iarinskii, and possibly also their relatives, descended upon the villages of the monastery. They were usually so drunk that they ruined their horses.[19] Peasants complained bitterly about torture, the raping of their wives, and "all kinds of crime."[20]

Thus, it appears that the conflict over the liturgical books at the Troitsa Monastery must be understood in the context of significant acts of violence perpetrated by Ioasaf's relatives and protégés. The petition writers probably sought to attract the tsar's attention in order to rid themselves of Ioasaf's personal regime. Their timing was excellent. Ioasaf's competitors immediately investigated the archimandrite for opposing Nikon's reforms, in order to weaken Ioasaf.

The case of the Troitsa Monastery indicates that the introduction of Nikon's liturgical reforms did not generate significant social discord per se. Use of the old books was seized as an opportunity for protest in order to get rid of an oppressive church official. Contrary to the assumption of many historians, the "masses," and in particular rank-and-file priests and monks, *defended* the new liturgical books.

It must be emphasized that conditions found in the Troitsa Monastery were by no means unique during this period. Other monasteries also were deeply divided over issues of resources and power. But in only one other monastery did such conditions lead to conflicts over the revision of liturgical books: the Solovki Monastery, which was then the second-most-powerful monastery in Russia.

A few excerpts from a report on the Solovki Monastery became part of the protocols of the Troitsa case.[21] Was this purely a coincidence? Or did the officials investigating the Troitsa Monastery see a link to similar developments at Solovki?

While the excerpts provide only scanty and inconclusive information about the conflicts at Solovki, they do contain the names of some of the players. In particular, the elder Savvatii Obriutin and the watchman (*budil'nik*) Tikhon, known as opponents of the new liturgical books, seem to have played roles similar to those of the elders Averkii and Vavila at Troitsa. In June 1658, Savvatii and Tikhon—conspiring with their archimandrite—forced the Solovki priests and monks to sign a statement outlawing the new liturgical books from the entire territory of the monastery.[22]

Could there have been contact between the monastic elite at the Solovki and Troitsa monasteries? If so, this might explain Ioasaf's change of mind regarding the new liturgical books.[23] We may never know if Ioasaf was influenced by Solovki. But in both monasteries ordinary priests and monks welcomed the new books, whereas the archimandrite and members of the monastic elite remained hostile.

Whereas Archimandrite Il'ia of Solovki used his power to force the monks and priests of the monastery to reject the new books, Ioasaf of Troitsa apparently refrained from doing so. Some of the Solovki priests wrote a complaint to the tsar in which they maintained "they all told the archimandrite to start saying Mass according to those [new] Service Books himself and they would do the same. But the archimandrite and his advisors did not want to hear about those books. . . . "[24] The priests described the hopelessness of their situation:

> The archimandrite and his advisors started yelling at us as if they were wild animals and they slandered and scolded us, Your pious servants, with indecent words: "You dirty little priests (*popentsa de khudye*), you miserable creatures (*stradniki*)! We dare you to celebrate the heretical Latin Mass! You won't get out of this refectory alive!" And we, Your pious believers, were intimidated by their threats and prohibitions and gave our signatures.

Those who did not obey were thrown into prison, where they were tortured, starved, and beaten with whips.[25]

Soon after Il'ia's death, the priests who had called for the introduction of the new books unexpectedly found an opportunity when the new Archimandrite Varfolomei took charge. In October 1661, Varfolomei demanded that liturgies be conducted "according to the revised printed books", but his decision had little impact.[26] When he left on a trip to Moscow in February 1663, the elder Savvatii began to threaten priests who said Mass according to the new rites. The complaint of a priest named Gerontii has survived:

> [Savvatii] . . . summoned me, the local peasants surrounded me, and [he] began to speak: "Today these peasants . . . came to me and complained that you were still performing the liturgy according to the new books and that you have begun to respect the new rules (*stal pochitat' noviny*). . . . " They warned me to beware, that all the brethren and peasants had risen up against me; and others told me: "They want to stone you—protect yourself." And I, Lord, fearing lest somebody do something vile (*pakost' uchinit'*) sit here now in my cell isolated from the outside world . . . , and in despair and tears I no longer see the daylight. . . . [27]

Savvatii and his allies were sufficiently powerful to prevent the use of the new forms of worship at the Solovki Monastery. The number of liturgical books purchased by the monastery during the 1650s dropped off dramatically.[28] By the year 1660, such books were apparently no longer purchased, and for approximately sixteen years thereafter, the monastery and its hinterlands practiced the old liturgical rites. Again we observe that the use of the old rites was not the result of spontaneous mass protest, but of manipulation and intimidation.[29]

In December 1662, a similar investigation involving criticism of the Nikonian reforms was conducted in Moscow.[30] The proceedings began soon after Nikon, in one of his numerous attempts to defeat his opponents, had excommunicated Metropolitan Pitirim for acting as patriarch. In a letter to the tsar Pitirim wrote:

> When he [Nikon] imposed these condemnations he stirred up the flock of true Christian believers and caused considerable revolt (*miatezh ne mal*) in the church. At last he has deprived himself of the honor and office befitting a prelate . . . and his condemnation is unconscionable, is not the decision of the council, and cannot therefore have any validity. The same happened to the divine martyr, Bishop Pavel of Kolomna, and many others when he was still acting as patriarch.[31]

As conveyed by this letter, Pitirim believed Nikon's anathema had the potential to create revolt within the church. Indeed, during these years Nikon must have enjoyed some popular sympathy because "books about Patriarch Nikon's life" were rumored to be circulating among inhabitants of Moscow.[32]

In this tense atmosphere, agents of the tsar's Secret Chancellery became aware that Terentii, a priest from Moscow, had called Pitirim the Antichrist, arguing that Pitirim had been justly anathematized by Patriarch Nikon. However, Terentii was also a determined opponent of the new liturgical rites. What must have puzzled church officials was Terentii's conviction that Pitirim, and not Nikon, was responsible for the hated change of rituals. This feature of Terentii's dissent is peculiar if one considers that the traditionally studied Old Believer texts denounced Nikon as the Antichrist.[33] Clearly, Terentii was not familiar with this central leitmotif of Old Believer rhetoric.[34]

Did Terentii's preaching against the revision of liturgical books generate significant popular support? In order to answer this question, I find it helpful to reconstruct the events that led to Terentii's arrest. On December 14, 1662, the clerk Ivan Moshchintsev invited guests to his home to celebrate the baptism of his newborn child. The celebration started with dinner and ended in the early hours of the next day. At some point during the dinner Terentii embarked on a long sermon which began with a biblical exegesis (*uchil ot Bozhestvennogo pisaniia*) on the birth of Christ and continued long after the dinner was over. Terentii insisted that the "priestly office was great" (*velik de sviashchennicheskii chin*), contrasting its purity to the "unworthiness" of Metropolitan Pitirim. According to some eyewitnesses, he began calling Pitirim a "fornicator" (*bludnik*) and insisted that the metropolitan owed his position entirely to "his flattery of the tsar." Continuing in this vein, Terentii also called Pitirim the Antichrist, and began to denounce the new liturgies.[35]

A late guest, who arrived at Moshchintsev's house after midnight, found that the party had gotten out of hand: "The clerk Savka Semenov was shouting and complaining that the secretary Andrei Bogdanov was beating him in order to prevent his singing a Greek song. The priest [Terentii] began to assault Savka and pounded his face."[36] According to the testimonies of other guests, Terentii had been quarreling with Savva Semenov "about old and new books" for some time when Bogdanov arrived on the scene.[37] Bogdanov made the mistake of intervening on Terentii's behalf, and the already volatile situation exploded.

Later the secretary recalled the unanticipated dangers: "The clerk Savka began to scold [me] and called [me] a 'scribbler.' [I] got into a fight with him for that, and in fear of being murdered by him, [I] left Ivan's home soon afterward."[38] Another guest, Aleksei Ostav'ev, recalled that Moshchintsev had tried to defuse the situation by secretly giving him Terentii's stick (*batog*) for safekeeping. However, when Ostav'ev arrived home a very drunk Terentii knocked at the door and demanded his stick, apparently planning to return with the weapon to Moshchintsev's dinner table.[39]

What do these incidents reveal about societal attitudes toward the revision of liturgical books? First, it is clear that only a small number of guests participated in the controversy over the new books. The clerk Eremei left immediately after Terentii and Savva began to quarrel "about the Christian faith . . . and other ecclesiastical matters." Viktor Leont'ev from the Taganka settlement left as soon as the atmosphere became tense. Departing dinner guests included Kuz'ma Podoshevnikov, a member of the merchant guild who had stayed for only about an hour, and Vasilei Shilovtsov of the cloth-merchant guild (*sukonnaia sotnia*), who gave the following explanation:

> I was a guest at Ivan's house for only about two hours. . . . While [I] was there the priest of the Vvedenskii Church [Terentii] began to talk with the clerk Savka about books. But what exactly they were speaking about [I] cannot say because [I] do not know how to read and write.[40]

Other guests also admitted their lack of understanding of the matter under discussion, and this may account for their early departures.[41]

Some guests, however, left explicitly because they strongly opposed Terentii's criticism of the new forms of worship. A man named Dmitrii, for example, told Terentii to go away and teach "other fanatics" (*iarykh inykh*); but when Terentii threatened him, he quickly departed.[42] A certain Mikhail left angrily, warning that "the words of this priest were not good. They were, after all, officials (*prikaznye liudi*) and he told them several times . . . [that] they would pay (*im khudo budet*) for the words of this priest."[43] Still, enough of Terentii's opponents must have stayed behind to enable Savva, Terentii's main adversary, to throw out the powerful secretary Bogdanov.

The fact that Bogdanov sided with Terentii in criticizing the new liturgy is noteworthy not only because he appears to be the only dinner guest to have done so.[44] His behavior also refutes the historiographic assumption (derived from Old Believer texts) that the "masses" were most responsive to the revision of liturgical books. Bogdanov, for one, did not represent the "masses"—he was a powerful official in the Banditry Office (*Razboinyi prikaz*), a post that most likely involved him in suppressing a social uprising in Moscow in 1662 (the Copper Rebellion).[45]

The unwillingness of most guests to get involved in a discussion about liturgical issues stands in marked contrast to the emotional involvement of the two main characters in this drama, the priest Terentii and the clerk Savva Semenov. Their quarrel can be better understood by observing their different relationships to Metropolitan Pitirim. Savva, who served in the Patriarch's Office, owed his position entirely to Pitirim.[46] Knowing that he enjoyed Pitirim's protection, Savka acted with assurance by applauding the new books and by singing Greek songs to provoke Terentii.[47] Terentii, on the other hand, had apparently suffered under Pitirim. In his testimony, of which we unfortunately have only small fragments, he complained that "[Pitirim] said wild things about [us] priests to the tsar[. . .]called [us] criminals, and disciplines [us] with cruel punishments. Many are being disciplined even though they are innocent."[48] As an example, he pointed to financial ruin, a typical concern of parish priests during these years, as previously discussed. A monk loyal to Pitirim had falsely implicated Terentii "in having committed a theft and other things," and as a result Terentii had been deprived of five rubles, a large sum for a simple parish priest.[49]

Terentii's outburst of anger over the new liturgies remained an isolated incident echoing the power struggle between Patriarch Nikon and his challenger Pitirim. It can be attributed largely to Terentii's personal dislike of Pitirim and the priest's mistaken impression that Pitirim, not Nikon, was responsible for the liturgical reforms. In addition, Terentii clearly had a strong ego, as demonstrated by the aggressiveness with which he tried to dominate the dinner conversation at Moshchintsev's home.

The three cases discussed so far were preceded by a another investigation targeting a priest named Nikon from a small hermitage in the Kostroma district. The case sheds some light on the thinking of a provincial clergyman and the arbitrary and condescending treatment he received at the Kremlin.[50]

In April 1660, priest Nikon came to Moscow to acquire new liturgical vestments and books after losing everything when his hermitage burned down. However, before the priest received these objects he had a conversation with Archpriest Luk'ian, the confessor of the tsar, who asked "how it was to say Mass according to the new printed books" (*kakovo de sluzhit' po novym pechatnym knigam*). Without thinking, Nikon replied "that it was fine to say Mass according to the new books, but that it was also not bad to say Mass according to the old books."[51] Even though, as the priest later insisted, he had said nothing else about the new liturgical books, he was promptly arrested and confined to a monastery "until he completely regained his sanity."[52]

Why was priest Nikon declared insane? Such a drastic punishment seems out of proportion to his remarks. After all he did not openly reject the new liturgical rites, as did his contemporaries Terentii and Sila, nor preach against them. The problem was simply that Nikon did not attribute any great significance to the liturgical books—it apparently did not matter to him which way he said Mass.

Without Luk'ian's intervention, it is very likely that priest Nikon would have returned to his hermitage with the new liturgical books, as many other hermits did during this period.[53] Why he was arbitrarily singled out for persecution remains unexplained. The priest apparently had talked too much at the wrong time.

There is no evidence that the Kostroma area, where priest Nikon lived, was particularly sensitive to the introduction of new liturgical texts. In fact, the opposite appears to be true. During the 1650s, numerous priests from Kostroma and environs traveled to Moscow to buy the new Service Book.[54] Also in July 1658, the archimandrite of the powerful Ipat'evskii Monastery received one hundred Service Books for distribution to local parish churches; there is no evidence that this distribution generated any animosity toward the archimandrite.[55]

There is also no apparent connection between priest Nikon and the handful of legendary preachers, such as the runaway monk Kapiton and the peasant Daniil Filipov, who were active in the vicinity of Kostroma during the 1650s. Kapiton preached spiritual purification through sexual abstinence and fasting, and had apparently attracted a small following of runaway monks and peasants.[56] Daniil, declaring himself to be Christ, preached against marriage and drunkenness. Eighteenth-century religious radicals, the Khlysty, saw Daniil as the founder of their movement.[57]

Priest Nikon lacked the religious fervor and charisma of both Kapiton and Daniil. An average rural hermit, he exerted no influence; he remained an isolated individual with the misfortune of having aroused the displeasure of a powerful church official. Thus, under no circumstances can we assume he was punished for his involvement in a mass movement of discontent.

I have documented that few Muscovites were interested in the issue of new liturgical books; and those few who were interested, commanded little popular support. This point is further demonstrated by the example of a little-known early dissenter who strongly condemned the new books, not only in verbal conflicts with his contemporaries, but also in writing.

The Chudov monk Savvatii attracted the attention of the highest Kremlin authorities shortly after Nikon's abdication. The reason was neither his popularity nor his possible influence on larger audiences, but simply that he was engaged in a bitter personal feud with the churchmen who were revising Muscovy's liturgical books. He apparently had been agitating for several years against the editors, many of whom lived with him at the Chudov Monastery, arguing that "their stupidity" and "lack of expertise" (*nerazumie*) had ruined the honor of the tsar. In particular, he polemicized against the Chudov monk Evfimii, who played a leading role at the patriarchal printing press.[58] Savvatii also accused the powerful archimandrite of the Chudov Monastery of being semi-literate. Subsequently chased out of the Chudov Monastery and exiled to the northern Kirillov Monastery, Savvatii wrote a long petition to the tsar in 1660.[59] This petition shows an unusual familiarity with the process of liturgical reform, unsurpassed in its detail even by the petitions of later Old Believers.[60]

Although Savvatii was included as an Old Believer in Avvakum's *Vita*, his thinking does not fit smoothly into the Old Belief tradition.[61] The characteristic feature of Savvatii's petition was a meticulous linguistic analysis of the new liturgical books; later Old Belief petitions focused more exclusively on liturgical features. Also, he had apparently never heard of the founding fathers, and did not identify with their cause.[62] It is therefore not surprising that Savvatii's petition was not included in later seventeenth- and eighteenth-century Old Belief text compilations.[63]

Savvatii attributed larger theological meanings to certain phonological and morphological changes he had observed. For example, he discovered that the new texts tended to use a compound perfect past tense of the auxiliary *byti* (to be) instead of the older imperfect or aorist forms.[64] The new Triodion included the following phrase: " . . . *na prestole byl esi Khriste so otsem i dukhom*," in which the compound perfect form replaced the aorist *beiashe* found in pre-Nikonian texts.[65] This change probably reflected the penetration of a vernacular linguistic element into a sacral text, a tendency observed by linguists as characteristic of the seventeenth century. Savvatii, who must have been trained in Church Slavonic, (if not in Greek), saw the change as a digression from the rules of the liturgical language of Muscovy.[66] To him, the use of the perfect implied a question about the eternal duration and timelessness of Christ's reign. The person of Christ, he concluded, had been isolated from the other components of the Trinity because "they say that He is not always sitting on the throne together with God the Father and the [Holy] Spirit."[67]

As Savvatii correctly discerned, some linguistic changes did profoundly distort the original meaning of the liturgical text. One example he cited is the following passage from the new Psalter: " . . . *ne poznakh knizhnaia zakonnaia pisaniia.*"[68] This wording seriously distorted the original variant: " . . . *ne poznav knizhna cheloveka vediashcha zakonnaia pisaniia.*"[69] Some changes represented clear grammatical mistakes, possibly suggesting that the editors did not have a solid knowledge of Church Slavonic.[70] Other revisions showed the influence of the spoken language, indicating that employees of the printing press had "Russified" some esoteric Church Slavonic language elements. Another example Savvatii cited is the rephrasing of the psalm "*leta nasha, iako pauchina pouchakhusia (*pauchakhusia*)*," or the colloquial pronunciation of the vowel /a/ as [o] in *doronosima (*daronosima*)*.[71]

Savvatii was an unusual figure who, unlike his less learned contemporaries, keenly observed that Nikon's revision of liturgical books did not necessarily produce better or more authentic texts. His observations were later confirmed by the scholar S. A. Belokurov, who demonstrated that much of the revision process was in the hands of individuals poorly trained in languages.[72] Belokurov would probably have agreed with Savvatii's comment that the term "corruption of books" (*knizhnoe neispravlenie*) was more appropriate than "correction of books" (*knizhnoe ispravlenie*), the term used in seventeenth-century sources to describe the revisions.[73]

Savvatii's linguistic knowledge is not surprising, considering his background. According to data provided by the Russian scholar Veselovskii, Savvatii was the same person as the secretary Tret'iak Vasil'ev, who had retired in 1654 from a long career of bureaucratic service.[74] Vasil'ev served in the Foreign Office from 1640–46, a period of intense literary and linguistic activity in this particular office. This experience seems to have influenced his interest in linguistic and liturgical issues. Among his papers we find not only a glossary of Polish terms, but also notes about a liturgical controversy between Patriarch Filaret and Ukrainian Archpriest Lavrentii Zizanii. Vasil'ev's learning was known to one of his closest friends, Prince Semen Ivanovich Shakhovskoi, a leading intellectual figure of seventeenth-century Muscovy.[75] In a letter Shakhovskoi addressed Vasil'ev as "a man of very great mind (*prevysokii v razume*) and knowledgeable in the divine dogmas."[76] Shakhovskoi's assessment is confirmed by the petition Vasil'ev submitted to the tsar after assuming the identity of Savvatii.

No other seventeenth-century Muscovite gave such a detailed and knowledgeable linguistic critique of the new liturgical books. However, Vasil'ev's—or Savvatii's—sophistication was not only unappreciated by his colleagues at the patriarchal printing press, but was lost to posterity because later critics of the new liturgical books were uninterested in his observations. He is known to us through a limited number of texts that have survived in only a few manuscript copies. These texts were directed to the tsar, or to men generally known as loyal executors of the tsar's policies. As a result, their message could have affected, at best, only a very small and defined milieu.[77]

The archival evidence discussed here strongly contradicts the traditional claim that the introduction of new liturgies triggered an immediate large-scale movement of protest against the church. The specific behavior, character traits, and ideas of those who opposed the new books between 1658 and 1666 defy generalization. The Moscow priest Terentii, for example, was a self-appointed prophet and appears to have had much in common in attitude and determination with the tailor Sila. These men thought their mission was to educate their contemporaries about the depravity of the church hierarchy, and used the new liturgical books as a topic for their sermons. Other dissenters were powerful churchmen, such as Archimandrite Ioasaf of Troitsa and the Solovki elder Savvatii, who used the denunciation of new books to intimidate and harass the monks and priests under their control. There were also a few protesters who lived in the immediate vicinity of the patriarchal printing press. The most important of these was the Chudov monk Savvatii, who may have initially welcomed the liturgical reform process, but later withdrew his support because he distrusted his colleagues' philological and theological expertise.

There is no evidence that these isolated individuals convinced—or even tried to convince—large audiences to protest the new liturgies. In fact, they had difficulty rallying anyone to their defense when they got into trouble. I conclude that the number of opponents to Nikon's reforms did not substantially increase after his abdication in 1658. Certainly, the "masses" had not been alienated by his reforms. In fact, there are indications that in the two largest monastic territories of Muscovy, Troitsa and Solovki, just the opposite was true: the lower clergy and peasants sought the support of church leaders to defend themselves against the efforts of their masters to maintain the old liturgies.

THE REVIVAL OF OLD BELIEF: THE PARADOX OF BISHOP ALEKSANDR OF VIATKA

The dissenters discussed so far in this chapter did not identify themselves as Old Believers. They did not mention the first Old Believers by name or refer to their work, and did not speak or write in the apocalyptic idiom found in the writings of Ivan Neronov and other Old Believers. Even the obscure priest Terentii, who expressed concerns about the state of Christian morals in Muscovy similar to those voiced by Neronov, did not speak negatively about Patriarch Nikon. The principal reason for the re-establishment of Old Belief after Nikon's abdication in the summer of 1658 was the emergence of a new group of Old Believers.

Neronov and Avvakum were far removed from the centers of Muscovite religion; Neronov was mostly withdrawn in his remote hermitage outside Vologda, and Avvakum still in Siberian exile. Each reappeared on the stage of history only briefly during the period discussed here—Avvakum in the summer of 1664 and Neronov shortly thereafter—and then both were condemned by the Church Council of 1666. Thus neither played a significant role in the formation of what might be called the founding community of Old Belief.[78] Indeed, this new Old Belief community proved much more stable, and therefore had a more lasting impact on the Muscovite religious landscape, than the small communities previously established by Avvakum and Neronov.

There is little evidence that the new generation of Old Believers ever supported Avvakum and Neronov during Nikon's patriarchate. In fact, some of them had accepted the new liturgies during the early 1650s and turned against them only after Avvakum and Neronov had disappeared from the scene.[79] The revival—and possibly even survival—of seventeenth-century Old Belief was largely the work of Bishop Aleksandr of Viatka. The name of Aleksandr, paradoxically, has been expunged from the collective memory of the eighteenth-century Old Belief Church (*staroobriadchestvo*), probably due to his recantation of beliefs at the 1666 Church Council.[80]

The story of Aleksandr's life helps to delineate the social parameters of early Old Belief. At first glance, Aleksandr's conversion to Old Belief appears unlikely because he was a favorite of Patriarch Nikon and built a remarkable career under his protection. By the early 1650s, even though he came from a remote northern provincial town, he had risen to archimandrite of an important Vologda monastery. Precisely because he was a man without other important social or political connections, Aleksandr may have been one of the most reliable executors of Nikon's orders.[81]

Several unusual circumstances help to explain Aleksandr's change of heart. First, he was probably better informed about the fate of the first Old Believers than any other Muscovite hierarch of the 1650s. In the late summer of 1653, Aleksandr was given the responsibility of supervising Neronov's imprisonment. There are no indications that he felt any sympathy for Neronov. In fact, he had Neronov brutally beaten for continuing to speak out against the degeneration of Christian morals and the changes in church liturgies. But in his capacity as incarcerator, Aleksandr had numerous personal encounters with Neronov and we cannot exclude the possibility that he was impressed with the selfless courage and genuine religious fervor with which Neronov endured even the most vicious humiliation. It is conceivable that the first seeds of doubt were sown during this time.[82]

A second development in Aleksandr's career was probably even more important for his later conversion to Old Belief. In July 1655 Nikon rewarded him for his unyielding treatment of Neronov by promoting him to bishop. Nikon spent an enormous amount of money on Aleksandr's ordination, turning the ceremony into a great spectacle. Soon afterwards Aleksandr was assigned to the unoccupied bishop's seat at Kolomna. This time his mandate was to dismantle the bishopric and subsume its lands in the private "domain of the patriarchs" (*patriarshaia oblast'*).[83] This assignment eventually turned Alexandr against Nikon. Not only did Aleksandr come to resent the fact that his appointment was only temporary, but he also gained first-hand insights into the brutal treatment of his deposed predecessor, Bishop Pavel of Kolomna.

Pavel's tragic story is known to later Old Belief primarily through information Aleksandr gathered during his stay at Kolomna. Apparently Aleksandr was the first to compile such records, which were confiscated from his palace long after he had been forced to leave Kolomna for the remote town of Viatka. Among these records one finds, for example, a scroll entitled "On the Deposition of the Bishop of Kolomna." Another pamphlet (*tetradka*), which dealt more specifically with the removal of Pavel from his bishopric, was titled "On the Expulsion of the Bishop of Kolomna."[84]

Who was Pavel? According to later Old Belief sources, he was a powerful ally of Avvakum during the early 1650s. Indeed, Avvakum's *Vita* as well as letters by Fedor Ivanov, all written during the 1670s, asserted that Nikon had Pavel expelled from his bishopric because he was so threatening to the patriarch.[85] The earliest Old Believer necrologies (*sinodiki*), which date from the early eighteenth century, mention Pavel as the first martyr of Old Belief and record that he was burned in Novgorod in April 1656. This assertion was further developed in Denisov's *Vineyard*, which begins with Pavel's biography.[86] That early eighteenth-century Old Believers thought highly of Pavel can be deduced from the fact that Denisov wrote a second history of Pavel's life, *The Legend of Pavel of Kolomna* (*Skazanie o Pavle kolomenskom*), which circulated widely among Old Believers.[87]

There is little documentary evidence that Pavel openly opposed the new liturgies. In fact, his signature is on the original manuscript of the

Conciliar Act of 1654, which contains the official decision to embark upon the revision of the liturgies. Pavel's signature is missing only from the printed version of the act that was published in 1656, two years after the church council.[88]

Still, Pavel's sympathy for early Old Belief is likely on personal grounds. Pavel's brother-in-law, Metropolitan Ilarion of Suzdal', who probably knew Pavel better than any other contemporary, related in his *Vita* that Pavel was close to Neronov and had admired him since youth. Neronov and Pavel had frequent contact in the home of the Nizhnii Novgorod priest Anania, who was Neronov's close friend and favorite teacher. Indeed, church investigators later confiscated a note (*otpiska*) in Pavel's hand that was addressed to Neronov and written on eight scrolls.[89]

It is even possible that Aleksandr knew his predecessor, since Pavel also had once belonged to Nikon's inner circle. Pavel was, in fact, one of the first bishops Nikon appointed, specifically chosen to replace a personal enemy whom Nikon forced to abdicate soon after he came to power.[90] It should be emphasized that Pavel, like his successor Aleksandr, was at first a loyal executor of patriarchal policies. We know, for example, that he defended the prerogatives of the church against the Kolomna voevoda. When this secular ruler wanted to arrest a priest for drunkenness, Pavel intervened on the priest's behalf—probably following Nikon's orders—and had him returned to his parishioners. While this peculiar incident bears little resemblance to the reform zeal of Neronov and Avvakum, the fact remains that Pavel was soon to share their tragic fate.[91]

After Aleksandr's arrival in Kolomna in late 1655, someone must have related the details of Pavel's sudden fall from power, his subsequent maltreatment by the authorities, and mysterious disappearance. If we can believe later Old Believer sources, Pavel was a fervent believer and was prepared to die for his religious ideals.[92] In this regard Pavel must have reminded Aleksandr of Neronov, and for the second time Aleksandr found himself confronting a man of superior religious strength and conviction. Nevertheless, Aleksandr was clearly proud of his promotion to bishop and did nothing to save Pavel's life. Indeed, it was shortly after Aleksandr took up residence in Kolomna that Pavel was hounded to death by agents of the patriarch.[93]

During the next two years, Aleksandr helped Nikon to dissolve the eparchy of Kolomna. Under Aleksandr's auspices, special emissaries from Moscow began to describe the assets of the bishopric, and one may still find these carefully compiled registers in the archive of the Patriarchal Treasury Office (*Patriarshii kazennyi prikaz*). They list all the churches, monasteries, villages, and towns of the Kolomna eparchy that were to become the property of the patriarch.[94] The taxes, services, and other obligations that had once been owed to the bishop of Kolomna were now recorded in the income books of the patriarchal court. All of these documents were approved by patriarchal secretaries (*d'iaki*) without protest from Aleksandr.[95] In fact, Aleksandr signed the protocols of the Church Council of October 1657, which officially abolished the Kolomna eparchy.[96]

One might say that Aleksandr sealed his own fate by assisting Nikon in the destruction of one of the oldest Russian bishoprics—an act unprecedented in the history of the Russian church. Even though the bishopric was restored in 1674 and elevated to an archbishopric, it apparently never recovered from Nikon's destructive blow.[97] In the first year of Nikon's rule, the Kolomna bishopric was richer than either the Pskov or Tver' eparchies. By the end of the seventeenth century, however, Kolomna ranked a distant last among the old dioceses of Muscovy in both assets and population, while the Tver' and Pskov eparchies had grown almost tenfold. Thus, Kolomna, which had been an ecclesiastical center since 1350, ceased to play an active role in Muscovite church politics.[98]

Having helped to destroy what might have become a lucrative power base, Aleksandr was forced to accept a much less rewarding assignment as the first bishop of Viatka. He had to adjust to a very different way of life after moving to this church outpost established by Nikon in the remote northern forests. For the first time in his ecclesiastical career, Aleksandr no longer enjoyed undisputed authority, and certainly had no access to wealth. At Kolomna he had lived in a luxurious palace, but now he had to be content with a dilapidated monastery.[99] Viatka was also a perilous assignment because of its location in an outlying area that Aleksandr had been ordered to integrate into the power structure of the Muscovite church and state. Indeed, Nikon justified the establishment of the new bishopric as follows: "It is a vast stretch of land with many people. There are many remnants of pagan customs, and it is said that idol worship has survived as well."[100] Thus, Nikon had again chosen Aleksandr for an assignment requiring loyalty, this time in the face of religious anarchy.

There is good evidence that Aleksandr was miserable in Viatka. An undated letter written by one of Aleksandr's supporters to the Morozovs, an influential boyar family in Moscow, requests their intercession on behalf of the bishop and his clients:

> You should reach out and help our father, Bishop Aleksandr of Viatka, who has been badly treated by Nikon and has suffered a long time. . . . Aleksandr urgently needs the calm of a monastic cell because

his bishopric is in great disarray (*nestroenie*). Officials and men of all ranks who belong to his household live in the homes of local traders, but they stay only a month or two and then move on because the townspeople . . . are rude and self-centered and chase the bishop's men from their households with dishonor. The bishopric here is new, . . . and they don't have the royal generosity required to build their own buildings. Their homes in Kolomna have been seized for the patriarch. And now these poor creatures have lost their last pennies and are wandering from home to home in great poverty. When I look at them, I can only cry.[101]

Aleksandr felt deprived of income he considered belonged to him, and soon after his arrival in Viatka he developed a personal grudge against his former benefactor.[102] In a letter of December 1659 to the tsar, Aleksandr complained bitterly about tithe lands (*desiatiny*) that should have been assigned to his new bishopric, but had remained under the control of the neighboring diocese of Vologda:

[Nikon] . . . told me before an image of God that the bishopric of Viatka and Perm' had few tithes and that he wanted to add new ones. Then he sent me from Moscow to Kolomna to promptly dissolve that bishopric's administration. . . . After my departure the patriarchal secretary Ivan Kalitin, who wanted to please the archbishop of Vologda, compiled an incorrect inventory [of tithe lands] in various towns and districts. . . . After fabricating this false list the patriarch forgot the council's decision, his word, and his signature on my petition . . . , and now the bishopric of Viatka has only 143 churches, that means 277 churches less than the Kolomna bishopric. . . . I, your humble servant (*bogomolets*), have begged you before, Sire, and have given you many petitions to provide for my new existence and to feed my household.[103]

As documented by this and other letters in the patriarchal archive, Aleksandr's transformation into a critic of the new liturgical books was preceded by a significant change in his personal well-being. Poor and in constant danger of being molested by the local population, it appears that Aleksandr's admiration for the Old Believers Neronov and Pavel grew in proportion to his declining fortunes.[104]

While bishop of Kolomna, Aleksandr had enjoyed being in the limelight of patriarchal politics. He had participated in the Church Council of 1656, which officially excommunicated Neronov. In the same year he had assisted Nikon in elaborate church ceremonies at the Uspenskii Cathedral in the Kremlin that apparently had the purpose of demonstrating to Muscovites the superiority of the new liturgies.[105] Aleksandr also had seen to it that the new books were introduced in the parishes of his diocese. In 1656, for example, he bought fifty of the controversial first edition Service Books (*sluzhebniki*), which contained many mistakes. The following year, he bought an additional fifty Service Books.[106]

It is only *after* being recalled from his post in Kolomna that Aleksandr changed his mind about the new liturgies. Once he had arrived in Viatka, the reduced number of liturgical books acquired for the bishopric suggests that Aleksandr made no serious effort to introduce the new liturgical rites. In 1660 Aleksandr purchased only one copy of a new Psalter; a close associate, deacon Kiprian, bought two such books; and two clerics from the cathedral choir (*pevchie*) of Viatka each bought one book. While it could be argued that the volume of sales had declined in general, not just for Viatka, other bishops bought significantly more Psalters.[107] Even as late as 1671, the failure of Viatka monasteries to obtain new books was brought to the attention of the tsar's Secret Chancellery.[108]

While Aleksandr did not improve his personal situation by opposing the new liturgies, he greatly contributed to the cause of Old Belief. In fact, one might say that by the late 1650s he was the single most important Old Believer in Muscovy. There are two reasons for Aleksandr's claim to fame. First, he established a small, informal network of intellectuals who opposed the Nikonian reforms. The principal figures in this network were Abbot Spiridon Potemkin, Abbot Feoktist, and Archimandrite Nikanor. Second, he commissioned several individuals to compile critiques of the new liturgical books.

In early 1666, church investigators confiscated an undated scroll addressed to "Aleksandr, the lord and most holy bishop of Viatka and Perm'" (*gosudar' preosviashchennyi Aleksandr episkop viatskii i velikopermskii*). Upon opening it they found a treatise juxtaposing phrases from two printed Service Books, one issued in 1623 under Patriarch Filaret, the other under Nikon in 1656. No detail had escaped the anonymous author, who pointed out that traditional theological terms such as *blagodat'* (blessing) and *blagostyn'* (alms) had been replaced by the more familiar *milost'* (grace) and *blagost'* (goodness). The author found changes in prayers upsetting. One prayer, for example, no longer asked God's blessing "for all of us" (*o vsekh nas*), but "upon all of us" (*na vsekh nas*). Apparently a theological purist, the author also noted the arbitrary replacement of age-old sentences with entirely new ones, as well as the elimination of entire phrases. A remark concluding the careful discussion of one important prayer sums up his irritation that the revisions followed no clear pattern: "the prayer has been completely ruined" (*vsia ta molitva perebita*).[109]

An even more comprehensive critique was assembled under Aleksandr's auspices soon after he moved to Viatka. In this tract, which deals particularly with the Book of Needs (*trebnik*) of 1658, another anonymous author pointed to numerous deviations from earlier Muscovite and Kievan editions. He was quite emotional, and left the following indignant remarks in the margin: "False!"; "Ridiculous and scandalous"; "The editors must have been drunk . . . !"[110] The fact that such writings were not unique can be reconstructed from entries in an inventory of texts confiscated from the bishop's palace. There one finds, for example, several pamphlets "concerning the incoherent passages of the newly printed books" (*o ne-ispravnykh rechakh novye pechati knig*).[111]

This inventory is one of the most remarkable documents about early Old Belief, and resulted from a careful search conducted in Viatka in February 1666 by Moscow special agents. Instructed to look "in all of the bishop's cells, in all places and vessels . . . to inspect all kinds of writings and seize all of the written materials except church and housekeeping books of the bishopric," one might say they discovered the first Old Belief library. This library consisted of eighty-seven manuscripts, more than half of which had been assembled with the explicit purpose of showing "the disagreement" (*nesoglasie*) between the old and new books.[112]

The inventory also included numerous texts attributed to the first Old Believers. In fact, Aleksandr compiled two special collections of writings (*pisaniia*) by Neronov and Avvakum. The bulk of the "Collection of Grigorii Neronov" comprised twenty-nine pamphlets (*tetradi*), among them Neronov's letters from exile and essays on the power of the Holy Spirit (nos. 2, 19).[113] The "Collection of Archpriest Avvakum" contained seven pamphlets, including four pages of unedited excerpts from Scriptures (no. 15). One also finds a letter to Neronov (no. 39), three undated petitions to the tsar (no. 46), and a few other notes. The memory of these courageous fighters against Patriarch Nikon, who had suffered "in the name of Christ" (*Khrista radi*), was clearly important to the new generation of Old Believers.[114]

Other texts listed in the inventory recall the apocalyptic themes formulated in Neronov's letters. For example, we find excerpts from the Apocalypse (no. 29), as well as evidence from Latin chronicles about the impending destruction (*razorenie*) of Muscovy (nos. 13, 26). Also included were handwritten notes about the twelve Sibylls, a popular mythology in medieval Christian literature about the imminent end of times (no. 8). Other texts were devoted to the sacredness of Muscovite religious traditions, among them excerpts from a sixteenth-century church council and a liturgy for saint Filipp (nos. 4, 35). One finds an epistle to His Holiness Hermogen, who was patriarch of Moscow and all Rus' during the Time of Troubles (no. 18). And finally, there are copies of documents illustrating the denunciation by Patriarch Filaret of western-Russian and Ukrainian books (nos. 23, 28). These and other texts had been used as source materials by Neronov during the early 1650s, and they survived to become the basis of later Old Belief writing, thanks largely to Aleksandr's efforts.[115]

While it is impossible to identify all the authors and contributors, the contents of Aleksandr's library illustrate that he had obtained substantial support for the liturgical cause among the highest clergy of Muscovy. For example, one finds a note written by Archimandrite Tikhon of the Danilov Monastery in Pereiaslavl', who had tonsured Neronov a monk despite the latter's excommunication by Patriarch Nikon.[116] Aleksandr corresponded with Archimandrite Pafnutii of Perm', who unfortunately remains unknown to us, about the painting of icons.[117] Other works belonged to Abbot Feoktist, who had once been in charge of the Zlatoustovskii Monastery in Moscow; and several more came from the pen of Archimandrite Spiridon Potemkin, the spiritual leader of the Pokrovskii Monastery in Moscow.[118] Finally, there are indications that Aleksandr received texts from Archimandrite Nikanor of Solovki.[119]

We find ourselves confronted by a paradox that contradicts later Old Believer polemics against the "Nikonians": many of the earliest texts of Old Belief were sponsored or written by hierarchs who—throughout most of the 1650s—had acted as loyal executors and supporters of Patriarch Nikon's liturgical reforms. Why would former friends and clients of the patriarch turn against his reform work?

One likely answer is that Aleksandr made an extra effort to convince these men to join his cause. We know, for example, that the bishop did not stay in Viatka, but spent much of his time in Moscow, where he had his own palace. Given Aleksandr's long-standing connections with the patriarchal see, he had access to the Chudov Monastery in the Kremlin and met regularly with other hierarchs in the Uspenskii Cathedral—the very nerve center of the Muscovite church.[120] Aleksandr's sojourns outside his bishopric became so frequent that in February 1664 the tsar gave orders for Aleksandr to move back to Viatka and stay there.[121]

Aleksandr's recruiting efforts were not successful among the large majority of hierarchs. Most bishops and monastic leaders probably despised Aleksandr as a minion of the much-hated Nikon. After all, he had been Nikon's principal accomplice in the destruction of the Kolomna bishopric—an act considered by post-Nikonian church leaders to be so great a crime that it became one of the main justifications for Nikon's exile. Aleksandr was, however, successful in winning over a few of Nikon's former friends who, like himself, had suffered a dramatic fall from power after Nikon's removal from the Kremlin. Only *after* their status in the hierarchy had been significantly diminished did churchmen such as Archimandrite Nikanor and Abbot Feoktist become concerned about the revision of books.[122]

Nikanor, who became one of Aleksandr's most important allies, had also been a favorite of Nikon. In the spring of 1653, the patriarch appointed him archimandrite of the powerful and wealthy Solovki Monastery.[123] Nikon apparently installed a loyal follower so as to curb the unruliness of the Solovki monks. But in doing so, he also eliminated the previous archimandrite, Il'ia, who had been uncooperative during Nikon's tenure as metropolitan of Novgorod.[124] Despite Nikon's protection, however, Nikanor was soon deposed and forced to return to Moscow. There, he was rewarded for his loyalty with an appointment as archimandrite of the newly built Savva Storozhevskii Monastery, the favorite monastery of the tsar and thus one of Muscovy's most prestigious ecclesiastical institutions.[125]

Nikanor received high-ranking visitors from Constantinople and frequently hosted Patriarch Nikon at the Savva Monastery. He conducted long liturgies and other religious ceremonies for his eminent guests, a fact recorded in a variety of sources, including the diary kept by one guest, Pavel of Aleppo.[126] It is very likely that the archimandrite used the new liturgical books in the presence of these guests. Entries in the sales records of the patriarchal printing press confirm that the Savva monks acquired new liturgical books during Nikanor's tenure.[127] Thus, it appears that Nikanor both practiced and advocated the new liturgical rites.

Nikanor lost his position at the Savva Monastery in 1660, the same year that other friends of Nikon lost their ecclesiastical posts. Indeed, Nikanor was exiled to the Solovki Monastery together with other deposed clerics, suggesting that he was punished for his close ties with the patriarch.[128]

Only while in exile did this one-time favorite of Nikon change his attitude toward the new liturgical books. We might speculate that the previously mentioned Solovki elders, who rejected Nikon's reforms, influenced Nikanor to follow their example. In any case, soon after his arrival at Solovki, the learned Nikanor began to assemble excerpts from various old liturgical books to refute the innovations introduced by Nikon. Having established contact with Aleksandr, he then contributed texts to Aleksandr's library.[129]

The same pattern applies to Abbot Feoktist, who also owed his career to Patriarch Nikon. Appointed abbot of the important Zlatoustovskii Monastery in July 1654, a few months after Nikon had officially embarked on the revision of liturgical books, Feoktist lost this position in 1658, the same year that Nikon left the patriarchal throne.[130] Feoktist was arrested in 1666 as a protégé of Aleksandr.

During his tenure as abbot, Feoktist bought new liturgical books directly after their release from the patriarchal printing press. In fact, in September 1656 he and Metropolitan Pitirim of Krutitsa were the first to buy the new Service Book. Feoktist also kept a new Lectionary (*prolog*) in his monastic cell, and he subsequently donated it to the parish church in his home village of Pavlovo in the Suzdal' district.[131]

Similar observations can be made about Abbot Spiridon Potemkin, who later became a legendary figure among Old Believers. Spiridon headed one of Nikon's favorite monasteries, the Pokrovskii Monastery, which had been founded by the tsar's personal endowment in 1656. The patriarch was in close contact with the monastery and visited its shrine, which indicates that he probably had a good relationship with the archimandrite.[132] This monastery also bought the new liturgical books, as documented by entries in patriarchal printing press sales records.[133]

Why Spiridon started writing on behalf of early Old Belief is not clear. His name appears in investigative records only once, shortly after his death: in November 1665, the metropolitan of Riazan' denounced him to the Secret Chancellery for composing "subversive writings" (*vypiski khul'nye*) against the new Nikonian religion.[134]

Even though he was overlooked by official investigators, who focused on more visible personalities such as Nikanor and Aleksandr, Spiridon was probably the first important Old Belief theologian. His work has been little studied, but there can be no doubt that he laid the foundation for later Old Belief thinking. We know, for example, that texts attributed to Spiridon and listed in the Viatka inventory were assembled in a manuscript book during the late 1660s.[135] Important Old Believers such as Fedor Ivanov and Avraamii, who later compiled influential manuscript books of their own, acknowledged Spiridon's influence and called him "father and prophet."[136] Not surprisingly, the *Book* (*Kniga*) of Abbot Spiridon became one of the most widely copied and disseminated texts of the Old Belief tradition. In fact, the anonymous editor of the first version of the *Book* introduced the abbot as a "new theologian" and "extraordinary teacher."[137]

Spiridon's writings were addressed to all "Orthodox Christians" of Russia. He warned them to avoid contact with "those who are damned for renouncing their faith"; the "damned apostates are expecting the Antichrist and exchange sophistries with the Jews (*s zhidami mudrstvuiut*)." He also exhorted his contemporaries to seek the truth and to remember the power of God: "The word of God is like a spiritual sword (*mech dukhovnyi*). Those who denounce the Holy Spirit commit a dishonorable act (*nechestie*) that cannot be pardoned in this century or in future [centuries]. Read these lines with attention so that you will understand the [power of] the spiritual sword and the word of God."[138]

To Spiridon the world was divided into two parts: on one side were "unfeeling Christians who called themselves Orthodox ... but did not grasp" the truth. They understood only "worldly philosophy [and] external wisdom," but not true inner Christianity. On the other side were Spiridon's heroes, whom he called "the seekers of Christ" (*khristoliubtsy*), or "those faithful to Christ, the Pastor." Only the latter were in a position to understand "the extraordinary mind of Heaven" (*razum nebesnyi*) and "divine philosophy."[139]

There is evidence that Spiridon saw himself continuing the tradition established by archpriests Neronov and Avvakum. He personally copied what is probably the only theological work by Avvakum that survived from the 1650s. Here, in response to a follower who had abandoned Old Belief, Avvakum described how his own deep faith in Christ had guided him through the turmoil of his early career.[140]

Spiridon undoubtedly shared Avvakum's faith, but he was much more erudite. Indeed, if we can trust his unpublished *Vita*, this man of boyar origins had been trained by Polish Jesuits in his native Smolensk. He was so well read in Latin and Greek theological texts, "Jesuits and cardinals all feared him and were not able to combat his speech with words." His subsequent flight to Muscovy seems inspired by the destruction of his home town by Polish troops and fears of an impending eastward expansion of the Catholic Church. Once in Muscovy, Spiridon used his considerable learning to polemicize against changes in Russian liturgical worship, which he attributed to the Jesuits (and the Jews), but also against the Catholic Church. This world view, rooted in the anti-Catholic polemic traditions of his native White Russia, created many of the thought patterns that guided later generations of Old Believers.[141]

One might say that Old Belief began to define, and in fact, to create itself as a movement based largely on the texts in Aleksandr's library. Evidence suggests that even Avvakum relied on this library. He most likely recovered copies of texts that had been lost during the hardships of his life in Siberia when he was in Moscow in 1664 enjoying a short reprieve from exile. In any case, Avvakum resumed his writing after nearly ten years of silence. Notes that he had gathered with Archpriest Daniil in 1653 became the source for an extensive polemic against the new sign of the cross.[142] Earlier attacks on the corruption of morals and loose clerical behavior were developed in the "little letter" (*pisaneitse*) of 1664. This important text, recently rediscovered by Soviet historians, became the blueprint for many of Avvakum's future writings.[143]

The texts in Aleksandr's library influenced other seventeenth-century Old Believers as well. Most importantly, they provided much of the raw material for the compilation of the *Shield of Faith* (*Shchit very*) which, like Spiridon's *Book*, became one of the most significant pillars of seventeenth-century Old Belief culture.[144]

One of the texts in the *Shield* was Feoktist's *Molebnoe pisanie*, which offered a succinct summary of the main arguments of early Old Belief. Given the clarity and brevity of this text, it was probably well suited for instruction: later teachers of Old Belief could find not only a list of Nikon's major reforms, but also diatribes against "Latin" influences, and references to alleged heroes of the Russian ecclesiastical past such as sixteenth-century Metropolitan Makarii and Nikon's patriarchal predecessors. The treatise glorified the pious achievements of Tsar Ivan the Terrible and the fight of Ukrainian Prince Konstantin of Ostrog against the Catholic Church. Feoktist conveyed a strong sense of the religious conviction and self-discipline of a churchman who had spent "much time since his youth to strengthen [himself]" in all tenets of Orthodox theology. Indeed, his text reads like an urgent appeal to posterity, underscoring the importance of learning: only those who studied texts and thus familiarized themselves with the details of Nikon's reforms, as well as with Orthodox history and theology, would be able to defend the cause of Old Belief.[145]

Ten years after the arrest and exile of the first Old Believers, their cause was still alive. Some of their letters survived, thanks to the efforts of Bishop Aleksandr and a small network of high-ranking hierarchs. These churchmen also began to write critically about the new books and to deposit their writings in a secret central library.

Thus, the growth of early Old Belief was not due to the popular appeal of ideas advocated by Neronov and Avvakum, but rather to support from influential church hierarchs. Among them were men who had been loyal executors of Nikon's liturgical reforms during most of the 1650s but had changed their minds after losing positions of power in the wake of his abdication. The fact that one of his closest allies, Bishop Aleksandr, became founder of a movement that subsequently equated Nikon with the Antichrist remains one of the great paradoxes in the history of Russian religion.

BISHOP ALEKSANDR AND HIS SUPPORTERS: CONVERSIONS TO OLD BELIEF BEFORE 1666

The small circle of church hierarchs around Bishop Aleksandr found support for their cause among a few rank-and-file churchmen. The Old Believer hierarchs encouraged some members of the Moscow parish clergy to express negative views about the new liturgies. I have also found that Aleksandr's influence reached directly into the Patriarch's Office, which was the Kremlin headquarters of the Russian Orthodox Church. In addition, there were a handful of followers in Russia's provinces.

One of the most fervent supporters of this circle was the Kremlin deacon Fedor Ivanov, whom later Old Believers would consider one of the legendary founding fathers of their movement along with Avvakum.[146] In a letter addressed to Abbot Feoktist, his "lord and dear friend," Ivanov declared both Aleksandr and Feoktist would receive eternal compensation because they were fighting so bravely "for our mother the holy ecumenical church," and because their cause was "the cause of God and not a human affair." He also asserted his willingness to do anything in his power to promote their ideas.[147]

Ivanov's most important contribution was his work with texts critical of the Nikonian revisions. After familiarizing himself with the contents of Aleksandr's secret library, he began to assemble a library of his own: he copied and edited older texts, such as a manuscript book that had belonged to Neronov, and also gathered materials for new texts from the manuscript collection of the Kremlin church in which he served. How prolific he was in these literary activities can be assessed from the fact that at the time of his arrest in December 1665, church investigators seized a large trunk filled to the brim with copies of "many letters" and "many words taken from the Holy Scriptures."[148] Several more manuscripts must have escaped official attention because during his trial at the Church Council of 1666 he drew on another set of texts to support his position.[149] Later, during his exile at Pustoozero, Ivanov used this surviving archive to compile the *Answer of the Orthodox* (*Otvet pravoslavnykh*), which became a pivotal text of Old Belief culture during the remainder of the seventeenth century.[150]

These activities were not of immediate importance for contemporary Muscovites, but had a long-term impact on the literary culture of Old Belief. Even though Ivanov is known to have preached in public, his social connections were rather limited.[151] Ivanov was friendly, for example, with the extended family of Archpriest Avvakum; he knew most of Avvakum's

sons and daughters and their spouses and children. He was close to Neronov's son Feofilakt, who apparently kept Ivanov informed about the fate of
his father. In addition, Ivanov spent time with the fools-in-Christ Fedor
and Afanasii, two of Avvakum's most zealous followers. Through the fool
Fedor, who was hiding in the household of the widow Feodosiia Morozova, Ivanov established contact with this remarkable boyar woman. In
Iaroslavl', Ivanov was in touch with Abbot Sergei of the Tolgskii Monastery, a hierarch whom he may have converted to the cause of Old Belief.[152]

Ivanov also maintained contact with the exiled Avvakum and Neronov.
Avvakum began to write secret letters which Ivanov first copied for his
own use, and then deposited in Aleksandr's library.[153] Neronov informed
Ivanov about the tribulations he suffered after verbally attacking a protégé
of the archbishop of Vologda. When Ivanov learned that Neronov's opponent had publicly proclaimed the justness of Christ's crucifixion, he
expressed his fury in a petition to the tsar, accusing the Vologda preacher
of "blasphemous and Jewish speeches" (*bogokhul'nye i zhidovskiia rechi*).[154]
Thus, Ivanov not only promulgated the cause of the exiled "zealots," but
also helped connect them with the newly emerging community of Old
Believers in Moscow.

We don't know much about this community, but it appears that a
number of Moscow priests were inspired to become Old Believers by
following Ivanov's example. One of these priests, Tikhon, wrote an apocalyptic tract in which he prophesied the advent of "the Antichrist and the
Last Judgment."[155] Another sympathizer was the parish priest Isidor, who
exchanged several letters with Avvakum during the 1670s. Two other
priests, Koz'ma and Stepan, also converted to Old Belief during this
period, as indicated by their later correspondence with the "Pustoozero
prisoners."[156]

These priests were in the minority, as Ivanov's sad experience demonstrates. Ivanov's family had produced parish priests for several generations,
and his relatives must have taken pride when, in 1659, he was appointed to
the Blagoveshchenskii Sobor in the Kremlin. However, these relatives
turned against him as soon as he openly rejected the new liturgies. His
uncle, the Kremlin priest Ivan, got so angry that once "when he was drunk
[he] chased [him] with a knife and a pole-ax (*sekira*)." On another occasion, Ivanov's uncle and aunt tearfully implored him to accept the Nikonian reforms because otherwise he "would bring dishonor on [their] kin
(*na rod nash bezchestie navedeshi*)." Two cousins, who were both clients of
Metropolitan Pavel of Krutitsa, sided with their father against Ivanov. The
reason for these relatives' concern was clear to Ivanov: they wanted to pur-

sue lucrative careers in the Kremlin and were willing to sacrifice religious truth to do so. The fact that Ivanov overcame this family pressure illustrates the strength of his religious conviction. Like Avvakum, he called himself a "fighter in the name of piety (*blagochestie*)."[157]

The uncompromising attack on clerical corruption begun by Neronov and Avvakum during the early 1650s was now—nearly ten years later— revived and taken up by another courageous duo: Ivanov and the obscure priest Irodion. Irodion, who served at the Rizpolozhenskii Sobor, one of the tsar's private churches, shared Ivanov's ideals. He was also in close contact with Aleksandr, as evidenced by several letters and notes from Irodion found among the texts in Aleksandr's library.[158]

On December 27, 1660, Boyar Fedor M. Rtishchev, one of the leading minds behind the liturgical reforms, brought a letter to the patriarchal court demanding that priest Irodion be seized and interrogated. The next day Iosif, the archimandrite of the Novospasskii Monastery, found a pamphlet lying on the ground (*na doroge*) when returning from the Kremlin to his monastery. Officials of the patriarchal court quickly established a connection between the two documents and proceeded to question Irodion about them.[159]

Irodion freely admitted authorship of the documents, one of which strongly condemned the secular behavior of the Muscovite clergy:

> There is not one bishop left who lives as a bishop should. There is no priest who lives in priestly fashion, no monk living a genuine monastic life. . . . Abbots have abandoned their monasteries and fallen into fraternizing with lay women and girls. Priests, abandoning their teaching responsibilities, . . . like to display to everyone their disgusting and repulsive way of life (*merzostnoe i kal'noe svoe zhitie*) . . . and they do not want to hear the Word of God.[160]

Irodion's denunciation of such ecclesiastical practices went hand in hand with his glorification of the priesthood: "The office of the priesthood plays the same role in the world as the soul in our body. We should all be aware that a bishop represents God before everyone and that the priest represents Christ. . . ."[161]

What inspired Irodion to choose such zealous words? Against whom were these lines specifically directed? The pamphlet contains some clues. First, he denounced specific changes in the wording of a gospel text, a Lectionary (*prolog*), and the Menaion (*mineia obshchaia*) of the month of August, and identified the editor, Arsenii the Greek, as the main perpetrator of this "heresy" (*arsenieva eres'*).[162] Second, the pamphlet criticized changes in the consecration of holy water. During his interrogation Irodion called this liturgical change "the heresy of the editors," but without implicating Arsenii.[163] We know that this change was associated with the name of the Greek archimandrite, Dionisii, an important translator and editor at the patriarchal printing press and also a personal enemy of Irodion.[164]

The conflict between Dionisii and Irodion was known to Aleksandr's circle. Ivanov wrote about it, but the most detailed account is found in a later letter by Avvakum. This letter relates a story so scandalous that editors of the text have often chosen to delete it.[165] Irodion had been serving as the spiritual father to employees of the patriarchal court and the patriarchal printing press. On one occasion a patriarchal clerk, who is not identified, confessed to Irodion that he had suffered a violent assault by the Greek archimandrite: "The archimandrite committed numerous acts of sodomy and fornication. One day, through an act of the Devil, he committed the filthy business in the sanctuary area with a boy whom he had dressed in the liturgical vestments worn by prelates. . . . "[166]

There is no independent proof that Dionisii ever committed such an act; what is significant is that Irodion believed the story. He went around town from party to party (*po pirushkam khodia*) telling the story to anyone who happened to be present.[167] Given Irodion's religious ideals and his strained relationship with Dionisii, it is not surprising that he attacked Dionisii on liturgical grounds. Irodion's writings were directed against the abuses and immorality of one of Muscovy's most powerful churchmen, just as the sermons of Avvakum and Neronov had been directed against the misdeeds of Patriarch Nikon.[168]

There is no indication that Irodion mobilized, or even angered, ordinary Muscovites by exposing the behavior of one of the most important book reformers. In fact, Irodion stopped opposing the new liturgical books after he received a Moscow parish position in August 1664.[169] His fervent polemic against the church's new rites thus primarily exerted a literary influence: copies of Irodion's writings were given to Aleksandr's agents and deposited in his library; later Old Believers incorporated Irodion's observations about Dionisii the Greek into their writings.[170]

Aleksandr's most important ally outside Moscow was the priest Nikita Dobrynin of Suzdal'. Dobrynin was an admirer of Bishop Pavel of Kolomna and thus learned of Aleksandr's fate after his assignment to the Kolomna bishopric.[171] Dobrynin actually met Aleksandr in Suzdal' in August and in October 1659, when the bishop led a fact-finding mission to investigate the alleged crimes of Nikon's friend, Archbishop Stefan. It was apparently not difficult to convince Dobrynin to fight against the new liturgies; like most Suzdalians, Dobrynin was extremely angry about Stefan's behavior. Indeed, he was engaged in a personal feud with the bishop that would soon destroy his life.[172]

Why did Dobrynin get into trouble with Stefan? One thing is certain: the introduction of the new books in the Suzdal' bishopric did not immediately play a role in this conflict. Dobrynin was upset about many other issues including the ruthlessness with which the bishop secured ecclesiastical posts and sources of income for himself and his family—a motive familiar from Neronov's and Loggin's battles against church corruption. Dobrynin raised the issues of greed and nepotism in a petition he sent to Moscow in early 1659. This petition in his own hand has survived in church archives:

> Together with his brother, the treasurer and monk Khristofor, and his nephew, the clerk Vasilii, . . . he beats priests, monks, and all sorts of people under his authority (*vsiakikh domovykh liudei*). And when his brother and nephew ride into the bishop's estates, they inflict beatings for their own limitless gain . . . many people have died from their blows, others are still languishing with injuries. He chased away many innocent abbots and installed his relatives instead, without Your royal approval. Similarly, he removed innocent priests from their churches and completely ransacked their homes without mercy. . . . They also squander the treasury of the bishopric . . . and distort the books recording incomes and expenditures. . . . [173]

At about the same time, Dobrynin sent another petition—surviving only in his own hand—accusing Stefan of plundering the graves of the Suzdal' church patrons. He gave the following account, which was subsequently confirmed in a report written by Aleksandr:

> The archbishop of Suzdal', Stefan, and his brother, the treasurer Khristofor, broke into the graves of the Grand Princes and the Shuiskiis and Skopins inside the cathedral. . . . They took their remains from the coffins, secretly carried them out of the church during the night, and buried them in various places. . . . The Great Lords and Princes of Suzdal' made provisions for our spiritual well-being and built the cathedral, endowing it with many lands. . . . Even after their death, they still give us drink and food and now their relics have been destroyed for no apparent reason. Merciful Tsar, . . . [give orders] to retrieve the relics of our great princely benefactors . . . from their secret hiding places. Have them buried again with honor in the cathedral and have their coffins restored as they were in the past. . . . Lord Tsar, have pity![174]

Dobrynin attributed much of Stefan's behavior to heretical freethinking. In a short petition to the tsar he accused Stefan of "slandering the

Christian faith." Stefan had been overheard saying that it was indecent to make visual representations of Christ's crucifixion, and had taught that it was possible to say Mass outside of church buildings.[175] He also had attacked the veneration of the Mother of God, a cult that enjoyed much popularity in seventeenth-century Muscovy. Stefan not only questioned the legitimacy of the cult, but plundered Marian shrines for personal enrichment.[176]

Finally, Dobrynin was outraged about Stefan's assault on local altars. Stefan had given orders to replace the altar cloths, and had thugs demolish altars and church interiors. In fact, he had participated in some of these acts: "[The bishop] broke the altars open and hurled them around. He also threw around the altar cloths and sometimes stuffed them into his pocket. He flung around icon stands, royal doors, and threw local icons as if they were simple boards."[177] In short, Archbishop Stefan acted like an enemy of the Orthodox faith.

Dobrynin's verbal attacks recall the heroic rhetoric and religious zeal of Avvakum and Neronov. Like them, Dobrynin wanted to maintain the spiritual integrity of the Orthodox church; and like them, he suffered greatly for his religious idealism. Initially, Dobrynin's complaints were taken seriously by Nikon's enemies, who saw an opportunity to punish one of the patriarch's cronies. Dobrynin even became a principal witness for the prosecution against Stefan at the 1660 Church Council. Soon afterward, however, he was severely punished for his outspokenness and barred from exercising the office of the priesthood, as documented by a petition the defrocked priest submitted after his arrest in early 1666:

> In 1659, I informed you, Sire . . . about the many wrongdoings against the church by Stefan, the archbishop of Suzdal'. You gave orders to investigate the archbishop's faults and Stefan himself admitted his guilt at the council in front of you and the prelates. Because of my denunciation, I . . . was prohibited from saying the divine liturgy until a church decree was issued. And I . . . have not said Mass and have been without the communion of the divine sacraments of Christ's body and blood for more than six years. I have been dying spiritually (*dushoiu pogibaiu*). During all these years, fearing the hour of death, I have been asking you and the hierarchs to absolve me, but the order has not come. . . . Have mercy on me and order the divine hierarchs to free my soul. . . . [178]

The dramatic deterioration in his fortunes helps to explain why Dobrynin became Aleksandr's ally. Before his encounters with Aleksandr in late 1659, Dobrynin had taken only a cursory interest in the liturgical reforms. He had willingly participated in church services using the new liturgical books and had limited his criticism to assembling a few notes about the books for his own personal use. Only after discussing Nikon's reforms with Aleksandr was Dobrynin inspired to write a long treatise against them. He then sought the advice of Aleksandr's learned protégé, Ivanov, who apparently helped him edit a compilation of detailed notes comparing old and new liturgical books.[179]

Dobrynin shared with writers such as Spiridon Potemkin and Abbot Feoktist a great anxiety about the deterioration of Russian religion. He agreed that the future of true Christian piety in Russia was threatened by Patriarch Nikon and his minions, and developed a motif that is also found in Neronov's writings: Nikon was about to bring the Russian Orthodox Church into union with the Catholic Church of Rome. The misdeeds of the corrupt higher clergy were seen as part of a Roman conspiracy, and all profanities in Russian church life attributed to the fact that Patriarch Nikon wanted to emulate the Roman pope (*v papy dostignuti*).

According to Dobrynin, Nikon's removal was insufficient for restoring the true religious mission of the Russian clergy. The first step was thought to be a drastic separation of the old sacred tradition from the profane innovations of the previous decade. In particular, clerics should visibly display their adherence to the old ways and no longer dress in vestments that made it impossible to distinguish them from "a Roman, Pole, or Jew" (*rimlianin, ili liakh, ili zhidovin*).[180]

Thus, Dobrynin had absorbed what might be called the rudiments of seventeenth-century Old Belief theology. He probably became a fervent critic of Nikon's reforms because Aleksandr's circle—most importantly, deacon Fedor Ivanov—offered an explanatory model for his own experiences at the hands of a corrupt hierarch. He accepted the argument originally made by "zealots" such as Neronov and Avvakum that there was an intrinsic connection between ecclesiastical corruption and the corruption of liturgical texts. Maintaining the purity of liturgical books and their ancient language was thought to be one way of fighting against the secularization of the church.[181]

Dobrynin not only wrote against ecclesiastical corruption; he also fought against it with great courage. His fate was closely linked to his continuing protests against the outrageous behavior of Archbishop Stefan. While Stefan was temporarily removed from Suzdal' and quarantined in the Kremlin, Dobrynin stayed behind to confront Stefan's minions, who continued to run the affairs of Suzdal'. In doing so, he quickly fell victim to violent assaults that recall similar attacks on Avvakum and Neronov.

In 1660, Archbishop Stefan's brother and nephews took their revenge.

They beat Dobrynin and locked him out of the cathedral, depriving him of his livelihood. Stefan's family even threatened to murder Dobrynin, and the frightened priest expected that his house would be destroyed at any time by a raving mob. Dobrynin also had serious troubles with the archbishop's officials, who still controlled church affairs in the town.[182]

These violent confrontations apparently did not intimidate Dobrynin, and Stefan's cronies had to look for other ways to get rid of him. This is demonstrated by a case brought against Dobrynin by the episcopal secretary Boris Vasil'ev in July 1663.[183] Boris and his brothers, the episcopal clerks Andrei and Ivan, claimed that the defrocked priest had become an unbearable troublemaker: once he "came toward [him] with a sharpened stick and maliciously (*nariadnym delom*) tried to murder [him]." Fortunately, brother Andrei was on the scene and prevented the murder. Nevertheless a public humiliation had not been avoided because "Nikita started to beat [him] with a cudgel and to tear [his] overcoat." All three brothers swore by their honor that "at that point, Sire, [Nikita] said things that are of great concern to the Sovereign (*skazal za soboiu tvoe, velikogo gosudaria, slovo*)."[184]

Dobrynin's version of this incident was quite different. He insisted that he had tried to defend the church treasury against the criminal deeds of these corrupt clerics:

> On July 2, secretary Boris Vasil'ev was about to take the treasury with silver money from the archbishop's palace. He, priest Nikita, heard about this and called out to many people in an attempt to save your treasury, Sire, and that of the bishopric. Boris Vasil'ev [and other officials] had planned the robbery: They had already broken a tunnel through the floor from the ice cellar into the palace; . . . and they had climbed in and were about to take the treasury of the archbishopric, the silver money, and all manner of valuables out of town. . . . They pretended that a fire had broken out in the palace and they called witnesses to justify them with a lie. But they called no one except their own men, such as Boris' father-in-law, the Archpriest Simeon Ivanov; his godfather, the key-keeper Dmitrii Vasil'ev; and his spiritual father, Fedor Ivanov.[185]

This act of heroism, which recalls Avvakum's earlier fights to rescue the patriarchal treasury, probably sealed Dobrynin's fate. No one believed Dobrynin's story, because he was put under surveillance (*na krepkie poruki*) and investigated by agents of the tsar's Secret Chancellery. It is possible that the unfortunate priest was allowed to stay in Suzdal', but there is no further documentation of his situation before his arrest in early 1666.[186]

Dobrynin had no chance to win in this conflict. His arrest and trial for rejecting the liturgical books signaled his complete defeat in the struggle against Archbishop Stefan and his cronies. In fact, Dobrynin's removal from Suzdal' set the scene for Stefan's triumphant return.[187] The Church Council of 1668 fully reinstated Stefan and, in celebration of this event, the later Patriarch Ioakim read Mass over the relics of Arsenii of Elasson, the legendary first Greek bishop of Suzdal'.[188]

Dobrynin became a permanent social outcast, and was thus in no position to organize a mass movement of protest against the new liturgical books. In fact, like Neronov before him, Dobrynin became completely disillusioned and recanted his beliefs to escape further suffering. His lasting contribution to the cause of Old Belief was not that he became a popular hero, but that he wrote a comprehensive treatise critical of the new books which left its mark on the literary tradition of seventeenth-century Old Belief.[189]

The direct involvement of Bishop Aleksandr in the Suzdal' affair reveals another interesting dimension in the social history of early Old Belief. It appears that Dobrynin was assisted not only by the bishop, but also by agents from Kremlin church bureaus. When Aleksandr traveled to Suzdal' he was accompanied by one Parfenii Ivanov, a secretary (*d'iak*) of the Patriarch's Office. This powerful man had a discussion with Dobrynin about the singing of the hallelujah, and gave him an old Greek text about this part of the liturgy. Parfenii Ivanov is mentioned again in the protocols of the 1666 Church Council as one of Aleksandr's closest allies, but since he died before the beginning of the proceedings against him, we know little about his activities.[190]

Parfenii was not the only ally of Aleksandr within the church administration. There was at least some sympathy for the cause of early Old Belief among other high-ranking officials. Deacon Fedor Ivanov, for example, related from his own experience that there were doubts about the liturgical reforms in the highest echelon of the Patriarch's Office. Metropolitan Pavel of Krutitsa, who headed the office at the time of Fedor's arrest, said the following to his prisoner: "Deacon, even we know that the old church piety is righteous and holy (*pravo i sviato*). The [old] books are immaculate (*neporochny*). But the tsar would punish us and we therefore stand behind the new books." This encounter took place in the Kremlin headquarters of the Russian patriarchate and was witnessed by Boyar Il'ia Avraam'evich Bezobrazov and the secretary Dionisii Diatlovskii.[191]

While at least some high church officials were apparently wavering on Nikon's liturgical reforms, only one of them, the clerk Fedor Trofimov, openly severed his ties with the patriarchal see and compiled a petition against the new liturgical books. Why did Trofimov, whose writings also made their way into Aleksandr's library, throw his support so openly to the cause of Old Belief?[192]

The answer is, in part, that he shared the reform zeal of men like Avvakum. Trofimov was particularly upset about the loose sexual morals of clergymen and church officials in the Kremlin. One shocking example was Vasilii Ivanov, the deacon of the Uspenskii Cathedral. This Vasilii "lives in the 'Latin' fashion (*po latyni*). When he was with his wife he does not wash himself. In fact, he celebrates Mass and all services coming directly from his woman to the church altar. That is obvious 'Latin' behavior."[193] Trofimov also observed homosexual practices among his colleagues who, instead of working at their desks, sneaked into Kremlin churches to fornicate with other clerics:

> Our brethren, the clerks, kiss and fondle with subdeacons, deacons, and the archdeacon in the altar area. They don't see any sin in this. In fact, they practice sodomy with Nikon's favorites (*ugodniki*) visiting them in their cells, and fornicate with each other in their homes. The wives of those who are married have complained to my wife about this sodomy. . . . It is an abomination of desolation that they live in "Latin" impurity and practice sodomy instead of supporting the Church of God.[194]

These accusations, which Trofimov formulated in two notes (*rospisi*) to the Kremlin, illustrate the influence of Old Belief ideas.

Trofimov also picked up an interpretive model that Neronov had used in some of his writings during the early 1650s: attributing what he saw as the general decline of religious morals in Russia to a "Latin" conspiracy. Following the example of other early Old Believers, Trofimov equated the Russian Orthodox Church with the Roman papacy.[195] His writings abound in attacks on powerful church lords to whom he attributed pope-like ambitions. One of these was his direct superior, the patriarchal secretary Ivan Kokoshilov. As the most influential bureaucrat of Nikon's patriarchate, Kokoshilov's brutal activities left a strong imprint on church policies of the 1650s.[196] Trofimov described Kokoshilov as an ambitious and unprincipled sycophant who would do anything to please Nikon. Indeed, he had even been ready to deny that Jesus was the son of God simply because Nikon demanded it. Trofimov considered this blasphemy and identified the secretary as the first of several "heretics and apostates" surrounding the patriarch.[197]

Unlike Trofimov, Kokoshilov had somehow survived Nikon's removal and continued to wield great power. Efforts to remove him finally succeeded in 1661, the same year that Trofimov submitted his petition to the tsar.[198] The original text of Trofimov's petition has not survived, but a copy was deposited in the central archive of Old Belief at Aleksandr's Moscow palace. The inventory of this archive indicates that the petition was accompanied by a request to restrain the power of other patriarchal bureaucrats (*prikaznye patriarshie*) as well.[199]

Trofimov was removed from his position and exiled to Tobol'sk in Siberia, possibly because he had annoyed Kokoshilov by his petition. There, he quickly came into conflict with the bishops of Siberia, who were among the most formidable church magnates of seventeenth-century Muscovy.[200] The exiled clerk witnessed helplessly—and with great anger—how these bishops and their supporters used ecclesiastical authority to enrich themselves. Trofimov's bitter complaint about their deep-rooted nepotism and corruption has survived:

> [Metropolitan] Kornilii brought with him an adopted son, a Pole by birth, a young man by the name Iakov. He married him to the wife of Grigorii Gruzdev and thus procured great wealth for himself. [For] Grigorii and Archbishop Simeon [Kornilii's predecessor] had bought up all goods in the [Siberian] towns with money—many thousands of rubles—which the tsar had donated for the construction of churches. . . . Kornilii frequently visits his new daughter-in-law and has made his son a chief (*boiar*) in the church administration. Grigorii's home, where Iakov lives, is located right next to the archbishop's court, adjacent to the town wall. And one day Kornilii found it too dark in the courtyard and simply gave orders to cut through the wall. They made a gate and . . . now bring him alcoholic beverages [through this gate].[201]

It is noteworthy that Trofimov's conversion to Old Belief was very similar to that of his mentor, Aleksandr. Trofimov had also once been a protégé of Nikon and had wielded considerable power. Indeed, he had supported the new liturgical order and was deeply shaken when Nikon abdicated in July 1658. Trofimov did not become an Old Believer simply because he admired Avvakum and Neronov; in fact, we don't know whether he had heard about these early "heroes" before he made contact with Aleksandr. Trofimov became a reform-oriented zealot only after he had become a victim of church authority. Indeed, the once-proud churchman suffered both in Moscow and in Siberia at the hands of Muscovy's most powerful hierarchs. Thus, we again see the paradox that some former supporters of Nikon became important promoters of early Old Belief.[202]

Documentary information is very scanty about other lower-ranking churchmen who had contacts with Aleksandr's circle. For example, we know virtually nothing about the clerk Vasilii Iakovlev to whom Aleksandr sent an undated memorandum, a copy of which was deposited in the first Old Belief archive. Archpriest Konon of Nizhnii Novgorod, who was in contact with Aleksandr and sent him at least one polemic text, has not left any further traces in historical records. I have been unable to locate biographical information about Archpriest Mikhail of Galich, who lived in Kazan' at the time of the 1666 Church Council and kept in touch with Fedor Ivanov. Several rank-and-file monks, mentioned in surviving records in Aleksandr's library, remain similarly unknown: monk Trifilii of the powerful Simonov Monastery in Moscow; monk Onufrii, who had a vision about the new sign of the cross; monk Ignatii, who wrote to Abbot Feoktist and appears to have corresponded later with the "Pustoozero prisoners"; Feoktist's brother, monk Avraamii from the town of Ustiug, with whom Feoktist left some of his papers at the time of his arrest; and finally, monk Zosima, who lived at the patriarch's court in the Kremlin and apparently gave Aleksandr books from the patriarchal library.[203]

There were several others who assisted Feoktist and Aleksandr in their efforts to build a network of Old Believers.[204] One was probably the little-known priest Lazar', a friend of Neronov's who later became a client of Archimandrite Nikanor of the Savva Monastery. After Nikanor's exile to Solovki in 1660, Lazar' was arrested and exiled to Siberia. In Tobol'sk he became friends with the discontented Fedor Trofimov and soon began to compile lists (*rospisi*) documenting the differences between old and new liturgical books.[205] Lazar's name is not explicitly mentioned in descriptions of Aleksandr's library, but he very likely contributed several of the texts that are listed anonymously.[206]

The men Aleksandr attracted to his cause had certain experiences and qualities in common. First, they learned about the tragic stories of Neronov and Avvakum, either through personal acquaintance or by reading their texts in Aleksandr's library. Second, they appear to have gone through experiences very similar to those of the two "zealots." Most had suffered great misfortune at the hands of powerful church lords; others were appalled by these lords' failure to abide by what were considered basic moral principles. As a result, all of Aleksandr's supporters shared one dominant concern that they voiced in letters, petitions, and short treatises: the Russian Orthodox Church had become a corrupt and "Latinized" institution that was in need of urgent reform; otherwise, the church would be taken over by the Catholics or Jews. It was the combination of this fear and extraordinary reform zeal which, more than anything else, distinguished the first Old Believers from the other dissenters discussed in this book.

THE EVIDENCE ADDUCED in this chapter suggests that early Old Belief became a somewhat organized phenomenon during the eight years between Nikon's abdication and the 1666 Church Council. The explanation for this strengthening of Old Belief must be sought in the activities of a few high-ranking hierarchs, most of whom had once been closely affiliated with Nikon. Active proponents of the new liturgies during Nikon's patriarchate, these hierarchs became Old Believers for a variety of reasons including declining political and financial fortunes; personal encounters with victims of Nikon's violence; anti-Catholic sentiments; disgust with moral corruption within the church; or simply, strong religious conviction. The most important Old Believer of this period, if not the most important leader throughout the entire history of seventeenth-century Old Belief, was the later forgotten Bishop Aleksandr of Kolomna and Viatka.

Old Belief became important during this early period not because of its social influence, which was still very limited, but because Aleksandr had gathered a few learned and highly motivated *literati* around him including later legendary figures, such as Archimandrite Spiridon Potemkin and deacon Fedor Ivanov. These men made two lasting contributions to the history of Old Belief: first, they assembled and copied surviving letters and pamphlets from the pen of the exiled archpriests Avvakum and Neronov. Second, they elaborated on familiar themes from the archpriests' work by writing polemic works of their own. All of these old and new writings were deposited in one central library or archive in Aleksandr's palace.

One might say that Aleksandr created the "founding archive" of Old Belief.[207] During this early period Old Belief had one primary goal: to gather and write texts that would keep alive the opposition to Nikon's reforms. Contributing to the growth of Aleksandr's archive was considered the ultimate achievement, while access to these texts—which was largely a reflection of good personal relations with the bishop—defined membership in Old Belief.

The principal rank-and-file supporters of early Old Belief were churchmen from Moscow and environs, the centuries-old center of Russian Orthodoxy. They had held—or still held—influential positions within the official church: the secretary Parfenii Ivanov and the clerk Fedor Trofimov were employed by the most powerful bureaucratic body of the Muscovite church, the Patriarch's Office; deacon Fedor Ivanov and the priest Irodion served in the tsar's churches of the Kremlin; Nikita Dobrynin was cathedral priest in the ancient town of Suzdal'. Most of these men were involved in bitter personal feuds with powerful Russian hierarchs, convinced they were promoting "God's cause" (*delo Bozhie*) by exposing the corruption and lack of piety of these hierarchs. In short, the early Old Believers were religious idealists who wanted to create a better church.

Aleksandr's circle was probably much wider than earlier networks that had formed around Neronov and Avvakum: his influence reached into Moscow parishes, a handful of monasteries, and towns such as Perm' and Tobol'sk. Still, Old Belief could hardly be described as a large movement of popular protest. Those who took up the cause of Old Belief during this period were Aleksandr's personal friends and clients; the few lay sympathizers included family members and friends of Avvakum and Neronov, and the remarkable boyar woman Feodosiia Morozova.

Finally, there were dissenters who should not be confused with the early Old Believers. They had no access to the historical and theological texts in Aleksandr's palace and probably had never heard of Avvakum and Neronov. Certainly, the priest Terentii or the Chudov monk Savvatii might have made good allies, but they were not part of Aleksandr's circle and were consequently forgotten by later generations of Old Believers. The differences in world view between Old Believers and these other dissenters were especially pronounced in the case of Archimandrite Ioasaf of Troitsa, who shared none of the Christian ideals of men like Ivanov. Ioasaf took an interest in the old liturgies without, however, changing his way of life. In fact, he and his associates and relatives acted as violently toward local residents as did other Muscovite hierarchs. Finally, the rural hermit Nikon, who was simply ignorant of the difference between old and new rites, was turned into a dissenter by an arbitrary decision of church investigators.

One might say that the "interpatriarchal period" (*mezhpatriarshe vremia*), the time between Nikon's abdication in 1658 and the appointment of a successor shortly after the 1666 Church Council, witnessed seventeenth-century Old Belief at its zenith. During these eight years Old Belief had powerful protectors and mentors within the Orthodox Church hierarchy who penned many of Old Belief's most important texts. Even the charismatic authority enjoyed by the exiled Avvakum and Ivanov during later decades never quite compensated for their real loss of power as a result of the Church Council of 1666.[208]

The extraordinary church council that began at the Kremlin in April 1666 was a catastrophe for Old Belief. Aleksandr was the first to be tried and the first to admit the falsity of his views under cross-examination.[209] His supporters quickly followed his example, submitting written recantations as well. One of Aleksandr's most important allies, Dobrynin, wrote three recantations imploring Russian hierarchs for mercy and offering "to kiss [their] beautiful feet."[210] There appear to have been only two Old Believers who adhered to their beliefs, Archpriest Avvakum and the priest Lazar'. They were later joined by Ivanov, who revoked his written "repentance" (*pokaianie*) a few months after the conclusion of the church council.[211] These three heroic figures were exiled to the isolated prison colony of Pustoozero in the far north and became known as the legendary "Pustoozero prisoners."[212]

How did these few exiled Old Believers manage to preserve a community greatly weakened by the decapitation of its leadership? How did Old Belief survive not only into the next century, but well into the twentieth century? The answer is not that the "Pustoozero prisoners" were the leaders of a mass movement, but rather that they wrote and disseminated authoritative texts. These texts, which have been repeatedly studied by historians, defined the ideological mission and historical destiny of Old Belief.[213]

To accurately assess the influence of Old Belief on Russian society during the remainder of the seventeenth century, it is necessary to reconstruct the dissemination of Old Believer texts. According to new research by Russian philologists, three phases of dissemination can be distinguished. First, the "Pustoozero prisoners" circulated copies of the texts found in Aleksandr's library amongst themselves and their few remaining supporters in Moscow. They immediately eliminated texts by men they apparently considered unreliable, or even traitors to their cause. Among the censored texts we find, for example, a few of Dobrynin's petitions as well as Trofimov's writings.[214] This conscious intervention in Old Belief's textual heritage also resulted in the elimination of explicit references to the men who had recanted their beliefs in 1666.[215]

Next, texts accepted by the Pustoozero leadership were emendated and used for the compilation of new texts. Finally, the Pustoozero Old Believers began to copy and disseminate both old and new texts. This was a time-consuming and tedious process since these Old Believers, unlike European dissenters of their time, had no printing press to expedite their work. Instead, Avvakum and his fellow exiles had to rely on supporters such as the monk Avraamii and Feodosiia Morozova who, after daring efforts to smuggle texts out of the prison camp, made additional copies of the Pustoozero writings.[216]

Given the limited number of copies, these texts did not reach large audiences during the seventeenth century.[217] It appears that knowledge of Old Belief became more widespread in Russian society only around the turn of the century. This was largely due to the emergence of several centers of scholarship that used the Pustoozero texts and some of the texts in

Aleksandr's archive as a "sacred canon."[218] These communities—foremost among them the famous Vyg Community under the Denisov brothers—again provided Old Belief the stable organization it had lost with the collapse of Aleksandr's circle.

Many scribes were employed by these communities to further copy the texts of seventeenth-century Old Believer writers and make them available to the Russian population at large. Historian N. S. Demkova has recently spoken of a "chaotic spread of [Old Believer] texts" at the beginning of the eighteenth century.[219] It is important to remember that this process could not have occurred without Aleksandr's groundbreaking, albeit largely forgotten, work.

Even during the first decades of the eighteenth century, though, knowledge about Old Belief may not have spread very far. It is true there were now ordinary Russians—even outside the established Old Belief Church—who owned icons of Archpriest Avvakum, or who proudly identified themselves as readers of Abbot Spiridon Potemkin's works.[220] But they appear to have been the exception. Many Russians who could read, or at least prided themselves on the ownership of books belonging to Muscovy's old liturgical tradition, had not come across the writings of the early Old Believers.[221] In other words, many of the dissenters who denounced the official liturgical order during the reign of Peter I. probably did not see themselves as part of a larger Old Belief community.[222]

I turn now to these other dissenters who defended the old liturgies for reasons of their own and without contact with Old Believers. The remaining decades of the seventeenth century did not so much witness the expansion of Old Belief as the growth of a phenomenon official investigators described as a schism (*raskol*), which has often been confused with Old Belief.

CHAPTER THREE

Meanings of the Term Raskol

Historians often use the term *raskol* (anglicized as Raskol), or its English equivalent "schism," as an appellation for the Old Believer movement. In traditional scholarly discourse, Old Believers are called the "founding fathers of the Raskol," "Raskol fathers," "the teachers of the schism" (*raskolouchiteli*), or "the leaders of the schism."[1] This widespread equation of Raskol and Old Belief—indeed the use of the peculiar compound "Raskol-Old Belief" (*raskol staroobriadchestva*)—was first codified in pivotal nineteenth-century publications on the Russian Schism.[2] Its origins can be traced to polemic texts written in the aftermath of the 1666 Church Council, which condemned Old Believers as creators of a "schism" (*raskol*) and as dangerous "schismatics" (*raskol'niki*).[3]

I will demonstrate that Muscovite church polemicists did not apply the Church Slavonic lexeme *raskol* exclusively to Old Believers. In fact, when the word was first introduced into official discourse during the early 1650s, it was not meant to describe Old Believers but rather *all* men and women who had somehow failed to obey church authority. The meaning "Old Belief" was added more than a decade later, and coexisted with the original meaning of "general dissent."

This failure of church terminology to differentiate between Old Belief and other forms of dissent has strongly influenced the traditional view of the Russian Schism. Most historians—with a few notable exceptions, such as Robert Crummey—have tacitly assumed that the epithet *raskol'niki* signified Old Believers.[4] In fact, the polemic language of the church has been used explicitly to argue that the preaching and writing of a few charismatic men—such as Avvakum and Neronov—split the community of Russian Christians into two irreconcilable camps, the adherents of the official church and the schismatic Old Believers.[5]

It is important to remember that the term *raskol* was coined by seventeenth-century church hierarchs, and primarily reflects the perceptions of the Muscovite church elite regarding religious and social developments of their time. Church texts thus need to be read very carefully, and their descriptive terminology understood, before any general observations about the Russian Schism can be made.

This chapter presents a brief inquiry into the conceptual history (*Begriffsgeschichte*) of the term *raskol*, (hereafter referred to as schism). How did the term enter official discourse about Old Belief and other forms of dissent? Who employed the term? And finally, which issues and concerns did this term signify to those who used it? Once I have answered these questions, I proceed, in subsequent chapters, to study the social and religious realities that seventeenth-century churchmen associated with the outbreak of a schism.

The first usage of the term schism during the period under study here probably occurred in an encyclical (*okruzhnoe poslanie*) issued by Metropolitan Iona of Rostov in August 1652, a few weeks after Nikon became patriarch. Iona had just been appointed to the metropolitanate of Rostov, and the text expressed his priorities and expectations as new leader of Muscovy's third-largest eparchy. The encyclical was addressed to the populace of the Rostov eparchy, whom Iona addressed paternally as "my children" (*chadtsa moia*). The intended recipients, however, were the abbots and archpriests entrusted with the supervision of ordinary clerics and lay Christians.[6]

This text was mainly concerned with the correction (*ispravlenie*) of Christian morals. Parish priests and deacons were to educate their flocks in basic tenets of Christian belief by reading biblical texts and preaching. Church liturgies were to be conducted without haste, and parishioners were to show due respect. Monks and laymen (*mirskie liudi*) had to belong to Christian communities; they were to take communion and go to confession three times a year. Last but not least, the encyclical polemicized against the rampant drunkenness of clerics and laymen, which was to be fought with all available resources.[7]

A short reference to the outbreak of a schism is found in the following passage:

> Be it known to you: if anywhere—in town, village, or elsewhere—
> there appears an opponent of God's cause (*Bozhie delo*), or if anybody

begins to oppose sermons based on the Holy Scriptures, or slander a true pastor and teacher—archimandrite or abbot, priest or deacon: we are ready for such schismatics (*raskol'niki*) and with God's help we will catch these wolves. . . . [8]

Whom did Iona perceive to be a schismatic? The text provides no clear identification, but offers instead only a broad programmatic concept: a schismatic was any individual who questioned the authority of the church and its representatives. The term schismatic could be replaced by synonyms denouncing individuals who were disobedient to the religious precepts of the new bishop. For example, other passages of the same text demonized opponents of Iona as "murderers of God's Being" (*ubiitsy Bozhiia estestva*), "spiritual criminals" (*dushevnye razboiniki*), "evil-minded men" (*zloumnye*), and "troublemakers" (*bezchinniki*).[9] Thus, the first reference to the dangers of a schism was used by a powerful church leader who placed great emphasis on obedience to his authority.

The next documented usage that I have been able to identify contains the same general meaning of disobedience to ecclesiastical authority. However, the text in which it is found provides a clearer idea about the actual identity of those accused as schismatics. In early 1655, Archbishop Misail of Riazan'—who, like Iona of Rostov, was one of Nikon's earliest appointees—received a petition from a few inhabitants of Murom requesting his help. The petition denounced the population of Murom as being schismatic for having earlier chased one of the bishop's officials out of town. This official was none less than the previously mentioned Old Believer Loggin, who had been the archpriest of Murom until his dismissal in late 1653:

> Many great misfortunes have befallen us recently, as well as the attacks and persecutions of evil haters. Nobody defends us and the number of enemies is constantly growing. They call themselves priests and Christians, but are in fact schismatics because of their evil manners and habits. They are opposed to the divine traditions of the Holy Apostles and Holy Fathers. They offend everything that is pious, rebel against the church, hate the light, drink, blaspheme, and use foul language. Now they see that our father, pastor, and teacher, Archpriest Loggin, has been expelled and they have begun to insult everyone who leads a pious way of life. They persecute us with misfortunes, attacks, and slander.[10]

The concerns expressed in this petition coincide with those formulated by Iona. The writers saw the danger of a schism arising from the degeneration of Christian morals, and they discerned a serious split in the religious community of Murom:

There is a division (*razdelenie*) in our Orthodox Christian faith . . . God's enemies, drunkards, and blasphemers . . . aspire to descend with deceit upon the blessed spiritual authority in the town of Murom. [They are] against the Holy Apostolic Church and the archpriests because they want to completely destroy the Orthodox Christian Church and eradicate all piety without a trace.[11]

The schism referred to by Loggin's friends must be seen in the context of disciplinary policies introduced by Archbishop Misail. Even though Misail was not sympathetic to the Old Believers' cause, he was, like Loggin, a radical advocate of Christianization. In fact only a few months later, he paid with his life for trying to convert Mordvinian tribesmen to Orthodoxy.[12]

The outbreak of a schism at Murom was discovered soon after Misail, with the support of his agent Loggin, had tried to regulate the behavior of its Christian population. He had given the order that Orthodox Christians should go to church instead of spending their time drinking and playing games. Those who did not comply with this order were refused access to Christian sacraments, including Christian burial. Also, Misail had called for the closing of taverns and the confiscation of alcoholic beverages.[13] The schismatics who dislodged Loggin were, in all likelihood, angry defenders of popular customs Misail had attempted to eradicate.

It should be emphasized that none of the above-mentioned usages of the term schism applies to Old Belief. Indeed, one of the cited texts was written by supporters of former church official Loggin, who was an early Old Believer. This peculiar fact illustrates an important reality: Old Belief and the church apparently shared a common language for denouncing dissenters. When referring to schismatics during the 1650s, both sides agreed that schismatics were men and women who did not care to be "good" (*dobrye*) Christians. It is likely that this usage of the term schism originated in the official reform rhetoric of the 1630s and 1640s which, as N. F. Kapterev has shown, influenced both official churchmen and Old Believers.[14]

There is *no* evidence, however, that the term schism was widely used during the patriarchate of Nikon (1652–58).[15] We know, for example, that the patriarch himself referred to any opposition to his rule as heresy or criminal behavior. The notion of a schism was apparently not part of his rhetorical lexicon.[16] However, the language of the two above-cited texts reflects a concern similar to that of other official texts printed and disseminated under Nikon. For example, in October 1655 the patriarchal printing press published various editions of a treatise titled *Prayer for the Pacification and Unification of the Orthodox Faith*.[17] The text expressed great concern about the unity of the church and predicted a dire scenario, namely the loss of church unity. The term schism is not used in this tract, but other similar terms abound. Several passages, for example, employ the word *skhizma*, the Greek equivalent of the Church Slavonic *raskol*.[18] The Greek Orthodox concept of *apostasis* (apostasy) appears on almost every page: Muscovite church and religion were being undermined by countless "apostates" (*otstupniki*) and "apostasies" (*otstupstva*).[19]

It remains unclear who exactly was being accused of endangering the church. In part, the language of this tract recalls phrases usually applied to non-Christians living in Muscovy. For example, we find that the enemies of the church are identified as "faithless and godless Agarians" (*agariany*) and " . . . pagans who oppose the Cross of Christ" (*kresta Khristova soprotivnyia iazyki*).[20] However, the text makes clear that the dangers about to destroy the well-being (*blagosostoianie*) of the church had their origins in the Christian community:

> The apostates mercilessly whet their teeth and open their jaws wide like wild animals as if they were about to tear up and devour Your church. . . . We cannot endure these demons and their demonic arrows. We are encircled by apostates, have no protection, and cannot find refuge anywhere. . . . [21]

Christ's intercession is solicited to maintain the harmony of church life:

> Give peace to Your holy church. Do not allow it to be cursed . . . and grant quickly like-mindedness, concord, and consent to Your faithful slaves, Oh Christ, so that Your church will become secure. . . . Hunt down and completely eradicate heresies and apostasies, implant and multiply piety everywhere . . . and raise the Christian horn. . . . [22]

The mind-set reflected in this widely disseminated text was by no means unique to the 1650s, and it would be a mistake to assume that the apostates mentioned in the text were identical with the first Old Believers. In fact, the Manichaean bifurcation of the world into the forces of good and evil was a literary construct typical of many official texts of seventeenth-century Russian Christianity. A good example is the influential *Instruction* (*Pouchenie*) by Patriarch Iosif, Nikon's predecessor, which circulated among Muscovite hierarchs during the 1640s.[23] The text called upon the Muscovite clergy to fight "heretics" (*eretiki*), "blasphemers" (*bogokhul'niki*), and "rebels" (*miatezhniki*) who were undermining the welfare of the church. Anyone who opposed the teachings of the church was threatened with anathema.[24] The text also emphasized the improvement of Christian morals, which were seen to be under attack by the forces of evil and the machinations of the Devil. The primary offenses committed by enemies of the church were drunkenness (*p'ianstvo*) and sexual misbehavior such as fornication (*blud*), incest (*srodnoe bluzhenie*), and sodomy (*skotobluzhenie*).[25]

Thus, the notion of a schism developed in a cultural milieu that produced and disseminated texts painting a very pessimistic picture of Russian religious reality: the church was not in control but was in constant danger of being destroyed or at least destabilized. The eradication of non-Christian behavior was perceived as the best way to consolidate the church. Or, in the words of the Murom petition, the fight against drunkards and other "abusers of piety" (*blagochestiiu rugateli*) was considered the best way to prevent the outbreak of a schism.[26]

Clearly the word schism signified a widespread lack of piety as well as religious indifference. The only difference between Old Believers and churchmen on this issue was that Old Believers apparently meant what they advocated in their writings. Or to be more specific, Loggin promulgated his ideals in public even when his sermons provoked violent abuse by schismatics. Iona, by contrast, only gave lip service to the dominant reform rhetoric. For him, the term schismatic functioned as a convenient label that he could attach to disobedient members of his flock.[27]

It is significant that the cited texts do not use the term schism, (or words derived from the same Church Slavonic root *raskol*), to refer to Nikon's liturgical reforms. The term refers, instead, to the perceived limits of ecclesiastical power over Muscovite society; accordingly, the danger of a schism derived not from liturgical changes, but from the notion that Muscovites had never been properly Christianized.

There is no question that the term schism soon acquired the more specific meaning of opposition to the Nikonian reforms. This meaning was developed in polemic texts written during the controversy, which began in the late 1660s, over the revision of liturgical books. Each side of this highly literary controversy accused the other side of adhering to a schism. For example, an influential petition by the Old Believer Avraamii insisted that a schism had been introduced by Patriarch Nikon, and that the end of the world was imminent.[28] Other Old Believer texts employing the term *raskol* with this meaning could be cited.[29] Such Old Believer treatises have certainly contributed to shaping scholarly discourse about seventeenth-century Russian religion. But ultimately, the polemic texts produced by the other side of the controversy, that is, the official church, may have been even more important. These official texts interpreted Old Belief and other acts of religious dissent as part of a uniform movement of protest called *raskol*.

The first official reference to a schism in connection with the revision of liturgical books can be found in the Church Slavonic translation of a letter by the Greek Patriarch Paisii, which was printed in the revised Service Book of 1655. Paisii debated whether a schism could occur as a result of liturgical changes, and concluded that it depended very much on whether the Muscovite church classified opposition to the changes as schismatic. In other words, Paisii maintained that the church had the power to either create, or prevent, a schism. He pleaded for the acceptance of liturgical differences, and recommended that the church refrain from taking drastic measures and exercise tolerance:

> If one church happens to be different from another in a few unimportant and unessential rites, . . . that does not indicate any division, so long as the same faith has been immutably preserved. The church did not adopt from the very beginning all the rites that it keeps today, they were gradually introduced in various churches at different times . . . but this does not mean that they became heretical and schismatic (*raskol'nicheskimi*). . . . [30]

Paisii's plea for tolerance may have been heeded by Nikon, who chose not to designate opponents of the new books schismatics. However, it had little influence on Nikon's successors, who proceeded to speak with great alarm about the outbreak of a powerful and all-encompassing schism. Nearly ten years after Paisii wrote his letter, church texts contained the leitmotif that Muscovite religion and society were threatened, not by a handful of Old Believers, but by a widespread conspiracy of schismatics rejecting the new liturgical books. Particularly noteworthy are a few influential treatises written in connection with the trial of the first Old Believers in 1666. These treatises were codified by the Church Council of 1667, which officially excommunicated the Old Believers as schismatics.[31]

The notion of Old Believers as the leaders of a large movement of schismatics originated in the works of Simeon Polotskii, a White Russian monk who had been in the service of the tsar since early 1664. Simeon dominated the proceedings against the Old Believers. He set the agenda for their trial and provided visiting Greek hierarchs with a Latin translation of one of the most systematic Old Believer critiques of the new liturgies, Nikita Dobrynin's petition to the tsar.[32] He also translated into Russian a Latin response to Dobrynin's petition by the Greek theologian Paisii Ligarides.[33] Most importantly, Polotskii wrote *Staff of Rulership* (*Zhezl pravleniia*) as well as *Acts of the Church Councils of 1666 and 1667*, which laid down the guidelines for all future definitions of protest against the new liturgical books. The original manuscript containing these two works bears the Latin title *Demonstratio verae fidei contra schismaticos*, an indication that Polotskii's definition of the schism may have been influenced by Western models.[34]

Polotskii's basic approach was to interpret the Old Believers' rejection of liturgical books as part of a conspiracy to undermine the stability of the church. For example, his *Staff of Rulership* attributed a cataclysmic role to the relatively esoteric writings of Nikita Dobrynin. In Polotskii's eyes, Dobrynin assumed the proportions of a Goliath about to pounce upon the church with his troops (*s svoim polkom*). Learning a lesson from the story of David and Goliath, the church would defeat the schismatics by trusting in God's help.[35] The *Acts of the Church Councils* developed a similar argument. An elaborate preamble commissioned by the tsar compared leading Old Believers with Luther and Calvin. The events in Muscovy were thus equated with those of the Western Reformation, the great schism dividing the Latin world, with which the White Russian Polotskii was familiar from his experience in the Polish-Lithuanian Commonwealth.[36] Analogous to the great religious controversy in the West, Polotskii foresaw the unfolding of an apocalypse: Muscovite church and society were threatened by no less than the Devil and his minions, the Old Believers, and a titanic battle over the revision of liturgical books was unavoidable.[37]

Polotskii's views greatly influenced how seventeenth-century churchmen were to view, and then describe, contemporary religious realities. His texts became basic reading for those engaged in the supervision of local religious affairs. Evidence from the archive of the Novgorod eparchy, for example, illustrates that printed copies of *Staff of Rulership* were distributed to all major monasteries and hermitages in northern Russia.[38] Ivan, a priest from Kolomna who in 1667 or shortly thereafter wrote a polemic against a local preacher, probably had a copy of Polotskii's book at his disposal. The targeted preacher was an isolated prophet with no significant popular following. But in Ivan's eyes, he became a dangerous agent of Satan, a propagator of the schism who, in unison with the Old Believers, threatened the stability of the church (*mutiashche tserkov'*).[39]

The newly appointed Patriarch Ioasaf (1667–72) was one of the first Russian hierarchs to assimilate the language of Polotskii. Old Believers had considered him on their side in the polemic over the revision of books,[40] but Ioasaf's agenda as patriarch, outlined in a foreword to *Staff of Rulership*, was to wipe out the "obscene schisms" (*nelepiia raskoly*) and "seditious revolts" (*kramolnyia miatezhi*) that were undermining the church, and to restore church unity.[41] Circulated to Russian eparchies and monasteries, Ioasaf's promulgations painted a gloomy picture: Old Believers were the "leaders of the schism" (*raskolonachal'niki*) and were taking great numbers of Orthodox Christians into perdition (*v debr' geenny*). As a result, the Church of God was in an uproar and in danger of suffering great harm.[42] The patriarch's *Voice* (*Glas*), addressed to Orthodox clerics and laymen alike, described the Old Believers as conspiring with the Devil:

> The Devil, the eternal enemy of Christ's church, has mobilized his supporters, who are the vessels of his deceit and cunning, to speak ill (*obkhuzhdati*) of the revision of books and to create a great schism in the church. . . . [43]

Thus by the late 1660s, widely circulated texts repeated the idea that the Old Believers had caused a schism. Ioasaf's successor, Patriarch Ioakim (1674–90), continued the polemic tradition established by Simeon Polotskii. The 1670s and 1680s saw the production of numerous tracts portraying the grave danger of a schism, most of which were issued by the patriarchal printing press.[44]

The most important of these texts, *Spiritual Exhortation* (*Uvet dukhovnyi*) by Archbishop Afanasii of Kholmogory, was printed in thousands of copies in September 1682—five months after the execution of some of the most important Old Believers at Pustoozero. This polemic work, which singled out the executed Archpriest Avvakum as well as the priests Lazar' and Nikita Dobrynin as the main perpetrators of the schism, was to be distributed to all Muscovite parish priests; they, in turn, were supposed to instruct their parishioners about the dangers posed by these three men. The dead preachers were demonized as "soul-destroying wolves" and schismatics because "they had dared . . . to teach apostasy (*otstupleniiu*) from the holy church in order to make a rebellion (*vozmushchenie*). . . . " People should be wary of their followers "who again had escaped punishment. . . . [These] evil schismatics have been enraged (*vozbesnesha*) [by the execution] and again Satan has gathered them from the bushes and from the breezes (*is kustov i ot vetrov sobra*) to fall upon the immaculate (*neporochnuiu*) church." The text warns ordinary Russians against anyone who told them not to go to church, to pray, or to accept the holy sacraments.[45]

Spiritual Exhortation, which became standard reading for the Muscovite clergy under Patriarch Ioakim, fails to make any distinction between Old Believers and other schismatics. Indeed, anyone who raised his voice against the church was potentially considered a schismatic, that is, an agent of Old Belief. The introductory pages of the treatise suggest that the Old Believers provided a dangerous model: many ordinary Russians—denounced by the text collectively as "simple peasants," "know-nothings" (*nevezhdi*), and "unlearned simpletons" (*neuki-prostaki*)—had been encouraged to "follow their own laws and customs and to insist upon their own will," and were now behaving like Avvakum and other Old Believers.[46]

The generalizing language of these polemic texts created the guidelines for church and government officials, who soon began to classify diverse manifestations of dissent as part of a unified phenomenon—the schism. In October 1666, for example, officials of the tsar's Secret Chancellery denounced an obscure priest from the vicinity of Viazniki and his parishioners as schismatics for refusing to obey the orders of a newly appointed local abbot to use the new liturgical books.[47] Then in early 1667, the Patriarch's Office issued a list of all individuals accused of opposing the new liturgical books, many of whom had nothing to do with the Old Believers.[48]

A similar confusion is found in an order dated August 26, 1667 and issued by the Service Chancellery (*Razriadnyi prikaz*). This order announced that both the well-known Old Believer Archpriest Avvakum and the obscure Archpriest Mikifor of Simbirsk were to be exiled for refusing to ask forgiveness "for their schismatic acts against the church" (*v raskol'nikh tserkovnykh vinakh*).[49] Not only had Mikifor had no prior contact with Avvakum, he also had not been arrested for holding Avvakum's views. Mikifor had failed to introduce the new rites in the frontier province of Simbirsk, as noted by traveling Greek hierarchs who had visited in September 1666, and for this disobedience he was arrested and taken to Moscow.[50]

There can be no doubt that the idea of the schism quickly superseded older, probably more accurate, and less stereotypical modes of viewing dissent. To illustrate the dramatic impact of this new discourse, it is helpful to remember earlier practices of defining religious deviance. Before the pivotal Church Council of 1666, incidents involving the rejection of liturgical books had not been attributed to a schism. The preachers Sila, Fedor, and Aleksei, for example, who were arrested by Metropolitan Iona in 1657, were investigated for offending the name of the patriarch (*gosudarevo velikoe delo*).[51] The investigating officials interpreted the preachers' behavior within the traditional framework of proceedings designed to protect the honor of the patriarch. This practice had entered Muscovite church life under Patriarch Filaret, whose name and honor were frequently defended in trials.[52]

In another instance, the unfortunate priest Nikon from the Kostroma district was suspected of opposing the new books because he was insane; he was imprisoned for "madness" (*bezumstvo*), an indication that church officials viewed Nikon's behavior as a reflection of his personality, and not as part of a conspiracy against the church.[53] The priest Terentii was arrested and interrogated for uttering "unruly and indecent words" (*bezchinnye i nepristoinye slova*), and his behavior was understood primarily in terms of his attitudes toward his superior, Metropolitan Pitirim.[54]

After 1666, similar acts of dissent were universally classified as manifestations of the schism. Church investigators focused so intensely on the failure to use new liturgical books as a litmus test that they overlooked, for example, the similarity of many schism cases to those previously classified as "spiritual offenses" (*dukhovnye dela*) or "crimes" (*vorovstva*). Transgressions against the new liturgical norms would probably have been better understood if they had not been thrown together with a wide variety of phenomena previously attributed to very different causes.

Despite Polotskii's normative influence, the original meaning of the word schism—as used in the Rostov encyclical and Murom petition—continued to exist as an important linguistic substratum. In fact, the old notion that schism signified disobedience to church authority began to merge indistinguishably with the new meaning, "failure to use the new Nikonian rites." This is not surprising since there were indeed unknown numbers of Muscovites who had little, or no, contact with church institutions. In particular, there was widespread failure to attend church services, or go to confession and communion.[55] Because of such minimal contact with churchmen, many ordinary Muscovites had never been told to change the sign of the cross and other rites that they used in their daily lives.[56]

This dual meaning of the term schism appears frequently in the charters of northern bishoprics, which began to assert control over local parish life during the 1680s. In 1682, for example, Metropolitan Kornilii of Novgorod instructed the new archimandrite of Solovki to discipline residents of the monastery's hinterlands, who throughout most of the seventeenth century had failed to fulfill basic church demands and had not accepted the new rites:

> Priests must be strictly ordered to see to it that their male and female parishioners and children over twelve attend Mass during the Lenten season, fast, go to confession and, if worthy, take communion. The parish priests must send lists to our legal office (*sudnoi prikaz*) which indicate by name whom they serve as spiritual fathers, and which parishioners are opposed to this order. . . . Adherents of the schism who do not obey this order are to be exiled to monasteries where they are to be kept in confinement under strict supervision until they abandon their stubbornness, repent, and cease to behave like schismatics (*raskol'nichat' prestanut*). . . . [57]

During the early 1690s, parish priests from the remote Pogost regions of the Novgorod eparchy, (primarily the area around Lake Onega), had to send lists to their metropolitan reporting all parishioners who failed to go to confession and communion. These negligent parishioners were usually called schismatics because they had also failed to assimilate the new Nikonian religion. In April 1693, for example, priest Mikhail from the Vyshnevolukii Pogost wrote that he had named everyone whose behavior deviated from the set norms. He added proudly that " . . . other than those on this [list] there are no other schismatics in our parish, neither among our parishioners, nor among newcomers who belong to other parishes."[58]

The language of the documents cited—if understood only in the sense of Polotskii's equation of schism and Old Belief—obscures the underlying causes of the behavior. It would be misleading to assume that parishioners who were absent from church services were fervently opposed to the new books. While this may have been true for some, there were certainly many other reasons for absence from church services. These reasons, some of them as profane as sickness, drunkenness, or laziness, were usually not investigated by seventeenth-century churchmen.[59] Clearly, these schismatics had nothing in common with the highly disciplined and moralistic Old Believers, except that they happened to use the old liturgical rites.

A similar use of the term schism can be found in a letter by the Greek Patriarch Makarii, who visited the town of Nizhnii Novgorod and its environs in June 1668. His note, which was translated into Russian, calls for "the consolidation of the holy church and the Orthodox faith." The Christian population "of this land" must be saved from "the schismatics and enemies of the church" who could be found in multitude among "the simple and uneducated people as well as the priesthood."[60] Makarii explained the large number of schismatics by saying that "regulations about the improvement and consolidation of the Orthodox faith have still not arrived in these regions." To ameliorate the situation, he suggested printing instructions in the Christian faith in large quantities and distributing them among the local population (*napechatat' v dovol'nost' i rozdavat' v narody*).[61]

Makarii's complaint is of great historical importance because it inspired the founding of a new diocese in Nizhnii Novgorod a few years later.[62] Filaret, the first bishop of Nizhnii Novgorod, sent the tsar a letter of distress soon after his arrival at his isolated post. He insisted he was unable to cope with the large number of schismatics who disobeyed him and resisted his demands with force, and he pleaded with the tsar to have mercy and send government officials to his aid. Filaret did not identify the schismatics, but he very likely found himself in a situation similar to that of the Old Believer

Loggin in Murom: surrounded by people who either were indifferent toward the church, or did not want rules of proper Christian behavior forced upon them.[63]

Thus, the stigma schism frequently—in fact, in most cases, as I will demonstrate in the following chapters—did not refer to Old Belief, but rather the inability of church leaders to control the behavior of local populations in regions where religion had traditionally been practiced outside the structure of the church. There was often a clear correlation between the weakness of the church as an institution and the absence of the new Nikonian religion. For example, when Archbishop Afanasii of Kholmogory began to probe the hinterlands of his new diocese during the last two decades of the seventeenth century, he discovered more than 430 votive chapels (*chasovni*) that had been built by local peasants without official permission. None of these chapels owned the new books. Afanasii also noticed the absence of new liturgical books in many regular parish churches.[64] Thus, disobedience to the demands of the hierarchy and failure to assimilate new liturgical books were frequently related phenomena in the rural areas of Muscovy.[65]

This broad meaning of schism as a general failure to assimilate basic church demands—both liturgical and non-liturgical—continued in usage throughout the seventeenth century. One might say that the official notion of a schism was artificially superimposed on occurrences of disobedience to church authority. This is also suggested by the fact that local churchmen, that is, priests and monks who lived far from Moscow, were slow in adopting Kremlin definitions of dissent. In fact, they often failed, at least initially, to classify deviations from the new liturgical norms as manifestions of a schism.

The old ways of viewing religious disobedience and dissent continued to exist in the provinces, and great discrepancies sometimes remained between local and official interpretations. For example, Zakharii, a rural priest from the vicinity of Nizhnii Novgorod, described members of his parish who burned themselves alive in a religious frenzy as "criminals" (*vory*), "blasphemers" (*bogokhul'niki*), and adherents of a "heresy" (*eres'*).[66] In contrast, the official Nizhnii Novgorod chronicle interpreted this same event as part of the schism, citing the peasants' failure to attend church and to take communion, as well as their exposure to schismatic preachers.[67]

Another tract commenting on dissent outside Nizhnii Novgorod was written in Moscow shortly afterwards "on orders . . . of Tsar Aleksei Mikhailovich and with the consultation of the Holiest Council [of Bishops]." Moscow hierarchs were even more inclined than the local *literati*, who had compiled the Nizhnii Novgorod chronicle, to see peasant suicides as a result of a conspiracy by schismatics. In their eyes, the ordinary Russian Orthodox should "listen [to church demands] and guard themselves (*bliustis'*)" against the preaching of those who had consciously "severed themselves from the unity of the church." They should particularly avoid Mokii Vasil'ev, who "not only was a former follower (*poslushnik*) of Ivan Neronov, but also a friend of Archpriest Avvakum."[68] Clearly, diverse and unrelated occurrences of dissent—in this case a peasant suicide in a remote rural village and a lone Old Believer preaching in the town of Nizhnii Novgorod—had merged in the minds of Muscovite hierarchs.

We don't know when the local clergy assimilated official terminology for describing dissent, but it may not have been before the end of the seventeenth century.[69] Outside the cultural milieu of the church, the concept of schism was apparently even less familiar. For example, Don Cossacks, who had been coerced into using old books by their leaders, said they had never heard of the existence of a schism and gave illiteracy as the reason for their ignorance.[70] The priest Samoil, who fled from Moscow to the Don River, made the inconsistent statement that "he had never perpetrated any church schism" (*nikakogo raskolu tserkovnogo ne uchinil*), except that he had always used the old liturgical books.[71] A prisoner of war from Polotsk who lived at the Solovki Monastery until 1670, a man named Antipii, said he had been forced to use the old sign of the cross. In his eyes, he was guilty of a spiritual offense (*dukhovnoe delo*), but not of participating in a schism.[72]

The generalization inherent in the label schism created the false impression that the church was confronting a unified world of dissent. In reality, the Russian Schism was composed of infinitely varied phenomena, although few seventeenth-century contemporaries would have been aware of this diversity. Those most sensitive to the nuances were Old Believers, who made every effort to delineate themselves from other religious dissenters.[73] At the end of the seventeenth century, we find the Old Believer Efrosin creating new classifications of Russian religious dissent: "Old Believers" (*starovertsy*), "Priestless sect" (*bezpopovshchina*), "False Christs" (*lzhekhristomuzhi*), "Self-emasculators" (*skoptsy*), "Spirit worshippers" (*dukhomol'tsy*), and others.[74]

Awareness of the descriptive inadequacy of the stigma schism became widespread only at the beginning of the eighteenth century. The Old Believer Andrei Denisov, for example, strongly rejected the leveling implications of the label. In one of his works he underscored the distinct identity of the Pomor'e Old Believers, who were forced by the authorities to call themselves schismatics.[75] The keen observer of early eighteenth-century dissent, Metropolitan Dmytryi Tuptalo of Rostov, was bound by church convention to apply the stigma schism. But he often used it in the plural to indicate the impossibility of generalizing about religious realities in his eparchy, which stretched from Rostov to the distant reaches of northern Russia. He observed:

> The true Ecumenical and Apostolic Church has shrunk in size due to so many schisms (*raskoly*). It is almost impossible to find a true son of the church: almost every town has its own particular belief (*osobaia vera*), and simple peasants and women who don't know anything about the truth quarrel over dogma and teach. . . . [76]

It is the task of the historian to keep a sharp lookout for the specific religious, social, and other factors that contributed to the diversity of dissent phenomena subsumed under the omnibus category schism by seventeenth-century churchmen. In its original meaning, the term schism very broadly signified any failure to recognize the spiritual authority of the church, and this meaning remained intact throughout the seventeenth century. The writings of Simeon Polotskii appended the meaning of opposition to the new liturgical books. Polotskii accused the Old Believers, in particular priest Nikita Dobrynin and Archpriest Avvakum, of creating the schism, and this semantic dimension powerfully influenced subsequent historical thinking.

But Polotskii and other church polemicists greatly exaggerated the role of the Old Believers in the Russian Schism. With the analogy of Luther and the Western Reformation in mind, they viewed men like Avvakum as superhuman figures capable of far-reaching influence. After 1666, anyone who failed to use the new liturgical books was perceived not only as an enemy of the church, but as a member of an organized movement to destroy it. A handful of Old Believers, deemed the leaders of this movement, was duly executed in the Pustoozero prison camp in early 1682. Yet in the eyes of the church, their legacy remained a formidable challenge to Russian church and religion.

I conclude that the indiscriminate use of the term schism (*raskol*) in seventeenth-century church texts may have misled historians to see diverse manifestations of dissent as a unified movement of protest commonly called Old Belief, or Raskol. I question whether such a coherent movement of dissent existed during the seventeenth century. Looking beyond the stereotypes and generalizations contained in polemic texts, I analyze specific case studies in the following chapters in order to reconstruct the social origins of the Russian Schism.

CHAPTER FOUR

Muscovite Monasticism and Dissent

The acts of the 1666 Church Council signify a clear turning point in official attitudes toward the issue of liturgical books. Before 1666, the church investigated failure to use the new books only when such cases interested high-ranking hierarchs. After 1666, church officials made a more systematic effort to eliminate dissent. One important reason for this change was the influence on local churchmen of Simeon Polotskii's polemic concern with the schism (*raskol*). As a result, instances of liturgical dissent — now commonly regarded as manifestations of the schism — were more frequently documented, and we can thus form a clearer picture of how liturgical changes introduced during the 1650s affected Muscovite society during the remaining decades of the seventeenth century.

To illustrate the multifaceted dynamics of dissent, I will focus on one milieu that produced a relatively large number of schismatics (*raskol'niki*): seventeenth-century Muscovite monasticism. The connections between traditional monastic life and dissent have not yet been the subject of a systematic historical analysis. So far, only two scholars have paid attention to this phenomenon, A. P. Shchapov and I. Smolitsch. Shchapov observed that seventeenth-century monasticism provided ordinary Muscovites with an important alternative to official religious structures and, in particular, that the hidden hermitages of the forests gave men and women a chance to escape the demands of church and state.[1] Similarly, Smolitsch argued that monasteries enjoyed "great religious authority in the eyes of the people (*Volk*) . . . and always remained the center of popular religiosity and piety."

Although limited by what was available in the published literature at the time, many of Smolitsch's observations are insightful and could provide the basis for further research.[2]

We know very little about the social and psychological world of monastic dissenters. There are several factors—among them the mobility of nuns and monks, the geographic isolation of monasteries, and unwritten local customs—that make their stories difficult to reconstruct. However, on the basis of archival data gathered by seventeenth-century churchmen, we can piece together some of the circumstances that caused seventeenth-century monks and nuns to become dissenters.

I will first consider small monasteries and hermitages, which were significant outposts of dissent; then large monasteries. Large monasteries adhered to official liturgical policies, with a few notable exceptions that I will highlight. Finally, I will discuss the circumstances of unaffiliated monks and nuns, from whose ranks some of the most influential preachers against the new liturgical books were recruited.

SMALL MONASTERIES AND HERMITAGES

Three principal features of small monasteries and hermitages (*pustyni*) explain why they were particularly likely to develop incidents of liturgical dissent. First, these communities had been viewed by the church with suspicion even before the introduction of the new liturgical books; in fact, throughout the seventeenth century small monasteries were in constant danger of losing their autonomy. Second, the leaders of these monastic communities wielded considerable influence over their clients, be they monks or laymen. I have observed that local attitudes toward the Nikonian reforms were often shaped by an abbot's personal stand. Third, these monasteries were usually located in isolated villages or trading settlements beyond the reach of church authority. Attempts to eradicate the schism in small monasteries were designed to supplant local religious loyalties with centralized ecclesiastical control.

It is unlikely we will ever know the total number of dissident monasteries, or where they were located. Most of these monasteries owned less than twenty-five peasant households (*dvory*), and left no traces in the standard seventeenth-century land surveys and census records.[3] The reasons small monasteries and hermitages were founded remain equally obscure, although one factor must have been the prohibitively large donations (*vklady*) required of entrants to the larger monasteries. Usually founded by the spontaneous initiative of local peasant communities and trading settlements (*posady*), small monasteries provided grassroots access to monastic life for those who would otherwise have been excluded.[4]

An exceptionally detailed census book (*pistsovaia kniga*) from the 1670s describes the monastery in the small Volga town of Rybinsk as locally endowed and comprising six cells with nuns—all apparently from the community.[5] A similar monastery, the Luk'ianova Pustyn', was supported by the inhabitants of Aleksandrova Sloboda. This monastery must have had very few inmates: census takers registered its property as comprising only one household.[6] There is also evidence of obscure monasteries of similar size in the towns of Vologda and Pereiaslavl'.[7] But most small monasteries probably existed in the countryside, both inside and outside of villages.

It is difficult to ascertain how many small monastic communities had come under official scrutiny before the 1666 Church Council. The following cases demonstrate that some clearly had raised suspicions at the patriarchal court much earlier. The Riabina Il'inskaia Hermitage outside the small town of Liubim (Rostov eparchy), for example, attracted numerous local visitors during the early 1630s after the monks planted a rowan (*riabina*) tree on the grave of a locally venerated martyr, Abbot Adrian, who had founded another popular monastery in the area. This combination of relic and tree worship seemed suspicious to church officials, and reported miracles and healings were so dubious that Patriarch Filaret ordered a systematic probe into the matter.[8] While we do not know the outcome of this investigation, higher ecclesiastical power over the religious life of such monasteries was very limited. The abbot of the Preobrazhenskii Monastery in the village Danilovskoe (Kostroma district) was confronted by angry monks and their relatives when he tried to carry out the patriarch's call for discipline, and he apparently was forced to leave the village.[9]

The Troitskii Monastery, also in the vicinity of Danilovskoe, gained notoriety because it had been founded by the monk Kapiton, later considered by church leaders to be a dangerous dissenter. Kapiton came from the village and apparently enjoyed fervent local support. When orders were given in 1639 to instruct Kapiton and his monks "in the Christian faith and the rules of monastic life" (*v vere i inocheskikh pravilakh*), they refused to comply and ran away. The fugitives soon formed a new monastic community in the vicinity of Kostroma, which was destroyed in 1651.[10] Kapiton again escaped, and there is some evidence that he found temporary refuge outside the Blagoveshchenskii Monastery in Viazniki, a small community investigated for schism in 1666.[11]

The relatively well-documented life of Kapiton—and Kapiton's case was not unique—suggests some continuity between the dissent of the preceding decades and the schism discovered in small monasteries after 1666. Numerous monastic communities that were only loosely attached to the official church, or existed completely outside its institutional structure, were reluctant to cooperate with church demands, including, of course, the demand to use the new liturgical books.

Dissent in small monasteries, described as schismatic after the Church Council of 1666, would simply have been classified differently earlier. This change in official perception can be illustrated by the difference in the fate of two small monasteries from the Suzdal' district. In 1658, the abbot of the Kazanskii Monastery was arrested for "impolite words" (*nevezhlivye slova*) against the archbishop of Suzdal', and for illegally converting a parish church to a monastery. The monastery was sealed and the monks chased away.[12] About ten years later, church investigators discovered deviant behavior in a small monastery near the Sakhtoshkii Lake. These monks vigorously denied that Christ was still the savior of Christian believers and, like the monks of the Kazanskii Monastery, opted out of the accepted structure of the Orthodox Church. Unlike in the earlier case, however, the monks of Sakhtoshkii Lake were perceived as opponents of the new liturgical books and punished as schismatics.[13]

There appears to be a connection between the 1666 Church Council and a growing trend toward eliminating monastic autonomy. True, numerous small monasteries had already been absorbed during the 1650s by Nikon's huge monastic foundations: the Krestnyi, Voskresenskii, and Iverskii monasteries. But other large monasteries, the patriarchal see, and local eparchies also began to assume control of small monasteries during the following decades.[14] This trend continued well into the Petrine period, as evidenced by the "investigations concerning the ascription of monasteries with few brethren" (*dela o pripiske malobratstvennykh monastyrei*), which affected the Suzdal' and Murom areas during the early 1720s.[15]

The list of monastic communities that disappeared during the late seventeenth and early eighteenth centuries is quite comprehensive.[16] It is significant that several of these monasteries had previously been investigated for schism. Among them we find, for example, the Zolotnikovskaia Pustyn', which was located outside Suzdal' and owned only six peasant households. Other cases involved the Vvedenskii and Borisoglebskii monasteries in the Viazniki district.[17]

The case against Avraamii, the superior (*stroitel'*) of the Monastery of the Kazan' Mother of God, illustrates in greater detail one power struggle that resulted in the loss of monastic autonomy. The Kazan' Monastery, located outside the village of Lyskovo in the vicinity of Nizhnii Novgorod, had remained small and inconspicuous since its endowment by the local community. The number of brethren had grown from seven during the 1620s to about twenty during the 1660s, and the community probably owned not more than twenty-four peasant households. Despite the monastery's small size, Superior Avraamii wielded considerable local power—a circumstance that brought him into conflict with church agents.[18]

In fact, patriarchal investigators had tried unsuccessfully to remove Avraamii in 1659 and again in 1660. The administrative records of Boyar Boris Ivanovich Morozov, who claimed power in both Lyskovo and the monastery, reveal that this initiative was supported by the highest Muscovite authorities.[19]

Morozov was unhappy with Avraamii for a number of reasons: it was generally known that he gave shelter to runaway serfs and assumed authority in legal matters. Morozov was incensed, for example, when Avraamii arrested and beat a peasant girl from Morozov's estate for stealing from her stepmother.[20] The last straw for Morozov was apparently when Avraamii put barriers across the road that passed his monastery, thus impeding Morozov's peasants' access to Lyskovo, an important trading outlet on the Volga. While we can only guess about Avraamii's motives (perhaps he wanted to collect money from the peasants), his action prompted Morozov to complain to the tsar. In September 1659, a royal charter ordered Avraamii to clear the road immediately; he was then to be arrested and sent to Moscow.[21]

Avraamii never arrived in Moscow, even though inhabitants of Lyskovo vouched with their signatures (*za porukami vyslat'*) that he had departed for Moscow. Ivan Kalitin, one of the most powerful patriarchal officials of the seventeenth century, was enlisted, and he immediately sent a note to the voevoda of Nizhnii Novgorod requesting assistance in locating Avraamii. The evidence suggests that the voevoda, Semen Artemeevich Izmailov, interrogated the monks and several local peasants, who again insisted Avraamii was en route to Moscow with a petition for the tsar requesting relief from poverty for his monastery. Despite these extraordinary efforts, there is no indication that Avraamii's whereabouts were ascertained.[22]

The deep rift between the church and the monastery at Lyskovo did not heal even after Avraamii's disappearance. The monks insisted that Avraamii had not been at fault, and complained about the great injustice he had suffered by being forced to leave his position. They also refused to accept the new abbot selected by the church, Ven'iamin, arguing that Ven'iamin's roguery (*plutovstvo*) was known throughout Morozov's estate and that he had been beaten and expelled by the peasants of a neighboring village.[23]

Ven'iamin probably belonged to a pool of Moscow-educated clerics who shared the moral reform values of the Old Believers. There is good evidence that Morozov repeatedly attempted to appoint such clerics to the parishes of his estate.[24] However, these appointees did not usually fare well because they expected regular church attendance and performance of the Mass in its proper length.[25]

The monks who defended Avraamii must have known their lives would be made easier by the return of their former superior. Avraamii, unlike Old Believers, made no effort to discipline them for neglecting their duties.[26] The monks got their wish: as soon as the monastery was no longer under church scrutiny, Avraamii returned. He resumed control of the monastery until 1666, when the Moscow church council began a vigorous campaign against the newly defined schism. This time the church succeeded in capturing Avraamii and interrogating him.

Confronted with the charge of being a schismatic, Avraamii pleaded innocent, claiming he had used the old liturgical books only because he was not yet familiar with the new ones. He insisted that he was not opposed to the new liturgies, and promised to "correct all aspects of the church service according to the newly revised and printed books."[27] However, Avraamii's credibility was seriously compromised when it was learned that he had instructed many local people (*mnogikh liudei*) about the falseness of the new liturgical books. In fact, his preaching attracted so many visitors that the Zheltovodskii Monastery, a powerful outpost of the patriarchal church not far from Lyskovo, was in danger of losing its local influence.[28]

The fact that Avraamii was accused of introducing a schism is interesting in several respects. First, if Avraamii had not been known to patriarchal authorities because of prior conflicts with Moscow, his failure to use the new books might have gone unnoticed, and he would have had no reason to argue in favor of the old liturgies. Second, Avraamii's preaching added a new dimension to the influential role he already played: he became a charismatic figure for the inhabitants of his monastery and village, far more powerful than the unpopular monks of the Zheltovodskii Monastery across the Volga.[29]

At some point after 1666 Avraamii's monastery was subjected to the authority of the Dukhov Monastery, which belonged to the archbishops of Nizhnii Novgorod.[30] About the same time, several other small monasteries and hermitages in this area were also put under the control of larger monasteries. The neighboring Tolokontsovskii Monastery, for example, was absorbed by the powerful Savva Storozhevskii Monastery. In 1723, Petrine authorities counted thirty-two monastic communities in the eparchy of Nizhnii Novgorod that had lost their autonomy during the seventeenth century.[31]

Avraamii's disobedience can be understood within the context of local resistance to church interference and widespread refusal to assimilate the official rhetoric of reform. There had been longstanding tensions between his native village of Lyskovo and the official church over a variety of issues. For example, the Zheltovodskii Monastery attempted to tax and control the distribution of alcohol in the village; the reason given was that the monks, pilgrims, and traveling merchants who visited the area were frequently victims of violent attacks by drunken peasants. In addition, the villagers were accused of engaging in "devilish games" (*besovskie igry*) involving dancing bears and minstrels (*skomorokhy*).[32] In October 1670, the conflict burst out into the open when the villagers, with the help of Cossack and peasant rebels under the command of the insurgent Stepan Razin, laid siege to the Zheltovodskii Monastery.[33]

A similar scenario, albeit with less violent overtones, can be observed in the village of Murashkino which, like Lyskovo, was under the control of Boyar B. I. Morozov. Abbot Ivan Kurochka, who was in charge of the Spaso-Preobrazhenskii Monastery, was arrested and taken to Moscow in 1666 for adhering to the schism. Unlike Avraamii, Kurochka quickly succumbed to church demands and signed a statement promising to immediately start using the new liturgical books. However, there is reason to believe that he secretly continued using the old rites. According to an inventory of the monastery church from 1672, only six of the twenty-one books were new editions; these six included a Service Book that had been printed in 1668 and was undoubtedly a gift to encourage the monks to use the new liturgies.[34]

The nuns of the Troitsa Convent in the same village also came to the attention of Muscovite officials during the 1666 investigations because they had been hosts to Kurochka and Avraamii on at least one occasion and their priest, Nikita, had made jokes about the new liturgical books.[35] The nuns were disciplined and warned to use the new books. However, it is not clear that they actually did so; a 1672 description of the convent's sacristy indicates they owned mostly old liturgical books.[36]

It is impossible to establish when liturgical books arrived in the small monasteries of Muscovy because census records and church inventories documenting the ownership of new books date only from the 1670s.[37] However, the documents available for the village of Murashkino reveal a curious situation: even monasteries targeted by the Church Council of 1666 continued to own old books, and the number of new liturgical books was insignificant.

The fact that the old liturgical tradition continued at the Murashkino monasteries after 1666 was probably due to their ties to the local community. Murashkino peasants were known to have been uncooperative with church and state demands; local parish churches owned very few, if any, new liturgical books. The monasteries were richly endowed with old liturgical books, as well as vestments, bells, icons, and other religious artifacts, and they could ill afford to act against the preferences of their generous benefactors.[38] Thus, liturgical dissent—or schism as church officials called it—at the Murashkino monasteries had its roots not in Old Belief propaganda, but in local support for traditional practices.

An additional circumstance may explain why the monks of the monasteries in Lyskovo and Murashkino were considered dangerous schismatics, while other monasteries in the same area were not even investigated. We know that Patriarch Nikon came from a small settlement about halfway between these two villages.[39] Nikon maintained contact with his family in the area, and some of the priests and monks in Lyskovo and Murashkino owed their positions to him.[40] Avraamii, for example, came from the same district, and it was due to Nikon's influence that he first became leader of the Spasskii Monastery in Murashkino, and one year later of the Kazan' Monastery in Lyskovo.[41] Avraamii's personal affiliation with the region's famous native son may have brought him additional prestige, but it may also have brought him the unwanted attention of Moscow investigators. Quite possibly the Murashkino monks and nuns were singled out for investigation because of their ties with Avraamii.

The attempt to forcefully introduce new liturgical books foreshadowed the fate of these three monasteries: during the following decades they seem to have lost vital links with the local communities that had nourished and supported them. Inventories from the eighteenth century indicate that these once richly endowed monasteries had fallen into poverty, a fact that led eventually to their transformation into parish churches.[42]

Another case illustrates both the rootedness of dissenting monasteries in their surrounding communities and the strong local influence of their leaders. In conjunction with the 1666 Church Council, an effective investigation was conducted against Moisei, the abbot of the Blagoveshchenskii Monastery in the trading settlement (*sloboda*) of Viazniki (Vladimir district).[43] Moisei was remarkably well connected; his monastery received monetary donations from influential persons such as the archimandrite of the Chudov Monastery, the Moscow boyar clan of the Miloslavskiis, and the metropolitan of Kazan', as well as local peasants and traders. In particular, Moisei maintained connections with the Blagoveshchenskii Cathedral in the Kremlin, a center of ecclesiastical reform efforts during the 1640s and 1650s.[44] Despite these ties, Moisei seems to have ignored both official reform rhetoric and patriarchal authority, doing everything in his power to establish personal control over the religious affairs of the settlement.

The central church became aware of its powerlessness in Viazniki when a priest named Vasilii Fedorov sent a denunciation to Moscow.[45] Fedorov wrote that Moisei and his brother, Archpriest Merkurii, had ordered the population of Viazniki to stay away from priests who said Mass according to the new Service Books.[46] We do not know to what degree their orders were obeyed in local parishes. There is evidence, however, that all two hundred nuns of the local Vvedenskii Monastery obeyed.[47]

The mysterious murder of Fedorov soon after his denunciation illustrates the considerable power Moisei and Merkurii wielded. It is likely that Merkurii hired a murderer to dispose of Fedorov. During the murder investigation, which remained unresolved, considerable attention was paid to Merkurii's relationship to the suspects.[48] Numerous inhabitants of Viazniki and the surrounding area were interrogated. All those confronted by church investigators, including the parish priests of the area, gave the same answer: They did not know " . . . if [Fedorov] had been criticized, or if anybody had made boasting speeches against him."[49] No one dared even to question the authority of Moisei and Merkurii.

Dissent in Viazniki and environs might have disappeared without a trace if, as stipulated by the Church Council of 1666, Moisei had been permanently exiled to the distant Kola peninsula. But for unknown reasons, possibly his connections with high-ranking Moscow clerics, Moisei was allowed to resume his position. Reinstated as abbot of the Viazniki monastery in August 1667, he continued to dominate local religious affairs for many years without raising any suspicions. Only in December 1686 was Moisei forced out of office. Shortly afterwards, Patriarch Ioakim gave orders to inspect the monastery's book collection and found that only ten of forty-two liturgical books were newly printed copies (*novoizdannoi pechati*).[50]

When Peter I. had the settlement of Viazniki investigated a few decades later, his agents discovered Moisei's legacy: the community of Viazniki had become home to old-book advocates such as the traders Petr Iakovlev and Moisei Timofeev, both of whom specialized in smuggling old books to dissenting communities in Poland and Turkey.[51]

The Troitskii Monastery at Shuia (Suzdal' eparchy) was never investigated for schism, despite indications that the monastery—or other inhabitants of Shuia—had never acquired new liturgical books.[52] It appears that religious matters in Shuia remained largely unregulated until the reign of Peter I. Although the patriarchal court and the large Troitsa Monastery maintained small offices (*podvor'ia*), their presence—as well as efforts to interfere by the powerful Shartomskii Monastery not far from Shuia—yielded no results.[53] Shuia monks and priests acted without regard for the dictates of Muscovite churchmen. The monk Savvatii, for example, was viewed by local authorities with suspicion after losing his monastic habit while gambling in a tavern.[54] However, the abbot of the Troitskii Monastery, Savvatii's superior, may not have behaved much better; the archbishop of Suzdal' experienced great difficulties when attempting to discipline him in 1684.[55]

Throughout the seventeenth century this area was known as a hideout for brigands, and was therefore very dangerous for Muscovite officials. In 1628, Boyar Ivan Gundorov was murdered when he came to Shuia.[56] In October 1665, shortly before the church council, the tsar accused a local peasant elder of tacitly tolerating and hiding "criminals" who were known murderers. Even as late as 1682, the powerful Boyar Artamon Matveev hired several extra bodyguards to protect him when he traveled between Shuia and Aleksandrova Sloboda.[57]

Given these circumstances, we can understand why the accusation of schism was not raised in connection with Shuia until the eighteenth century. Intervention by official authorities under Peter I. finally resulted in the registration of local dissenters.[58]

The Vologda eparchy had a high concentration of small, remote monastic communities. Founded by charismatic individuals who attracted local followings, these monasteries were closely associated with peasant villages and settlements. The hermitages around the trading village of Tot'ma provide good examples of the limitations of church control. Even though two of the Tot'ma abbots were officially canonized in 1715 and 1729, it is unlikely that they perceived themselves and their communities as part of the official church structure.[59] During the seventeenth century, the Tot'ma area was dangerous for outsiders because of its many bands of brigands and robbers. In 1667 under the leadership of their elder, Estafei Firsov, the villagers outright refused to provide transportation services and to pay taxes.[60] A bailiff from a large monastery in Ustiug, sent to collect money from local peasants, was burned and tortured. Boyar Savelei Kozlovskii barely escaped with his life when he passed through by ship.[61]

The Tot'ma area is known as the birthplace of the monk Kornilii, whom Old Believers discovered during the early eighteenth century and later venerated as one of the legendary heroes of their tradition. Kornilii's *Vita*, which was written by Old Believers, leaves out some of the sinister aspects of Tot'ma life. It describes how a few monks living in the forests around the village influenced Kornilii's decision to embark on a monastic career:

> Since his early childhood he had listened to [stories about] the exploits of the holy fathers with great attention and had always admired the monastic way of life. . . . Father Kornilii had a brother named Michael who admonished him to take a wife and to look after his own home. Konon [=Kornilii] in turn advised Michael to leave the world and live as a monk (*inochestvovati*). . . . Whenever Konon found a monk, he would ask him about the salvation of the soul and how one could be saved. . . . God gave him fathers who were able to tell him everything about the right way of salvation, which leads to the Kingdom of Heaven.[62]

As indicated by Kornilii's later association with Andrei Denisov, one of the most important Old Believers of the early eighteenth century, it is likely that he became an Old Believer toward the end of his life. However, Kornilii was first and foremost a product of the religious world that existed in and around the village of Tot'ma. He spent time in large monasteries, including the eminent Troitsa and Chudov monasteries (where he worked as a baker), but he did not care for the life there and adhered to the religious models of the Tot'ma monks. Most of the time he lived as a hermit in the forests. During the 1690s, he became a cofounder of the unofficial hermitage of Vyg, which—thanks to the missionary activities of the Denisov brothers—was transformed into an important outpost of Old Belief.[63]

There were at least two other small monasteries in the Vologda eparchy with some connection to Old Belief: the Ignat'eva and Pokrovskaia hermitages. Both were associated with Ivan Neronov, who (as mentioned above) was tried as a dangerous schismatic by the Church Council of 1666. The Ignat'eva Hermitage, located in the village of Neronov's birth, was founded on top of the relics of a monk venerated in the area, Ignatii. Data on the hermitage are meager. We don't know when it was founded, or when it was transformed into a parish church. During the nineteenth century, a local historian (*kraeved*) from Iaroslavl' inspected the church building and found that the peasants had preserved an old gospel book (*naprestol'noe evangelie*) with an inscription dedicated to Abbot Neronov. Thus, Neronov was still remembered by this community more than two hundred years later.[64]

After his trial, Neronov, as archimandrite of the large Danilov Monastery in Pereiaslavl', began implementing official church policies; meanwhile the Ignat'eva Hermitage became an important outpost for opposition to the new liturgical books.[65] During the 1670s, a monk of this hermitage assembled one of the earliest compilations of Old Believer texts. This compilation contains Fedor Ivanov's *Answer of the Orthodox (Otvet pravoslavnykh)*, a letter by Avvakum, two brief notes regarding the economic affairs of the Ignat'eva monks, and one by the editor polemicizing against Simeon Polotskii's *Staff of Rulership*. This curious document probably indicates the editor's perception of official concern over the schism (which Polotskii had inspired) as a threat to the autonomy of the hermitage.[66]

The Pokrovskaia Hermitage came into conflict with the church in 1675, when the patriarch gave orders to arrest Abbot Feodosii for adhering to the schism. Formerly a close affiliate of Neronov, who had shorn him a monk, Feodosii left the Ignat'eva Hermitage in 1669 to establish his own monastic community. His influence in generating resistance to the new liturgical books must have been quite significant, as indicated by the special attention his case received in both Vologda and Moscow, and by the church's continued alarm, even after Feodosii had recanted his beliefs.[67] The brethren of the powerful Pavlov Monastery outside Griazovets, where Feodosii was taken for instruction in the new liturgical rites, were told to make absolutely sure that "he was not secretly adhering to some form of schism *(ne obretaettsa li v taine kakova raskola)*".[68]

Feodosii's arrest did not change the behavior of the community he left behind. His example, as well as that of his mentor Neronov, became important components of local religious identity. At the beginning of the eighteenth century, a monk of the monastery wrote a history *(skazanie)* that glorified the activities of Neronov. One of his greatest contributions, according to the unknown author, was that Neronov had infused Feodosii with his ideals and thus contributed to the flourishing of the community.[69] We do not know whether, or for how long, the community continued to adhere to the old rituals. But the fact that such a tribute to officially condemned dissenters was written so many years later illustrates that Feodosii—and for that matter, Neronov—had succeeded in creating a strong, local religious consciousness that was not dependent on their physical presence.

These two cases were exceptional because they involved Old Believers, yet they confirm that dissent in small monasteries and their environs was often due to the influence of a single individual. In both cases we see the Old Believer Ivan Neronov at work, a man who was unpopular in most other parts of Muscovy. Expelled from Moscow and other towns, he chose to withdraw to his native village and there to found his own religious community. Clearly Neronov enjoyed great support at home, even after he had recanted his beliefs at the 1666 Church Council. His charisma probably did not stem from his purist ideals, but rather from his status as a native son who—after more than thirty years of close association with the Moscow patriarchs—had returned home a hero in the eyes of his fellow villagers.

A further example of the influence of charismatic and powerful individuals is provided by the missionary activity of a monk named Iov, who in 1651 founded the Rakova Hermitage not far from Tver'. Like Neronov, Iov was a monastic leader of unusual stature. He had grown up in a Catholic noble family of the Polish-Lithuanian Commonwealth and was brought to Muscovy as a young man by Patriarch Filaret, who apparently took an interest in him. During the 1620s and early 1630s, Iov had enjoyed the tutelage of Filaret and—after converting to Orthodoxy and becoming a monk—had served as the patriarch's personal assistant (*pri kelii ego derzhav*).[70]

We know nothing about Iov's life between the time of Filaret's death in 1633 and Iov's reemergence from historical obscurity with his establishment of the Rakova Hermitage. We may assume that he enjoyed a certain reputation because the archbishop of Tver' officially recognized him as abbot. He also received a considerable church endowment that allowed him to equip his monastery with "all kinds of amenities" (*vsiakie pripasy*). During Nikon's patriarchate Iov commanded considerable local influence. Not far from his hermitage, for example, he founded a new monastery that attracted numerous local peasants as monks. In 1666, he came to the attention of the Muscovite church for fostering dissent in the area. But unlike other dissident abbots, Iov managed to avoid capture and soon became known as the founder of numerous monastic communities identified as schismatic.[71]

Iov escaped in the direction of his native Poland. In 1669 and 1671, his presence is confirmed in Sloboda Ukraine not far from the town of Ryl'sk, where he founded the L'govskii Monastery. According to a later account that originated in the official church, this monastery attracted strange groups of religious dissenters. For example, Iov's monks were said to have "two mad dogs" (*dva psa besnovatykh*) that they brought regularly to church services. As soon as the dogs began to yowl (*zavyvali*) so loudly that it was impossible to hear the priest performing the liturgy, the monks rejoiced in the firm conviction that God had spoken to them.[72]

In 1677, we find that Iov had moved farther south into the steppe. He founded another monastery on a tributary of the Don River that survived even after his death in 1680.[73] All efforts of Muscovite officialdom to disband this community were unsuccessful. When a military detachment razed the monastery buildings in 1688, the monks and nuns simply moved on and found a new habitat farther south on the Kuma River.[74] Few small monasteries of the seventeenth century displayed such resilience. It appears that a new form of monastic dissent had emerged, one that relied more on tightly knit communities than on the support of local settlements. Iov had created a truly separatist community that could survive without ties to specific villages and trading posts. His example is therefore of great importance because it signifies, more than other documented cases, how seventeenth-century dissent in small monasteries was eventually transformed into the sectarian separatism of the eighteenth century.

Several other examples illustrate the important role of small monasteries in seventeenth-century religious dissent. Iov's follower, Ioasaf, established new monasteries in Sloboda Ukraine. The communities of Vetka, survived well into the eighteenth century.[75] The existence of numerous other dissenting hermitages in the Nizhnii Novgorod area is beyond doubt, even though there is little information about them. Suffice it to mention Otereva Pustyn', not far from the above-mentioned village of Lyskovo; the founder of this monastery, Pafnutii, was captured on the Don River by Muscovite agents during the early 1680s.[76] P. Pascal found evidence of the existence of a dissident community at the Krivoezerskaia Pustyn', which later was converted into an important church outpost in the eparchy of Nizhnii Novgorod.[77] The final attack on such monasteries came under Peter I., when Archbishop Pitirim proceeded to convert large numbers of them into outposts of official authority.[78]

Several small monasteries in the Novgorod eparchy were accused of adhering to the schism when subjected to closer scrutiny during the 1670s and 1680s; among them was the Anzerskaia Pustyn' on the White Sea littoral.[79] Other hermitages came to the attention of church officials when the area around the Solovki Monastery was searched during the early 1680s.[80] The work of the Old Belief historian Filipov illustrates that in the northern forests a number of hermitages adhered to the old liturgical books.[81] The *Vita* of the monk Kirill, who was a cofounder of the Vyg Monastery, reveals a network of hidden hermitages and isolated small monasteries that probably guaranteed the survival of the old liturgical tradition in the area. Kirill was constantly on the move from one small monastery to the next before the late 1650s, when he established his own hermitage on the Suna

River, not far from the trading settlement of Kandopoga on Lake Onega. There he attracted a considerable following from among the local population before he came under attack by church officials who felt threatened by his popularity.[82]

The case of Evfimii, although less extensively documented, presents a striking contrast to the above-cited successful attempts of powerful monks and abbots to control local liturgical practices. In early 1666, the tsar's Secret Chancellery received information that Abbot Evfimii was sheltering runaway nuns at the small Pokrovskii Monastery in the trading village of Ivanovo (Suzdal' district), and using violent means to enforce use of the old liturgical books. The report also mentioned Evfimii's conflict with the disobedient deacon Luk'ian, who called for use of the new books. Evfimii silenced Luk'ian with a severe beating that left him bleeding (*do krovi*), and gave orders to lock Luk'ian out of the church "so that he would not hear [Luk'ian's] singing of the liturgy" (*chtob on evo pen'ia ne slyshal*).[83]

Unlike monastic leaders such as Avraamii, Moisei, Feodosii, and Kirill, who enjoyed considerable support in their communities, Evfimii's power did not extend beyond the walls of his monastery. He clashed with a strong-willed parish priest, Mikhailo Davydov, who accused him of leading people astray by making the sign of the cross with two fingers. Unable to control local attitudes toward the new liturgical books, Evfimii cursed Mikhailo for refusing to obey him.[84] Thus, Evfimii tried, but failed, to use the controversy over new books to increase his personal status.

Since historical data about small seventeenth-century monasteries and hermitages are scattered, we probably will never know the extent to which rejection of Nikon's reforms was successful in this milieu. However, both seventeenth-century Old Believers and official churchmen recognized small monasteries and hermitages as significant adherents of the old liturgical tradition.

In a letter to the family of Archpriest Avvakum, the Old Believer Fedor Ivanov used the prophecy of a hermit named Mikhail to explain Avvakum's arrest and exile within a larger historical context. Mikhail, who lived in a hermitage in the Suzdal' area during the 1640s, had predicted the end of the world and the advent of the Antichrist years before the revision of books. According to Ivanov, Mikhail's prediction had now come true. Hermit Mikhail and his ideas were obviously very important to Ivanov. It is therefore not surprising that Mikhail's name can be found in the necrologies (*sinodiki*) of the eighteenth-century Old Belief, which list all individuals considered to have died for the old faith during the seventeenth century.[85] The co-opting of Mikhail into the Old Belief tradition is unusual only in that he died several years before the introduction of the new liturgies. However, it indicates that the Old Believers perceived hermits such as Mikhail to be important allies in their efforts to defend the old rites.[86]

One of the major church polemicists of the seventeenth century, Metropolitan Ignatii of Tobol'sk, equated schismatics who led hermitages and small monasteries with wizards and sorcerers (*volkhvy i charodei*).[87] He related the tale of an unnamed "teacher and enemy of God" who enticed many women and girls to join his monastery. Exerting tight control over them, he began to preach free love and infanticide. Ignatii described the gruesome killing of a newborn child in the following:

> They brought the hermit the still throbbing and beating heart of the newborn child on a wooden platter. That evil man, that imitator of the Armenians, took a knife and cut the heart into four pieces with his own hands. Then he told them: "Take these, dry them in an oven, and crush them into a powder". . . . [88]

There is no documentary evidence that such an event occurred, and it is conceivable that the learned Ignatii made use of a stereotype common in Western Christianity.[89] However, there is more than a kernel of truth in his observations. First, he correctly discerned that leaders of small monasteries and hermitages wielded considerable power over their communities and that they often used this power to impose their own ideas, including opposition to the new liturgical books. Second and more importantly, Ignatii understood from firsthand experience that these alternative monasteries were often beyond the reach of church authority. Considering that these monasteries existed in virtually every region of Muscovy, one is inclined to agree with Ignatii's assessment that the church was confronted by a major threat to its authority.

I conclude that small monasteries and hermitages were significant outposts of dissent during the second half of the seventeenth century. The reason for this development was not—with very few noted exceptions—contact with Old Believers, or familiarity with Old Believer texts. Rather, these monasteries were highly prone to conflict with church authority due to their close affiliation with local communities and their domination by strong and independent-minded abbots. Refusal to accept the new liturgical books can therefore be understood in the context of a longstanding failure to communicate with—and indeed, obey—the centers of Muscovite church power. In fact, one might see official efforts to eradicate the old pre-Nikonian rites in small monasteries and hermitages as attempts to integrate these local religious institutions into the fold of the Orthodox Church.

LARGE MONASTERIES

In contrast to small monasteries and hermitages, monasteries owning more than one hundred peasant households (*dvory*) appear to have been reliable adherents of official liturgical policies throughout the seventeenth century.[90] They bought and distributed the new liturgical books, and also provided prison cells to hold captured dissenters. Why did a small percentage of these monasteries resist the liturgical innovations while the overwhelming majority accepted them? In the following section, I discuss the few exceptional cases among large monasteries and the circumstances surrounding their opposition.

One such exception occurred at the distant Kozheozerskii Monastery in northern Russia. Priest Nikon from Kostroma was exiled to this monastery in 1660 after his arrest for making ambiguous remarks about the new liturgies. All the arrangements were meticulously made, and Nikon arrived at the monastery as planned. But then a strange thing occurred: orders were given to return Nikon to Moscow as quickly as possible. A prison cell was reserved for him at the Andron'ev Monastery, a place that gained some notoriety a few years later when the Old Believer Avvakum was imprisoned there.[91] What motivated the decision to return the exiled prisoner to Moscow?

The case of the Kozheozerskii monk Bogolep, brought before the 1666 Church Council, provides one explanation. Bogolep, whom the assembled hierarchs viewed as a dangerous schismatic, was accused of preventing use of the new rituals at his monastery. The officials who took priest Nikon to Kozheozero were probably the first to discover this, having been misled by the fact that the monks had dutifully acquired the new Service Book and other revised books from the patriarchal printing press. They must have concluded that the environment was not conducive to educating their prisoner in the new rituals.[92]

In particular, Bogolep was said to oppose the tripling of the hallelujah, which had officially superseded the traditional double hallelujah in church ceremonies. According to a denunciation by a visiting monk from the prestigious Savva Storozhevskii Monastery, he went so far as to call the new mode of singing the hallelujah "a Roman heresy" (*rimskaia eres'*). He had also rejected all demands by the metropolitan of Novgorod and former *locum tenens* of the patriarchal see, Pitirim, to adopt other new rituals, insisting stubbornly that he did not care how many orders Pitirim sent.[93]

A member of a powerful boyar clan, the L'vovs, Bogolep had entered the Kozheozerskii Monastery during the tenure of Abbot Nikon, who later became patriarch. Bogolep was loyal to Nikon, and remained cooperative as long as Nikon was his superior. But when Nikon left the monastery in 1646 to accept a powerful ecclesiastical position in Moscow, Bogolep quickly assumed control over the monastery's affairs.[94] Most importantly, he gave protection to runaway servitors (*sluzhilye liudi*) and had them shorn monks. The runaways formed Bogolep's retinue, and with their help he suppressed any disagreement with his personal rule. For twenty years he had been so busy with secular matters that he did not attend church services or take communion. Nor did he participate in meals at the refectory table (*trapeza*) of the monastery and, for at least ten years, he had not had a spiritual pastor.[95]

In 1649 when his patron, Nikon, became metropolitan of Novgorod, Bogolep used the occasion to force out the Moscow-appointed Abbot Ioasaf, and to install his own candidate, Dionisii. Dionisii's only known act is to have surrounded the monastery with fortifications (*ograda*); shortly thereafter, he was replaced by another of Bogolep's clients. None of the abbots at the monastery enjoyed long tenure: between 1649 and 1661, Bogolep appointed six different abbots.[96] Thus, Bogolep achieved his goal of exercising absolute control over the monastery and its hinterlands. Indeed, by 1666 he was a wealthy man, probably because he plundered the territories and assets of the monastery.[97]

It appears that Bogolep accepted the new liturgies—and supplied the monks and priests under his control with the new books—as long as his rule remained unchallenged. The situation changed dramatically once the power of his protector, Patriarch Nikon, was on the wane. In 1660, the same year in which the patriarch was condemned by a Moscow church council, Bogolep refused to discipline the exiled priest Nikon for using the old books.[98]

Two other events helped to focus Bogolep's attention on liturgical issues. First was the arrival of an ambitious new abbot, Pavel, who was supported by the church leadership in Moscow. This abbot stood up to Bogolep and prepared a list of his digressions from the canon of the Orthodox Church. High on the list were Bogolep's sexual exploitation of minors, failure to attend church services, and random use of violence.[99] Bogolep had, for example, driven a monastic retainer named Panteleimon to suicide after threatening to torture him for stealing money. Bogolep was also accused of robbery: his monastic cell held an arsenal of weapons and booty from numerous raids.[100]

Second, and more important, was the appointment of the *locum tenens* of the patriarchal see, Metropolitan Pitirim, as the new head of the

Novgorod eparchy.[101] Pitirim pressed the issue of liturgical conformity, and suddenly Bogolep, a man who had never cared much about the Mass, became an active defender of the old liturgies. His behavior can thus be interpreted as a determined effort to maintain his personal power.

The 1666 Church Council ordered Bogolep's arrest, and denounced him for having "led many astray by his way of life" (*mnogikh zhitiem svoim soblaznil*).[102] Despite the council's great concern, Bogolep's influence over liturgical practices at the Kozheozerskii Monastery was short-lived. After his removal from the monastery, Abbot Pavel faced no opposition upon reinstating the new liturgies, suggesting that the monks had complied with Bogolep merely to avoid his beatings.[103] The monastery soon became a place of exile where schismatics were instructed in the use of the new rituals.[104] We may therefore conclude that the outbreak of dissent at the Kozheozerskii Monastery was an isolated event resulting from the clash of a powerful boyar monk with the metropolitan of Novgorod.

Several analogous cases of unruly behavior are documented in sources dating from the same time period. For example, another protégé of Patriarch Nikon, the cellarer of the Kornil'ev Monastery in the Vologda eparchy, was accused of avoiding church services, and also of drinking and molesting children.[105] Semen Osiev, who had recently become a monk at the Nuromskii Monastery outside Vologda, was blamed for not having a confessor and not taking communion.[106] Unlike in Bogolep's case, however, neither the church nor the monks involved regarded the liturgical books as an important issue.

There is evidence that abbots of a few other large monasteries in northern Russia refused to assimilate the new books. Dosifei, abbot from 1662–70 of the Besednyi Monastery outside the Tikhvin trading colony (*posad*), managed to evade the demands of the 1666 Church Council for several years.[107] This is a remarkable accomplishment, considering that Besednyi was located only about three kilometers from the Bogoroditskii Monastery in Tikhvin, one of the largest and most powerful monasteries of northern Russia and a loyal executor of the liturgical reforms.[108]

In March 1668, the archimandrite of the Bogoroditskii Monastery received orders from Metropolitan Pitirim to stop the local baking and distributing of hosts bearing the old shape of the cross. All Tikhvin parish priests were to be interrogated about this practice. Priests whose hosts did not bear the four-ended cross were to be arrested and sent to Novgorod; women (*prosvirni*) who baked the questionable hosts were to be confined to the Vvedenskii Convent.[109]

A number of factors suggest that the distribution of old hosts was not a spontaneous local response to the Nikonian reforms. The residents of Tikhvin were known to be rather negligent in liturgical matters. Few men and women actually went to communion or confession, or observed fasts, and these circumstances did not change when priests began distributing the old hosts.[110] During the 1650s, repeated efforts to educate the local population in proper Christian behavior had failed. Clerics and laymen alike had been instructed to stop smoking and stop consuming alcohol—habits known to have distracted many seventeenth-century Muscovites from attending Mass. However, the average priest and parishioner of Tikhvin spent little time in church services.[111] Therefore, we may assume that the impulse for distributing old hosts came from those few individuals who were sensitive to the liturgical changes.

Dosifei was without question the most prestigious and influential individual in the region to reject the new liturgies. Under his leadership the Besednyi Monastery had emerged as an important player in local religious affairs. In 1663, Dosifei had severed ties with the archimandrites of the Bogoroditskii Monastery, who claimed authority over Besednyi affairs.[112] Although many small monasteries in the area lost their autonomy to the Bogoroditskii Monastery, Besednyi experienced tremendous growth. An inventory from 1661 indicated only four peasant households; census records from 1678 registered 113.[113]

During these years, the rigorous taxation policies of the Bogoroditskii Monastery generated popular hostility in the town of Tikhvin. In fact, there were several unsuccessful community revolts, and in February 1666, the "poor and powerless populace" (*bednye i malomochnye*) of Tikhvin wrote a petition to the tsar asking for relief from their horrendous tax burdens.[114] Thus, a joint antagonism placed the local trading colony of Tikhvin and the Besednyi Monastery in similar positions vis-à-vis the Bogoroditskii Monastery. The distribution of unauthorized hosts may therefore have represented a symbolic rejection of the archimandrites' exploitative power.

It is likely that Dosifei inspired the outbreak of dissent in Tikhvin. After his departure in 1670, no further protests against the new liturgies were recorded in the community. Without Dosifei, the Besednyi Monastery also gave up its resistance. The monastery eventually shrank to its former size and lost its local appeal, indicating that the Bogoroditskii Monastery was able to reestablish control.[115]

Unlike Avvakum and other charismatic defenders of the old rituals, Dosifei eluded capture by church officials. There is evidence that he headed at least two schismatic communities in northern Russia: during the early 1670s, he was the leader of the Kurzhenskaia Pustyn', a small monastery that later came under the influence of Old Belief; in 1682, he was abbot of the Troitsa Monastery in the vicinity of Olonets.[116] Thus, long after manifestations of the schism had disappeared at Tikhvin, Dosifei still opposed the new books. By assimilating the model of the small unofficial monastery, which seems to have been the most successful form of seventeenth-century dissent, Dosifei helped keep the old liturgical tradition alive.[117]

Another example of the schism emerged at the Ferapontov Monastery during a controversy with Moscow over the status and treatment of the exiled Patriarch Nikon.[118] The deposed patriarch had arrived at Ferapontov in early 1667—the same year that Avvakum arrived in the prison colony of Pustoozero—and encountered similarly miserable conditions. Nikon lived under constant guard, and his contacts with the outside world were carefully controlled. His letters from this period, largely unstudied by historians, have survived in the archive of the tsar's Secret Chancellery. They betray a mixture of religious determination and self-pity familiar from Avvakum's letters. In the summer of 1667, for example, Nikon sent the following lines to Tsar Aleksei Mikhailovich:

> Like in his time the Apostle, I steadfastly praise my physical suffering, for God is again answering me, and the will of God is fulfilled. I welcome my physical agony and the maltreatment I experience, because when the outer man is embittered, the inner man renews himself. I live alone, expelled and exiled. They put me in a stinking cell in the monastery's hospital building, the windows have been sealed, bugs and fleas multiply endlessly. . . . I sit in silence and am mindful of eternal darkness and relentless worms. The intense heat and smoke in my cell recall the fires of hell, but I am not disturbed. They took away my robe, and the crutch that supported my old age. In all of this I remember the word of God: "Blessed are they who are persecuted for righteousness' sake, for theirs in the Kingdom of Heaven."[119]

There was one significant difference between the exiles of Nikon and Avvakum: whereas Avvakum was kept in isolation, Nikon had contact with an established religious community in the monastery where he was imprisoned. Initially, Nikon's contact with the Ferapontov monks was limited to requests for food and books. Over time, however, Nikon's living conditions improved. By 1672, he had managed to find himself a cook, a tailor, a cobbler, and a clerk to write his letters; at least five clerics lived and celebrated Mass with him. He spent large sums of money on fancy foods, clothing, and hunting and fishing gear. As his favorite pastime became horseback riding, the monks provided him with expensive horses and saddles.[120]

In August 1672, the head of Nikon's military guard accused Afanasii, the abbot of the Ferapontov Monastery, of adhering to the schism. He maintained that Afanasii "was acting against the will of the Great Sovereign and the Apostolic Church [because] he performed the divine liturgy incorrectly. . . . " The guard's urgent request for help from Archbishop Simon of Vologda has survived in the church archives. Nikon's correspondence also reveals the liturgical preferences of the Ferapontov monks. In April 1673, for example, Nikon mentioned in a letter to the tsar that church services in the Ferapontov Monastery were being conducted according to the old liturgical rites. He requested permission to celebrate Mass by himself in a separate church building.[121]

However, there is no evidence that Nikon came into serious conflict with the schismatics. Quite the contrary: Abbot Afanasii and his monks regarded Nikon with reverence and respect. In January 1675, it came to the attention of Patriarch Ioakim that the inhabitants of the Ferapontov Monastery were addressing Nikon as "the most holy patriarch" (*sviateishii patriarkh*).[122] Ioakim was so alarmed that he promptly dispatched an investigative commission. Interrogations fully confirmed the reports: the schismatic monks did perceive Nikon as the true and only patriarch of Muscovy. Their high regard stands in marked contrast to Old Believer texts' depiction of Nikon as the Antichrist.[123]

Patriarch Ioakim's commission found that the deposed patriarch exercised authority over both religious and secular affairs at the Ferapontov Monastery. When Abbot Afanasii brought Nikon a popular local icon showing the patron saint Ferapont, for example, Nikon ordered the icon destroyed, arguing that Ferapont was not a legitimate saint. Nikon arranged marriages for "girls and destitute women," sometimes over the objections of their future husbands. He forced at least one young woman to become a nun, and provided the money for her to live in a convent. Nikon's usurping of the monks' role in local religious practices did not prevent them from demonstrating their loyalty by kissing his hand.[124]

The bonds between Nikon and the Ferapontov monks were hard to loosen. When investigators tried to arrest the abbot and other monks, Nikon instructed his guards not to cooperate and severely scolded the leader of the commission. Erupting in a fit of rage, Nikon denounced Ioakim as "the little patriarch" (*patriarshishkom*), and called the orders to arrest the monks "criminal." Reminding the commission that he, Nikon, had brought Ioakim from Kiev to the Iverskii Monastery, he claimed Ioakim as "his monk" (*svoim cherntsem*).[125] Ioakim's emissaries later attributed the failure of their mission to Nikon's intervention.[126]

It is interesting that Nikon neither instructed the monks to use the new liturgical books, nor admonished them for their failure to do so. He was apparently more concerned with defending his spiritual monopoly against outside interference. For example, he ordered monks and peasants to construct crosses along roads and waterways leading to the monastery bearing the following inscription: "This life-giving cross of Christ was erected by humble Nikon, patriarch by the mercy of God, exiled and imprisoned for the benefit of the word of God and the holy church in the Ferapontov Monastery at Beloozero." Similar words appeared on liturgical and other vessels used at the monastery.[127] Thus, we observe a communion of interest between the deposed patriarch and the Ferapontov schismatics: both wished to keep their distance from the official church.

Following Nikon's arrest in the summer of 1676, opposition to the new liturgies all but disappeared at the Ferapontov Monastery. Nikon was confined to a small cell in the neighboring Kirillov Monastery, a community that absorbed numerous exiled schismatics during the seventeenth century.[128] To prevent him from making contact with the outside world, Nikon lived under the close supervision of " . . . two smart, good, and trustworthy monks." These monks were instructed to ensure that the former patriarch would have "only correct printed books" in his possession.[129] Does this mysterious stipulation mean that Nikon had not only tolerated liturgical dissent at the Ferapontov Monastery, but even participated in it? Whatever the meaning—and we will probably never know for certain— Nikon's assertion of independence from the church clearly contributed to a favorable climate for dissent.[130]

Any discussion of the Russian Schism would be incomplete without mention of the Solovki revolt. The rejection of new liturgical books by Russia's second largest monastery culminated in armed resistance in 1668. Government troops surrounded the heavy fortifications with the aim of conquering the monastery and enforcing the new rites—a task that was successfully accomplished only eight years later. What inspired the monastery's determined refusal to assimilate the new books? Why did the monks pick up arms rather than succumb to church demands?

Looking through the sale records of the patriarchal printing press, one finds that new books were bought by other large monasteries in northern Russia, such as the Aleksandrov-Svirskii, Antoniev-Siiskii, and Kirillov monasteries.[131] Acceptance of the new liturgical books can also be documented for the territories surrounding the Solovki Monastery and its patrimony (*votchina*). The Pomor'e district, where many of the monastery's lands were located, acquired a disproportionately large number of new books; book merchants from Kholmogory, an important trading town not far from Solovki, bought more of these books than merchants from any other town in Russia.[132]

How, then, are we to explain the Solovki monks' rejection of the new books? There is little doubt that at least some of the monks vehemently opposed Nikon's reforms. As documented in several petitions to the Kremlin, these monks requested permission to continue using the old books and also indicated they would fight to the death to do so.[133] Similar requests can be found in the testimonies of captured insurgents as well as in a few eyewitness accounts by emissaries sent to the monastery from Moscow.[134]

At the same time, however, there is good evidence that monks and priests were coerced by a group of powerful elders (*sobornye startsy*); one method was to draw up petitions against the new books and force everyone to sign them.[135] According to monks who fled during the siege, many inhabitants of the monastery had not wanted to fight church orders. In fact, low-ranking clerics had bought new books from the patriarchal printing press: in 1669, when the monastery's leaders gave orders to search all monastic cells, more than four hundred of the new books were confiscated.[136]

The Solovki Monastery had been in conflict with the Muscovite church long before the uprising. The church's efforts to subdue the unruly community had begun several decades before the clash over liturgical books. In 1621, an indignant Patriarch Filaret observed that numerous monks were rebelling and refusing to live according to monastic rule. Filaret's attempt to appoint a new abbot was not backed by sufficient coercive power, and proved unsuccessful.[137] During the late 1640s and early 1650s, the monastery became the target of several investigations. The elder Iosif Pleshcheev was arrested and sent to Moscow for interrogation. Orders were given to "put thieving and conspiring monks into chains and throw them into prison."[138] And the metropolitan of Novgorod, (later Patriarch Nikon), threatened to enlist the support of the tsar if the Solovki monks continued to disobey his orders.[139]

Another factor contributing to the Muscovite church's troubles was the presence of a large number of exiles (*ssyl'nye*) at the Solovki Monastery. The influx of exiles that had begun under Patriarch Filaret continued without interruption until 1668, the year the monastery was encircled by troops.[140] Among the exiles were former boyars such as members of the Godunov, L'vov, and Pleshcheev clans, and monks from the largest and most powerful monasteries of Russia such as the Troitsa, Chudov, and Kirillov monasteries.[141] Many high-ranking hierarchs ended up at Solovki, among them the notorious Archbishop Iosif Kurtsevich who had ruined the Suzdal' eparchy with his ruthless violence and greed.[142] Deposed leaders of monasteries included Nikanor, archimandrite of the Savva Storozhevskii Monastery. Finally, there were men such as Gerasim Firsov, who had been sent to Solovki after embezzling precious stones and sables from Moscow merchants.[143]

The monastic elite of Solovki made no serious effort to keep the exiles under guard. Metropolitan Nikon complained that prisoners were free to walk around the monastery and to participate in monastic affairs. In fact, exiles could easily join the monastery's ruling council.[144] In a charter dated 1651, Nikon wrote:

> By order of the tsar, monks and people of diverse ranks are sent to your monastery for punishment (*pod nachal*), and you do not keep them under control as you should according to the will of the tsar; you don't handle them strictly (*ne krepko*), but give them freedom in all respects. You ignore the order of the tsar by not submitting them to strict supervision, and these exiled outlaws are the source of great trouble (*smuta mnogaia*). And now the Lord Tsar and Great Prince of All Russia, Aleksei Mikhailovich, has ordered us to write you swiftly and categorically that all those sent to your monastery for punishment are to be held under strict surveillance and do labor service.[145]

If we consider that many of the exiles had been sent to Solovki by church decree, we should not be surprised to find that they were hostile toward the church. Their hostility no doubt contributed to the polarization that eventually culminated in open revolt.[146] The symbiosis between Solovki elders and exiles was described in a complaint addressed to the tsar in July 1666:

> These [exiles] provoke many rebellions here in our monastery because their number has increased, and this has led to great lawlessness. And members of the monastery's council, the monks Aleksandr, Gennadii, and even the deposed monk Efrem, live together with these men fallen from grace. They stage revolts, compile seditious letters, and develop schemes with the intention of doing great harm to your devout monastery.[147]

As a result of their lenient treatment, exiles played a significant part in the revolt. Gerasim Firsov, for example, became known as one of the most notorious Solovki troublemakers. "Without him," some angry monks told investigators, "there would be no troubles and no rebellion." Archimandrite Varfolomei, who had been toppled through the combined efforts of elders and exiles, reported that Firsov was their leader: "he formed a secret pact with rebellious monks, scoundrels, and individuals fallen from grace."

Not only was Firsov responsible for plundering the monastery's treasury, but he also advocated "great and every conceivable lawlessness." According to information gathered by church investigators, he drank alcohol and smoked tobacco, and was known for seizing money from peasants; he even stabbed a fellow monk with a knife.[148]

Archimandrite Nikanor, the one-time ally of Aleksandr of Viatka, began to advocate the use of violence. He could be seen "walking incessantly from tower to tower, consecrating the [monastery's] cannons with incense and sprinkling them with water." During the uprising, Nikanor ordered sharpshooters to kill the leader of the Muscovite musketeers. Providing them with spyglasses (*trubki*), he exhorted them to show no mercy: "As soon as you see him, shoot at him; because when we cut down their shepherd, the warriors will scatter like sheep."[149]

In many respects, the revolt at Solovki resembled occurrences of dissent at the Kozheozerskii and Ferapontov monasteries. The principal difference was the presence of many powerful figures at Solovki, all of whom behaved as defiantly as Bogolep and Afanasii had individually, a fact that explains why the Solovki Monastery managed to resist church demands for so many years.

The suppression of the revolt was brutal and absolute: almost all of the captured rebels were summarily executed by decapitation or hanging. The church finally succeeded in integrating the monastery into the ecclesiastical structure of Muscovy by appointing a new monastic elite recruited from other large northern monasteries.[150]

Some of the Solovki monks did manage to escape, and they founded new monastic communities of their own. Gennadii, for example, withdrew to the distant reaches of the White Sea littoral where he lived for many years in his own hermitage. A close friend of Gerasim Firsov, he had been one of the principal organizers of the Solovki revolt. We know nothing about his new monastic community, but we may assume—since many peasants died under his leadership at Solovki from ruthless acts of violence and torture—that his rule over this community was similarly cruel.[151] The number of other monastic communities founded in the wake of the Solovki revolt remains unknown. But it appears that a mushrooming of small dissident monasteries occurred in northern Russia.[152]

Historical evidence is scarce on occurrences of dissent in other large Russian monasteries. We know only of isolated individuals, both abbots and monks, who expressed sympathy for preserving the old liturgical rites and were promptly imprisoned. Particularly illustrative is the case of Abbot Sergei of the Tolgskii Monastery in Iaroslavl'. In 1670, Sergei was imprisoned in a dungeon at the same monastery over which he had previously ruled for several years. There he stayed until at least 1681, when he was let out of confinement to greet Patriarch Nikon who, by then frail and dying, was passing through on his way to Moscow. Sergei fell to his knees, asked for Nikon's blessing, and proclaimed in front of a large crowd that the patriarch had appeared to him in his dreams.[153] Sergei's refusal to recant, and his ability to endure a long imprisonment, marked a great spiritual achievement but had no larger societal impact.

Personal concerns probably also guided a handful of nuns who were disciplined by the abbess of the Vvedenskii Convent in Tikhvin during the 1680s.[154] In another case, monk Serapion of the Simonov Monastery in Moscow apparently received no sympathy from his fellow monks when he was arrested for questioning the three-finger sign of the cross and other liturgical changes, and nobody defended him when he was subsequently exiled to the Zheltovodskii Monastery. There he met another isolated dissenter, the monk Savva Romanov, known for having written a few texts denouncing the new liturgical order.[155]

One could enumerate many examples of captured schismatics who were handed over to large monasteries for disciplining. Suffice it to mention that rebellious monks from the Solovki Monastery were confined to several large northern monasteries including the Antoniev-Siiskii and the Krestnyi.[156] In addition, large monasteries—such as the Spaso-Prilutskii, Pavlov Obnorskii, and Kornil'ev monasteries found in the eparchy of Vologda—informed on outbreaks of the schism in their villages and hamlets.[157]

The information presented here suggests that manifestations of the schism occurred in large monastic institutions only under exceptional circumstances. All of the large dissident monasteries were located in northern Russia, a fact suggesting that these remote monastic institutions were poorly integrated into the ecclesiastical structure of Muscovy.[158] And in all of these cases, the outbreak of dissent can be viewed as resulting from strong anti-church sentiments independent of the book issue.

Liturgical dissent was thus an important phenomenon in monastic milieux on the fringes of official religious society. Indeed, the regional distribution of such schism cases reflects the relative power of the Muscovite church: the more authority the church maintained over local monastic life, the more likely was compliance with Nikon's reforms. In the great centers of official monastic life, the impulse toward schismatic behavior was relatively weak; smaller and more isolated monastic communities demonstrated stronger adherence to the old liturgical rites.

MONKS AND NUNS OUTSIDE OF
MONASTIC INSTITUTIONS

In seventeenth-century Muscovy many monks and nuns lived beyond the reach of the hierarchical church. Some lived in small monasteries and hermitages, but an unknown number were unaffiliated, or only temporarily affiliated, with monastic institutions. The latter wandered from one village or town to the next, covering large distances. They sometimes found temporary refuge in hermitages, parish churches, or peasant huts; just as often, however, they attached themselves to groups of itinerant clerics, or to charismatic founders of small monastic cells in the forests. Even before the Church Council of 1666, the official church had scrutinized the behavior and religious practices of these monks and nuns; after 1666, many were singled out and persecuted as schismatics.

Those monks and nuns labeled schismatics were actually very different from the reform-oriented Old Believers. Many of them shared characteristics with unruly clerics who, prior to 1666, had been prosecuted for drunkenness, sexual misconduct, and violence. I also find that itinerant monks and nuns were motivated by popular beliefs, and largely ignored official church rhetoric. Finally, I outline factors that led ordinary Muscovites to assume a monastic way of life outside of officially sanctioned church institutions.

Who were these unaffiliated monks and nuns? And why were there so many of them during the seventeenth century? It is impossible to describe a typical profile. There were as many types of behavior and belief as there were reasons for joining the growing ranks of the unaffiliated.

Muscovite authorities were already concerned about unaffiliated monks and nuns during the decades preceding the emergence of liturgical dissent. In June 1652, the tsar observed that Moscow and other cities were crowded with monks who " . . . walk along the trading places and streets and sit at the crossroads. By doing so they desecrate the monastic way of life."[159] In 1639, the archbishop of Vologda complained about "monks who are troublemakers (*bezchinnye*) and live in the homes of ordinary laymen. They sit in pubs, get drunk and lead idle lives. Others wander about the world and create great disorder (*velikoe bezchinie*) . . . roaming the streets without wearing their monastic habit."[160] A decade earlier, church authorities had arrested two monks as heretics just after their arrival in Vologda: accused of dangerous preaching and of distributing outlawed Ukrainian books, such as the works of Trankvillion Stavrovetskii, they had claimed to be in direct communication with the Holy Spirit.[161]

One important reason for the large number of unaffiliated monks and nuns was that seventeenth-century church authorities made unprecedented efforts to regulate the behavior of those cloistered in large monasteries.[162] Patriarch Filaret (1619–33) repeatedly gave orders to punish monks engaged, for example, in black magic and other heterodox practices.[163] Under Patriarch Iosif (1642–52), the Kremlin issued numerous orders to discipline unruly monks and nuns. Drunkenness, empty churches, and random violence—considered intolerable offenses—were to be eradicated.[164]

During the 1650s, Vologda officials tried to systematically register all local nuns; in 1656, a nun who had aroused considerable suspicion after roaming the streets became the target of an investigation.[165] Documents from this period also abound in attacks on deviant sexual behavior.[166] These condemnations were much more stringently enforced than in earlier periods, as illustrated by the appointment of a new generation of Moscow-trained abbots determined to implement church orders[167], and also by the growing number of monks punished by exile.[168]

What happened to these expelled monks? A significant number of them probably became opponents of Nikon's liturgical reforms. As the following case histories demonstrate, schismatic monks were constantly on the move, eking out a living. They were prone to use violence and displayed a deep-seated hatred of official religion and its representatives.

I will start with the case of the monk Ivan. In June 1670, arsonists tried to blow up the powder house in the town of Murom. The fire was discovered in time to avert a major explosion and consequent destruction of the cathedral located next to the powder house. None of the arsonists (*zazhigal'shchiki*) was captured, but the military commander of the town connected the incident with his imprisonment of a schismatic monk, Ivan, and demanded military enforcements from the tsar:

> This criminal act of arson was the work of the same criminals and unknown schismatics. I, your servant, had ordered the musketeers and traders of Murom to stand guard day and night at all town gates, but now, oh Lord, it has become dangerous for me to hold that monk Ivan. ... Sire, if this monk Ivan and his unknown companions, the brigands and schismatics, create another fire or scandal I do not want you to punish me by fines or disgrace. ... [169]

We have no reliable identification of Ivan. However, he was probably the same person as Ivashko, who had eluded capture two years earlier after small monastic cells in the forest near Murom had been discovered and destroyed.[170] The escape of Ivashko and his followers had alarmed local churchmen and they endeavored to learn their whereabouts. A child, who had lived with Ivashko, was tortured but remained silent. An itinerant monk, who also knew Ivashko, was sent to Moscow for interrogation. When this monk broke out of confinement at the Simonov Monastery, the tsar's Secret Chancellery issued an urgent order to all noblemen in the Murom district to search for the schismatics. It is thus plausible that Ivashko was finally captured and imprisoned in Murom under the name of Ivan. If so, the attack on the cathedral in Murom could have been a desperate effort by his followers to liberate him.[171]

From the perspective of church officials, one of the most frightening schismatics was the monk Iev, also known by his secular name Ivan Saltykov. In July 1674, Iev escaped from a cell at the Kozheozerskii Monastery where he had been imprisoned for his participation in the Solovki revolt. The tsar's court became involved in the search and officials in various areas of Muscovy, including the town of Murom, were instructed to stop itinerant monks and interrogate them about Iev.[172] We do not know if Iev was ever recaptured; he may very well have found refuge among fellow dissenters. But we do know quite a bit about his previous activities at the Solovki Monastery.

Originally from Moscow and possibly a member of the Saltykov boyar clan, Iev belonged to a circle of radicals who used physical force and intimidation to control Solovki. Soon after the siege of the monastery began, Iev and some monks broke into cells of other residents and forced them to give up *all* their liturgical books—including old Kievan imprints and editions printed *before* the reign of Patriarch Nikon. This coercion culminated in the following scene, which betrays a mix of violence and religious radicalism:

> Wherever there were pages with images of Christ, the Mother of God, and the Saints they tore them out of the [liturgical] books. [Then] they took the books to the landing pier behind the monastery where they ripped them apart, cursed, stamped on them with their feet, and pierced them with their lancets. The book covers they threw into a fire, but the books themselves they sank in the sea after cutting an ice-hole. About the Great Lord [tsar] they made abusive remarks. . . . [173]

Iev's propensity for violence scarcely distinguished him from other Solovki monks who were wont to use force against their opponents, although the degree of his fanaticism may have been unusual. Iev was arrested en route to Sweden soon after the Solovki revolt. It is not inconceivable that he had contact with radical Protestants in Sweden, a circumstance that might explain why his hatred of liturgical books focused on images of Christ, the Mother of God, and the Saints.[174]

A number of schismatic monks participated in the Moscow revolt of 1682. According to one Kremlin observer, "ignorant monks who are vagrants and drunkards (*brodiagi i p'ianitsy*)" played important leadership roles.[175] Patriarch Ioakim accused these monks of threatening his life when they, along with a few priests, led a mob of Muscovites into the Kremlin. Carrying icons and lit candles, the mob surrounded the Arkhangel'skii Cathedral where the patriarch and the most important Muscovite hierarchs were celebrating Mass. Ioakim later described the scene:

> They intended to stone us. Some of us who had ventured out . . . reported that they were carrying stones on their bosoms or in their pockets and began to throw them. . . . We also sent Archpriest Vasilii from the tsar's palace to read to the people our admonition and instructions regarding their misguided behavior (*prelest'*). Not only did they not give him a chance to read them, but they even wanted to kill him. . . . [176]

The patriarch and other church leaders escaped unscathed, and some of the rebellious monks were captured soon afterward.

Dorofei was one of the monks seized after the 1682 Moscow revolt, but he had been on the run for many years and had repeatedly defied the authorities. He had first raised alarm at the patriarchal court by escaping from the Andron'ev Monastery in Moscow. From there, he had made his way to Astrakhan', where he apparently established connections with rebellious Cossacks. Temporarily held prisoner in Nizhnii Novgorod in 1671, he again escaped. During the 1670s, search warrants describing Dorofei in some detail were sent to many monasteries. The archbishop of Vologda, among the most zealous in his efforts to recapture Dorofei, searched the small monastic communities in the hinterlands of his eparchy.[177] In 1682, Dorofei explained that he had hidden in a private home in Iaroslavl' before finding refuge on the Don River with his close friend, the monk Ilarion. In the meantime, he had also visited the rebellious Solovki Monastery and apparently become acquainted with the issue of liturgical books.[178]

Dorofei and other monks who participated in the revolts of the seventeenth century probably learned their use of violence while living on the frontiers of Muscovy.[179] There was clearly a relationship between frontier areas, where central controls were relatively weak, and violence-prone monks. In 1648, for example, during the massive revolt of the northern Ustiug region, several monks were accused of participating in robbery and murder; the monk Tikhon was identified along with the archpriest of the town, as being responsible for murdering an official. During the same year, several monks were arrested for participating in a rebellion in Kursk. In

Siberia a monk named Kornil, who had been arrested for gambling, broke out of prison and apparently abducted several women.[180]

Church officials had the greatest difficulties in the southern steppe region. On the Don River, where Dorofei spent much of his life, monks — and to a certain extent nuns — fought in the cohort of the Cossack rebel Stepan Razin. When several of these Razin supporters came to the Ferapontov Monastery to recruit followers from among clerics living with the deposed Patriarch Nikon, the Muscovite church reacted with panic.[181] Such rebel monks were probably among the most wanted schismatics of the seventeenth century.

The cases that follow suggest that many unaffiliated monks acted in ignorance — or defiance — of official church rhetoric, including prohibitions against drinking and sexual promiscuity. Their actions, more often rooted in popular religious beliefs and practices, reveal a proclivity toward taking religious matters into their own hands. They lived in a monastic world that had little in common with the ascetic ideals advocated by Avvakum and others.[182]

After the Church Council of 1666, for example, dissident monks escaped from the Nilova Hermitage close to Tver'. According to a letter by their Abbot German, they were notorious drunkards who could not endure living under his regime, which demanded soberness and monastic discipline. German also complained that they had taken along old liturgical books.[183] But clearly, these monks had not assimilated the reform rhetoric of Old Believer texts.

In January 1668 local officials in Kostroma were notified to search for the monk Feodosii, who had escaped from a Moscow monastery with quite a bit of booty, including liturgical vessels and other utensils (*utvar'*). The search for Feodosii yielded no results; however, the investigators did capture another runaway monk called Varlaam who was hiding at the small Nastas'in Monastery in Kostroma. A peasant, who had denounced Varlaam, described the monk as a great drunkard (*pop'et de vsiakie pitiia*) and troublemaker fond of disrupting the local community.[184]

A search of Varlaam's hideout yielded two barrels of alcohol and several letters "blaspheming the name of God" (*bogootmetnie pis'ma*). While detailed contents of these texts were not disclosed, Varlaam's views were clearly disconcerting to the church. Under interrogation, Varlaam revealed that he had fled from the Kirillov Monastery in northern Russia in early 1667. Around Easter of the same year, he had found refuge at the Florishcheva Hermitage in the vicinity of Nizhnii Novgorod and become a choral singer (*kryloshanin*). He had quickly realized his mistake: Ilarion, the hermitage's abbot, was a rigorous disciplinarian and an appointee of Stefan Vonifat'ev, the zealous confessor of the tsar.[185]

Varlaam had left as soon as possible for Moscow, and then moved on to Kostroma. There he became acquainted with the monk Semen of the Nastas'in Monastery. Semen asked Varlaam, who had apparently received the holy orders of the priesthood, to assist him in the baptism of children. Varlaam fulfilled Semen's request and in return received shelter at the monastery. Varlaam's reluctance to submit to the monastic discipline required by Ilarion probably explains his feeling at home at the Nastas'in Monastery, where he could drink freely and otherwise act independently.[186]

The reform-oriented Abbot Ilarion was probably scandalized by Varlaam's behavior. He later reported to Moscow that many schismatic monks and nuns were hiding in the villages surrounding the Florishcheva Hermitage. They lived separately from the rest of the community in log cabins (*v izbakh*) in groups of ten to fifty, and engaged in fornication (*blud*). These women and men emerged from their hideouts only to disrupt church services and offend churchgoers; a favorite practice was to use the exterior walls of church buildings as latrines (*isprazhniaiutsia u tserkvei blizko*).[187]

It is important to note not only Varlaam's wanton behavior, but also his receptivity to popular heterodoxy. While on the road near the Florishcheva Hermitage, he met a group of bear trainers (*medvezhie povodil'shchiki*). These men, frequent visitors at local folk festivals in the Nizhnii Novgorod area, intrigued Varlaam and he carefully listened to their teachings. They appear to have inspired him to write the pamphlets, subsequently lost, that church investigators confiscated from him after his arrest.[188]

What these pamphlets contained can only be surmised from an angry petition written by the Old Believer Ivan Neronov, who observed the activities of bear trainers while serving as parish priest in Nizhnii Novgorod during the 1630s.[189] Neronov complained that such men mocked the powerful Pecherskii Monastery by staging a pagan festival in its immediate neighborhood:

> Oh Sire, men and women from the town, various rural settlements, and villages gather at the Pecherskii Monastery. Salesmen of alcohol, oh Sire, set up pubs with all sorts of beverages; strolling players, bear trainers, and minstrels (*skomorosi*) with their devilish instruments all come together. They celebrate in the following fashion: the bear trainers dance with bears and dancing birds, the minstrels and players with masks, shameful sexual paraphernalia, tambourines and pipes. . . .[190]

While Neronov deplored the anti-ecclesiastical implications of such festivals, Varlaam felt comfortable with them.

There was indeed a peculiar affinity between monasticism outside the official church and popular religion. Neronov observed with disgust that women and men dressed as nuns and monks participated with rowdy crowds that invaded local parish churches, and he strongly denounced these mobs of "criminals" (*razboiniki*):

> They are destroying the church. They roar with laughter, scream and squeak, thereby creating great disturbances in our churches. . . . Some walk about with an image of God hanging from their necks . . . and others pretend to collect money for the building of churches, but later many of them are seen in the company of drunkards . . . , they act as if they were mad, but then you see that they are in full command of their minds . . . , they smear their feet with manure, mix blood and brain and crawl over the floor of our churches making squeaking noises. . . . [191]

This largely submerged cosmos of popular religion around the town of Nizhnii Novgorod witnessed some of the most radical forms of seventeenth-century dissent. In early 1672, a parish priest from the village of Pomry in the Nizhnii Novgorod district related that members of his community, apparently while in a religious frenzy, had burned themselves to death. He attributed their action to the teachings of itinerant monks and nuns who had visited them. According to the testimony of a few survivors, the peasants had followed the example of a nun named Paraskoviia, who had burned herself and her son to death in a nearby barn.[192]

We know nothing more about Paraskoviia, except that she had predicted the end of the world. A semiliterate pamphlet (*gramotka*), probably written by a peasant, that was rescued from the fire suggests the nature of her preaching: as the Day of Judgment was imminent, the only way to escape eternal perdition was to die for the true Christian faith (*pomrem za veru Khristovu*). The text cites the revision of books as the sign that the end was near.[193]

Other itinerant monks and nuns from the Nizhnii Novgorod district promulgated a similar radicalism. On January 12, 1666, an official of the tsar's Secret Chancellery wrote the following note (*zapis'*):

> In the forests [of the Nizhnii Novgorod district] there were six [sixteen?] people in one monastic cell (*kel'ia*). . . . When Danilo Betniakov and his musketeers approached the cell and attempted to seize them, they barricaded themselves inside and did not allow anyone in. And they themselves burned this cell down from inside. . . . [194]

Shortly afterward, a patriarchal emissary sent to the Nizhnii Novgorod area related that a nun named Evpraksiia was preaching horrendous blasphemies. According to the emissary's report, "such things, Sire, cannot be written down or spoken by human lips. Even among the ancient heretics such heretics cannot be found."[195]

Evpraksiia, who may have been the former abbess of a small monastery in the nearby settlement of Kozmodemiansk, had come to the attention of the Muscovite church a few months earlier. Records from December 1665 identify her as the teacher of many false prophets (*lzhivye proroki*) outside Nizhnii Novgorod.[196] In early 1666, she was located in the vicinity of the Florishcheva Hermitage, suggesting that she might have participated in the activities described by Abbot Ilarion. However, she repeatedly eluded arrest, a fact attributed by the frustrated patriarchal emissary to her enormous mobility.[197] Evpraksiia's students included monks and runaway nuns from local monasteries who wandered through the forests finding temporary refuge in peasant homes.[198]

The preacher monks Vavila and Leonid, probably Evpraksiia's students, were known to convince peasants—including members of their own families—to lock themselves into huts and refuse food and drink until they died of starvation.[199] In their interrogations, Vavila and Leonid said the change in liturgical books had been the greatest shock of their lives. There is no reason to question their testimony; their shock does not, however, explain why they led others to commit suicide.[200]

None of the four preachers of death identified in the vicinity of Nizhnii Novgorod seems to have been literate; they had spent their lives in the oral semi-Christian world of the Russian peasantry.[201] The Old Believer Efrosin later denounced such preachers as "disgusting teachers . . . of foul peasant life and village stupidity," and compared them to pagans (*pagantsy*).[202] But he was not completely off the mark; several pieces of evidence point to the existence of pre-Christian elements in the religious practices of Muscovy's wandering monks and nuns during the seventeenth century.

A nineteenth-century archaeologist excavated monastic cells and hermitages in the area where Evpraksiia and her students had been active, and noticed that most of them had been founded in the immediate vicinity of, or even on top of, prehistoric graves (*kurgany*).[203] It is hard to believe that the location of these monastic cells was mere coincidence. Perhaps these gravesites dating from pre-Christian times served as constant reminders of death, and inspired not only monastic renunciation of the world but also thoughts of suicide.

While much of our current knowledge about this phenomenon must remain speculative, there are a few indications that wandering monks who preached against the revision of books were influenced by peasant beliefs in prophecy and magic. In 1679, the metropolitan of Riazan' lectured the schismatic monk Mikhail Mikulin in front of the entire population of Riazan'. Mikulin's crime had been composing seven scrolls of "all kinds of indecent speeches about the most holy Godhead." When asked about the origin of his ideas, which were unfortunately not reported, he pointed to a local peasant visionary (*snovidets*).[204]

In another case in 1675, officials of the bishop of Viatka tracked down nine monks and nineteen nuns who were wandering through the woods of the eparchy. They were identified as dangerous schismatics, and the order was given to defrock them. Porfirii from Kazan', the leader of the group, had been carrying human bones in his bag. When questioned under torture, he admitted that the bones were the remains of preachers who had been burned in Kazan' a few years earlier. He claimed that he used the bones to recruit followers and to maintain power over his community. He ground the bones into a powderlike substance which he then added secretly to food and drink. With this magical trick, he purported to have seduced numerous peasant girls in the villages of the Kazan' district.[205]

Many monks and nuns who were far less radical—and typically non-violent—also became dissenters, but for reasons having little to do with the religious ideals of the Old Believers. These reasons included the experiences of plague and death; widowhood; social isolation; and limited access to official monasteries.

In January 1666, for example, a military detachment captured four monks, two nuns, and one novice (*belets*) living in an isolated monastic cell in the forest. The monks signed a joint statement that they had not been to communion or confession because they opposed the introduction of new liturgies; the novice and the nuns did not refer to the liturgical changes.[206] There can be little doubt, however, that these clerics would have remained outside the mainstream of official Russian religion even without the new books. During the early 1650s—several years before the new books were distributed—they had abandoned their secular lives and been made monks and nuns by Abbot Isaiah, the founder of their community. Three of them came from the same village in the Nizhnii Novgorod district and identified themselves as peasants of Boyar Il'ia Danilovich Miloslavskii; one monk was from the trading colony (*posad*) of Nizhnii Novgorod. While the men were silent about their reasons for becoming monks, the women said they had entered monastic life during the plague of 1654.[207] Very likely, these nuns had been deeply shaken by their experiences.

The hope for a religious escape from a world infused with suffering was an important leitmotif during the seventeenth century, and the experience of death was omnipresent. The Russian scholar S. A. Belokurov discovered a handful of letters written by monks during the Time of Troubles (*smuta*) in which the instability of that period, especially as indicated by occurrences of murder and military assault, was frequently mentioned.[208] There are no studies indicating whether the *smuta* experience and subsequent traumas—of which there were many during the seventeenth century—increased the monastic impulse in Muscovite society. We do know, though, that the Old Believer Ivan Neronov and his wife joined monastic communities because of the devastation caused by the pestilence: from a population of approximately forty-six hundred in the town of Pereiaslavl' Zalesskii, where Neronov was shorn a monk in 1656, only 939 survived.[209]

Encounter with death appears to have influenced many women to join unofficial monastic communities,[210] and widows were particularly likely to exhibit animosity toward the new books. We do not know exactly how many of the nuns accused of schism were widows, but a significant number had lost their husbands—either due to the pestilence, or to the numerous wars of the period.[211] Monastic communities also provided a form of security for widows who, especially if they were pregnant, were suspicious to church authorities.[212] There were other ways to find similar protection and security, as demonstrated by the example of a widow living with her children in the house of a German pastor in Nizhnii Novgorod.[213] But joining groups of wandering monks or building monastic cells in the forest must have been an important means of escaping social sanctions.[214]

In December 1680, for example, an estate administrator of Boyar Mikhail Iakovlevich Cherkasskii complained to Moscow that three widowed nuns and their children had built a monastic cell in the forest not far from the manor house. The administrator regarded them as a nuisance because they lived in abject poverty and resorted to begging. According to the nuns' testimonies, they had left the world to save their souls (*dushu svoiu spasti*) and to please God (*bogu ugodit'*). When asked about the new liturgies, they answered that they had refused to take the sacraments or go to confession ever since the new books had been introduced. In contrast to many other schismatics of this period, they did not recant their beliefs. Even after their children were taken away from them, they maintained their opposition to the new books. After fruitless efforts by numerous priests and monks to convince them to accept the new liturgies, they were finally burned at the stake, preferring death to compromising with a world they had long ago forsaken.[215]

Dissent occurred even in circles that could afford access to official monasteries; such nuns included the boyar widows Anna Khilkova, Marina

Potemkina, and Feodosiia Morozova.[216] Some of these noble widows made conscious efforts to promote opposition to the new books.[217] For example, the widow Avdot'ia Vasil'evna Pozharskaia gave refuge on her estate to several nuns and their children who were practicing the old rites. The young boyar woman Evdokiia Leont'eva was unmarried, but "she had fallen into great grief" after her father's sudden death. In despair, she embarked on a spiritual quest and soon began defending the old rites and supporting a persecuted nun, apparently also of noble origins.[218] The widowed aunts and mothers of two noblemen from the Novgorod area were accused of teaching family members about the old liturgical books. They were sent to the Pokrovskii Convent in Suzdal', a monastic prison that absorbed female noble dissidents during the seventeenth century.[219]

Another scenario of dissent was discovered in connection with the investigations of the 1666 Church Council: several unmarried or otherwise unaffiliated women and men had found refuge in monastic cells. These small, informal communities seem to have provided orientation and a sense of belonging; opposition to the new books may have been a secondary consideration. For example, among the followers of the above-mentioned preachers Vavila and Leonid, a monk named Nikita sought to escape adversity after being victimized at the monastery where he had previously lived for sixteen years:

> About five years ago robbers came to that monastery and burned [me].
> Ever since, [I] have been sick and have stopped going to church. The
> brethren began reproaching [me] that [I] did not attend Mass, and soon
> [I] could not take it and left to live in a hermitage. . . .[220]

Other members of the monastic community included Nikita's unmarried brother, Nikifor, who had been a monk for thirty years and joined Vavila and Leonid in order to care for Nikita. The nuns Antonida, Vera, and Golendukha stated that they had been homeless ever since their small monastery was destroyed by order of Prince Ia. K. Cherkasskii, on whose land they had settled without permission. The nun Galasiia indicated that she had been on the road for more than three years, and that an itinerant priest had dressed her in monastic habit; she had knocked at the doors of numerous monasteries before finding shelter with Vavila and Leonid. One peasant girl had apparently left her village after going out of her mind (*soshla vne uma*). She had begun dressing in black monastic habit by her own initiative.[221]

The stories of Galasiia and the unnamed peasant girl find parallels in the statements of other schismatics, and represent familiar themes of seventeenth-century religious dissent.[222] During the decades preceding and following the Council of 1666, the church paid considerable attention to the spontaneous and unregulated proliferation of nuns and monks. In 1640 the monk Lavrentii, who headed a small monastic community in the settlement of Mikhailov in the Riazan' eparchy, was angrily denounced by the local archbishop for making anyone a monk or nun who requested his services (*vsiakikh chinov liudei, kto evo prizovet, postrigal*). The law code (*ulozhenie*) of 1649 stipulated that " . . . pretenders (*samozvantsy*) [who] put on monastic habit or skullcaps on their own authority" were to be severely punished.[223] In 1671, Ivan Krasulin, who had been exiled to the Kola peninsula for comparing the tsar to Satan, was suspected of dressing as a monk without official sanction. The Krasulin affair was seen as so serious that Patriarch Ioasaf intervened himself.[224] Hierarchs attending the Church Council of 1681 observed: "Women are becoming nuns outside of monastic institutions (*vne monastyrei*), right in their homes, and now they wander from house to house, sit along the streets and on streetcorners, asking for alms."[225]

The success of schismatic monks such as Vavila and Leonid reflects a religious dilemma of the seventeenth century: while access to official monastic institutions became more limited, the urge to renounce the world and lead a monastic life apparently increased. This discrepancy between popular need and official church policy can be illustrated with two examples. In 1657, a Vologda woman refused to live with her husband and threatened to commit suicide unless she was made a nun. Instead of offering to help, the archbishop of Vologda had the woman arrested and interrogated.[226] During the late 1660s, a peasant woman named Kapka appealed to the abbot of the Ferapontov Monastery to make her a nun. When he refused, she turned to the monk Loggin, who belonged to an unofficial monastic community in the neighborhood, and became the nun Kilikiia.[227]

The surplus of nuns during the seventeenth century was observed by numerous travelers. Stopping in Arkhangel'sk in the 1670s, the Dutch visitor van Klenk likened unaffiliated nuns to the Beguines (Begijnen) of his homeland. Amid the bonanza of this boom town, he discerned the desperate poverty of the women selling icons in front of the Kreml' building and asking for alms.[228] Such nuns flocked to Patriarch Iosif when he traveled through Vladimir in 1643. In 1652 on his first visit to Vladimir, Patriarch Nikon was confronted by hordes of beggars that included dislocated nuns.[229] During the pestilence of 1654, the authorities put up roadblocks to prevent access to the city of Moscow and the Troitsa Monastery, a provision that strongly affected wandering nuns.[230] These "homeless nuns" (*bezmestnye staritsy*) tried to find shelter at parish churches and small nunneries, but there seems to have been little room for them.[231]

Despite its polemic focus on Old Believers, the Orthodox Church appears to have been aware of the connection between the proliferation of schismatic dissent and the dramatic demographic surplus of unaffiliated nuns and monks. After the Church Council of 1666, for example, a few bishops made efforts to control unaffiliated nuns by gathering them in nunneries.[232] The Church Council of 1681 called for the building of new monasteries—especially nunneries—as a crucial component in the fight against the schism.[233] Archbishop Pitirim of Nizhnii Novgorod issued the following circular to local archpriests and abbots:

> There are many schismatics in almost all settlements—probably they number, all in all, in the thousands. In the districts of Balakhna and Iur'ev about ten thousand schismatic monks, nuns, and novices live without peasant households. ... In the forest there are about four thousand nuns. They should all be seized and put into a monastery. ... Orders must be given in all districts that monks, nuns, and novices are not allowed to live outside of monasteries—be they in settled, or in deserted places. No one is to live [a monastic life] in the forests, fields, trading settlements, or homes under penalty of death. And whoever wants to live in a monastic cell in the forest without belonging to a monastery has to seek written permission from the archbishop. ... [234]

Archbishop Pitirim was probably more familiar than other churchmen with the popular roots of schismatic dissent. He had once lived among self-declared nuns and monks in the Nizhnii Novgorod forests and had, in fact, been himself accused of schism.[235] He may also have learned from the observations of Nizhnii Novgorod's first bishop, Filaret, who in 1672 wrote that the absence of ecclesiastical controls in the area was leading to the proliferation of dissent. Both Pitirim and Filaret were right: the large number of unaffiliated monks and nuns in the forests was a clear sign of ecclesiastical failure. Had the church been willing, and able, to build monasteries in greater numbers earlier, the rapid spread of *raskol* in the provinces might have been prevented.[236]

Instead, the assembled hierarchs at the Church Council of 1681 decided to curb the mobility of schismatic nuns and monks who were wandering everywhere "without permission of the higher clergy." The most dangerous monks were to be confined to monastic prisons surrounded by high fences. Itinerant monks roaming the streets of Moscow were to be rounded up and held under guard at the Troitsa Monastery. Local bishops were to erect similar detention centers for unruly nuns and monks in their own dioceses.[237] But such measures neither put an end to the "monk-vagrants" (*cherntsy-brodiagi*), nor alleviated the fears they inspired among Russian prelates. As one frustrated and angry church polemicist of the period stated, "they continue to wander about according to their own free will . . . not living anywhere under monastic supervision."[238]

More than any other social group, itinerant monks and nuns were responsible for the vitality and the ongoing dissemination of liturgical dissent. Their activities can be observed not only in the central regions of Muscovy, the areas around Nizhnii Novgorod, Murom, and Suzdal', but also in the distant reaches of northern Russia,[239] Siberia,[240] the Don River,[241] and Sloboda Ukraine.[242] It is impossible to say how many of them existed, since they frequently eluded detection and seventeenth-century churchmen lacked the necessary resources to track them down. Furthermore, we may assume that the line between dissenting and non-dissenting behavior was easily crossed. Pitirim of Nizhnii Novgorod may have been correct when he estimated the number of schismatic monks and nuns in his diocese to be in the thousands.

I HAVE DEMONSTRATED that after the Church Council of 1666, which introduced the notion of a schism (*raskol*), Muscovite churchmen became particularly apprehensive about the failure of monks and nuns to assimilate the new liturgical books. This failure—contrary to official church treatises—cannot be attributed to the influence of Old Belief leaders; rather, it must be understood within the larger context of monastic nonconformity.

Countless small, locally endowed monasteries had been viewed with suspicion by the church even before the introduction of the new books. Often located in communities that were hard to control by outside authority, the presence of schismatic monasteries in the midst of unruly villages and trading posts, such as Lyskovo and Murashkino near Nizhnii Novgorod, was hardly a coincidence. During the second half of the seventeenth century, the founding of large monastic complexes, such as Nikon's Iverskii and Voskresenskii monasteries, threatened the autonomy of these small monasteries.

A number of monks and nuns fled from large monasteries—usually due to the increased enforcement of monastic discipline by newly appointed abbots and abesses—and began to roam freely. These monks and nuns were not only independent-minded, but also prone to heterodox ideas and violent anti-ecclesiastical behavior. There were also countless men and women who could not afford—or were not permitted—to enter regular monasteries and convents. Many of them took matters into their own hands: they either convinced wandering clerics to make them monks and nuns, or they simply began to dress in black monastic habit of their own accord.

Not surprisingly, some of the most fervent and influential preachers against the new liturgical books were recruited from these milieux: radical nuns, such as the prophetess Evpraksiia, who wandered from village to village in the Suzdal' area; and popular abbots, such as Superior Avraamii, who was hidden from church agents by the villagers of Lyskovo. How many of these charismatic figures existed during the second half of the seventeenth century cannot be established with any certainty. What is certain, however, is the tremendous influence they wielded over attitudes toward the new books. In fact, the church was so alarmed by their activities that the imprisonment of dissident monks and nuns was viewed as crucial in the fight against the schism.

Study of alternative monastic life during the seventeenth century not only sheds light on the socioreligious preconditions of dissent; it also helps us to understand the origins of eighteenth-century sectarian communities. This continuity can be illustrated, for example, by the missionary activities of Abbot Iov. After founding a number of short-lived, small monasteries, he succeeded in creating a tightly knit and highly mobile community on the Don River that proved capable of surviving brutal persecution. A similar continuity can be found in the north, where monks such as Kornilii and Kirill founded the famous Vyg Community. Even though this community—thanks to the rigorous disciplinarian measures of the Denisov brothers—was soon transformed into an outpost of Old Belief, its origins were inseparable from the traditions of alternative monastic life.[243]

Indeed, one might say that eighteenth-century Old Belief benefited from existing forms of monastic dissent. The folklore of later Old Belief communities glorified hermitages and small monasteries as idyllic alternatives to a world rotten and doomed.[244] Accounts of "invisible" monasteries in the woods of the Tver' area became a mainstay in the post-Petrine Old Belief recruitment of followers. These legends were similar to the widely disseminated tales of "invisible" towns where monasteries and churches constantly rang their bells.[245] Stories of wandering monks and nuns also seem to have enjoyed particular popularity among eighteenth-century Old Believers.[246]

Thus, the monastic way of life that produced much dissenting behavior during the seventeenth century, provided important—albeit highly idealized—models for the dissemination of Old Belief during later centuries. Still, this later development should not obscure the fact that the schismatic monks and nuns of the seventeenth century had little, if any, contact with Old Believers.

CHAPTER FIVE

The Russian Priesthood and the Official Church

The proceedings of the 1666 Church Council expressed great concern that Muscovite parish priests were not cooperating with the new liturgical policies. Simeon Polotskii, author of the proceedings, alerted church officials that priests were among the worst proponents of schismatic behavior:

> [They] . . . have inflamed the souls of large numbers of unstable people, . . . they call the former holiest patriarch of Moscow, Nikon, bad names (*zlosloviat*) . . . and humiliate the entire hierarchical order. With their craziness they bring the 'common people' (*narod*) into an uproar and they say churches are not churches, prelates are not prelates, and priests not priests, and many other similar obscenities (*bliadeniia*).[1]

I will argue that this concern on the part of the church was greatly exaggerated. In fact, parish priests were much more willing to acquiesce to the church's liturgical demands than were monastic clergy.

The alarm with which assembled church hierarchs viewed the behavior of the priesthood had two principal causes. First, a small number of radical priests did indeed attack the liturgical reforms—and advocates of the reforms—both verbally and physically. Most of these schismatic priests had previously been defrocked and were thus forced to look for alternative ways of exercising their profession, such as roaming the roads of Muscovy to spread the message of dissent. Second, a considerable number of parish priests had not yet switched from the old to the new liturgies for the simple reason that they had never been instructed to do so. Such priests included the clergy of distant and isolated Russian parishes that had not yet received new liturgical books. Not surprisingly, the seventeenth-century church considered the education of priests in liturgical matters to be a priority in its fight against the schism.

We are thus dealing with two historical problems that will be discussed separately. On the one hand, marginalized priests spoke out fervently against the established church. Almost all of these priests were without parishes: they lived as vagabonds, finding occasional shelter under the tutelage of powerful protectors, or eking out a living while hiding in the forests. On the other hand, church officials in Moscow and other centers of Muscovite religion were out of touch with large segments of the parish clergy. More than any previous reform measure, the introduction of the new liturgical books exacerbated this problem because the church could now clearly ascertain whether its reforms were being transmitted on the local level.

Since liturgical education was a priority of the seventeenth-century church, I will begin with a discussion of the measures taken by churchmen to ensure cooperation of the parish clergy. These measures were ultimately of much greater historical importance than the persecution of dissident priests, and in the long run, enabled the church to exert greater control over local parish life.

EDUCATION OF PARISH PRIESTS AND REGIONAL EXPANSION OF CHURCH POWER

The acts of the Church Council of 1666 established a connection between the absence of proper controls over local priests and liturgical dissent. In particular, the council pointed to the ignorance of rural parish priests and urged archpriests and abbots to make frequent visits (*dozirati pochastu*) to village churches. They were to make sure that these priests obeyed church orders and instructed ther parishoners to "subordinate themselves completely to the Holy Eastern Church without any doubts."[2] Subsequent councils continued to target parish priests.[3] The acts of the Church Council of 1681, for example, described many priests and deacons as bad representatives of the Christian faith who did not care to follow church precepts:

> They do not live according to the rules (*bezchinno*), drink in excess, and are so impertinent that they celebrate the Mass and other liturgical services even before they are sober. . . . The holy sacraments of baptism, unction, marriage, confession, communion, and the last rites (*eleosviashchenie*) they perform drunk. They show no signs of repen-

tance and continue in their unruly drunkenness, paying no attention to the Holy Scriptures and despising the prohibitions of their prelates. . . . [4]

Successful implementation of the liturgical changes in Russian parishes was thus part of a larger program: the reform of priestly behavior. The underlying assumption was that once priests began to pay more attention to the responsibilities of their priestly office, they would also celebrate proper church services. The acts of the Church Council of 1666 instructed priests not only in the use of the new sign of the cross and the new Service Book, but in many other matters of behavior.[5] No priest was allowed to say Mass without wearing liturgical vestments; church buildings had to be kept clean, and sacraments properly stored. Also, parish priests were to refrain from drinking and to adopt new modes of personal hygiene, such as regularly washing their hands.[6] The cleanliness and sobriety of priests was designed to ensure that rituals and sacraments would not be defiled. Hand-in-hand with these instructions went threats to punish parish clergy who engaged in trade or commerce—an effort to focus priests' attention on the proper performance of their religious duties.[7]

Efforts to reeducate Muscovite parish priests had already begun before the introduction of new books. During the second half of the 1640s, the ecclesiastical elite undertook a major initiative to reform the modes of church singing. Each litany had to be sung separately by distinct voices, not recited by several priests and deacons simultaneously as before.[8] This change significantly lengthened church services, and thus generated considerable discontent. Tensions grew to such an extent that by 1649, the church leadership was forced to convene an emergency session of prelates and the measure was withdrawn.[9]

The Church Council of 1651 attributed the general unpopularity of this reform to the failure of local priests and deacons to understand and effectively transmit the rationale for the change to their parishioners.[10] In particular, the council associated the failure of priests to implement church demands with their inability to read. From then on, only literate priests were to be selected for parish positions; those who lacked a basic knowledge of reading and writing were to be sent to school (*uchilishche*) to enable them to instruct their parishioners in basic matters of "faith and Christian living."[11]

Under Patriarch Nikon, these reform efforts were accompanied by increased authority of church officials over priests. For example, new decrees restricted access to parish positions. One such instruction was sent to the metropolitan of Novgorod in 1654:

[This] decree determines who can be appointed to the offices of priest or deacon. . . . [The candidate] should be literate and humble. He should be well-versed in the rules of the church and be able to talk about the Books of God. He cannot be a drunkard, gambler, thief, robber, or murderer. . . . [12]

Nikon also obliged priests to acquire official ordination papers.[13] These more stringent rules help to explain why unknown numbers of priests were imprisoned during Nikon's patriarchate.[14]

After the 1666 Church Council, the patriarchal printing press began to print and disseminate numerous short didactic pamphlets to Muscovite parish clergy. These texts combined admonitions about proper Christian behavior with instructions about the correct use of the new liturgies.[15] In fact, it was required of every priest to read and sign one of the most influential of these pamphlets, the *Oath to Patriarch Ioakim* from 1679, before he could receive an official appointment charter.[16] The *Oath* demanded unconditional loyalty and obedience to the patriarch as well as evidence that the candidate was familiar with the new liturgies. It spelled out in detail the necessity of mastering liturgical performances such as the three-finger sign of the cross, the distribution of the new hosts, and the tripling of the hallelujah. And, from the standpoint of the church most importantly, priests had to promise the patriarch they would educate their parishioners about the new liturgies in accordance with the will of local bishops.[17]

Despite these exhortative measures, it often took considerable time for parish priests to adopt the new liturgical order. In 1683 after visiting parishes in many villages and small towns of his diocese, Metropolitan Pavel of Riazan' observed to his astonishment that almost nowhere were the rituals consistent with the new liturgical books. Pavel did not discern any serious crisis, nor did he attribute the problem to the priests' hostility. He merely pointed to their ignorance in religious matters, and informed his officials that the new liturgies would take hold as soon as the local clergy learned more about proper Christian behavior. Insisting that priests be taught they were doing God's work on earth as an extension of God's will (*prilezhit delu Gospodniu*), he expected them to behave differently once they were convinced of the sanctity of their office.[18]

After the Church Council of 1666, the metropolitans of Riazan' had intensified disciplinary actions against parish priests. An undated order of Metropolitan Ilarion, who signed the acts of the council, instructed local officials to force disobedient priests into compliance, and promised as many armed emissaries as might be required (*svoikh pristavov skol'ko prigozhe*).[19] Despite the threat of force, some priests ignored all efforts to discipline them. In 1671, for example, the priest Zinovii of a small village in the Murom district was enjoined to stop exercising his office because of his false denunciations (*iabedy*) and illegal sales (*prodazhi*). In 1675, he was reprimanded for not possessing official ordination papers. In 1677, parishioners reported that Zinovii had become a widower and although they had not allowed him to serve as their priest, he stubbornly refused to step down.[20]

Zinovii's noncompliance—even with the requests of his own parishioners—is echoed in other cases. In 1678, a parish priest in Murom beat up the gatekeeper of the metropolitan's court.[21] In 1680, a nobleman from Nizhnii Novgorod complained to the metropolitan that a priest named Fedor was hiding a runaway peasant woman.[22] Such examples help to explain why liturgical reforms were not immediately adopted. The archive of the Riazan' metropolitanate suggests that priests abandoned the old liturgies during the 1680s and 1690s when ecclesiastical supervision over their parishes was increased. Thus, the temporary failure to introduce the new liturgies was overcome as soon as more regular contacts with local priests were established.[23]

The archbishop of Vologda worked for many years to establish official liturgical reform policies in local parish life. During the late 1670s, he required all parishioners of his eparchy to sign papers guaranteeing that their priests would use only the new Nikonian rites.[24] Priests had to provide evidence that they owned copies of the revised liturgical books. The priest Sergei, who ran a parish in the hinterlands of the Pavlov Monastery, dictated the following statement to his semi-literate son, who recorded it in extremely poor handwriting: "In my Church of the Resurrection of Christ there is no printed or handwritten copy of an old Service Book printed before the patriarchate of Nikon. This is what I have to say."[25] On April 2, 1678, the priest Leontii from the Beloozero district signed a paper at the bishop's court in Vologda indicating he owned a copy of the new Service Book. He also confirmed that he had given the old Service Book to the abbot of the Novoezerskii Monastery, who was apparently responsible for overseeing religious affairs in the Beloozero district.[26]

Probably Leontii did not acquire the new liturgical book much earlier than 1678, and it is possible that he represented the exception rather than the rule.[27] The archbishops of Vologda had traditionally had trouble exercising their authority in the rural environs of Beloozero. On previous occasions, for example, priests living in the immediate vicinity had responded with force when the bishops tried to discipline them for disorderly behavior (*bezchinstvo*). One, Grigorii, took out his rifle when threatened with arrest and, according to a report in the diocesan archive, an armed gang of his parishioners proceeded to "dishonor" the leader of an episcopal search party "by beating him in the face and by pulling his beard (*za borodu drali*)." In the end, Grigorii did not use his rifle, but the bishop's agents were lucky to escape. At about the same time another priest, Ivan, and his parishioners welcomed visitors from Vologda with a barrage of bullets. Ivan and Grigorii apparently continued to live according to their own rules; whether they ever used the new liturgical books has not been recorded.[28]

The transition from the old liturgical order to the new took place gradually in the Vologda eparchy. There are no indications of any dramatic conflicts over the introduction of new books in local parishes: the voluminous archive of the bishopric is silent on the subject. In fact, evidence suggests that parish priests willingly sold their old liturgical books, and that their parishioners supported them in this endeavor.[29]

Before priests would comply with orders of the archbishop, two conditions had to be fulfilled: contacts between Vologda and local parishes had to be intensified and regularized, and priests had to be made accountable directly to their bishop. In particular, the archbishop insisted that priests could serve in parishes only after they had received official appointment or ordination papers. By the 1680s, most priests had apparently accepted this policy. Documents in the diocesan archive include hundreds of requests by priests to be admitted to the holy orders or to serve in particular parishes, and anxious requests for the replacement of lost or stolen appointment papers.[30]

The diocesan archive of Vologda also contains a large number of petitions by parishioners to confirm, or select priests.[31] Among them is a typical request by the parishioners of the St. George Church in the Shilegotskaia Volost', dated March 1670:

> Lord, Most Holy Simon, Archbishop of Vologda . . . have pity on us and give orders, oh Lord, that Fedor Kharitonov, the widowed priest of [our] St. George Church, may continue to serve at that church. . . . He is the spiritual pastor of all parishioners and has been a good man to all [of us]. He is humble, lives a decent and spiritual life, and takes good care of God's church; he is neither a reveler (*brazhnik*) nor a drunkard, but is very attentive to all our spiritual needs. Our parish is small and poor . . . , but our priest Fedor Kharitonov works for the sake of God (*rabotaet Bogu*). . . . His father, grandfather, and great-grandfather were born and have died here. Lord and Great Prelate, have mercy![32]

The petition was examined and countersigned by the priest-monk (*ieromonakh*) Kirill, who was sent by the bishop to visit the parish. Kirill testified that Fedor had confessed to him, and was worthy (*dostoin*) of continuing to serve as priest. A clerk of the archbishopric added in his handwriting: "March 23, 1670: orders were given to let him serve for one year from this date."[33]

Thus, parish appointees were subject to on-site inspection as well as to bureaucratic regulation. Under these circumstances, it is unlikely that any priest who did not accept the new liturgical books could have served in a Vologda parish during the late seventeenth century. We can conclude, therefore, that the appointment policy developed in the wake of the 1666 Church Council ultimately ensured the success of official liturgical policies in the Vologda eparchy.

In the isolated parishes of the former Novgorod see, the old liturgical rites disappeared later than in the Vologda eparchy. During the late 1670s, for example, Metropolitan Kornilii of Novgorod repeatedly warned parish priests and deacons of the distant Kargopol' area to say Mass " . . . according to the rite, as presented in the newly printed Book of Needs."[34] But the new liturgies were probably not implemented until after the Church Council of 1682, when the vast eparchy was subdivided into three smaller bishoprics led by bishops seated in Novgorod, Ustiug, and Kholmogory.

In 1683, parish priests of the Novgorod eparchy were directed to teach their parishioners the three-finger sign of the cross. In 1686, episcopal officials received orders to hand out new liturgical books, and make sure that parish priests used the right liturgies in ceremonies such as the consecration of church buildings. During the same year, emissaries were sent to inspect and describe (*dosmotr i opisanie*) all parishes of the reconstituted eparchy.[35] By the end of the century, parish priests had begun to cooperate with church demands. During the 1690s, for instance, they were sending regular reports to Novgorod describing the religious practices of parishioners, including their liturgical preferences.[36]

Shortly after the new archbishop of Ustiug assumed his office in 1682, he ordered all parish priests " . . . to sing and speak with one voice at a time—articulately and not confusedly (*miatezhno*), but according to the newly revised books."[37] From 1684 to 1722, a central administrative office in the home of the archbishop at Ustiug regulated all parish appointments. The surviving archive of this office contains numerous petitions by priests asking to be allowed to stay in their parishes. There is no mention of conflicts with parish priests over the new liturgical books, suggesting that the books had been generally assimilated.[38]

Nowhere can the gradual transition from the old to the new liturgies be better observed than in the newly created archbishopric of Khol-mogory.[39] During the 1680s, soon after the diocese was established, epis-copal emissaries received written orders to distribute new liturgical books to parish churches. Poor priests, unable to afford such books, were given free copies. Kholmogory was also the first Muscovite eparchy to systemati-cally confiscate old liturgical books remaining in the possession of parish priests.[40]

These measures did not, however, ensure immediate acceptance of the new liturgical order. Archbishop Afanasii found he first had to increase supervision of his priests. Much like the archbishops of Vologda, he pro-ceeded to regulate appointments of the parish clergy. Afanasii made no effort to disrupt the election of priests by peasant communities, but all candidates proposed for the priesthood had to obtain his approval before they could assume parish positions. For this reason, parishioners, or their candidates, wrote countless petitions to Kholmogory.[41] Prospective priests and deacons typically had to travel to Kholmogory where their compe-tence—liturgical and other—was tested by the archbishop himself, or by his officials.[42] Usually these interviews resulted in orders to undergo addi-tional instruction in the fundamentals of church services; as a result, many candidates stayed at the episcopal palace to study the new liturgical books before they were granted permission to go home.[43]

No seventeenth-century Russian bishop understood as well as Afanasii that education of priests was the key to eradicating the old liturgical order, and efforts in this regard continued throughout his tenure. In 1694 and 1695, special charters were issued to archpriests and other local church offi-cials to distribute copies of a Book of Rites (*chinovnik*) to all parish priests under their supervision. If priests did not understand what was expected of them, they were to be given further instructions.[44] In 1700, the archbishop sent copies of the Liturgical Exegesis (*tolkovanie liturgii*) by the Greek Patri-arch German to all parish priests. His intention was not only to unify liturgical practices, but also to raise the level of priests' awareness.[45]

Available evidence suggests that the old liturgical order may have per-sisted for several more years. As late as 1715, for example, the liturgical practices of the cathedral church at Kholmogory had to be declared nor-mative for the whole eparchy, and another Book of Rites was prepared for general distribution.[46] Thus, it took a long time before the efforts of Arch-bishop Afanasii led to widespread acceptance of the new liturgies by local parish priests.

We do not have sufficient data to map the progress of the new liturgi-cal rites in Russian parishes during the decades following the Church

Council of 1666. But it is likely that the regional advance of the new liturgies was directly linked to the growth of ecclesiastical controls over the priesthood. In the Vologda bishopric, increasing contact between church and outlying parishes probably led to widespread acceptance of the Nikonian reforms by the end of the 1670s. Further north, in the Novgorod and Ustiug eparchies, the transition from old to new practices in worship seems to have taken place during the 1680s and 1690s. In the most northern parishes, in the eparchy of Kholmogory, the old liturgies disappeared during the first decades of the eighteenth century.

DISSIDENT PARISH PRIESTS AND PARISHES

There are comparatively few examples of active resistance, or refusal to cooperate with the demands of the church, on the part of parish priests or their parishes. In this section I discuss the few examples of resistance found in available sources. I will argue that special historical circumstances—for example, a prehistory of tension with the church rather than Old Believer influences—motivated disobedience to their hierarchs.

One unruly area was the land belonging to the rebellious Solovki Monastery. In 1669, a church official from Novgorod toured these parishes in an apparently futile effort to collect taxes for the metropolitan see. He noticed the general absence of liturgical books from church services as well as the failure of the Novgorodian metropolitans to implement other basic reforms, such as the singing of liturgies in one voice.[47]

This situation was no different from that observed by the metropolitan of Riazan' a few years later. However, there was one additional circumstance that may have contributed to the emergence of more serious conflicts in Solovki: neither priests nor parishioners prayed for the health of the tsar and his family. As early as 1647, the peasants of Solovki had collectively refused to swear the oath of allegiance.[48]

Given the traditional hostility of Solovki peasant communities toward the tsar, their reaction to the new books should come as no surprise. We are best informed about the aggressive opposition of both priests and parishioners in the small trading community of Kem' on the White Sea. In November 1668, an emissary from Novgorod named Vasilii made the mistake of saying Mass from the new books in the parish church of Kem'. He later justified his action by explaining that Semen, the parish priest, had left on a trip to an isolated village. Shouting from two elected peasant leaders, the church elder (*tserkovnyi starosta*) Nikita and the community elder (*mirskoi starosta*) Maksim, interrupted Vasilii's service. Soon pandemonium broke out. Everyone scolded Vasilii, calling him "a student of the Anti-christ."[49] Another official from Novgorod, the monastic priest Iona, was sent to Kem' several months later "for the correction of the divine church liturgy" (*dlia ispravleniia Bozhestvennogo tserkovnogo peniia*). But he fared no better—the peasants did not even bother to attend services.[50]

Priest Iona tried to locate Semen, who had disappeared upon Iona's arrival—allegedly to distribute alms among the poor of the Solovki hinter-lands—in an effort to remedy the situation. After a systematic search of the area, Semen was found hiding in the home of the peasant Fedor Fokin. When musketeers tried to arrest him, the following scene ensued:

> About fifty or more peasants gathered and took the priest Semen from the musketeers by force. The peasant Fetka grabbed an ax and wanted to cut them down. [The peasants] wanted to kill the musketeers, and called them heretics and apostates (*otpadshimi*).[51]

It is uncertain whether the capture of Semen would have convinced him to say Mass according to the new liturgy. He managed to escape to the Solovki Monastery, and apparently participated in the armed uprising there. Other parish priests from Kem' also sought refuge at the rebellious monastery.[52] Monks who defected to Kremlin troops during the uprising testified that "the priest Matvei [from Kem'] was the source of great crime in the Solovki Monastery: he strengthens the criminals in the monastery and gives all sorts of fabulous and conspiratorial speeches."[53]

It is clear that the Kem' parish priests played a vital role in inciting their parishioners to violence against the church. The popularity of these priests endured even after they were forced to leave the parish church. In fact, several parishioners joined their priests at the Solovki Monastery. In June 1671, a church official, who had been sent from Moscow to Kem', made the following observation:

> The peasant Savka Lavrov from the small town of Kem' hired himself out to go to Murmansk by boat. ... However, it came to [my] knowledge that Savka was in the Solovki Monastery. Five other people also recently disappeared from Kem', but I found out the truth about them . . . ; and others who left Kem' without a trace in various months and years have all appeared in the Solovki Monastery.[54]

During the summer of 1673, two emissaries were sent from Moscow to capture and discipline the local parish priest, who was perceived as the source of continuing troubles in the trading colony. At the same time, soldiers made their way to Kem' to seize the "brigand Khariton and his accomplices." We do not know exactly who Khariton was, but he appears to have been the parish priest; after Khariton and his supporters were arrested, the opposition of the Kem' parishioners to the new liturgies ceased.[55]

The stubborn refusal of Kem' and other Solovki parish priests to accept the new liturgies can be seen as an extension of the revolt of the Solovki monks: the priests merely followed the example set by the monastic elite. There is good evidence that the monks controlled parish affairs within the monastery's territory. In prior decades, church interference in local parish life had been, if not impossible, very difficult at best. During the 1620s, for example, Patriarch Filaret observed that church emissaries could not discipline the Solovki parish priests; they lived according to their own free will and put the money they collected for the metropolitan of Novgorod into their own pockets.[56] By the middle of the seventeenth century, local parishes were addressing petitions to the archimandrite of Solovki, not to the metropolitans of Novgorod.[57] Only after the military defeat of the monastery in 1676 was the church able to change the loyalties of the Solovki priests.[58]

The Solovki parishes were integrated into the archbishopric of Kholmogory during the early 1680s. There is no evidence that the more than two hundred northern parishes transferred to this new eparchy displayed an unruliness similar to that of the Solovki parishes. Only the parishes of the Vaga district had, coincidentally, come to the attention of the metropolitan of Novgorod during the 1670s.[59] The hierarch had complained about the continued use of the old liturgical books, as well as about the random drunkenness and "laziness" (*lenost'*) of the parish priests which resulted in frequent cancellation of church services.[60] To ameliorate the situation, parish priests were subjected to clerical supervision and instruction: liturgical performances were to be checked by regular visits, and peasants had to sign written statements promising to pay for new liturgical books.[61] Thus, failure to use the new liturgies was not perceived as a conscious act of opposition, but merely an indication of the indifference of local priests.

In other areas of Muscovy, refusal of parish priests to accept the Nikonian reforms was rarely recorded. The few exceptions may be attributed to ecclesiastical impatience, or use of excessive force.[62] Rather than relying on the gradual education of priests, some local officials interfered more drastically in parish life. One case that attracted attention in Moscow was the attempt to discipline the parish priest of Feduevo, a remote village in the Poshekhon'e district. Like the priests of Kem', this priest enjoyed considerable prestige, and efforts to seize him led to active local resistance.

In December 1682, a large military detachment under the leadership of the voevoda of Torzhok, Mikhail Chelishchev, descended upon Feduevo. Musketeers sealed off the church and occupied the home of the parish priest, Peter, who had disappeared along with the sacristan and the son of the church clerk. The military occupation culminated in a Mass conducted by a church official, which peasants and their families were forced to attend. They endured the new liturgies until communion was distributed. Perceiving a sudden change of mood, musketeers and church officials began to force hosts into the mouths of parishioners. Only the church clerk swallowed the host; most spat it out. Some parishioners sneaked out of the church before anyone could lay hands on them, others ran away shouting and making horrible noises (*s gamom*).[63]

Soldiers withdrew from Feduevo, leaving behind a new priest and a number of church emissaries under Superior Rafail. The representatives of the new religious order occupied the home of the missing parish priest. Soon afterward, the following situation occurred:

> [The villagers] beat Superior Rafail and the bailiff in the priest's courtyard, threw logs through the priest's windows into his cabin, and chased away the superior's horses. At the gates of the priest's property a crowd of about fifty peasants approached the superior, the church clerk, the bailiff, a servitor, and an elder. [The peasants] were carrying spades, raised pitchforks, and cudgels and were ready to attack them, screaming at the superior and eager to beat them. . . . [64]

Thus, a dramatic show of force was followed by resistance to the churchmen who were propagating the new liturgies.

We know very little about the outcome of this conflict. But it is likely that the deposed priest, Peter, continued to direct the religious affairs of his parishioners even after a new priest had been installed. According to a report that reached Moscow, Peter had at first hidden in the home of a peasant elder, and then sought refuge in the swamps surrounding the village. Given Peter's local prestige, we may assume that some parishioners joined their former priest in his hideout. It is also possible that the suicides of several peasant men and women that occurred not far from the village a short time later were related to renewed efforts to capture Peter.[65]

In the absence of further evidence, we can only speculate whether other parish priests in the area were uprooted by force, or whether the military assault on Peter's parish was an exceptional occurrence. We know that leaders of the Dolgorukov boyar clan, who owned the parish, complained bitterly about the harsh treatment of Peter.[66] We also know that during the late 1670s and early 1680s, the countryside of the Poshekhon'e district was in an uproar: several peasant suicides were recorded during those years, and it is possible that these dramatic acts of despair were caused by the destruction of parishes and the arrest of priests.[67] At least a few parish priests from the area did become important advocates of liturgical dissent. One of them, Prokopii, came from a family of priests that had served in parishes of the Poshekhon'e district for generations.[68]

Military attacks on priests and their parishes could result in behavior classified by church officials as schismatic. However, violent interventions in parish life occurred only rarely. Only one parish priest and his parish were ever identified and attacked for schismatic behavior by the archbishops of Vologda, and this was in 1690, after most other parishes of the bishopric had already moved from the old to the new liturgical order.[69]

Similarly, the leaders of the vast Novgorod metropolitanate had no reason for concern about the success of their efforts to reeducate priests in the new liturgies: the archive of the metropolitans contains only one case indicating parishioners were unhappy with their priest's use of the new rites, but this case was precipitated by an official complaint from the priest about the inadequacy of the income his parishioners provided. It is likely that the priest was eventually forced to resign his parish position.[70] In general, however, the expulsion of priests by their parishioners cannot be attributed to priests' readiness to accept the new liturgical books. There were many other reasons for discord between seventeenth-century priests and their parishioners; foremost among them were conflicts over income, use of violence, and theft.[71]

Another exceptional case demonstrates the solidarity of priests and their parishes against outside assault. In the year 1666, shortly after the church became concerned with the outbreak of a schism, the parish of the small village of Pirovo in the Suzdal' eparchy not far from Viazniki was attacked. The attacks were apparently instigated by the new archimandrite of the Blagoveshchenskii Monastery, who was trying to ingratiate himself with Moscow by implementing the new liturgies as soon as possible because his predecessor, Moisei, had been exiled for not doing so. In September 1666, a procession of priests and monks from Viazniki, clerks from the local administrative office, and some gunners (*pushkari*) moved to the parish church of Pirovo. The procession was to culminate in a service at the church but Dmitrii, the parish priest, managed to prevent the service. He was assisted by his parishioners who blocked the entrance to the church, shouting that they had their own priest (*u nikh de est' svoi pop*) and that nobody would be allowed to say Mass according to the new books in their church.[72]

This confrontation was essentially a continuation of an earlier antagonism. The previous summer, the new archimandrite had sent several soldiers to the parish to seize Dmitrii and his son. Dmitrii had locked himself in the parlor (*gornitsa*) of his home while his wife jumped out of a window to call for help. A crowd of peasants had soon assembled, forcing the soldiers to withdraw.[73] This occurrence indicates how deeply rooted Dmitrii was in the community, and how official efforts to replace him led to protests by his parishioners against the new liturgies.[74]

Another case, recorded in the parishes in and around the town of Galich during the mid-1670s, demonstrates that violence and coercion could mobilize fierce opposition to the new liturgies.[75] In fact, this case caused such a stir in Moscow that both the patriarch and the tsar became involved. An entire region temporarily fell under the dominion of parish priests rebelling against the Nikonian reforms—a scenario that to my knowledge did not occur anywhere else during the seventeenth century.

It all began with a petition submitted by the priests and deacons from the town and surrounding districts requesting that the voevoda, Perfilii F. Rakhmaninov, be replaced. The petitioners complained: "He arbitrarily sends his bailiffs and errand-boys (*rozsylshchiki*) in great numbers; they . . . enter our houses and ruin them; our wives and children are scolded and dishonored; they beat and torture us . . . and we sit in chains and irons."[76] While petitions of this kind may not have been unusual in seventeenth-century Muscovy, it certainly was an uncharacteristic response to immediately send two of the most powerful Muscovite officials, the boyars Ivan F. Lyzlov and Afanasii L. Ordin-Nashchokin, to Galich to investigate.[77]

One reason for the capital's interest may have been Rakhmaninov's persecution of local priests who used the old liturgical books. Rakhmaninov's victims, almost exclusively local parish priests, noted that neither Patriarch Ioakim nor the tsar had condoned Rakhmaninov's violence.[78] When Rakhmaninov physically abused them for wearing old liturgical vestments, such as Russian skullcaps (*skuf'i*), he was unable to justify his action on the basis of written authority.[79]

There is no obvious explanation for Rakhmaninov's use of force. His reaction to priests' continued use of the old books may have been exacerbated by his difficulties with the ecclesiastical establishment of Galich: Rakhmaninov was engaged in a bitter feud with Sil'vestr, the influential archimandrite of the local Paisiev Monastery, over who should exercise local spiritual authority. The archimandrite apparently advocated a gradual transition from the old to the new liturgical order and resented the fact that the voevoda had taken control of the local church tithe office (*desiatichnii dvor*).

In particular, Sil'vestr complained that Rakhmaninov made random accusations of schism without justification. Sil'vestr himself had been accused of being both a notorious drunkard and a schismatic. In fact, "he had not the least thought of schism in his mind and he also did not find the least trace of drunkenness in his life."[80] The enraged Rakhmaninov retorted that "[Sil'vestr] does not care how priests behave in church, and whether or not they say Mass correctly . . . he scolds [me] all the time and dishonors [me] by [treating me] like a brigand . . . and calling me the lowest gentryman from Riazan' (*poslednim synom boiarskim*). . . . "[81]

The feud between Rakhmaninov and Sil'vestr was the prelude to the voevoda's attack on local priests. The first to be targeted was the archimandrite's closest ally in the community, the priest Evdokim, who served at the Bogoiavlenskii parish church in the Galich merchant colony. Evdokim was a formidable opponent for the voevoda. He was, after the archimandrite, the most powerful figure in local church life. Priests and other residents told investigators Evdokim was such a powerful man (*chelovek mochnoi*) that it was not a good idea to contradict him.[82] His power probably resulted from his strong connections to both the religious and secular leaders of Galich. Evdokim was related by kinship and marriage to the land elder (*zemskii starosta*), the archpriest, and the clerk of the local tax office (*s'ezzhaia izba*), all of whom offered support and protection once Rakhmaninov began his assault.[83]

When the voevoda attempted to seize Evdokim, the powerful priest spread the rumor that Rakhmaninov had made heretical remarks about the Holy Spirit. This accusation, which may have been entirely fabricated, proved very effective. Everyone—including the tsar and the patriarch— believed it. Under considerable pressure from both the local community and from Moscow, Rakhmaninov may have tried to exonerate himself by accusing other priests of introducing a schism.[84]

Almost every parish priest in the area sided with the persecuted Evdokim. In fact, it appears that local priests refused to accept the new books merely out of loyalty to him. This can be concluded from the curious fact that hardly any of them spoke about liturgical books when interrogated by the Moscow emissaries. They typically stated they had felt under attack and had wanted to save their skins. The local elder of priests (*starosta popovskii*), Iosif, defended himself in the following way: "[We] never sit drunk in the church tithe office and [I am] not in the least involved in a schism. If someone drinks in his home, fine, let him drink. If not, not (*khto p'et tot p'et, khto ne p'et tot ne p'et*)."[85] The priest Grigorii, who headed the Rozhdestvenskii Church, complained that the voevoda had called him and other clerics drunkards and rogues (*pluty*). The priest of the St. Barbara Church reported that Rakhmaninov had put him and his brother in chains for conducting an inquest and postponing a funeral.[86] Thus, the priests' primary concern was to guard themselves against the voevoda's arbitrary interventions.

Unfortunately, we do not know the outcome of this conflict. But by accusing the voevoda of heresy, Evdokim had clearly made a clever move. In addition to mobilizing the local community, his accusation deflected the attention of church investigators from the dissenting priests. Ordin-Na-shchokin, the tsar's special envoy, personally interrogated Rakhmaninov about his heresy, and the investigation increasingly focused on that issue.[87] Rakhmaninov's repeated assertions that Evdokim and his friends had lied were apparently to no avail; his credibility had been compromised.[88]

Evdokim may have succeeded, at least temporarily, in keeping the new books out of Galich and its environs—a feat no other parish priest of seventeenth-century Muscovy could claim to have accomplished. The schism of the Galich parish priests can be seen as a conflict between an ambitious voevoda and the men who had traditionally run ecclesiastical affairs in the region. Opposition to the new books was principally the work of one powerful and cunning priest who commanded significant loyalties among other priests as well as the general population.

In the traditional historiography, Muscovite parish priests have too often been viewed as subservient and socially insignificant.[89] While this may have been true of many, there were also independent-minded, highly influential priests such as Evdokim. Local bishops repeatedly had to intervene in conflicts generated by these priests. However, almost none of the recorded cases concerned the issue of new books.[90] One possible conclusion, supported by the Galich case, is that unless the issue was forcibly introduced by outside authority, it remained insignificant.

A case involving the attack on the village of Dedilovo outside Tula by Iosif, the new archbishop of Kolomna, leads to the same conclusion.[91] While the archbishop was traveling through the area in March 1674, the parish was, for unknown reasons, denounced for adhering to the old liturgical order. Since the persistence of the old liturgies was not unusual in provincial parishes during the 1670s, the singling out of this parish was unfortunate. The archbishop, a notoriously bloodthirsty and brutal tyrant, probably wanted to set an example. He moved into the village with his entourage, and proceeded to interrogate and torture suspects personally. Vlas, the parish priest and main target of the investigation, had disappeared. But according to Iosif, Vlas had remained in the community "moving [from house to house] . . . with his entire family." The archbishop learned, to his great frustration, that members of the parish were gathering in secret to attend Vlas' liturgies, and he conceded that Vlas remained the spiritual leader of his parish even after going underground.[92]

Could the tense situation at Dedilovo have been resolved without conflict if Iosif had been less inclined to use force? Vlas had powerful protectors in the community, including the leader of the local musketeers (*streletskii sotnik*), Fedor Elishev. Other priests stood firmly behind him. And, just as in the case of Evdokim, Vlas' real power derived from his kinship and marriage connections: the Cossack Kuzem'ka Samkov, who probably served under Elishev's command, was Vlas' brother-in-law.[93] Given these circumstances, it would have been difficult to discipline Vlas under any circumstances. His persecution for adhering to the schism naturally provoked local resistance.

I conclude that a small number of parish priests and their parishioners fought in defense of the old liturgical order. In order for such rebellions to occur, certain historical conditions had to be present. One of these conditions was the sudden use of force by outside authority. Another was the stubborn refusal of local priests to yield their power in the community to outsiders. Finally, protection offered parish priests by higher authority, such as the local archimandrite or a military leader, was required. However, these circumstances rarely coincided. The mobilization of parish priests and their parishioners against the new liturgical order therefore remained the exception rather than the rule.

DEFROCKED AND ITINERANT PRIESTS

As a rule, priests with parishes did not pose a great threat to the new religious order. They were eventually educated in the Nikonian rites and transformed into local pillars of the ecclesiastical center. However, there were numerous priests who had never received a parish, had been deprived of their parishes, or been removed from the priesthood. This milieu of defrocked and marginalized priests produced some of the most dangerous dissenters of the seventeenth century.

The church councils of 1666 and 1667 expressed great concern about priests on the roads of Muscovy: "[They] . . . must not wander from church to church without the blessing of their prelates. Those who continue to do so should become alien to the priesthood."[94] However, these elusive priests had not only established themselves on the roads; they were performing church services in homes according to the old liturgies even under the nose of the patriarch in Moscow.[95] The Church Council of 1681 warned laymen of all ranks to close their doors to itinerant priests. Priests who continued to say Mass without official permission were threatened with banishment to distant monasteries, where they would do forced labor or live out the rest of their lives under "heavy guard" (*krepkii nachal*).[96]

There were many reasons for priests' inability to procure parishes; these priests had in common only that they lived outside the institutional network of the established church. For example, some were unsuccessful in receiving or renewing official appointment papers. Others obtained appointment papers—but no parishes—by lying to their bishops about local peasants having elected them, or by simply forging the papers.[97] There were also many widowed priests who, according to the rules of seventeenth-century church life, could serve as parish priests only with the explicit permission of their hierarchs. Finally, a large number of priests had been deprived of their parishes as a form of punishment; usually such priests were placed under official interdiction (*zapreshchenie*) or expulsion (*izverzhenie*).[98]

Throughout the century, unaffiliated priests were seen as breeders of dangerous dissent. During the 1620s, the metropolitan of Novgorod complained to Patriarch Filaret that priests who had never been ordained encouraged northern peasants to disdain marriage. Widowed priests were investigated for heresy.[99] Defrocked priests became known as great troublemakers; some of them were, for example, accused of witchcraft.[100] Thus, we can observe that individuals acting as priests without official sanction were prone to heterodox or deviant religious behavior long before the introduction of the new liturgical books.

It may therefore come as no surprise that priests without employment repeatedly came to the church's attention in connection with investigations of schismatic behavior. In particular, such priests seem to have played crucial roles in the transmission of dissent to the peasantry. In 1666, for example, a priest named Ivan migrated from village to village in the Suzdal' district, teaching peasants they would fall prey to the Devil if they used the three-finger sign of the cross. We do not know much about Ivan's background, or the reason for his alienation from the church. We know only that he enjoyed the protection of local peasants, who shielded him when church investigators attempted his capture.[101] During the 1680s, Isidor, who had once served as parish priest in the village of Kozmodemiansk, enjoyed a considerable reputation in the isolated hamlets and villages around Nizhnii Novgorod. He soon became one of the best known opponents of Nikon's reforms in the area.[102] In 1684, the metropolitan of

Novgorod identified the defrocked priest (*raspopa*) Nikita, who was apparently hiding in a small trading colony (*pogost*) in the northern forests. Nikita wrote and disseminated pamphlets condemning the new liturgical order, and was therefore seen as a dangerous transmitter of dissent.[103]

There is evidence that itinerant priests served vital religious needs. Their services were particularly in demand by peasant families that, for one reason or another, did not choose to participate in the religious life of their parishes.[104] In 1691, for example, a parish priest named Tit complained to the archbishop of Vologda about the behavior of Iakov Shaban's family living in a remote village of his parish: Iakov and his relatives had not come to Mass or confession for many years, and they had personally insulted Tit. Iakov had repeatedly told Tit "they had always lived without abbot or priest and would not need any now." Iakov's wife apparently shared this opinion, and spoke openly about priests in very derogatory terms. Despite its strongly stated anticlericalism, the family drew on the services of priests in secret—a fact that understandably made Tit very angry.[105]

Tit discovered that the family had hired a priest named Ivan Akinf'ev to perform a purification ceremony after Iakov's wife had given birth. According to Tit, the peasant family had asked for Akinf'ev's help because he said prayers and blessings according to the old liturgical books. Tit said Akinf'ev was known in the area; he wandered from parish to parish "saying [purification] prayers and baptizing children of other people in their homes, always fulfilling their wishes (*po ikh voliam*). . . . "[106]

A few similar cases demonstrate that the services of parishless priests were in demand among peasants not firmly integrated into their own parishes. For example, in early 1692, the peasant Ivan Grigor'ev was arrested along with his wife, son, and daughter-in-law for drawing on the services of the itinerant priest Trefil. Grigor'ev insisted he was not a schismatic and that his only wrongdoing, which he greatly regretted, was not having had a spiritual pastor for seven years. He claimed the priest Trefil was his brother, and had just paid a family visit. Whether Grigor'ev was speaking the truth could not be determined; by the time an official from Vologda arrived in the village, the itinerant priest had disappeared without a trace.[107]

Another investigation that attracted attention in the Russian north during the early 1690s began with the arrest of the schismatic peasant Ivan Kozel. Kozel, his wife, and their children had been hiding for many years in the forests and swamps of the Pomor'e district. Kozel had apparently not withdrawn from the world to lead a contemplative religious life, but rather to join a band of robbers armed to the teeth with rifles, bows and arrows, knives, and axes. Local peasants feared Kozel and his family because " . . .

they walk around with weapons and large dogs and defame our Orthodox Christian faith . . . and people who need to go into the forest cannot do so because they are terrified."[108] It is significant that neither Kozel nor his companions belonged to a local parish church. Their religious needs were apparently met by the deposed (*otstavnoi*) priest Samson, who had been present on at least four occasions to assist with the births and baptisms of Kozel's children.[109]

The scanty available information does not allow us to reconstruct the interaction of peasants and defrocked priests in greater detail. However, one may safely assume that itinerant priests fulfilled two major functions in the religious dissent of seventeenth-century peasants. First, they provided alternative worship for peasant families; without them, many peasant children might have remained unbaptized. Second, they spread the message of liturgical dissent by inculcating in peasant families the idea of the unacceptability of the new liturgical books.

Unaffiliated or defrocked priests also served as transmitters of dissident behavior to the highest Muscovite elite. For example, the peasant Ivan Grigor'ev bragged that his brother, the above-mentioned priest Trefil, was hiding in the Moscow household of Boyar Larion Semenovich Miloslavskii.[110] The defrocked priest Pron'ka Ivanov, who had formerly served in a Moscow parish church, gained some notoriety during the late 1670s by transporting the corpse of the boyar woman Evdokiia Leont'eva from the trading colony of Viazniki to the small village of Lenovo in the Moscow district. At Lenovo, which may have been the birthplace of Leont'eva, he buried her according to the old rites. Initially Pron'ka managed to conceal the identity of the woman he had buried. But when he repeatedly returned to her grave to say requiems, he was denounced to the tsar.[111]

The presence of runaway priests in the household of Feodosiia Morozova is well-documented, and there is other evidence about the employment of itinerant priests in the households of noblemen. The fact that priests who opposed the new liturgies found refuge in Muscovite elite homes may have inspired the church to regulate the employment of priests by aristocratic households.[112]

As the ecclesiastical infrastructure of the southern steppe was very poorly developed, Cossack warriors on the Don River also drew heavily on unemployed priests. Only the settlement of Cherkassk had a regularly endowed parish church, which had been built and consecrated on the initiative of Patriarch Nikon. All other settlements or trading colonies had temporary chapels (*chasovni*), if any at all. The priests serving at the

Cherkassk church received official appointment charters; elsewhere the employment of priests was left to the local Cossack communities. Under these circumstances, one can easily understand that the presence of officially sanctioned priests on the Don was attested only sporadically.[113]

Since the Cossacks could draw on a large pool of priests who had fled the centers of Muscovite religion, they did not need (or perhaps did not want) to depend on long-term appointments of priests. In March 1688, the metropolitan of Kazan' complained to Patriarch Ioakim that the Cossacks were hiring "runaway priests" (*beglye sviashchenniki*) who included individuals forbidden to perform the sacraments.[114]

The failure of official church authority to assert itself in the south led to the foundation of the new bishoprics of Voronezh and Tambov during the 1680s. Mitrofan, the bishop of Voronezh, attempted to emulate the appointment policies for priests, documented above, for the Vologda and Kholmogory eparchies. But unlike his northern counterparts, Mitrofan failed miserably: priests whom he sent to serve at the Cherkassk church had to be replaced every year because they apparently transferred their loyalties from the bishop to the local Cossack population.[115]

One of the priests hired by the Don Cossacks was the defrocked priest (*raspopa*) Samoil Larionov. In January 1688, Samoil was accused as a schismatic, and the following description was issued to Muscovite military detachments on the Don:

> [These are] Samoshko's features: reddish dark hair, skinny figure, dark-complexioned face, a small beard. He shaves his head, but unevenly; he wears a sheepskin coat that is covered with thick linen, old and sky-blue. His boots are straight and made of calfskin. His priest's cap is made of cherry-colored cloth stuffed with down, and looks old.[116]

The timing of Samoil's dissent is interesting because it sheds some light on motives that may have prompted unemployed priests to reject the old liturgical order. Samoil had previously served as priest in another southern trading settlement, and had apparently used the new liturgical books. We do not know why the church defrocked him, but he was subsequently hired by Ataman Lavrent'ev, a powerful Cossack leader embroiled in conflict with Muscovite officialdom. Virtually overnight, Samoil became known as an outspoken opponent of the new books. This transformation was clearly influenced by his relationship to his employer. When Samoil asked the assembled Cossacks under Lavrent'ev's command which books he was to use to say Mass, he was told to use only the old ones.[117]

The ataman, for his part, had no reason to be unhappy with the priest he had hired. One of Samoil's first acts was to threaten the handful of local priests and monks who enjoyed official church recognition. For example, he attacked a monk named Pavel, a loyal supporter of the metropolitan of Belgorod, as an agent of the Antichrist. When Pavel refused to be intimidated, Samoil called on his Cossack protectors who seized Pavel, put a chain around his neck, and tied him to a pole.[118] Samoil was also behind the confiscation of new liturgical books from southern steppe chapels and the Cherkassk church. Next he began an aggressive campaign against icons showing the three-finger sign of the cross; many icons had their paint scratched off and were then repainted. Soon Samoil had become the ultimate local authority in religious matters, and he made sure that the Cossacks no longer prayed for the patriarch and the tsar. Samoil's own aspirations to power are revealed by his curious call for the establishment of a new anti-Muscovite eparchy to be headed by Nikon's long-deceased adversary, Bishop Pavel of Kolomna.[119]

Several other unemployed priests under the sway of the Don Cossacks also became known as schismatics. While they apparently never gained the influence of Samoil, they were viewed by church authority with similar alarm.[120] Thus, the example of liturgical dissent on the Don demonstrates that priests who were not integrated into the institutional structure of the church could become formidable opposition forces, posing a great danger to local church representatives.

Samoil's aggressive actions recall the participation of radical priests in some of the violent social revolts of the seventeenth century, such as the Copper Rebellion or the Stepan Razin uprising, to mention just two examples. One important distinction was the significance Don Cossack insurgents of the 1680s attributed to the old liturgical order; they equated its opposite with the growing intrusion of Muscovite church and state into their local affairs. The priests among them were therefore singled out as dangerous schismatics.[121]

Dislocated priests played visible leadership roles in a few other large-scale rebellions against the new books. One such rebellion occurred in northern Russia: under the leadership of a deacon named Ignatii, peasants attacked and plundered the Paleostrov Monastery on the shores of Lake Onega. Ignatii had been affiliated with the rebellious Solovki Monastery, although he had departed before the monks resorted to arms. According to contemporary polemicists, he conducted an aimless and adventurous life "on the road leading from Vologda to Kargopol' " before attracting a local peasant following by his preaching and teaching. Those describing Ignatii's activities insisted his popularity was due to using witchcraft and advocating sexual promiscuity.[122] We do not know to what degree Ignatii tried to educate his listeners about the new books, but the denunciations of his adversaries may indeed hold a kernel of truth. The behavior of the peasant rebels suggests that Ignatii's hostility toward the church was probably not primarily concerned with liturgical books.

In January 1687, Ignatii and his spiritual ward (*dukhovnyi syn*), Emel'ian Ivanov Vtorogo, led a formidable force of twelve hundred men, according to the metropolitan of Novgorod, in an assault on the monastery.[123] Given their superiority in arms, including possession of a cannon, the rebels easily subdued the monks. Church officials were shocked by the ensuing developments. First, monks were beaten and driven out of their monastery. Next, the insurgents moved into the empty monastic cells and made themselves comfortable; they even brought in women, to the great dismay of church officials. Especially disconcerting was the conversion of the altar area of the monastery church—by means of a hole cut in one of the altar walls—into a lavatory. We do not know whether defilement of sacred objects was the purpose of the assault. The attack on icons seems to have been inspired by robbery: the images were left intact, while the silver and gold frames (*oklady*) were broken off. Subsequent plundering of the monastic treasury confirms that the insurgents had more in common with robbers than with religious rebels.[124]

When a military detachment from Novgorod finally overpowered the monastery, a raging inferno broke out.[125] We do not know how many of the insurgents perished, nor what became of Ignatii. Contrary to later legend, it is possible that Ignatii escaped along with some leaders of the revolt and his friend Vtorogo, who took along a considerable part of the booty.[126]

Ignatii and his contemporary Samoil on the Don both displayed remarkable hostility toward the church, and both condoned the use of violence. Their behavior was not shaped by the teachings of Old Believers, who advocated peaceful submission and suffering, but by the milieux in which they lived.[127] Ignatii shared the strong hostility of local peasants toward the Paleostrov monks; he must have known that preaching against the new liturgical books was like throwing a spark into a powder keg. Samoil served the interests of the Don Cossacks by expelling officially appointed clerics at the Cherkassk church. Employed to destroy the institutional presence of the Muscovite church on the Don River, he used the issue of liturgical books to efficiently accomplish this task.

How many dissident priests of this kind existed during the seventeenth century remains unknown, due to incomplete historical evidence.[128] But their potential appeal must have been frightening to the church. Nowhere is this more obvious than in the polemic against the defrocked priest (*izverzhennyi pop*) Nikita Dobrynin, a man who had previously received considerable attention as a supporter of the Old Believer Bishop Aleksandr.

Although there is little documentation of Dobrynin's activities after the Church Council of 1666, there can be no doubt that in 1682 he temporarily emerged from historical obscurity as one of the leaders of a Moscow revolt against Patriarch Ioakim. Unlike the "Pustoozero prisoners," Dobrynin was neither an ascetic, nor a peaceful sufferer who willingly accepted his fate. Indeed, there is evidence that this man, disowned by fellow Old Believers after his multiple recantations at the 1666 Church Council, had turned to drinking.[129] Both church sources and eyewitness accounts identify Dobrynin as an angry rabble-rouser responsible for inciting violence against patriarchal messengers, and for endangering the lives of the highest clergy of Muscovy.[130] Dobrynin mobilized a furious crowd, including large numbers of armed musketeers, to storm the Kremlin. In the ensuing dramatic confrontation documented by several eyewitnesses, Dobrynin severely beat the new archbishop of Kholmogory.[131]

The church, determined to set an example, had Dobrynin beheaded on Red Square.[132] Local ecclesiastical authorities were instructed to warn parish and other priests against following in his footsteps. In 1684, the patriarchal printing press issued a treatise against Dobrynin titled *Speech about the Defrocked Priest Nikita* (*Slovo o izverzhennom pope Nikite*).[133] This text was derived from a manuscript, *Sermon against the Priest Nikita* (*Pouchenie na popa Nikitu*), which had been sent to northern Russian parishes during previous years. Parish priests had to make handwritten copies of the text to read to their parishioners, apparently to prevent them from listening to wandering radical priests.[134]

The church may have overreacted by disseminating these printed warnings. As indicated above, most schismatic priests kept a very low profile. They made their living by quietly tending to the spiritual needs of peasants who maintained little contact with their regular parish priests. There is evidence from the Petrine period that these largely invisible activities did yield some long-term results. For example, peasants from the Kostroma and Nizhnii Novgorod areas, who were accused of schism in 1724, admitted they had been living independent religious lives ever since they had been baptized by itinerant priests who visited their villages. A woman reported that one such priest had made her a nun. Others conceded that schismatic priests had given them communion, and had acted as their confessors.[135] The runaway soldier Varlaam Levin, a notorious schismatic of the Petrine era, was taught by a wandering priest who had once secretly practiced the old liturgies in the household of a powerful boyar.[136] These priests contributed to the emergence of an alternative religious life that centered on the use of old liturgical books.

Still, it would be an exaggeration to speak of an organized schismatic church served by priests who had been expelled from the official church. Most of the priests discussed here influenced only a few individuals. For example, a small number of peasant families from the Vologda district drew on the services of the itinerant priest Akinf'ev, who never became a serious competitor of officially appointed parish priests in the area. Only a handful of priests without parishes were successful in commanding significant local followings, and then, as in the case of Samoil, only for a limited period of time. As a rule, dissident priests were not able to build permanent networks that might have challenged the authority of the established church.[137]

THE FAILURE of seventeenth-century Muscovite priests to assimilate the new books often reflected a crucial ecclesiastical dilemma: the institutional underdevelopment of the Russian Orthodox Church on the local level. Numerous parish priests continued to adhere to the old liturgical rites simply because the message of Nikon's reforms had never reached them. Not surprisingly, one of the principal measures against the schism was the introduction of more systematic ecclesiastical control of parish priests. With the standardization of appointments and increased supervision of priestly behavior, the old liturgies gradually disappeared from most parishes. How long this transitional period may have lasted can be inferred from the example of the northern eparchy of Kholmogory, where, despite rigorous educational efforts, parish priests did not complete their conversion to the new liturgical rites until the early eighteenth century.

There were schismatic priests who were deeply hostile to the church and could not be easily disciplined. Some resented their permanent unemployment; others were alienated because they had been defrocked. A number of established parish priests defended themselves with great force against any attempts to depose them, or reduce their authority. All of these priests committed acts of violence that frightened their contemporaries. They often acted in league with local strongmen, and thus enjoyed considerable protection. From the point of view of the church, the most dangerous schismatics of the seventeenth century were to be found among them.

CHAPTER SIX

Muscovite Lay Society and Dissent

This chapter focuses on two distinctive features of Russian lay dissent that set it apart from dissent in clerical milieux. First, lay dissent was often a highly personal matter of spiritual salvation.[1] Very rarely did members of the laity attempt to assert institutional or local religious autonomy—as was often the case with monks and, to a lesser extent, with parish priests. The cases I discuss here typically involved individuals or families who wanted to live religious lives free from church interference. Second, lay dissent repeatedly entailed—at least in peasant milieux—extreme outbursts of violence, which included the murder of church representatives and group suicides.

Before beginning a detailed discussion of these phenomena, I will briefly outline some characteristics of lay religion during the seventeenth century. Most important is the apparent indifference demonstrated by the average Muscovite toward official ecclesiastical matters. In fact, there is substantial evidence that church attendance was very low during most of the seventeenth century and that a significant number of Muscovites did not take communion, go to confession, or have their children baptized.[2]

Beginning in the 1640s, local church officials and priests were regularly ordered to instruct parishioners in basic Christian behavior. In 1642, for example, the archbishop of Suzdal' issued a memorandum to local supervisors of priests. The memorandum, which was widely disseminated in the eparchy, attributed the cutting of beards, the wearing of make-up, fornication, and other alleged acts of moral degeneration to the failure of laymen to assimilate basic church teachings.[3] During the 1640s and early 1650s, the new tsar, Aleksei Mikhailovich, urgently appealed to priests and town officials to fight lay indifference in church matters. A typical charter addressed to the voevoda of Sviiazhsk contained the following statement:

> It has come to our attention that Christians are living without pastoral fathers in towns, rural settlements (*sela*), and villages. Many die without repentance and do not feel in the least obliged to confess their sins, or to receive the Body and Blood of the Lord.[4]

Such orders continued to be disseminated after Patriarch Nikon's liturgical reforms. The Church Council of 1666 instructed priests to keep written records of baptisms and marriages, and to compile a "book of [all] living parishioners."[5] During subsequent decades, priests actually kept comprehensive lists (*rospisi*) of parishioners who did not attend church services, or failed to come to confession or communion.[6]

Although serious efforts were made to bind Muscovites more closely to their churches, such efforts were not very successful. In 1687, for example, the first archbishop of Ustiug sent a memorandum to his priests complaining that the parishioners of his new eparchy did not know the Lord's Prayer or the Hail Mary, and that few came regularly to confession or paid attention to fasts.[7] This memorandum strongly resembles an order (*nakaz*) in the same year that Metropolitan Kornilii issued at the Novgorod Cathedral. Other similar acts from the 1680s indicate the church's continuing concern with lay behavior, as well as the continuing efforts of many laymen to maintain only a minimum of contact with church representatives.[8]

Since liturgical reforms would have had little effect on the lives of men and women who rarely attended church, what was the nature of lay protests against the new books during the seventeenth century? Should we assume that only regular churchgoers were upset by the new liturgies? Or were there other reasons for lay discontent?

The distribution of documentary evidence in surviving seventeenth-century church archives demonstrates that the overwhelming majority of conflicts between church and society arose from secular matters.[9] The comprehensive archive of the Novgorod House of St. Sophia (*Novgorodskii Sofiiskii dom*), one of the most active church institutions, comprises a huge number of documents relating to taxation, peasant runaways, and land distribution. Other archives contain a large number of petitions requesting secular and religious leaders' interference on behalf of local communities.[10] These petitions, too, demonstrate that issues such as taxation and land ownership generated the most numerous grievances against the church.[11] Information on conflicts over religious issues, however, is scarce.[12]

The predominance of conflicts over economic issues is not so surprising, since the church hierarchy included among its archimandrites and bishops some of the largest landowners of Russia. The archimandrites of the Kirillov Monastery, for example, taxed more than fifty-five hundred peasant households in 1678. The metropolitan of Rostov owned 3,457 households in 1653, and had increased this number to 4,398 by 1700.[13] According to census records from 1678, the patriarch himself was the largest landholder of Muscovy. He held 8,610 households as his personal property, whereas the largest boyar landholders, N. I. Romanov and B. I. Morozov, owned about seven thousand and six thousand households respectively.[14]

If one considers that church leaders were just as inclined to tax their lands as were secular leaders, one can easily understand that financial burdens were a common source of peasant discontent.[15] Other groups also came into conflict with the church over financial matters. For example, northern merchants strongly resented having to compete with large monasteries that paid no trade duties. These merchants' complaints persisted, even after a legal act of 1646 had formally abolished the ancient trading privileges of monasteries. Thus, monasteries continued to dominate the commercial life of the Russian north.[16]

Since the church provoked antagonism by the sheer weight of its economic and financial power, was widespread socioeconomic discontent related to protests against the new liturgical books? Did peasants and merchants unhappy with the taxation of the patriarch, or local bishop, refuse to accept the new liturgies as symbolic expression of their grievances? Was the murder of clerics by schismatic peasants also an act of revolt against economic policies?

In my examination of urban milieux I find that social and economic grievances had little influence on dissenters: urban dissent was usually a personal religious affair and involved isolated individuals. The same was generally true for the countryside: peasant schismatics—with the notable exception of peasant rebels and brigands—were inspired by intense spiritual feelings not shared by others in their environment.

TOWNS AND MERCHANT COLONIES

After the Church Council of 1666, religious dissent in Muscovy's towns received serious scrutiny. Church historians, both Western and those of prerevolutionary Russia, have tended to perceive urban dissent as an extension of what they called the Old Believer movement. A few Soviet scholars, most notably Aleksandr I. Klibanov, must be credited with drawing attention to urban radicals who clearly had no association with Old Believers.[17] Still, Marxist predispositions have led Klibanov and others to generalizations about the progressive role of such dissident traders and craftsmen in the class struggle of burghers against the dominant feudal order.[18] Traditional scholarship has not addressed urban manifestations of the schism on their own terms. As a result, this form of religious dissent has either been overlooked, or reduced to reflections of underlying socioeconomic grievances.

My research indicates that dissent in the towns and trading colonies of Muscovy differed significantly from other manifestations of the schism. In this milieu we are dealing almost exclusively with personal religious activities ranging from the study of the Scriptures and liturgical books to the assumption of traditional clerical roles such as preaching and baptism. Unlike the vast majority of their lay contemporaries, these dissenters focused on spiritual issues and questions of salvation. Not surprisingly, they were often isolated and drew inspiration from outside sources, e.g. Protestant ideas gleaned from Western traders or pamphlets.

Inhabitants of Muscovy's trading settlements were no doubt among the first to accept the religious message of Old Belief preachers like Avvakum. One of these was Ivan Trifonov from the Moscow trading colony. On the eve of the Church Council of 1666, Trifonov read and circulated one of the first polemic texts against the new sign of the cross. The manuscript, which had been in his possession for some time before it was confiscated, bore evidence of much use: it contained several marginal glosses in different handwriting, indicating Trifonov had discussed the contents with others.[19] The fact that small conventicles of Moscow traders met under the auspices of Old Believers can be reconstructed from the testimony of Avvakum's friend, deacon Fedor Ivanov. The deacon counted among his allies a handful of men, such as Trifonov, who gathered regularly in the secrecy of their homes to "read sacred books."[20]

Trifonov's sustained interest in liturgical matters may have been exceptional. Although Old Believers preached in urban settings, they received only sporadic and short-lived attention.[21] For example, during his reprieve from exile in the summer of 1664, Avvakum attracted a number of adherents in the suburbs of Moscow; one documentary source implies that he had considerable support in the trading colony of Sadovniki.[22] However, this interest may have been due more to his charismatic presence—and his being a victim of official authority—than to his message. After Avvakum was re-arrested and deported to Mezen' in northern Russia, his influence quickly dissipated. According to Andrei Samoilov, one of Avvakum's few remaining friends, a considerable number of traders and craftsmen—Samoilov mentions eighty—forgot the preacher as soon as their parish priests instructed them to use the new books and the new sign of the cross.[23]

Another example suggests the limits of urban support for Old Believers. On the eve of the Church Council of 1666, the preacher Neronov was approached by several members of the Vologda trading colony. Far from being interested in his thoughts on liturgical questions, they had come to complain about the misdeeds of the local bishop.[24] One reason they brought their complaints to Neronov was that he was also known to have been a victim of the bishop. Originally from the area, Neronov had established ties with Vologda craftsmen and artisans when he hired them to rebuild his monastery, the Ignat'eva Hermitage.[25]

There is some evidence that writings of the first Old Believers continued to reach urban milieux even after their arrest and exile.[26] But to a large extent, the roots of dissent in the towns of Russia must be attributed to other factors. The following cases, in which Old Belief preachers play no discernible role, reveal more typical patterns of religious dissent in the towns of late Muscovy.

A court case that received considerable attention in connection with the Church Council of 1666 targeted the merchant Feodul Ivanov from the Kostroma trading colony.[27] Feodul, who specialized in millstones, had not been to church services since the town of Kostroma was devastated by pestilence in 1654.[28] Feodul had kept to himself, refused to go to confession and, at some point, taken up preaching in the community. A note in the patriarchal archive gives the following account:

> He says about the holy churches that there is no Church of God; and he teaches many simple people not to see the divine and holy life-giving sacraments as holy mysteries, but as ordinary bread and wine. And about his person he claims that he has in himself the living power of the Holy Spirit who gives him the authority to preach and teach. Many witnesses, priests and others, testify to this. Also, he says dishonorable things about priests.[29]

Even though Feodul was explicitly tried and punished for schism, his thinking was quite different from that of Old Believer followers, who gathered in homes to study liturgical books. In all likelihood Feodul saw no reason to use *any* church books, old or new, after his religious conversion. He relied on an internal voice that he considered to be the Holy Spirit. In this respect, he can be compared to spiritualist prophets from the West, such as Sebastian Franck and Kaspar Schwenckfeld.[30]

Radical religious ideas, such as those propagated by Feodul Ivanov, existed in other trading settlements of Muscovy as well. In 1651, a parish priest from the trading post of Viatka bragged about disciplining a local woman who claimed to have visions of God.[31] A resident of the small town of Staritsa on the Volga River was accused in 1689 of having called himself God.[32] A man from Pskov attracted great attention in the town of Izborsk when he ran naked into the market square, apparently in a frenzy, holding a smashed icon of the Mother of God. He later insisted he had acted while out of his mind (*v zabytii uma*), and did not recall giving "indecent speeches about the Holy Patriarch Ioasaf."[33]

Other cases of urban dissent reflect the influence of Western ideas. One such case involved the mystical preacher Quirin Kuhlmann, who was burned at the stake in 1689. Kuhlmann had moved from his native Silesia to the German suburb (*nemetskaia sloboda*) of Moscow by invitation of its residents. Throughout his stay in Moscow, he maintained close relationships with Russian merchants, whom he must certainly have told about his exchange of letters with eminent Protestant theologians at the universities of Helmstedt, Rostock, and Lübeck.[34]

As Kuhlmann's case suggests, the influence of radical Protestant teachings on some of the individuals discussed here may have come via contacts with displaced Western preachers. This impression is further supported by the circulation of works by German spiritualists and mystics, such as Jacob Boehme, in merchant milieux.[35] The above-mentioned radical, Feodul of Kostroma, probably acquired his ideas in this way.

On the eve of the Church Council of 1666, Isidor Kriuchkov from Kolomna was arrested and questioned for lapsing into schism. Kriuchkov was accused of writing apocalyptic "threats" (*grozy*) with charcoal on church walls. He was seized after he had dropped a handwritten pamphlet (*tetrad'*) in the Kolomna vegetable market (*ovoshchnoi riad*) in which he predicted the end of the world in the year 1670.[36] A copy of this pamphlet has survived thanks to the efforts of a zealous local parish priest, who made it his mission to fight Kriuchkov's deviant behavior.[37]

The text provides further insight into the psychological world of urban radicals, and illustrates, in particular, that their primary concern was not the revision of liturgical books. Kriuchkov referred to two Italian mendicant monks in the Sicilian city of Palermo (*Polimitarskii grad*) who had recently heralded the imminent end of the world. These monks, claiming to be messengers of God, preached that divine wrath was about to destroy the universe according to the following apocalyptic scenario:

In 1666, Africa will burn and rivers of blood will flow; in 1667, a great man will arise. In 1668, Europe and Africa will shiver with fear (*trepetat'*), and during the year 1669, the One and Triune God will reveal himself throughout the entire universe. And in 1670, the lights of Heaven will go out, and there will be only one flock and one shepherd. The Day of Reckoning will come and the Judge will pass judgment on each according to his affairs.[38]

How did Kriuchkov learn about this eschatological prophesy circulating in Italy? It is likely that he had copied a Russian translation of a foreign pamphlet containing the monks' prophesy. Supporting this hypothesis, we find at the top of the pamphlet a note stating that the original had been sent by a burgher of Palermo to the vice-regent of Hungary (*Ukharskiia zemli podkoroliu*). Kriuchkov may have received the pamphlet from a merchant who had been in Hungary and in some way acquired, and possibly also translated, the original leaflet.[39]

The contribution of foreign pamphlets and broadsheets—in particular, those issued by the printing presses of the Protestant duchies and cities of Germany—to religious radicalism in Muscovy's trading colonies is suggested by the following undated instruction issued by Patriarch Ioakim sometime during the last quarter of the seventeenth century:

Traders buy leaflets (*listy na bumage*) that have been printed in the German lands and sell them, even though they have been issued by the German heretics, those Luthers and Calvins. They do so because they have savagely and falsely formed their own damned opinion [on faith] ridiculing the [true] Christians. . . . Orders should be given to heralds . . . to proclaim that German heretical pamphlets must no longer be bought and sold in the market rows along the crossroads.[40]

While Ioakim was specifically referring to foreign depictions of saints and their destructive influence on Muscovite icon painting, one may assume that texts such as those in Kriuchkov's possession also circulated in Muscovy's marketplaces.[41]

During the 1680s, a letter written by the townsman (*posadskii chelovek*) Ivan Sidorov from Voronezh fell into the hands of the Foreign Office in Moscow. The letter expressed the following convictions:

The Lord God and Our Savior Jesus Christ will appear in [our] time. . . . Only five years of our earthly existence are left, and during these years God will come with great glory and in hosts of angels . . . [to fight] against the Antichrist and his supporters,[. . .]the proud apostates, persecutors and . . . bloodthirsty tormentors. In His righteous anger, He will exact double retribution . . . and drive the impious from the earth and eliminate all untruth. . . . He will reestablish His Kingdom where He will reign in all eternity with His entire Heavenly Host, and with all His saints and those who please Him. . . . [42]

Here again we may be dealing with influences from a non-Orthodox source. Other passages from Sidorov's letter elucidate the influence of Protestant apocalyptic ideas. For example, Sidorov asserted that God could be experienced with a "clean heart" (*chistym serdtsem*), a notion familiar from Western spiritualist tracts such as the *Theologia Deutsch*.[43] And Sidorov's conviction that anyone could be called to preach, or to interpret the Scriptures, bears a clear resemblance to Luther's notion of the priesthood of all believers.[44] The likelihood of such influences is stronger because Sidorov fled Russia and lived abroad during the patriarchate of Nikon. While we do not know exactly where he lived, he probably crossed the border into Ukraine, where southern Russian merchants had numerous contacts.[45]

In the early 1680s, Patriarch Ioakim issued a warning to church officials that many preachers were promising the imminent Second Coming of Christ.[46] One of these preachers was Koz'ma Kosoi, a blacksmith (*kuznets*) from the trading colony of Elets. Kosoi's case is noteworthy because he was condemned not only by the church, but also by itinerant monks who advocated use of the old liturgical books.

Muscovite officials learned about Kosoi when they confiscated liturgical and other church books in the possession of a wandering monk. Hidden among these books, they discovered a letter (*pis'mo*) addressed to "the monk Makarii and all the monks living on the Don River." The letter, briefly summarized by a secretary of the Foreign Office, was a warning from monks in Moscow to beware of the teachings promulgated by "a certain man, called Koz'ma." While we do not know much about the letter writers, they clearly viewed Kosoi as an outsider, and his teachings as a dangerous aberration from Christian doctrine.[47]

At some point the letter writers had met and interrogated Kosoi:

We questioned him [Koz'ma] many times about [his teachings]: "Who has spread this wisdom? Has it been handed down from the times of the saints, or endorsed by some church councils?" The arrogant Koz'ma was unable to cite the least evidence from the divine Scriptures. But he relied on deceived reason (*prelshchennyi razum*) and it was clear that he had thought it out by himself, and that it had nothing in common with the Holy Fathers. He is immensely haughty (*kichit bez mery*) and denigrates [everyone] . . . while setting himself up as great and knowing great secrets that have been revealed to him. . . . But he always says alien things and calls theological thinking a lot of cerebral nonsense (*premudrost'*) . . . insisting: "I own the original text (*podlinnik*) that God himself wrote with his own finger before the creation of the world and the building of the universe. Based on this text, I have written these pamphlets."[48]

The monks, who obviously knew much more about Orthodox doctrine than Kosoi, finally let the self-declared prophet go. Unfortunately, they did not deem it necessary to copy his pamphlets (*listy*), and burned them instead.[49]

A central tenet of Kosoi's belief was his claim to know when the world would come to an end. The monks recorded: "The ne'er-do-well (*bezdel'nik*) insists that he knows exactly when the last day and hour will be. He says that he does not care for the divine words of Christ in this matter, because . . . God kept things secret from the Apostles by simply not telling them."[50]

Following his arrest in 1687, Kosoi was interrogated at the Foreign Office in Moscow. There, the preacher proclaimed the imminent appearance of Great Prince Mikhail, whom he may have associated with the first Romanov tsar. The resurrected Tsar Mikhail was to convince the two present tsars of Muscovy, the brothers Ivan and Peter Alekseevich, to cleanse the universe of the infidels (*nevernye*). The Cossacks were to come to the aid of the tsars, killing those who would not join them.[51] In short, anyone opposed to Kosoi's apocalyptic teachings was to be slaughtered.

How did Kosoi arrive at this interpretation of seventeenth-century church life? He told his interrogators that he regularly studied the Bible, especially such apocalyptic texts as the prophesy of Daniel.[52] Presumably he formed his own opinions on religious matters without relying on the authority of priests or monks. We may also infer the influence of Protestant thinking: Kosoi's prophesy had much in common with the chiliastic teachings of radical preachers in the West, such as the Taborites and Thomas Müntzer. The myth of the risen Emperor and an avenging divine law played important roles in the religious utopias of such Western prophets.[53]

Judging from the concern of Muscovite officials, who compared Kosoi to the rebel leader Stepan Razin and tortured him more brutally than other schismatics, we may assume that he enjoyed considerable support among the Cossacks. This is not surprising, since the Cossacks used other preachers (for example, the aforementioned priest Samoil) to push their political independence from Moscow.[54] But did Kosoi leave any significant imprint on social or religious behavior in Moscow, where he lived temporarily, or in Elets, his hometown? The evidence indicates that he attracted only a small number of followers from a very specific milieu.

Kosoi was most successful within his immediate family. One of his brothers was burned at the stake in Moscow during the 1670s for advocating heretical ideas. Another brother, Demian, was probably a defrocked parish priest from Moscow or Elets and accompanied Kosoi to the Don to preach among the Cossacks. We also know that Kosoi formed tightly knit religious communities of "brothers and sisters," some of whom had withdrawn into the southern mountains to await the end of time.[55] Kosoi's only surviving letter addresses these men and women as his "dearly beloved" (*liubimtsy*), and asks for their blessings and prayers. These communities included an unknown number of relatives (*srodniki*), and probably also his wife.[56]

Other historical evidence suggests that lay dissenters who lived and preached in urban environments remained social outsiders. For example, Semen Smol'ianov, a town dweller from Murom, was repeatedly investigated for schism during the 1680s by officials of the Riazan' metropolitanate. Semen was apparently perceived as an odd, lone figure who set a bad example by not going to communion and confession. Since the bishop did not expel him from the community, he was clearly not seen as a threat. In fact, it appears that his behavior was viewed with less alarm than another Murom resident's denunciation of the tsar during the early 1660s.[57] Supervision of Semen's religious behavior and, in particular, regular church attendance, was entrusted to his neighbors and professional colleagues. In 1689, they signed a written pledge (*poruchnaia zapis'*) "that [Semen] . . . would no longer be a schismatic in the divine Scriptures."[58]

In other towns, the situation was similar. There are indications that a few isolated dissenters may have lived in the trading colonies of Suzdal', Vladimir, Iaroslavl', and Vologda.[59] These men led alternative religious lives in the privacy of their own homes, but convinced few others to emulate their behavior. Some of them came to the attention of church officials when they left their homes to live in the forests. For example, in 1675 the bishop of Viatka captured the itinerant preachers Simon Strel'nikov and Pron'ka Batashev, who had gathered a conventicle of eight followers.[60] A handful of schismatics from the town of Romanov attracted attention when they hired two widowed priests to say Mass in their homes. Stepan Chernoi, their leader, stunned church officials with his radical acts: on one occasion, he walked into the cathedral and "took a piece of blessed bread (*antidor*), chewed it in his mouth, and spat it on the floor."[61]

Evidence from the Moscow suburbs documents that a small number of craftsmen sympathized with the defenders of the old liturgies. One was the blacksmith Iosif Savel'nik, who gave refuge to wandering preachers in his home.⁶² In the town of Nizhnii Novgorod, a handful of local merchants may have shown sympathy for dissenting ideas; the salt merchant Mikhail Evdokimov attracted official attention after a friend had taught him about the apocalypse.⁶³ Merchants were probably also responsible for the growing trade in old liturgical books in both Nizhnii Novgorod and Moscow, although there is no evidence they were fervent believers. Most likely they saw an opportunity for making a profit, since the hidden monasteries of the forests always needed these books.⁶⁴

There were two important exceptions to the social isolation of urban dissenters, which can be documented for most towns of Muscovy. Lay preachers in the towns of Pskov and Novgorod seem to have attracted significant followings. This anomaly is all the more striking since other northern towns of similar size such as Kholmogory,⁶⁵ Olonets,⁶⁶ Kargopol',⁶⁷ and Arkhangel'sk⁶⁸ conformed to the prevalent pattern.

The preacher and merchant Ivan Merkur'ev represented a powerful spiritual authority in his hometown of Pskov. He baptized an unknown number of children, both newborns and some who had already been christened by an official priest. Pavel Kornyshev and the miller Kirka were among his admirers, and invited him to their homes to christen their infant daughters. Merkur'ev conducted the baptismal ceremony "according to an old Book of Needs" in the presence of family members. Many others came to him for confession, among them Aleksei Anisimov and his wife. Merkur'ev offered spiritual consultations and conducted an unspecified number of burials.⁶⁹ He thus assumed sacramental and confessional roles that the Muscovite church allowed only its priests to perform, and in fact, replaced priests for a number of local inhabitants.

Merkur'ev inspired a small number of other preachers to follow in his footsteps. Gerasim Pavlov, who had apparently been taught by Merkur'ev, proudly gave church investigators a long list of craftsmen and artisans who had hired him to baptize and bless their children.⁷⁰ Described by his interrogators as a "great talker" (*velikii slovesnik*), Pavlov bragged during his confession that many Pskovians had fled into the forests as a result of his preaching.⁷¹ Several years later, another of Merkur'ev's students, the trader Semen Menshikov, wielded significant influence in Pskov; local church leaders compared him to Nikita Dobrynin, the above-mentioned Old Believer priest who seemed more frightening to the church than any other seventeenth-century dissenter.⁷²

In the absence of sufficient data, we can only speculate about what inspired Pskovians to seek out Merkur'ev and his students instead of their parish priests. There is some evidence that tensions with the church may have run higher in the town of Pskov and its environs than in other urban areas. Archbishop Arsenii of Pskov complained in 1667 that local parishioners refused to pay their church taxes. His successor, Metropolitan Markell, later wrote to Moscow that he had serious difficulties exerting spiritual control over his parishes. In 1683, local insurgents demanded that church leaders and priests limit the ringing of church bells on pain of death. And ten years later, Pskovians complained bitterly to the patriarch about the church overtaxing them.[73] Merkur'ev and his supporters may thus have profited from these strong anti-church sentiments.

Although Merkur'ev enjoyed considerable local power, there is no indication that he used his power to attack the established social or political order. He had learned apocalyptic ideas from his father, who was convinced that the revision of liturgical books had destroyed the old Muscovite religion. During the 1680s, Merkur'ev began teaching his father's ideas to others. His first followers included a trader of foreign descent (*inozemets*), Martin Kuz'min, and two musketeers, one of whom—judging by his unusual name, Vasko Shlan—may also have been a foreigner. The four met regularly to read and discuss the apocalypse. They speculated about the return of Tsar Mikhail—as did the radical Kosoi—but without threatening vengeance, or predicting political turmoil.[74]

The second anomalous occurrence of urban dissent was recorded in Novgorod. There, the religious landscape was controlled to an even greater degree than in Pskov by merchants who began usurping the spiritual authority of the clergy. In fact, Metropolitan Kornilii sent an urgent appeal to Patriarch Ioakim during the early 1680s requesting help to break their power.[75]

Ivan Dement'ev, one of the most visible of these merchants, grew up in the trading town of Velikie Luki, located on the road between Pskov and Vitebsk not far from the Lithuanian border. His father had brought him from the Polish-Lithuanian Commonwealth to Muscovy upon entering the service of the tsar. The early death of Dement'ev's parents not only thrust him into poverty, but may also have led him to develop strong religious sentiments. After aimless wanderings, he found refuge with a relative in the Merchant Quarter (*torgovaia storona*) of Novgorod. He began selling loaves of white bread (*kalachi*), and also worked as a miller. He must have succeeded in business because he soon acquired enough leisure time to study books—among them the gospel, the works of church fathers, and Lectionaries (*prologi*). Dement'ev insisted that he had taken to heart (*vnimal sebe v razum*) everything he read during this intense study period.[76]

At some point during the early 1670s, Dement'ev became convinced that he had to teach other Novgorod merchants and craftsmen about the degeneration of the old religion. Some of the men and women interrogated after his arrest recalled that he had read to them in their homes from books "many times" (*po mnogie vremena*).[77] Since he could refute arguments and adduce evidence for his claims, he must have seemed an impressive religious authority to the families he visited. Considering his wealth, his learning, and his friendship—albeit short-lived—with the voevoda, it is easy to understand his local following.[78] Dement'ev soon commanded an extended underground network of alternative religious life. He moved from house to house, educating his disciples and baptizing (or rebaptizing) as many children as possible. Eventually he gave up his business to become a full-time teacher and preacher.[79]

Other Novgorodian merchants displayed a similar religious independence. Iakov Kalashnikov, who also traded in bread and with whom Dement'ev had stayed on various occasions, was convinced that priests were unworthy of holy orders (*ne iskusny*) because they spent their time in taverns getting drunk. He consequently refused to have anything to do with them.[80] The merchant Semen Gavrilov and his son, Ivan, were largely responsible for the local dissemination of pamphlets (*tetradi*) regarded as schismatic by the church. We do not know the contents of these pamphlets, but it seems the Gavrilovs shared Dement'ev's conviction that the world would come to an end in 1692. Considering that the Gavrilovs were powerful enough to convince a highly placed clerk in the metropolitan's household to copy their texts, their influence in the community must have been significant.[81]

These Novgorod examples confirm that dissent in urban milieux was largely a religious affair. But why were Novgorodians apparently so much more willing to assert their religious autonomy than were town dwellers of other areas? One explanation is suggested by the investigations that followed Dementev's arrest in 1683: some of the schismatics had, at one point in their lives, been in neighboring Swedish territory. For example, the merchant Semen Gavrilov traded regularly with Swedish partners.[82] The trader Vasilii Rukavichnik was captured in the forest in the company of a Russian who had lived in territory under Swedish domination.[83] One dissenter even sought the protection of the Swedish Crown, and the tsar had written to the King of Sweden in order to retrieve him.[84] This orientation toward Sweden had not escaped the attention of Metropolitan Nikon, who warned the tsar during the late 1640s that the inhabitants of Novgorod were on the verge of seceding from the Muscovite state.[85]

The religious fervor of Novgorodian and Pskovian merchants had much in common with the ideas advocated by lone preachers in other Muscovite towns and trading settlements. All of these individuals were guided by strong religious convictions, and in particular, by apocalyptic visions that may have been influenced by contacts with the Protestant West. But whereas wealthy merchants such as Dement'ev remained moderate educators, craftsmen—Kosoi, Kriuchkov, and others—became much more radical. With their frightening end time predictions, they called for the destruction of their enemies. One of these enemies, incidentally, was the Old Believer Avvakum, who denounced these prophets as dangerous heretics.[86]

Rather than comparing urban schismatics to Avvakum or other clerical critics of the new books, one would do better to consider parallels with their well-documented Western counterparts. Some of these schismatics resemble the self-proclaimed radicals and "masterless" artisans who roamed the streets of London and other English cities during the seventeenth century. Dement'ev and other merchants recall the heresiarch Waldes from Lyons, who gave up his considerable wealth to found a movement of spiritual renewal. The men who sat in their homes critically reviewing liturgical texts may be compared to the Italian miller Menocchio, who formed his own religious opinions through voracious reading.[87] Thus, religious dissent in Muscovy's trading colonies can be understood as a distinctly urban development that was by no means limited to Russia.

VILLAGES AND PEASANT HINTERLANDS

Rural dissent produced one response not found in other milieux: protests against the new books could assume the violent forms of social banditry and revolt. While Soviet interpretations attribute much of the Russian Schism to revolts of the oppressed peasantry, I maintain that the combination of religious dissent and social violence, though distinctive, occurred relatively rarely. In most parts of Muscovy, personal concerns of faith and salvation were the primary motivations for peasant dissenters. When violence did occur, it was only among the well-to-do and independent peasantry of northern Russia and western Siberia; I have not found examples among peasants of other regions, where either serfdom or tighter institutional controls existed.[88]

In April 1695, one of the most peculiar episodes of the Russian Schism came to the attention of officials in the northern frontier town of Olonets.[89] It was learned that Terentii, a peasant from the forest village of Ek, was torturing his wife Marfuta because—as the officials put it—"she would not go into the schism (*v raskol ne idet*) with her husband." Marfuta's mother testified that Terentii "had broken her [daughter's] right arm and severely bruised her breasts," and that he was about to break her legs in order to kidnap her. Soon afterward, this testimony was corroborated by interrogation and by inspection of the victim.[90]

Before his marriage to Marfuta, Terentii had lived with other schismatics in the dense forests around Lake Onega. Terentii and his friends, who also came from the immediate vicinity of the lake, soon became notorious for their interference with local life. They regularly emerged from their secret hideouts (*pristanishcha*) for forays into surrounding villages to seize food and other supplies by force. Occasionally they tried to persuade others to join them, and apparently resorted to coercion if they were refused. They once took a parish priest from the village of Kuzaran, for example, a spectacular act that attracted considerable local attention.[91]

At some point Terentii had left the schismatics and moved back to his home village. He married Marfuta, after having repeatedly promised both her and her mother that he was no longer interested in being a schismatic and that he would forget his former friends. But no sooner had Terentii settled down to a normal life than his past caught up with him. One day a man named Mitrofan, the leader of the schismatics with whom Terentii had previously lived, knocked at the door. He demanded that Terentii immediately return with him "into the schism" (*v raskol ego zval*). We do not know what transpired, but it appears that Terentii was sufficiently intimidated that he decided to return to the forest—a decision that brought him into severe conflict with his new wife.[92]

Who was Mitrofan, and what was his purpose in recruiting local peasants? Perhaps genuinely inspired by doubts about the revision of books, he and his followers insisted on using the old liturgical books, old hosts, and the two-finger sign of the cross.[93] At the same time, they continued to intimidate and rob local villagers, and no one dared oppose them. Violence, and not religion, seems to have been the foundation of this peasant dissenting community. Religion was a means to an end, in this case, a means to exercise control over the villagers.

In order to understand this peculiar fusion of religion and violence, we need to look further at peasant life on Lake Onega. The peasants on the shores of Lake Onega had developed a strong sense of independence. Freedom from feudal obligations and unregulated working conditions in trade and fishing had provided them good incomes and control over their own community affairs.[94] During the 1660s and 1670s, however, age-old autonomies came under serious attack.[95] A collective petition to the tsar dated May 1677 allows us to observe the growth of local discontent. In particular, the Onega peasants were unhappy about the introduction of random taxation and military service, developments that can be explained by the fortification of the nearby town of Olonets after the Peace of Stolbovo in 1649.[96] High on the list were also complaints about the intrusion of powerful monasteries—some as far away as Moscow and Novgorod—into local economic affairs:

> They have arbitrarily seized our, your orphans', lands, waters, fishing grounds, virgin forest, and all conceivable assets . . . many envoys from Moscow and Novgorod the Great, who are accompanied by numerous musketeers, pass through our districts and villages. They eat and drink in our houses with great rage at the expense of our entire community, and force us to supply them with many foodstuffs, fish, meats, chicken, sheep, and eggs. And, in addition, they take away many of our carts.[97]

Soon after this petition reached the tsar, officials protected by musketeers again made their way into the Pogost settlements of Lake Onega. This time, they encountered great hostility; by 1678, the Pogost of Tolvui was in open revolt.[98] Peasant attacks on the local Paleostrov Monastery attracted even greater attention in Moscow. I will take a careful look at this rebellion because the peasant insurgents who seized and destroyed the monastery were considered to be dangerous schismatics.

I have already observed that deacon Ignatii's preaching led to the first attack on the monastery in 1687.[99] The next attack occurred less than two years later under the leadership of Ignatii's student, Emel'ian Ivanov Vtorogo, who was supported by peasant strongmen from Tolvui and other Onega settlements. Vtorogo was a trader, but he was of peasant stock and his family came from the Pogost of Shunga.[100] Even though he had moved to the town of Povenets he spent much of his time on Lake Onega, where he was seen repeatedly in villages of the rebellious Tolvui Pogost. In September 1688, unconfirmed rumors reached the tsar that Vtorogo had gathered "an ugly gang" (*skvernoe soborishche*) in the forests behind Lake Onega, and that these brigands had seized the Paleostrov Monastery.[101]

What occurred at the monastery very strongly suggests peasant rebels taking revenge, rather than religious insurgents destroying the new liturgical order. As soon as the monastery had been seized, the occupiers began to systematically destroy everything of value: the mills (*zavody*), monastic buildings and cells, the small monastic village, barns with hay and food, and finally, the church building. When the church went up in flames, the rebels grabbed the abbot and his brethren, tied them up, and threw them into the fire.[102] Total devastation of the monastery resulted from an extreme outburst of violence that was unprecedented in the history of the Russian Schism.

How can the fury of the rebels be explained? I believe the answer lies in the grievances articulated in 1677. We know that the Paleostrov Monastery had traditionally owned the best timber, most fertile soils, and most lucrative fisheries in the area, and that the monks had expanded these holdings—at the expense of local peasants—during the seventeenth century. Anger over the Paleostrov monks' economic ambitions was compounded by the efforts of monasteries outside the area to enrich themselves locally. When the peasants took matters into their own hands, the Paleostrov monks became the obvious scapegoats. It was many weeks before the rebels were finally driven out of the monastery. After brutal exchanges of gunfire, which left many musketeers and rebels dead, the surviving insurgents withdrew into the forests.[103]

Soon the area around Lake Onega became infested with armed bands of schismatics, and several violent incidents were reported. For example, Misha, the son of a local parish priest, reported that his first wife had been kidnapped in the middle of the night by schismatic brigands. She had vanished into the forests beyond Lake Onega, and Misha had since remarried.[104] Misha described another visit by the same brigands:

> They came to the house of [my] father during the night while [I] was gone. [They were] the same brigands and schismatics, unknown people with guns . . . and began to break into [our] house in order to rob [us] (*dlia grabezha*). And [my] father, the priest Mark, fled through the back gate to the belfry and began to ring the alarm bell. People came running from surrounding villages and the brigands withdrew from our courtyard to the lake, shooting at us with their guns.[105]

Several weeks later, the brigands returned for the priest Mark and his son, Misha. The attackers were apparently prevented by Mark's parishioners from drowning him in the lake and taking Misha, who had been tied up, into the forest.[106] There is no evidence, however, that the attack was provoked by Mark's use of the new liturgies. Indeed, the brigands took along new liturgical books and utensils as booty—an occurrence that was repeated in another deadly attack on one of Mark's colleagues at a neighboring Pogost. Other schismatics destroyed new liturgical books, but these peasant outlaws plundered whatever fell into their hands: it apparently did not matter whether they seized a rifle, or a new Psalter.[107]

The Onega parish priests represented a threat because they did not hesitate to denounce escaped peasant rebels and brigands to official authorities.[108] Priests often risked their lives to deliver denunciations, but it is likely that in so doing, they acted on behalf of their parishioners.[109] One witness told investigators that many parishioners were unhappy "because their lives had been made difficult by the schismatics (*ot raskol'nikov zhit'e khudo*)."[110] The determination of one courageous local peasant, who shot it out with the dissenters rather than give them his land, appears to have been the exception rather than the rule; most peasants were intimidated by the armed rebel patrols that regularly appeared in their villages.[111]

I conclude that the initial motivation for the use of violence by Onega peasant schismatics was purely economic. But after their defeat at Paleostrov, they continued to use violence to intimidate priests and instill fear in the community. How, then, did the peasants on Lake Onega differ from peasants who used violence against the church and its representatives, but were *not* accused as schismatics? I will now consider several such episodes in order to illustrate the broader context of seventeenth-century anti-church violence.

During the 1620s, patriarchal officials noted acts of hostility directed against the bishop of Kolomna and the pillaging of church buildings in the southern town of Kozlov. In 1626, the murder of the patriarchal official Vasilii Podlesov in the vicinity of Vladimir by his own peasants attracted attention at the tsar's court. The Spaso-Evfimiev Monastery at Suzdal' reported the beating of monks and the destruction of an entire monastic village by local peasants. Another monastery, located in the Beloozero district, indicated that peasants had attacked one of its priests, and that robbers made its hinterlands dangerous. Tsar Aleksei Mikhailovich received repeated complaints about thefts from churches.[112]

In 1676, the archimandrite of the Trifonov Monastery in Viatka complained that the peasants Il'ia Rukhin and Nikifor Pervunin had gathered an armed band, and seized a local monastic cell and village.[113] The band destroyed the cell and tortured the monk in charge so severely that he nearly died. Monastic peasants and servants who refused to cooperate with the rebels suffered the same fate. Soon the rebels had the village and environs under firm control: armed sentries patrolled the area, and rebel leaders governed local affairs.[114] Most importantly, they robbed the priest, beat him, locked him out of the church building, and eventually expelled him from the community. The villagers were understandably very angry, but could do nothing in the face of deadly force. After the insurgents had left, their victims called them "apostates from the Orthodox Christian faith" (*otmetniki khristianskoi pravoslavnoi very*).[115]

The full extent of anti-ecclesiastical violence perpetrated by peasants and the regional distribution of such violence during the seventeenth century remains unexplored, but there can be no doubt that peasants demonstrated a remarkable willingness to use force against the church. The only difference between such anti-ecclesiastical acts and the behavior of the Onega schismatics appears to have been the latter's refusal to use new liturgical books. A look at a similar case from Siberia reveals how the rhetoric against the new liturgical books may have entered the minds of the Onega rebels.

During the late 1680s, Moscow church officials learned about the immolation of a crowded parish church in the Siberian village of Kamenka, located not far from the town of Tiumen'. On Easter Sunday of 1687, about four hundred peasants from several villages had gathered to celebrate in the Kamenka church, which was the spiritual center of a far-flung parish. The overcrowded church building had suddenly gone up in flames in the middle of the Mass. The fire spread so rapidly that the exit was obstructed and everyone was trapped inside. Panic broke out. Many who were not burned or suffocated were trampled to death, or died when they attempted to jump out of the windows. An investigation revealed that peasant schismatics had been the arsonists: they had spread powder (*porokh*) underneath the church building and then lit it.[116]

Who were these schismatics, and what incited them to this act of violence? We do not know for certain, but there appear to be some similarities to the outbreak of dissent on Lake Onega. Soon after this incident, officials heard that peasant dissenters, armed with all kinds of weapons, had barricaded themselves on Iosif Reshetnikov's farm, located in the Tiumen' district not far from Kamenka. According to contemporary estimates, there were approximately three hundred men, women, and children in the fortified compound. A band of forty to fifty heavily armed fighters regularly left the compound to rob and assault travelers on the main highway through the district. Other peasants in the area, who had apparently been beaten and robbed, appealed for protection.[117]

There is evidence that Reshetnikov's hopeless military stand was inspired by a peculiar mixture of social and religious despair. Reshetnikov and his father, Pakhomii, had once been affluent and independent peasants. One day, officials of the metropolitan of Tobol'sk had appeared and attempted to requisition a significant portion of their crops. Father and son refused to yield, determined to resist any military effort to remove their grain supplies. Claiming their lives would be ruined, they insisted they would prefer to burn their own fields rather than give in. They even threatened to burn the town of Tiumen' and destroy the local grain supplies.[118]

With their livelihood endangered, these men had also become strongly opposed to the new liturgical books. Metropolitan Pavel of Tobol'sk observed that Reshetnikov and his followers "were defaming the Church of God and the Holy Council of Prelates (*osviashchennyi sobor*) by making many indecent speeches that cannot possibly be committed to writing."[119] The metropolitan discerned, however, what was in all likelihood the source of the peasants' religious radicalism: two runaway monks, (one of them a rough-looking character with his ear cut off), who were living in Reshetnikov's compound.[120]

Thus, "normal" peasant revolts could apparently turn into revolts against the new liturgical order if peasants had contact with dislocated clerics. On Lake Onega, the defrocked deacon Ignatii (and possibly other priests as well) may have planted the seeds of religious dissent, though this is not conclusively documented. In western Siberia, one can clearly identify itinerant monks as the source of peasant discontent with the new liturgies. It is therefore likely that violent outbreaks of liturgical dissent occurred only if two conditions were met: first, the lives of well-to-do and traditionally independent peasants were suddenly shattered by the drastic economic interference of church authority; and second, there were radical clerics present who preached their own views on church and religion.[121]

Similar incidents of violence and destruction can be documented for other northern and Siberian locales.[122] Furthermore, there appears to be considerable correlation between outbursts of anti-church violence and another scenario of dissident violence: the group suicides of peasants. A look at the regional and temporal distribution of such suicides reveals that most occurred in northern Russia and Siberia beginning in the 1680s.[123] Of these, at least four cases were documented in the area around Lake Onega, that is, in the same milieu that generated violent attacks on churchmen.[124] The most spectacular case involved a series of suicides that resulted in the deaths of at least eight hundred people. I turn now to a more detailed discussion of the background of this case.

During the summer of 1693, a band of schismatic peasants accompanied by several monks emerged from the woods and attacked the settlement of Pudozh. They plundered most of the peasant homesteads and physically abused the two parish priests. After establishing absolute control over the parish, they instituted systematic changes in local religious life. First, they ransacked the interiors of the churches (*po nutru vverkh na glavy stavali*). They removed all liturgical books, icons, and crosses; altars were stripped of cloths (*antiminsy*), shrouds, and liturgical vessels. Then, a few selected icons—apparently those of local saints—were carried to the lake, carefully cleansed, and used to bless the water. Once this had been accomplished, the entire band jumped into the lake for a ritual bath. They forced all villagers to follow their example and be rebaptized. Peasants also had to swear in writing to obey orders absolutely.

Some peasants, who managed to escape, sought refuge with the voevoda of Olonets and related what had happened. A major military offensive ensued: the dissenters were driven out of Pudozh and chased into their forest hideouts. Surrounded, with no way out except to surrender, they set fire to their cabins.[125]

One must assume that many died involuntarily in these mass suicides, since numerous peasants had been kidnapped or coerced into joining the band. Especially in the case of the women and children who perished in these conflagrations, we may question whether we are dealing with suicides, or murders committed by authoritarian fathers and husbands.[126] Some evidence concerning the collective suicide of the followers of the Siberian radical Reshetnikov illustrates this point. After a military siege lasting many months, the fortified compound suddenly went up in flames; it appears the insurgents had intentionally lit cannon powder.[127] Most perished, but a few escaped to tell their stories. Among them was Stepanida, the wife of a local peasant; she had also taken one of her little children with her when she jumped out a window. Stepanida reported that she and her children had been forced onto a sled by her husband and driven to Reshetnikov's farm.[128]

These peasant suicides can be understood as part of the broader phenomenon of schismatic brigandage. This finding does not, however, rule out that other peasant suicides may have occurred for entirely religious reasons: these usually involved individuals, families, or small religious conventicles, who chose death over living in what they perceived to be a defiled world. Numerous tragedies of isolated peasants and their families have been obscured by the general epithet schism. I will briefly address a few of these cases.

Ivan Gundilov, a relatively affluent peasant who lived in the Mekhonskaia suburb (*sloboda*) of Tiumen', strongly resented the interference of the parish priest in his personal religious life. For example, having somehow learned that Gundilov refused to drink alcohol, the priest repeatedly tried to force him to drink. Gundilov responded that "he was not in the habit of drinking," and the priest threatened him and his son with violence. The conflict escalated when Gundilov and a few other peasants insisted on making the sign of the cross with two fingers, arguing that this was the way God had commanded them to cross themselves. In order to escape the priest's wrath, Gundilov and his supporters locked themselves in a cabin with their families. Armed guards promptly surrounded the cabin, determined to starve them into submission. However, the fervent peasants did not succumb. They somehow managed to survive on a diet of cooked rye and melted snow for seven weeks. At this point, presuming them to be dead, the guards withdrew and the cabin's inhabitants made their escape.[129]

We do not know whether these peasants would have chosen voluntary suicide to escape the harassment of their parish priest; we know only that other exceptional individuals were prepared to do so. For example, the peasant Ivan Korobeinikov from a village in the Tiumen' district was considered by some of his neighbors to be their teacher. When churchmen threatened to torture Korobeinikov for not teaching the new liturgical books, he responded: "It would be better for [me] to commit suicide . . . if God desired [me] to do so, than to testify against [my] brothers and neighbors, because [I] am unable to endure the pain and no longer know [who I am]."[130] Iakov Solom'ianin, who lived in the Olonets district not far from Lake Onega, had formed a small community of relatives and friends in his home. Before they were discovered and committed suicide, these men and women had observed a rigorous religious lifestyle which included giving alms to the poor.[131] Other such suicides can be documented.[132]

But we need not look only at acts of self-destruction to find peasant schismatics who displayed a similar religious fervor. For example, Avraamii Leont'ev from a village outside Kargopol' attracted attention in March 1684, when he and his brother stole their father's corpse from the powerful Spasskii Monastery.[133] How they managed to do this remains unclear, but the Leont'ev family had led a religious life distinct from the rest of their parish for many years. Their parish priest admitted that about fifteen years earlier, he had taught them to use the two-finger sign of the cross. Since then "he had learned the truth and begun to teach" (*uznav istinu pouchal*) his parishioners to use the new liturgies. He asserted that everyone except the Leont'evs had obeyed his teachings.[134]

Four peasants from the vicinity of Murom came to the attention of local churchmen in early 1672, after a runaway monk from the Polish-Lithuanian Commonwealth had been arrested in the area. Apparently they were eager to absorb the monk's teachings against priests and sacraments, and believed his assertions about the degeneration of Muscovite church life.[135] In July 1675, the peasant Iurii Tomilov and his son, from a village outside Velikie Luki, were arrested. Iurii's family had given refuge to a wandering monk, who had dispensed old liturgical books and hosts. When pressed to reveal the whereabouts of the monk, Iurii pointed to the homestead of Kondratii Lavrov in a neighboring village.[136] In 1676, the voevoda of Arzamas identified the peasant Stepan Remizov as a preacher of the old liturgical books. Several years later, a peasant trader from the village of Pavlov-Perevoz in the Nizhnii Novgorod area was blamed for writing and distributing "blasphemous letters" (*bogomerzkie pis'ma*) in Moscow.[137]

Other examples could be cited of peasants living independent religious lives, in open or secret defiance of official church demands.[138] In March 1666, agents of the tsar's Secret Chancellery captured some seventy peasant schismatics in the Vologda district. Almost all of them were pious believers who practiced a rigorous religious life in the privacy of home. Except for the fact that they were not wearing monastic habits, they behaved much like monks and nuns. Women and men lived without sexual contact and ate at separate tables. They also subjected themselves to regular fasts that included abstinence from meat, fish, and eggs. Most of the seventy men and women arrested came from families in different villages. They were isolated from each other, and probably did not even know one other.[139]

Among them were schismatics identified in the village of Bleshcheevo, which belonged to Boyar I. D. Miloslavskii.[140] All members of the Artem'ev family, these schismatics comprised the widower Foma, his four children, and two of their spouses. Foma had suffered greatly due to the loss of his wife and four other children. He may also have grieved the sudden death of the old parish priest, whom he had greatly respected.[141] We cannot exclude the possibility that Foma, left without spiritual guidance, found solace in the religious ideas of itinerant monks. Or alternatively, Foma might have succumbed to the religious fervor of his daughter, Stepanida. A strong-willed woman, Stepanida refused to eat or sleep with her husband, and refused to call on a priest because "she has a hand of her own with which [to] baptize without the help of a priest."[142]

There is no evidence that the behavior of Foma and his family was guided by social or economic grievances. One observes, instead, a retreat from regular parish life into the home. The fact that several schismatic families were headed by widowers or widows suggests that men and women deeply touched by personal grief may have especially yearned—as some of them put it—for spiritual salvation.

In a village that belonged to the Pavlov Monastery was another dissident family, the extended clan of the widow Aniuta Neusypaeva. Neusypaeva's influence seems to have reached beyond her family.[143] Local supporters included the Mikitin family as well as the widow Krestina, who apparently liked Neusypaeva's emphasis on a vegetarian diet since "meat [was] the one thing she [did]n't eat because she was old and toothless."[144]

In the village of Chechiulina, Stepan Vasil'ev had apparently convinced his wife and son, as well as his best friend, to live an alternative religious life.[145] Larion Antropov, who had lost his wife, played a similar role in another village. Antropov refused to eat with other people in order to ensure his spiritual salvation (*dlia svoego spaseniia*), and made a pilgrimage to the monastic community founded by the above-mentioned monk Vavila in the forest outside Viazniki. Antropov's widowed brother and niece apparently shared his religious zeal. The three celebrated Mass together in their home, centering their worship around private icons.[146]

Schismatic peasants in the Vologda district were much less independent than peasants of Siberia or the north. They lived in territories under the direct control of two powerful monasteries as well as several noble landlords. Judging from information in Vologdan monastic archives, these peasants struggled with economic and social hardships resulting from taxation, land distribution, and incidents of violence.[147] The hinterlands of the Kornil'ev Monastery, for example, were quite dangerous during the second half of the seventeenth century, since competing monk factions were fighting each other with the help of local peasants. However, social turmoil and hardship do not appear to have motivated peasant dissent in this area.[148]

Instead, confrontation with the sudden death of family members and friends appears to have been the most significant experience for peasant schismatics. We have already come across this factor in motivating religious conversions among a few urban dwellers and peasants turned monks. The horrors of death were palpable to most Muscovites, especially during outbreaks of the plague in the 1650s when entire towns, villages, and monasteries were devastated literally overnight.[149] The memory of these catastrophes did not fade for several decades. Popular tales about the plague continued to circulate, and worship at votive chapels dedicated to plague victims remained a dominant feature of popular devotion during the remainder of the seventeenth century.[150]

One is tempted to speculate about an intrinsic connection between the religious radicalization reported in this chapter and the plague—or the memory of its horrors. Several of the peasants accused of schism stated explicitly that the plague had led them to change their way of life.[151] Still, disastrous death tolls were common among all Muscovites living in plague-stricken areas. Why, then, did only a few express the strong religious sentiments described here?

The body of literature on the plague in Europe indicates there were usually two kinds of religious responses. One involved collective rituals to escape the nightmare of divine retribution: cross processions, relic worship, Te Deum Masses, community prayers, pilgrimages, and the construction of churches. Sometimes these celebrations led to religious mass hysteria or collective fantasies; good examples are the flagellants movement and the stories of miraculous intercessions by local saints. It appears these community-based responses mainly served to curb "collective panic," as well as to provide what one historian of Florence has called "thaumaturgical efficacy," that is, miraculous protection against a little-understood disaster.[152]

The other religious reaction to the plague was individualistic and intensely personal. According to one historian of the plague, some individuals "counted the hereafter more important than life on earth and, given the difficulties and brevity of earthly existence, salvation became paramount."[153] Instead of passive participation in spectacles of collective salvation, these individuals sought active self-transformation and direct communication with God. Some explored their conscience through introspection; others mortified their flesh through constant fasting, flagellation, and prayer. There is evidence that women were particularly receptive to this kind of religious experience, leading an interpreter of the plague to observe the "feminization" of private devotion.[154]

In Muscovy during the second half of the seventeenth century, contemporary evidence suggests that the vast majority of Russians reacted collectively to the plague. They participated, for example, in huge processions that culminated in the blessing of local streams and lakes with icons and relics. The Greek Patriarch Makarii, who led one of these spectacles on the Volga River, discovered the usefulness of relics and "various other holy objects" he had brought along from his native Antioch. Indeed, historian Nikolai Kapterev attributed the increased import of relics and icons from Greece and Palestine to popular fears about the plague and other epidemic diseases. He also noted the despair with which local communities begged the tsar for miracle-working "crosses with relics" (*kresty s moshchami*). It was commonly believed that such sacred objects, when properly used in public ceremonies, provided healing powers and protected against "sudden death" (*naprasnaia smert'*).[155]

There were two other popular Russian responses to the plague. One involved the discovery of local relics and the establishment of new shrines; this widespread phenomenon raised the suspicion of church hierarchs on several occasions.[156] The other response was the construction of churches in a single day.[157]

For example, the chronicler of the plague in the Vologda district noted the following:

> The residents [of Vologda] saw that a multitude of corpses were taken out [of town] every day. They screamed to God with tears and a grieving heart: "We have sinned, oh Lord, and confess our trespasses. . . . " They made a vow in their hearts that they would build God [a church] . . . dedicated to the glory of His name. They would work without interruption all day and night so that God would alleviate His just anger and show mercy to His people against the deadly plague. . . . It became known in both town and villages that a church would be built in the name of God. All people rejoiced in expectation of the assigned day.[158]

During the night before "the assigned day," large crowds gathered from the town and surrounding villages. Construction began after midnight, and was a highly emotional experience for the participants. Working feverishly and shedding many tears, they implored God to intercede on behalf of their community.[159]

The peasant dissenters discussed in this chapter did not follow this typical pattern; available evidence suggests that they reacted much more individualistically to the plague than did their contemporaries.[160] Indeed, these women and men took to heart the ascetic ideals of Orthodox Christianity in a world that appears to have focused on collective rituals. Rigorous worship and study, that is, the reading of old liturgical books, and constant prayer in front of old icons set them apart from both peasant community and church. This is particularly obvious in the case of Stepanida, who not only rejected all spiritual authority, but also broke completely with the mores of her social environment by insisting on a celibate life.[161]

The peasant widow Avdot'ia Baksheeva, from the small village of Konduska outside Tobol'sk, provides another example of such behavior. After the death of her husband, Baksheeva began hearing voices (*glasy*) from Heaven telling her to reject the moral corruption of her contemporaries. During the 1660s, this lone woman wandered the streets of Tobol'sk conjuring up horrible pictures of plague, famine, and fire. If the men and women of Tobol'sk would not mend their evil ways, she warned, they would all be destroyed by divine wrath (*gnev Bozhii*). While she was upset about the introduction of the new church liturgies, her main concern was that the Russian residents of Tobol'sk "did not fear God"; she desired them to repent and celebrate the divine liturgy "with pure hearts" (*s chistymi serdtsy*).

Baksheeva considered herself superior to Tobol'sk residents because of her piety and devotion. She accused them of focusing only on secular matters, and of blaming local elites for their economic and social hardships: "All kinds of people in the community say that famine and all varieties of poverty have been created by the men in charge (*nachal'nye liudi*). This was not caused by the men in charge. Rather, it was caused by God for the sinfulness of the world (*za mirskoe sogreshenie*)." The only way out of human misery, Baksheeva claimed, was to convert to true Christianity, that is, to "abstain from all evil things and untruths," as well as to return to the old forms of church singing (*staroe penie*).[162]

The religious enthusiasm of Stepanida and Baksheeva was motivated by profoundly personal reasons—certainly not because they had been influenced by Old Belief missionaries. In fact, I have found only one exceptional example of a peasant woman who was a declared admirer of Archpriest Avvakum, ready to die for him at the stake.[163] Perhaps these personal motivations are beyond the reach of historical analysis. However, it should be noted that the individuals under discussion here had much in common with another peasant minority during the second half of the seventeenth century: I have in mind the peasant women and men who suffered from a variety of extraordinary mental agonies.

One of the few contemporaries aware of their suffering was the deposed Patriarch Nikon. We know that after his exile to the Russian north in December 1666, Nikon enjoyed renown as a healer specializing in peasant diseases. Nikon's popularity among northern peasants contradicts Old Believer interpretations of the patriarch as an enemy of the "Russian people." The Old Believer view, however, is not the issue; more important is a brief description of the men and women who came to Nikon because "they had lost their mind (*bez uma*)."[164]

Some of these peasants stated they had been overwhelmed by a "great horror" (*strakh velikii*). Among them was the peasant Andrei from the Vologda district, who was trembling all over when Nikon examined him, but was not able to explain why he was so afraid. Others tried to describe their fears: the monastic peasant Trofim said he was horrified by the Devil; others claimed demonic possession; one peasant heard terrifying voices, which he attributed to demons conspiring to strangle him; another actually saw the demons and complained that they repeatedly tried to suffocate him.[165]

Among Nikon's visitors were also a number of deeply troubled women. For example, an unnamed peasant woman from outside Vologda was convinced that "everything she touched was pagan" (*do chego dotknetsia i to vse mnela byti pagano*); she refused to eat or drink, and had to be fed by others. A serf from a remote village in the Poshekhon'e district had stopped speaking; she had also renounced prayers, and no longer made the sign of the cross. Similarly, the peasant girl Anastas'ia had stubbornly refused to communicate with anyone for five years. The wife of a village blacksmith had hysterical fits, during which she beat herself. Finally, a thirty-year-old retainer of the Suzdal' Pokrovskii Convent "was screaming with all kinds of voices" (*vsiakimi glasy krichala*).[166]

Religious motives are not directly discernible in these cases, but from such mental agony it was sometimes only a small step to religious anxiety and mystical revelation. For example, the coachman (*iamskoi*) Peter Shadra from the Tiumen' district was about to get up one morning when a "great horror" befell him, and he became paralyzed. "It came to [me] like a furious storm. Some divine force grabbed [me] . . . and put [me] on a large field. There was a voice both terrifying and sweet. Then an intense light fell upon the field"; the light increased in intensity, and Shadra said he began to see an altar being lowered from Heaven, and "on this altar was an image of the Mother of God and the cross." Then, the image of the Mother of God began to speak: "You, Peter, tell the governor and those laymen who are intelligent and not stupid (*v mire umnym liudiam, a ne glupym*) that they are now saying Mass according to a new statute, and not according to the rules of the church fathers. Heretics are confusing the Orthodox Christian faith and polluting our churches. . . . " Unless the old religious order was restored, the voice continued, "God's wrath would fall on all people, and life would come to a halt. God would castigate people with great poverty, hunger, and thirst, and they would all rot horribly before the Day of Judgment (*pregniiut*)."

Shadra was terror-stricken, and trembled for many days after this extraordinary experience. Indeed, the vision immobilized him to the extent that he could not travel to the neighboring town. Shadra finally overcame his affliction when he realized that he had been chosen by God for a special preaching mission. He went with fervor to the local governor's office to report his news "to all the people of the town of Tiumen'."

After listening to him with amusement and curiosity, the Tiumen' officials set him free. A record of his statements was handed to the archbishop, who deposited it in the files of the Siberian Office, but apparently no one thought it necessary to punish Shadra. This official leniency, a striking contrast to the brutality meted out to most other peasant dissenters, may have resulted from the perception of Shadra as a harmless fellow whose religious despair was his own personal affair, or—as was so often thought in Western Europe—a proof of lunacy.[167]

Shadra's story reveals the inner religious turmoil of a seventeenth-century peasant dissenter. Such glimpses into the peasant psyche, while extremely rare, allow us to comprehend how deeply convinced some lay dissenters were of their right to seek religious alternatives or, on occasion, to speak out publicly against the church.

The evidence cited here does not support the global assertion that liturgical dissent was—as Soviet scholar Rumiantseva put it most recently—only a "peculiar religious cover" used by peasants to express their underlying discontent with the existing social order.[168] On the contrary, I have found that Muscovite peasant dissent was often a religious decision inspired by personal despair and the search for spiritual salvation. This explains why isolated dissenters and their families can be found living in all regions of Muscovy, regardless of local economic and social developments.

There is only one important caveat to this finding: socioeconomic grievances did play a decisive role in the emergence of liturgical dissent in the hinterlands of Lake Onega, and on the western Siberian frontier. In these two regions, anti-ecclesiastical violence developed from an explosive mixture of religious and social despair that was provoked, at least in part, by the economic ambitions of powerful northern monasteries and Siberian bishops. However, conditions in these remote frontier areas were exceptional, not normative. The typical rural dissenter was more likely to be a troubled and isolated individual in search of religious autonomy than an angry rebel in defiance of the established social order.

CONCLUSION &

Popular Opposition to the Russian Church

During the first quarter of the eighteenth century, the Old Belief historian Semen Denisov described what he perceived as the great crisis of the seventeenth century:

> When by divine assent the ship of the all-Russian church was entrusted to [Patriarch] Nikon ... he raised a very dark storm and tossed the Russian sea in extreme agitation, shaking the beautiful ship of the church with powerful whirlpools. ... He [Nikon] cut through the walls of our firmest divine laws with great fury and maliciously destroyed the church's sculls, the grandiose rites and liturgies inherited from our fathers. ... In his rage he shattered the entire ship of the Russian church and, in his great madness, created turbulence in our refuge. All of Russia was in revolt (*miatezh*), confusion, and doubt. There was great bloodshed, and many tears were shed. . . . [1]

Denisov painted a scenario familiar from seventeenth-century Old Believer texts, according to which Nikon's changes in liturgical practices shocked and demoralized much of the Russian population. The authors of these texts—most of them educated intellectuals such as deacon Fedor Ivanov—claimed they were writing in the name of "the majority of all the people" (*vsenarodnoe mnozhestvo*), providing the collective "answer of the Orthodox" (*otvet pravoslavnykh*) to the corrupt church. They proudly declared their God-appointed mission to guide the disillusioned and inarticulate Russian masses.[2]

Standard interpretations of the Russian Schism have tended to adopt Old Belief's own view of seventeenth-century dissent. A handful of Old

217

Belief figures are described with epithets such as "the leaders of the schism," "national agitators," "skilled propagandists," "the inspirers of the schism," etc.[3] Or, as Sergei Zenkovsky wrote with regard to Archpriest Avvakum, "his name [was] familiar to every Russian" thanks to the "moving quality of his epistles, sermons, and treatises, which circulated throughout Russia in a multitude of copies."[4] In a similar vein, Robert Crummey has recently spoken of an "Old Believer 'intelligentsia' " that provided the "images and rallying cries with which ordinary men and women could comprehend the rapidly changing and threatening world around them."[5]

Contrary to such interpretations, I have not found much evidence for Old Belief's mass appeal during the seventeenth century. Old Believer preachers such as Avvakum and Neronov never played the mobilizing roles that Luther and Calvin played in Western European societies. The archival records—in contrast to anti-Nikonian polemics—reveal quite a different picture of the Russian Schism. Seventeenth-century dissent was primarily an affair of independent-minded individuals and social outcasts who acted for their own reasons. These dissenters were neither inarticulate—that is, in need of learned spokesmen—nor did they identify themselves as part of a larger movement against the church. Rather, they gave angry expression to specific local and personal grievances.

During the years 1653–66, when Muscovite society was first exposed to the new Nikonian rites, I find that only a handful of individuals engaged in resistance, and that these individuals had little in common. Some had previously been victims of ecclesiastical intrigues, such as the monk Savvatii, who suddenly lost his influential position at the patriarchal printing press, or the Moscow parish priest Terentii, who suffered arbitrary violence at the hands of a powerful prelate. A few were exceptionally fervent men, such as the tailor Sila, who had been deeply disturbed by religious changes prior to the introduction of the new liturgies. Others simply happened to be at the wrong place at the wrong time, such as the rural hermit Nikon, who encountered the tsar's confessor when the latter was in a bad mood. Finally, there were a few powerful clerics who acted capriciously. For example, the archimandrite of Russia's largest monastic institution, the Troitsa Monastery, attacked and harassed monks and priests for using the new books after he himself had introduced the liturgical reforms.

None of these early dissenters commanded a popular following. In fact, there is evidence that such men were not merely ignored, but disliked. The monks and priests of the Troitsa Monastery complained bitterly about their archimandrite's interference with the use of the new liturgies, and the priest Terentii became embroiled in violence after preaching against the new books at a social gathering in a Moscow trading settlement.

The first Old Believers—that is, those few who identified themselves as defenders of the "old belief" (*staraia vera*)—looked with scorn upon the religious and secular behavior of ordinary Russians. Fervently convinced of the need to build a community of "true believers" (*pravovernye*) recruited exclusively from Russia's "elect" (*izbrannye*), educated clerics such as Neronov and Avvakum attacked acts of drunkenness, gambling, and fornication. Far from achieving popularity, they antagonized their contemporaries and were assaulted by enraged mobs.

Despite popular hostility, the first Old Believers succeeded in attracting a few devoted followers and organizing congregations of "brethren" (*brat'ia*) in Moscow and Nizhnii Novgorod. These brotherhoods had very limited numbers of participants and remained dependent on the personal charisma of their leaders, as well as on the tutelage of influential personages such as the boyars Pleshcheev and the merchant Zadorin. After the arrest of their founders, the first Old Belief communities quickly crumbled, and most "brethren" gave up resistance to the church.[6]

While the founding fathers wasted away in remote exiles during the late 1650s, a new group of Old Believers stepped into their places. Most important among them was Bishop Aleksandr of Viatka, a figure largely ignored by historians. Aleksandr, a former favorite of Nikon and loyal executor of the reforms, had risen to a high position. Nikon had put him in charge of incarcerating Neronov and destroying the power base of Bishop Pavel of Kolomna, an important Old Belief sympathizer. Only after Aleksandr's fall from grace and his removal from the Kremlin to a remote frontier town did he show any support for Old Belief. He then opened the doors of his palace to Old Believers and gathered surviving notes from the pens of the founding fathers.

Aleksandr's conversion to Old Belief, resembling that of the biblical Saul to Christianity, was by no means a unique occurrence. Other hierarchs such as Abbot Feoktist and Archimandrite Nikanor, as well as lower-ranking churchmen such as priest Nikita Dobrynin and the clerk Fedor Trofimov, also became Old Believers. Like Aleksandr, they had been supporters—and indeed loyal executors—of Nikon's liturgical policies before suddenly falling victim to church intrigues. Thus, support for Old Belief did not come from the popular masses, but from former members of the church elite and a few other clergy.

These disaffected churchmen made a crucial contribution to the history of Russian religion and laid the foundation for the Old Believer movement by creating a body of authoritative texts. These texts, which include Abbot Spiridon's famous *Book* and Dobrynin's lesser-known treatise, not only gave early Old Belief a unique identity but also ensured its survival despite the catastrophic impact of the 1666 Church Council, during which Aleksandr and most of his supporters recanted their beliefs. Though effectively deprived of their leaders, the few remaining Old Believers drew strength and courage from the texts they had inherited. During the late 1660s, Old Believers such as Ivanov, Avvakum, and Avraamii began creating miscellanies and polemic treatises from the first Old Believer text corpus, thus holding up the banner of Old Belief for future generations of Russians.

Indeed, one might well speak of the emergence of a "textual community" (Robert Crummey) that read, exchanged, and copied a corpus of sacred texts. But unlike texts by Western reformers that could be vastly multiplied by the printing press, the handcopied Old Believer writings did not widely circulate among ordinary Russians before the eighteenth century.[7] Their dissemination was probably limited to a few reform-oriented clerics and laymen who shared the uncompromising zeal and determination of Old Belief martyrs.[8] This hiatus between Old Believer *literati* and the rest of Russian society is further evidenced by the general ignorance on the part of ordinary dissenters about the existence of the founding fathers. The dissenters discussed in this book—with a very few exceptions—had never heard of either Avvakum or Neronov.[9]

Why did ordinary Russians participate in the Russian Schism? What explains their rejection of the Nikonian reforms if we cannot document the influence of Old Belief preaching and writing? There are no simple answers to these questions, but it appears that the Russian Schism resulted from official church policies. By suddenly and drastically intruding into age-old local and personal autonomies, the church generated popular opposition to its reforms. Rejection of the Nikonian reforms was therefore largely a response by communities as well as individuals to the church's insistence on controlling the religious affairs of Muscovy's hinterlands.

After 1666, which marked a turning point in relations between church and society, the church began an aggressive and systematic campaign to eradicate the last vestiges of the old rites in Muscovy. The 1666 Church Council had exaggerated fears that the Old Believers might find allies in Russian society and thus undermine the power of the Russian Orthodox Church. A collective paranoia overcame Russian hierarchs. Unaccustomed to any opposition, they became convinced that Old Believers posed a tremendous threat to the unity and stability of the church.

The most important church writer of the period, Simeon Polotskii, saw agents of Old Belief at work everywhere. His polemics denounced any failure to use new liturgical books—no matter what the reasons—as part of a dangerous Old Belief conspiracy against the church. Polotskii gave this conspiracy a name by calling it "schism" (*raskol*). While he may have had in mind the dangers posed by the Uniates of his native White Russia—as a point of fact, White Russian Orthodox applied the term *raskol* to converts from Russian Orthodoxy to Catholicism—he created a powerful model for interpreting seventeenth-century Russian dissent. From then on, Old Believers such as Avvakum and Dobrynin became known as "the leaders of the schism" (*raskolonachal'niki*).

Distributed to all dioceses and monasteries of the tsardom, Polotskii's texts significantly influenced local church agents. After 1666, hierarchs and officials began looking feverishly for manifestations of a schism in Russia's provinces. Eager to please their superiors, or perhaps sharing official anxieties, they applied the label schism rather freely to diverse phenomena of religious dissent.

So-called schism cases (*raskol'nye dela*), that is, cases involving opposition to Nikon's reforms, occurred in monastic environments more frequently than anywhere else. The rebellion of Russia's second largest monastery, Solovki, represents the most dramatic episode of the Russian Schism. Less dramatic rebellions occurred in smaller monasteries all over Muscovy. These confrontations with the Kremlin often ended in a military take-over of the monastery, the arrest and disciplining—if not killing—of monks, or deposition and expulsion of the abbot. Despite their failure, monastic insurgencies had long-term consequences: some monks eluded capture and became angry transmitters of dissent.

Among the largely anonymous crowd of clerics who rejected the church were many unaffiliated women who had declared themselves nuns (*samostrizhennitsy*) after their husbands' death, or because they sought a religious escape from the hardships of their lives. There were also numerous monks who had been chased out of regular monasteries because they were troublemakers or drunkards. The angry speeches and actions of these wandering ruffians posed a direct threat to local churchmen, who sometimes feared for their lives. The church also distrusted the leaders of unofficial hermitages (*pustyni*) who staunchly defended the autonomy not only of their monastic communities, but also of their villages and trading posts.

Archival records reveal a shortage of official monasteries and the concomitant proliferation of unofficial monastic communities and cells in the Russian forests founded by local peasants or charismatic holy men and women without the permission, or even knowledge, of church officials.

During the last decades of the seventeenth century, the church attempted to curb the growth of such communities by subordinating them to the control of officially sanctioned monasteries. The enforcement of Patriarch Nikon's new liturgies thus became a litmus test, a means of verifying whether the behavior of suspicious monks and nuns conformed to church standards.

Another target of aggressive church policies was the Russian parish clergy. Compared with monks and nuns, I have found that parish priests—with a few significant exceptions—were much less likely to dissent. The revolt of the Galich clergy, for example, can be explained as a response to violent attacks by the local voevoda. Or, one might consider the case of the priest, Peter, of the isolated village of Feduevo in northern Russia who rallied parishioners to his defense after a military detachment had taken over his family's home. But the typical parish priest in the Russian provinces was apparently a pillar of church support.

One probable reason for the loyalty of parish priests was that the expansion of church control over Russian parish life, which had begun before the 1666 Church Council, was executed systematically. In particular, bishops and their agents increasingly attempted to supervise appointments to parish positions. By the end of the seventeenth century, most parishes had accepted the new liturgies in token obedience to the Muscovite church center. Thus, the relatively low level of dissent among Russian priests can be seen as a reflection of successful disciplinary policies.

Still, we must consider that the controls imposed on the ordination of parish clergy also created a continuous surplus of unaffiliated priests, many of whom had been penalized or expelled from the body of the church for unruly behavior; others never got a chance because they lacked qualifications or connections. One might recall, for example, the priests of the Kholmogory diocese who failed to pass the basic reading and writing tests established by their bishop. Such unfortunate priests often became known as schismatics because they vented their anger by denouncing the new books. Thus, the discontented cleric on the fringe of the official church was a prime candidate for schism investigations.

I have found that the rural and urban laity were the least involved in schism cases. There were a few localized rebellions in the Lake Onega region and in Siberia that were organized by peasant strongmen or brigands and involved spectacular acts of violence, such as the kidnapping and murder of priests, the burning of a parish church, and the destruction of a monastery. Allowing for these and a few similar cases in frontier areas, the evidence on lay dissent primarily concerns individuals driven by extraordinary religious convictions. These zealous men and women were usually isolated from their communities, though some had the support of their families. They completely withdrew into the privacy of their homes to study books, fast, and worship in front of icons. Viewed with great suspicion by the church, these exceptional Russians were very similar to the heretics of the Western Middle Ages and the radical dissenters of Protestant Europe: they bypassed the clerical and sacramental authority of the church in order to search for God and salvation on their own.

Some of these zealots became self-proclaimed prophets and preachers who took to the road or marketplace to reveal truths they claimed to have received from God. Usually they were ignored or ridiculed, like the Siberian peasant Shadra who amused his interrogators with stories of voices from Heaven and visions of the Mother of God. Still, there were notable exceptions in the towns and hinterlands of Novgorod and Pskov, where powerful merchants sponsored alternative networks of lay religious activity. These wealthy men gave up their businesses to engage in preaching, and they became known as popular confessors, baptizers of children, and arrangers of burials. To church officials, the Novgorod and Pskov cases were among the most frightening manifestations of the schism. They were afraid that the two northern towns were on the verge of seceding to Protestant Sweden.

These findings demonstrate that there was no coordinated mass movement against the seventeenth-century Russian Orthodox Church. Once we remove the filters—ecclesiastical as well as Old Belief—that have distorted our perception of Russian dissenters, we can observe disparate acts of popular disobedience and defiance. Each manifestation of liturgical dissent was a distinct response to the growth of the ecclesiastical center and its penetration into local and personal religious autonomies. Instead of one great schism, one should probably refer to numerous small schisms that occurred in particular monasteries, parishes, and communities and involved individual monks, nuns, priests, and laymen.

It may be useful at this point to compare features of Russian dissent to better-known examples of heresy and dissent in the West.[10] Such comparisons elucidate several striking features of seventeenth-century Russian dissent, and suggest that we can understand the evolution of Russian religion only if we are careful in drawing analogies to contemporary Western developments.

First, Russian dissenters were the products of a society characterized by low literacy rates. Very few of the dissenters interrogated during the seventeenth century knew how to read or write. Unlike Western societies, Muscovy had not yet been touched by the print revolution. The only printing press in Russia was run by the patriarch in the Kremlin, and its principal products from the 1650s onward were the new liturgical books. Thus, Russians experienced the printing press as an instrument of control rather than as a catalyst for independent thinking and intellectual awakening.

In seventeenth-century England, as Christopher Hill points out in his study of popular culture during the English Revolution, "printing was a small man's occupation." The English market was flooded with pamphlets and broadsheets that even the poor could afford to buy. Under the influence of the printing press, England turned into "a nation of prophets." Ordinary men and women discussed matters of theology and envisioned the advent of the Kingdom of Heaven on earth after the overthrow of the state church. The enthusiasm of radicals who called themselves Ranters, Levelers, Fifth Monarchy Men, Quakers, and other names, originated in reading and writing: they studied the Scriptures and apocalyptic tracts before formulating their own views about the meaning of religion in human life.[11]

By contrast, glimpses into the beliefs and fantasies of Russian dissenters reveal—with the exception of a few learned clerics and town dwellers—a predominance of non-literate, or better, pre-literate, concerns. In the town of Suzdal', for example, the populace worshipped the graves of the ancient Suzdalian princes whom they revered as their protectors; attacks on this form of worship caused popular rebellion. In Moscow, icon worship was the principal source of solace during the devastating pestilence of 1654; when Patriarch Nikon dared to confiscate and mutilate icons, he triggered a mass frenzy. In Rostov, a tailor turned against the metropolitan when the relics of his favorite local saint failed to work a miracle. Many of the unofficial hermitages hidden in the Russian forests were built around burial sites, such as the graves of recently deceased holy men, or ancient mounds dating from pre-Christian times. The examples cited here illustrate that the thinking of Russian dissenters was not rooted in texts, but in custom and tradition.

Indeed, it appears that seventeenth-century Russians did not need to read or hear critical pamphlets before expressing discontent with their church. The willingness to resist ecclesiastical authority was already present, and revolts were often unleashed merely by the church's unbending insistence on obedience. If the dissenters studied here had one character trait in common, it was their utter lack of respect for church officials. Some used brutal means to fight and kill church representatives, others became preachers and religious leaders in place of the official clergy; many simply withdrew into the wilderness, or lived like vagabonds on the roads of Russia.

A second distinctive feature of Russian dissent was the paucity of theological rhetoric. Most of the women and men who defied church authority knew little, if anything, about the liturgical issues at stake. They also gave no thought to the religious and social life they desired if successful in keeping the church out of their affairs. Unlike the peasant rebels of Reformation Germany, for example, Russian dissenters did not invoke the gospel or abstract notions such as divine right. Demands for release from serfdom "as children of God" and declarations that all should "live together in brotherly love" appear to have been equally unimaginable: only occasionally were calls for the extermination of "all godless people" expressed in southern border areas, probably due to the influence of Western European radicals.[12]

According to Jean Delumeau's striking thesis, the inculcation of Christian teachings and ideals in the "masses" did not occur in the West during the Middle Ages, but was the characteristic achievement of the Reformation and the Counter Reformation.[13] In Russia, the systematic efforts of the patriarchate notwithstanding, seventeenth-century dissenters staunchly defended the way they had always conducted their lives and maintained a vigorous sub-culture. The fact that church efforts to evangelize Russian society did not succeed is an important historical feature that distinguishes Russian religious history from its Western counterpart.

A third distinctive feature of Russian dissent during the seventeenth century was the high degree of clerical involvement. Russian monks and priests, who for one reason or other did not enjoy official recognition, were the principal disseminators of dissent. Under their influence, unknown numbers of women and men adopted a monastic way of life, flocking to hidden monasteries in the forests. By contrast, Western dissent of the same period was essentially a lay effort to liberate piety from clerical domination. A better analogy can be drawn to Western European efforts of spiritual reform during the eleventh and twelfth centuries: like seventeenth-century Russian dissent, these efforts were essentially based on an imitation of clerical, especially monastic, religious practice.[14]

The crisis of the medieval Western church during the eleventh and twelfth centuries was triggered by the expansion of its authority over parishes and monasteries in outlying areas. The introduction of new controls over traditional religious autonomies significantly contributed to the emergence of European dissent.[15] Herbert Grundmann, one of the great authorities on Western medieval heresy, describes how the sudden regimentation of religious life led to an exodus from the official church. Religious women, for example, set up their own monastic communities in many regions of Europe, such as Flanders and the Rhineland. Laymen formed conventicles that practiced religion outside the accepted structure of the church. Preaching hermits roamed the countryside and attracted considerable followings.[16]

Five centuries later in Russia, a similar development was under way: the foundation charter of the patriarchate at the end of the sixteenth century called for the establishment of new bishoprics, and the church councils of the seventeenth century—especially the pivotal Council of 1666—created the blueprints for unprecedented institutional expansion. Episcopal sees were founded in remote areas such as the Novgorodian north, which was subdivided into the new bishoprics of Kholmogory, Ustiug, and Novgorod. The patriarchal see and episcopal chancelleries began to issue appointment papers for priests. Emissaries came to inspect local communities; priests were not only tested, but also disciplined for unruly behavior. Most importantly, the church began its assault on Russian monasticism, distinguishing between acceptable and non-acceptable forms of monastic living.

There is, however, a dramatic distinction between clerics who inspired outbreaks of religious dissent in Russia and the idealistic leaders of Cluny, or the apostolic poverty movements of the West. Only the Old Believer idealists shared the reform zeal of Cluny, but, as we have seen, Avvakum and Neronov often infuriated contemporaries by their sermons.

Many of the Russian dissenters were outlaws and brigands who resorted to acts of violence ranging from robbery to murder. In this they resemble the "primitive rebels" described by E. J. Hobsbawm rather than the holy men and women described in Old Believer texts and in the standard historiography of the Russian Schism. This phenomenon of "religious banditry" has no parallel in the history of Western Europe. True, figures such as Thomas Müntzer or the Münster Anabaptists were perceived as bloodthirsty criminals by contemporary polemicists. But none of these preachers went into hiding in the forests of Germany, or joined armed bands of robbers and highwaymen.[17]

Russian dissenters also displayed a remarkable readiness for self-sacrifice and self-destruction. When they were tracked down and surrounded by troops, they often barricaded themselves in log cabins and fought to the death. Some committed suicide by self-immolation when rumors reached them about approaching military detachments. An unknown number of women killed themselves after listening to the apocalyptic preaching of nuns like Evpraksiia, who migrated from village to village in the Suzdal' area.

The West produced numerous prophets of doom but, to the best of my knowledge, there were no preachers who openly called for suicide. Crusaders and flagellants may have been inspired by similar zeal and despair, but they never went to such extremes as to destroy themselves. Thus, Russian dissenters not only used violence against others, but also against themselves. Seventeenth-century Russia thus produced forms of religious violence unknown to Western Christianity.

In addition to shedding light on the distinctive features of Russian dissent, this book also suggests several revisions in Russian historiography. Scholars have often perceived Peter I. as an innovator for his expansion of bureaucratic controls over parishes and monasteries.[18] In fact, Peter I. merely continued, and possibly intensified, a trend that had already emerged during the second half of the seventeenth century. Furthermore, Russian society was by no means as church-oriented during the seventeenth century as some historians have assumed. The church did not play a "tremendous role in Russian life . . . that extended to the last minutiae of daily life."[19] Precisely the opposite was true: the church lacked contact with many individuals and communities. Indeed, it was this gulf separating church officialdom from ordinary clerics and laymen that inspired the Russian patriarchate to expand its power.

More importantly, the Russian Schism of the seventeenth century was not a clash between a popular movement of discontent headed by Old Believers on one side, and Muscovite church and state officialdom on the other. The texts written by Avvakum and other seventeenth-century figures who identified themselves as defenders of the "old belief" reflect a sophisticated and learned opposition to the church. However, the intellectual issues raised by Nikon's liturgical reforms, as the archival evidence I have cited demonstrates, did not engage large sections of Russian society. Rather, the reforms supplied a language of dissent for discontented and previously silent Russians: by rejecting the new liturgical books, they aggressively signaled to those with power their unwillingness to belong to the mainstream of Russian religion.

Given the multiplicity of discontented voices and the absence of overarching leadership, the Russian Schism of the seventeenth century was necessarily very fragmented. This fragmentation reflected, to a large extent, the unmended fissures and faultlines in late Muscovy's religious geography. Despite determined patriarchal efforts, ecclesiastical institutions remained absent or underdeveloped in numerous regions. Tsar Fedor

Alekseevich alluded to this dilemma in a letter to Patriarch Ioakim in September 1681:

> In faraway places, the Christian faith is not being disseminated, and as a result, the slanderers of the holy church are multiplying. . . . [T]hey cannot be disciplined (*ne imeiut vozbraneniia sebe*) because [even] in [existing] bishoprics, towns and hamlets are separated from each other by considerable distances.[20]

The tsar concluded that the gap between local society and the Kremlin had to be significantly reduced before the church could hope to erase the schism. The solution, which he suggested in several memoranda to church leaders, was to more than double, if not triple or quadruple, the number of Russian bishoprics.[21]

This unusually perceptive interpretation goes to the heart of the matter: central to the emergence of the Russian Schism were unanswered, and indeed unprecedented, questions of power and authority. Who should control local religious affairs? Should a powerful abbot, merchant, or peasant strongman obey the demands of the church? Should priests without employment, or monks outside of monasteries be allowed to determine their own religious practices? Should women give up a religious life merely because some church official decided they could not become nuns? The Russian church of the late seventeenth century did not tolerate autonomous decisions in these matters. But since some of these recalcitrant rebels had considerable local influence, e.g., the Solovki elders and the clergy of Viazniki, church agents encountered tremendous obstacles in attempting to establish religious conformity. Not surprisingly, conflicts engendered by the church's offensive sometimes ended in deadly confrontations.

In the final analysis, the most determined dissenters prevailed. One might say that a permanent schism or religious division gradually emerged as a result of their resistance. Absolute numbers are hard to establish in the absence of any reliable statistics: both the geography and numerical dimension of this schism were in constant flux, depending largely on the regional distribution and vehemence of assaults by the church. As persecution intensified even in remote areas, dislocation and chaotic mobility became the dominant features of seventeenth-century dissent. By the end of the century, an unknown number of dissident clerics and laymen found themselves on the move in order to escape arrest and punishment.

It was not until the first half of the eighteenth century that the contours and parameters of the schism became more fixed, largely as a result of the new intellectual centers of Old Belief that began to emerge, e.g., the so-called Priestist movement at Vetka and the Priestless movement at Vyg.

These centers disseminated seventeenth-century Old Believer texts and established schools where children were educated about the teachings of the founding fathers. Adults who failed to familiarize themselves with the basic dogmas of Old Belief were severely punished. This emphasis on systematic learning also produced a significant number of missionaries who were much better educated and disciplined than most of the Orthodox clergy. In fact, their educational models came from Western Jesuit schools via the Kievan Academy and eminent Ukrainian churchmen, such as Feofan Prokopovich and Dmytryi Tuptalo.[22]

Old Belief preachers, who could be found in almost every region of the empire, became a formidable force and drew more and more Russians into the fold of Old Belief. It was also largely due to their preaching that isolated Russian dissenters acquired a sense of belonging to a larger movement. Many became literate, bought icons of Archpriest Avvakum, or learned spiritual poems (*dukhovnye stikhi*) glorifying the heroes of the seventeenth century. In short, previously inchoate and amorphous phenomena of dissent acquired a new sense of direction and meaning. We might call this process the "routinization" (Max Weber) of Russian religious dissent.[23]

By contrast, the Russian Schism of the seventeenth century represented an amalgamation of diffuse phenomena: a serious crisis in the monastic world involving the rebellion of numerous monasteries and monks; the emergence of a significant surplus of unemployed and defrocked priests; the existence of strong anti-church sentiments in isolated villages and towns; the fusion of social banditry and religious radicalism; the quasi-Protestant quests of individual peasants, artisans, and merchants for religious salvation; the disillusionment of women with the church; and a widespread lack of popular knowledge about the basic tenets of the Orthodox faith. These features of seventeenth-century society point to a deep alienation between ordinary Russians and their church. It was this alienation— and not Nikon's reforms or Old Belief teachings—that led to the emergence of the Russian Schism.

REFERENCE MATERIAL

NOTES 🙠

The following abbreviations are used in the Notes. Complete authors' names, titles, and publications are given in the Bibliography, pp. 305–33.

AAE	*Akty, sobrannye v bibliotekakh i arkhivakh Rossiiskoi imperii Arkheograficheskoiu ekspeditsieiu Imperatorskoi Akademii nauk.*
AI	*Akty istoricheskie, sobrannye i izdannye Arkheograficheskoiu kommissieiu.*
BAN	Biblioteka Rossiiskoi Akademii nauk.
BE	Brokgauz, F. A.; Efron, I. A., eds. *Entsiklopedicheskii slovar'.*
Chteniia	*Chteniia v Imperatorskom Obshchestve istorii i drevnostei rossiiskikh pri Moskovskom universitete.*
DAI	*Dopolneniia k aktam istoricheskim, sobrannye i izdannye Arkheograficheskoiu kommissieiu.*
Delo	*Delo o patriarkhe Nikone.*
Dokumenty	Rumiantseva, V. S., ed. *Narodnoe antitserkovnoe dvizhenie v Rossii XVII veka. Dokumenty Prikaza tainykh del o raskol'nikakh 1665–1667 gg..*
GA Vologda	Gosudarstvennyi arkhiv Vologodskoi oblasti.
GIM	Gosudarstvennyi istoricheskii muzei.
GPNTB SO	Gosudarstvennaia publichnaia nauchno-technicheskaia biblioteka Sibirskogo otdeleniia Rossiiskoi Akademii nauk.
IIFIF SO	Institut istorii, filologii i filosofii Sibirskogo otdeleniia Rossiiskoi Akademii nauk.
IRLI	Institut russkoi literatury (Pushkinskii Dom) Rossiiskoi Akademii nauk.

LZAK	*Letopis' zaniatii Imperatorskoi Arkheograficheskoi kommissii.*
Materialy	Subbotin, N. I., ed. *Materialy dlia istorii raskola za pervoe vremia ego sushchestvovaniia.*
NA IIALI KNTs	Institut iazyka, literatury i istorii Karel'skogo nauchnogo tsentra Rossiiskoi Akademii nauk. Nauchnyi arkhiv.
NB MGU	Moskovskii gosudarstvennyi universitet imeni M. V. Lomonosova. Nauchnaia Biblioteka.
Opisanie MGAMIU	*Opisanie dokumentov i bumag, khraniashchikhsia v Moskovskom arkhive Ministerstva iustitsii.*
Opisanie svitkov	Suvorov, N. I., ed. *Opisanie sobraniia svitkov, nakhodiashchikhsia v Vologodskom eparkhial'nom drevnekhranilishche.*
Pamiatniki	Barskov, Ia. L., ed. *Pamiatniki pervykh let russkogo staroobriadchestva.*
PPBES	*Polnyi pravoslavnyi bogoslovskii entsiklopedicheskii slovar'.*
Prilozheniia	Rumiantsev, I. I. *Nikita Konstantinovich Dobrynin.* Vol. 2. *Prilozheniia. Materialy dlia istorii zhizni i deiatel'nosti popa Nikity Konstantinovicha Dobrynina.*
PSPVI	*Polnoe sobranie postanovlenii i razporiazhenii po vedomosti pravoslavnogo ispovedaniia.*
RGADA	Rossiiskii gosudarstvennyi arkhiv drevnikh aktov.
RGB	Rossiiskaia gosudarstvennaia biblioteka.
RGIA	Rossiiskii gosudarstvennyi istoricheskii arkhiv.
RIB	*Russkaia istoricheskaia biblioteka.*
RNB	Rossiiskaia natsional'naia biblioteka.
SPbFIRI	Sankt-Peterburgskii filial Instituta rossiiskoi istorii Rossiiskoi Akademii nauk.
"Sudnye protsessy"	Barsov, E. V., ed. "Sudnye protsessy XVII–XVIII vekov po delam tserkvi."
TODRL	*Trudy Otdela drevnerusskoi literatury Akademii nauk SSSR.*

Introduction

1. Ginzburg, *Cheese and Worms*, p. XIV.

2. The term "common man" as used here was coined by the German Reformation historian Peter Blickle in his *Revolution von 1525*, p. 179.

3. The beginnings of this process during the seventeenth century have been described in Kapterev, *Svetskie arkhiereiskie chinovniki*; Nikolaevskii, *Patriarshaia oblast'*. On subsequent developments, see Freeze, *Russian Levites*, pp. 46–77.

4. A good description of Nikon's reforms is found in Kapterev, *Patriarkh Nikon i ego protivniki*. The scholars working at the patriarchal printing press relied heavily—at least during the first years of the correction process—on Western compilations of Greek texts, even though they also used the Greek originals. On the use of Greek, Ukrainian, and Venetian manuscripts under Nikon, see Kraft, *Moskaus griechisches Jahrhundert*, pp. 130–31.

5. For a more detailed discussion, see the section on the historiography in this chapter. For additional orientation, see Cherniavsky, "Old Believers and New Religion"; Demkova, "Old Belief's Founder-Fathers."

6. Miliukov, *History of Russia*, 1: 193.

7. Daugny, "Les Raskol'niks"; Kapterev, "Tserkovno-reformatsionnoe dvizhenie."

8. Zenkovsky, *Russkoe staroobriadchestvo*, pp. 7–9; Cherniavsky, "Old Believers and New Religion," pp. 5, 16, 19. See, for example, the following typical statement by Cherniavsky: "The Old Believers were of the lower classes and represented the ideology and aspirations of the Russian masses" (*ibid.*, p. 39). Much has been written in the former Soviet Union about the alleged vernacular idiom of Old Believer writings and their easy accessibility by the "masses." See, for example, Eleonskaia, *Russkaia publitsistika*, pp. 73–75, 124; Vinogradov, "K izucheniiu stilia protopopa Avvakuma," p. 377. Recent research by UCLA linguist Emily Klenin demonstrates that the reading of seventeenth-century Old Believer texts required the knowledge of Church Slavonic, that is, the traditional language of Russian church learning. See also Chernov, "Na kakom iazyke pisal Avvakum?"

9. Zenkovsky, "Ideological World of the Denisov Brothers," p. 51; Demkova, "Old Belief's Founder-Fathers," pp. 9–10.

10. The third phase is described in Zenkovsky, *Russkoe staroobriadchestvo*, pp. 424–66; P. S. Smirnov, *Vnutrennie voprosy*, pp. 131–42, 170–81 and *Spory i razdeleniia v raskole*. On current attempts to revive Old Belief in Moscow, see the essays published by A. Antonov in the Old Believer journal *Tserkov'. Staroobriadcheskii tserkovno-obshchestvennyi zhurnal* (1992), nos. 1–2.

11. See, for example, Oparina, "Prosvetitel' litovskii"; Sarafanova, "Proizvedeniia drevnerusskoi pis'mennosti v sochineniiakh Avvakuma"; Niess, *Kirche in Russland*, pp. 22–43, 64–69.

12. Ginzburg, *Cheese and Worms*, *Night Battles*; Le Roy Ladurie, *Montaillou*.

13. Cf. essays by J. Le Goff, E. Delaruelle, R. Mandrou and other scholars in Le Goff, ed., *Hérésies et sociétés*, pp. 3–5, 147–57, 281–89.

14. The best survey on the church's development after 1700 is found in Smolitsch, *Geschichte der Russischen Kirche*.

15. Barsov, ed., *Novye materialy dlia istorii staroobriadchestva*; *Materialy*; Druzhinin, *Raskol na Donu*, pp. 262–316; *Prilozheniia*.

16. Such publications have been located with the help of the following indexes and bibliographies: Ogurtsev, *Iaroslavskii krai*; Masanov, *Bibliografiia Vladimirskoi gubernii*; Stepanovskii, *Vologodskaia starina*, pp. 453–566; A. V. Smirnov, *Ukazatel' soderzhaniia neoffitsial'noi chasti "Vladimirskikh gubernskikh vedomostei"*; Nikolaev, *Sistematicheskii parallel'nyi ukazatel'*; Karpov, *Sistematicheskii ukazatel' statei*; Shvedova, "Ukazatel' 'Trudov' gubernskikh uchenykh arkhivnykh kommissii"; Titov, *"Iaroslavskie eparkhial'nye vedomosti"*.

17. Nikol'skii, "Sibirskaia ssylka Avvakuma"; Pascal, *Avvakum*, p. XI; Pascal, "Po sledam protopopa Avvakuma."

18. *Pamiatniki*, pp. 78–85, 328–36; *Dokumenty*; Rumiantseva, ed., *Dokumenty prikazov o raskol'nikakh*. See also my review essay on Rumiantseva's publications in Michels, "The Puzzle of Early Old Belief."

19. Available descriptions of local seventeenth-century church archives are very poor and often simply assume that materials have been lost. See, for example, Zdravosmyslov, *Arkhiv i biblioteka Sviateishogo Sinoda*, pp. 12–13, 20, 42–61.

20. *Akty Kholmogorskoi i Ustiuzhskoi eparkhii*; *Opisanie del archiva Solotchinskogo monastyria*; *Drevnie akty Viatskogo kraia*; Ianovskii, "Opisanie aktov novgorodskogo Sofiiskogo doma."

21. SPbFIRI, f. 117, Kollektsiia P. I. Savvaitova; Kurdiumov, "Kollektsiia P. I. Savvaitova"; *Opisanie svitkov*.

22. For a history of the Solovki archive, see Liberson, "Deiatel'nost' Arkheograficheskoi kommissii po spaseniiu arkhiva Solovetskogo monastyria."

23. See the list of unpublished sources in the bibliography of this book.

24. RGADA, f. 163, Raskol'nicheskie dela, nos. 3–12. Other records in this fond date from the first half of the eighteenth century (nos. 13–16). Two documents from 1642 and 1651 (nos. 1–2) have no reference to the schism.

25. " . . . And [concerning] matters that used to be in the Patriarch's Office and involve schism, acts of opposition against the Church of God and heresies: if these matters persist they are to be administered by the Most Holy Stefan, Metropolitan of Riazan' and Murom" (cited from Kapterev, *Svetskie arkhiereiskie chinovniki*, p. 214). Cf. Nolte, "Spätpetrinische Altgläubigenunterdrückung."

26. According to N. N. Novikov, who studied this question at the end of the eighteenth century, we would have to look for patriarchal documents in a wide range of receiving archives and document collections, such as those of the Monastery Office (*Monastyrskii prikaz*) and the so-called Russian Spiritual Affairs (*Rossiiskie dukhovnye dela*), which were used in this study. See Novikov, "Moskovskie prikazy," p. 351.

27. For exceptions, see RGIA, f. 834, Rukopisi Sv. Sinoda which are described in Naster, "Kratkii obzor dokumental'nykh materialov."

28. The most substantial of these is the so-called *Raskol'nicheskaia kontora*, which was organized as a central collecting archive for all documents on religious dissent. The scholar of eighteenth-century dissent can also rely on systematically arranged local archives. For example, an inventory (*opis'*) of Raskol affairs published by the Vladimir Archival Commission comprises detailed listings of all cases conducted by local church and state agents during the eighteenth and nineteenth

centuries. Cf. RGADA, f. 288, Raskol'nicheskaia kontora (1723–1764); Nechaev, "Raskol'nicheskaia kontora"; Sakharov, ed., *Khronologicheskaia opis' del o raskole*; Tel'charov, "Fond Vladimirskoi uchenoi arkhivnoi kommissii."

29. An authority on the Great Schism of the fourteenth century observed about the events at Avignon in 1378 and their aftermath that "no other occurrence of this period left behind such an amount of written material" (Oakley, *Western Church*, p. 55, fn. 30). Similarly, the schism of the sixteenth century, commonly known as the Reformation, can be readily studied and reconstructed from a plethora of documents in German and Swiss archives. In fact, scholars are increasingly moving toward local studies of the Reformation, since city and county archives contain sufficient information to permit such studies. See, for example, Brady, "Social History." The term schism is still applied by some scholars to describe the Reformation period. Cf. Jedin, *Probleme der Kirchenspaltung*.

30. On the rich archival legacies of the Roman Inquisition see, for example, Hennigsen, ed., *Inquisition in Early Modern Europe*; Peters, *Inquisition*. When Ginzburg reconstructed the cosmos of the sixteenth-century miller Menocchio, he was able to learn in detail about Menocchio's reading habits, his thoughts, and his feelings. He managed to identify what he called "the complex of motifs that connect an individual to an historically determinate environment and society." Similarly, Le Roy Ladurie could study the "mentalities" of Cathar peasants, artisans, and shopkeepers in considerable detail because the Vatican archives yielded carefully preserved portfolios that recorded the heresy proceedings in minute detail. See Ginzburg, *Cheese and Worms*, p. XXIV; Le Roy Ladurie, *Montaillou*, pp. VII–XVII.

31. Cf. *Pamiatniki*, p. 122; RGADA, f. 125, Monastyrskii prikaz, opis' 1, g. 1669–70, d. 5; f. 163, d. 3, Sysknoe delo Posol'skogo prikaza o rostovskikh raskol'nikakh, fols. 1–53, esp. 33, 38, 51; f. 210, Razriadnyi prikaz, Prikaznyi stol, d. 416, fol. 57; Moskovskii stol, d. 421, fol. 41; f. 1201, Solovetskii monastyr', opis' 1, dd. 69, 80, 83; RNB, Solovetskoe sobranie, no. 20/1479, nos. 118, 122.

32. Le Roy Ladurie, *Montaillou*, p. XVII.

33. Russian officials also did not have much experience in investigating dissent. Heresy trials had been conducted only sporadically during previous centuries. See Hösch, *Orthodoxie und Häresie*; Kazakova and Lur'e, *Antifeodal'nye ereticheskie dvizheniia*; Zimin, *Peresvetov i ego sovremenniki*.

34. Western interrogators followed handbooks such as the *Directorium inquisitorium* compiled in 1376. The *Directorium* gave "the principles and details which should guide the inquisitor in all his acts. The book remained an authority to the last and formed the basis of all subsequent compilations" (Lea, *Inquisition in the Middle Ages*, pp. 354–55).

35. The first to write about the seventeenth-century schism were Dmytryi Tuptalo and Semen Denisov. See Dmitrii, *Rozysk o Brynskoi vere*; Denisov, *Vinograd rossiiskii*; Sullivan, "Vinograd rossiiskii," "Denisov's Russian Vineyard"; Iukhimenko, "Vinograd rossiiskii."

36. Articles and monographs published in Russia before the October Revolution are counted by the thousands. Since the 1960s a renaissance of schism studies has been under way in the West and the Soviet Union. See Sakharov, *Literatura istorii i oblicheniia russkogo raskola*; Prugavin, *Bibliografiia staroobriadchestva*;

Bibliograficheskii ukazatel' literatury po issledovaniiu pravoslaviia, staroobriadchestva i sektantstva; Heller, "Geschichte der russischen Altgläubigen."

37. Kapterev, *Patriarkh Nikon i tsar' Aleksei Mikhailovich*, 1: 447, 489. P. S. Smirnov observed what he called a primitive "literal and ritualistic faith" (*bukvo-obriado-verie*) and spoke, in particular, of "eschatological hopes" (*eskhatologicheskie chaianiia*), which were extensions of traditional Muscovite anti-Latinism and end time expectations evoked by Catholic aspirations in the East. See *Vnutrennie voprosy*, pp. CXXIX–CXXXIII.

38. See, for example, Shchapov, *Russkii raskol*, pp. 23–24, 81–91, 218–19, esp. 87.

39. *Ibid.*, pp. 159, 250–62, 365–80. For a typical generalization about the Nikon period (1652–58), the rest of the seventeenth century, and the first half of the eighteenth century, see *ibid.*, p. 9.

40. Shchapov, *Zemstvo i raskol*. On this and other journalistic works by the same author, see Wachendorf, "Regionalismus, Raskol und Volk bei A. P. Shchapov."

41. Andreev, *Raskol v narodnoi russkoi istorii*; Kablits, *Russkie dissidenty-starovery*.

42. Conybeare, *Russian Dissenters*, pp. 46, 55.

43. Zenkovsky, *Russkoe staroobriadchestvo*, pp. 27, 29, 169, 226, 302.

44. It is interesting to note that most of Cherniavsky's data are taken from early eighteenth-century sources. See Cherniavsky, "Old Believers and New Religion," pp. 7, 10, 18, 24, 27, 37.

45. Billington, *Icon and Axe*, pp. 139–40.

46. Most recently, see Uspenskii, "The Schism and Cultural Conflict." See also Neubauer, *Car und Selbstherrscher*, pp. 103, 137; Heller, *Die Moskauer Eiferer*, pp. 9, 21, 55, 95; Lupinin, *Religious Revolt*, pp. 11–14; Riasanovsky, *History of Russia*, pp. 218–20.

47. Pascal, *Avvakum*, pp. XVI–XVII, XXII, XXIV.

48. *Ibid.*, pp. X–XIII, 228–51, 442–52.

49. Hauptmann, *Altrussischer Glaube*, pp. 67–74.

50. Crummey, "Interpretations of Old Belief," p. 4.

51. Crummey, "Old Belief as Popular Religion," esp. pp. 706–7.

52. Crummey, "The Works of Avraamii."

53. Crummey, "Religious Radicalism," esp. p. 184.

54. Crummey, "Old Belief as Popular Religion," pp. 703, 705–7; "Interpretations of Old Belief," p. 6.

55. See, for example, V. I. Malyshev's numerous articles documenting the results of his archeographical expeditions and research on Archpriest Avvakum listed in Droblenkova, comp., "Spisok pechatnykh rabot Malysheva (1940–1971)," "Spisok pechatnykh rabot Malysheva (prodolzhenie)." In addition, see Malyshev, *Ust'-tsilemskie sborniki*, *Drevnerusskie rukopisi Pushkinskogo Doma*; Bubnov, ed., *Sochineniia pisatelei-staroobriadtsev*; Demkova, *Zhitie protopopa Avvakuma*; Pozdeeva, "Drevnerusskoe nasledie."

56. Robinson, *Bor'ba idei*, pp. 6–7, 21; idem, "Tvorchestvo Avvakuma"; Eleonskaia, *Russkaia publitsistika*, pp. 66–72, 89–95, 124.

57. Klibanov, *Narodnaia sotsial'naia utopiia*, pp. 110–25; Chistov, *Russkie narodnye legendy*, pp. 88–89; Rogov, "Narodnye massy i religioznye dvizheniia";

Shul'gin, "Kapitonovshchina"; Ankudinova, "Vzgliady pervykh raskol'nikov i narodnye massy."

58. Mel'gunov, *Religiozno-obshchestvennye dvizheniia*. For a discussion of populist and Marxist conceptualizations of the schism, see Pokrovskii, *Antifeodal'nyi protest*, pp. 5–7, 17–18.

59. Kartsov, *Religioznyi raskol*, 1: 76–101. See, for example, the following statement: "Under the leadership of Avvakum the Russian schismatic movement (*raskol'nicheskoe dvizhenie*) objectively assumed the character of a social protest. . . . " (*ibid.*, 1: 100).

60. See especially studies of the revolt at the Solovki Monastery such as Barsukov, *Solovetskoe vosstanie* or V. Chumicheva, "Stranitsy istorii solovetskogo vosstaniia."

61. Pokrovskii, *Antifeodal'nyi protest*, pp. 7–8, 31.

62. Druzhinin, *Raskol na Donu*, esp. pp. III–IX.

63. As indicated above Rumiantseva published most of the documents that form the backbone of her study. See also Michels, "The Puzzle of Early Old Belief."

64. Ankudinova, "Sotsial'nyi sostav pervykh raskol'nikov," esp. p. 61; Rumiantseva, *Narodnoe antitserkovnoe dvizhenie*, pp. 199–207, 219–22.

65. Zhivov, ed., *Pustoozerskaia proza*, p. 9.

66. Kalugin, "Ivan Groznyi i protopop Avvakum," esp. pp. 44, 46–47, 63; Klibanov, "Protopop Avvakum i apostol Pavel," esp. p. 22.

67. "Great movements have always great causes" (Conybeare, *Russian Dissenters*, p. 27).

68. On self-designations used by Western dissenters, see Moore, *Origins of European Dissent*, pp. 170–71, 227; Peters, ed., *Heresy and Authority*, p. 104.

69. See, for example, *Materialy*, 6: 62; 7: 32, 35; Borozdin, *Avvakum* (1900), pp. 269–70, 284; appendix, pp. 19–27, 65–70. The name *starovertsy* became the norm in early eighteenth-century texts. Cf. Denisov, *Vinograd rossiiskii*, fol. 7v and the so-called *Skazanie o starovertsakh zhivushchikh v zemli Moldavskoi* mentioned in P. S. Smirnov, *Iz istorii raskola*, p. 24, fn. 16. The name was apparently first used in a 1691 treatise by the monk Efrosin. See Chapter Three.

70. Zenkovsky, "Ideological World of the Denisov Brothers," p. 52.

71. See, for example, *Materialy* 6: 60–61, 81–82, 88–89; Borozdin, *Avvakum* (1900), appendix, pp. 34–35. The first to develop this language of belonging was apparently Ivan Neronov, in *Materialy*, 1: 53, 72–73 ["men of God" (*liudi Bozhie*) and "bondsmen of Christ" (*Khristovy raby*)].

72. I have decided not to adopt these terms because Neronov and Avvakum did not apply them consistently. In fact, they used the other terms mentioned here just as frequently. Cf. *Materialy*, 1: 79, 97, 102; Heller, *Die Moskauer Eiferer*, pp. 12–13, 32–33, 75; Kapterev, *Patriarkh Nikon i ego protivniki*, chaps. 1–2. On Avvakum's use of the term "zealot," see also Chapter One.

73. Zenkovsky, "Ideological World of the Denisov Brothers," pp. 63, 66.

74. In this sense, one can compare Old Belief to other reform movements within the Orthodox Church, such as those inspired by hesychasm and involving men like Nil Sorskii and Paisii Velichkovskii. See Ware, *Russian Orthodox Church*, pp. 62–70, 104–8, 117–18, 120–21. The term *ecclesia spiritualis* was coined by Western Christian reform movements that juxtaposed the ideal image of a purified church to

the existing church, which was usually deemed too worldly and corrupt. See, for example, Benz, *Ecclesia spiritualis* and Hammann, *Ecclesia spiritualis.*

75. The terms were probably invented by Andrei and Semen Denisov. See Liubopytnyi, "Katalog starovercheskoi tserkvi," pp. 2–11, 49–52; Karlovich, *Istoricheskie issledovaniia*, 1: 4, 15–16; Knie, *Russisch-Schismatische Kirche.* For a discussion of Karlovich's influential work, see "Novoe raskol'nicheskoe uchenie."

76. On the definition of Old Belief by a number of erudite eighteenth-century Old Believer scholars, see Druzhinin, "Slovesnye nauki"; *Pomorskie paleografy*; Chrysostomos, "Pomorskie Otvety als Denkmal des Altgläubigentums." In addition to the well-known Denisov brothers, Druzhinin mentions the names of other learned writers who have not yet been studied by historians.

Chapter One

1. Kapterev, *Patriarkh Nikon i tsar' Aleksei Mikhailovich*, 1: 106–14; Stroev, *Spiski ierarkhov*, col. 6; Golubinskii, *Istoriia kanonizatsii sviatykh*, pp. 267–68, 549.

2. For the standard dating of the schism see, for example, Kartsov, *Religioznyi raskol*, 1: 84 and Zenkovsky, "Russian Schism," p. 41.

3. *Materialy*, 6: 74; Borozdin, *Avvakum* (1898), appendix, no. 10.

4. A good synopsis of seventeenth-century Old Believer writings on these themes is found in P. S. Smirnov, *Vnutrennie voprosy*, pp. 1–15. For more detail, see Levitskii, "Pervye raskolouchiteli ob antikhriste"; Maksimov, *Rasskazy iz istorii staroobriadchestva*, pp. 39–80. For a popular eighteenth-century tale about Nikon, see the "Povest' o zhitii i konchine Nikona."

5. Cf. the very different approaches to the Nikon period in Meyendorff, *Russia, Ritual and Reform*; Uspensky, "The Collision of Two Theologies"; Kapterev, *Patriarkh Nikon i tsar' Aleksei Mikhailovich*, 1: 151–269, 432–90.

6. Makarii, *Patriarkh Nikon*, p. 15. The text of the original order has not survived. Makarii extrapolates its contents on the basis of Neronov's 1654 letters. Cf. a similar order dated June 2, 1654 which called for the confiscation of crosses in Moscow. See RGADA, f. 141, Prikaznye dela starykh let, opis' 3, g. 1654, d. 62, Pamiat' dumnomu d'iaku Almazu Ivanovu o vymene krestov blagosloviashchikh.

7. See, for example, an article added to the Liturgy of St. Chrysostomos, in RGADA, f. 1182, Prikaz knigopechatnogo dela, bk. 57, Kniga prikhodnaia novovykhodnym knigam (1655–61), fol. 190.

8. RGADA, f. 184, Arkhiv S. A. Belokurova, opis' 1, d. 1421, fols. 33–35; NB MGU, Sobranie knig kirillicheskoi pechati XV–XVII vv., no. 514, Sbornik Skrizhal' (1655), fol. 573. Priests and parishioners were told that the three-finger sign of the cross signified the Holy Trinity. The book was in all likelihood translated by Arsenii the Greek. Cf. Steinke, "Eine Dokumentation der Altgläubigen zum Zweifingerkreuz."

9. Makarii, *Patriarkh Nikon*, p. 83.

10. Makarii, *Istoriia russkoi tserkvi*, 12: 191–95.

11. Golubinskii, *K nashei polemike s staroobriadtsami*, p. 65.

12. *Puteshestvie antiokhiiskogo patriarkha Makariia*, 3: 137–38, 145–46, 184–85.

13. RGADA, f. 153, Rossiiskie dukhovnye dela, d. 48, Rospis' v obidakh sviateishogo patriarkha Nikona, fols. 1–3.

14. In Ukraine the three-finger sign of the cross was the dominant form, see Golubinskii, *K nashei polemike s staroobriadtsami*, pp. 171–72.

15. "Tsarskaia poslushnaia gramota krest'ianam Klinskogo uezda," *Akty Iverskogo monastyria*, cols. 57–61; "Otpiska patriarkhu Nikonu o neposlushanii pakhotnykh liudei," *ibid.*, col. 167 (after June 19, 1655).

16. *Ibid.*, cols. 39–41.

17. GIM, Sobranie Sinodal'noi biblioteki, no. 93, fols. 1–129, Kniga zapisnaia oblacheniem i deistvu velikogo gosudaria sviateishogo Nikona. See also Golubtsov, "Chinovniki moskovskogo Uspenskogo sobora," pp. XXXII–XXXV and Savva, *Ukazatel' Moskovskoi patriarshei riznitsy*, p. 219.

18. *Puteshestvie antiokhiiskogo patriarkha Makariia*, 4: 108–9.

19. Kozhanchikov, ed., *Opisanie sochinenii napisannykh raskol'nikami*, 2: 8–9, 52.

20. Cf. also the introduction of the new Creed. The early Old Believers were profoundly disturbed by the deletion of the word *istinnyi* ("true"); however, Nikon's contemporaries showed no such concern. In March 1658, the patriarchal printing press began to issue one-page leaflets with instructions on changes in the new Creed. Soon afterward thirty-six hundred copies had been sold—a fact indicating that a great number of priests and laymen were willing to buy such leaflets. See RGADA, f. 1182, bk. 57, fols. 597, 599v.

21. Kartsov, *Religioznyi raskol*, 1: 77–78, 84; Rumiantseva, *Narodnoe antitserkovnoe dvizhenie*, pp. 99–104. See also Makarii, *Istoriia russkogo raskola*, pp. 145–47 and Kapterev, *Patriarkh Nikon i tsar' Aleksei Mikhailovich*, 1: 146–50.

22. Gibbenet, *Istoricheskoe issledovanie dela patriarkha Nikona*, 2: 473–76, esp. 474. The original manuscript is preserved in RGADA, f. 27, Tainyi prikaz, d. 89, fols. 1–5.

23. "Looking at Nikon many priests have run away from their parish churches and Orthodox Christians are dying without confession and communion" (Gibbenet, *Istoricheskoe issledovanie dela patriarkha Nikona*, 2: 474).

24. One of the earliest examples is Fedor Ivanov's tract *O bogootmetnike Nikone* which was written in the late 1660s and refers to Nikon as "the precursor of the Antichrist who destroyed the Church of God. . . ." (*Materialy*, 6: 299–302).

25. Cf. Kozlov, "Delo Nikona," esp. p. 109; Rushinskii, comp., "Religioznyi byt," pp. 14–15.

26. Gibbenet, *Istoricheskoe issledovanie dela patriarkha Nikona*, 2: 474.

27. *Ibid.*, pp. 473–74.

28. This interpretation is further supported by the eyewitness account of Pavel of Aleppo who attributed the uproar against Nikon entirely to the destruction of icons, in *Puteshestvie antiokhiiskogo patriarkha Makariia*, 3: 136–37.

29. Another piece of evidence seems to support the notion of discontent in response to Nikon's liturgical books, but this evidence is not entirely trustworthy. Records pertaining to the speech in which Nikon announced his abdication as patriarch in July 1658, include the testimony of an eyewitness, Iov, the patriarchal sacristan (*riznichii*), who reported Nikon's words as follows: "When I traveled with . . . Tsar Aleksei Mikhailovich to the Kaliazin Monastery, a crowd of people gathered around Mount Calvary (*lobnoe mesto*) in Moscow and began to call me an iconoclast: 'You have removed and destroyed many icons.' They wanted to kill me for this. But I had seized only Latin icons before which nobody is permitted to

bow down . . . I am not an iconoclast. And they have been calling me a heretic ever since then: 'You gave us new books.' This is the punishment for my sins. . . . You may stone me, but I cannot save you with my blood. Rather than have you stone me and call me a heretic, I will henceforth no longer be the patriarch, and will leave you in the hands of the living God. He may save you" (*Delo*, p. 38). However, Iov may not have been a credible witness. He was the only witness, in fact, who interpreted Nikon to have said that the Moscow populace resented the revision of liturgical books. And when Iov's interrogators told him they found his testimony barely credible since none of the many other witnesses would confirm it (*ibid.*, pp. 20–49, esp. 23–24, 33), Iov withdrew his statement, admitting that Nikon had *not* mentioned the new liturgies in his speech (pp. 49, 68). Cf. Kapterev, *Patriarkh Nikon i tsar' Aleksei Mikhailovich*, 1: 489–90.

30. RGADA, f. 210, Prikaznyi stol, d. 298; f. 141, opis' 3, g. 1657, d. 69, Skazki ob iz"iatii ikon iz tserkvei. Published in part, in Kotkov, *Moskovskaia rech'*, pp. 294–312 and Kämpfer, "Verhöre." I thank Frank Kämpfer for calling my attention to this case.

31. RGADA, f. 210, Prikaznyi stol, d. 298, fols. 13, 46; Kämpfer, "Verhöre," p. 298, fn. 18.

32. RGADA, f. 210, Prikaznyi stol, d. 298, fols. 35, 37; Kämpfer, "Verhöre," p. 296.

33. RGADA, f. 210, Prikaznyi stol, d. 298, fol. 51; Kämpfer, "Verhöre," p. 296.

34. RGADA, f. 210, Prikaznyi stol, d. 298, fol. 3; Kämpfer, "Verhöre," p. 299.

35. *Delo*, p. 38; Makarii, *Istoriia russkoi tserkvi*, 12: 32; Kämpfer, "Verhöre," p. 301. This finding contradicts the later assertions of Old Believers about Nikon. See, for example, Archpriest Avvakum's statement that "[the] dirty dog Nikon, the enemy, has designed it so that one should paint the saints as though they are living, and arrange everything in a Frankish (*pofriazh'skomu*), foreign way" (*Pamiatniki istorii staroobriadchestva*, col. 283 as translated in Uspenskii, "Schism and Cultural Conflict," p. 124).

36. Some of the earliest Old Believer tracts attributed to Fedor Ivanov and Nikita Dobrynin underscore the discrepancies among the six editions of the Service Book, in *Materialy*, 4: 109; 6: 22–23. See also Kapterev, *Patriarkh Nikon i tsar' Aleksei Mikhailovich*, 1: 240–42.

37. Makarii, *Patriarkh Nikon*, p. 89.

38. "We were correcting many other books while we were working on this one and were therefore prevented from correcting it well" (*ibid.*).

39. The editors of the Psalter printed in 1658 insisted that the book "had been corrected with great care (*prilezhnim izpravleniem*) on the basis of Greek books" (RGADA, f. 184, opis' 1, d. 1421, fol. 34).

40. This notion was developed early on in the work of Old Belief intellectuals such as Semen Denisov. See, for example, the preface of his *Vinograd rossiiskii*, esp. fols. 12–13v.

41. RGADA, f. 1182, bk. 57, fol. 62a (sic). The priests are listed next to such eminent figures as the Serbian patriarch, the metropolitan of Krutitsa and one of the chief editors at the patriarchal printing press, Evfimii.

42. See the interrogation of the parishioners of the St. Nicholas Church, in RGADA, f. 210, Prikaznyi stol, d. 298, fols. 32–32v; Kotkov, *Moskovskaia rech'*, pp. 294–95.

43. RGADA, f. 1182, bk. 57, fol. 76v.

44. RGADA, f. 210, Prikaznyi stol, d. 298, fols. 26r-v; Kotkov, *Moskovskaia rech'*, pp. 305–6.

45. The sale of the original version of the Service Book was stopped temporarily in January 1656 because the patriarchal printing press thought it necessary to add further emendations. See RGADA, f. 1182, bk. 57, fols. 65v, 70v.

46. *Ibid.*, fols. 63r-v, 65, 72v, 74v, 80v.

47. Of the twelve hundred copies printed in the first issue (*vykhod*), 840 were purchased by bishops for dissemination in local parishes; one hundred were handed over to the tsar's court for the use of the royal family; fifty were given to Nikon. The editors, among them Arsenii the Greek and Evfimii, were given one book each (fols. 56v–57). Some other priests purchasing the books were not identified by place of residence. For example, it is difficult to say whether the priest Aleksei of the St. Elisius Church lived in Moscow or elsewhere (fol. 81).

48. *Ibid.*, fols. 63v, 69r-v, 70, 72, etc.

49. *Ibid.*, fols. 96, 215v, 447v; RGADA, f. 1182, bk. 59, Kniga bez zaglaviia. Vykhod i prodazha raznogo roda knig (1659–70), fols. 303, 564, 574, 592v.

50. RGADA, f. 1182, bk. 57, fols. 66, 208, 458v, 459v, 462.

51. *Ibid.*, fols. 65, 92, 96v, 215v. Both Shorin and Nikon conducted most of their business in the Nizhnii Novgorod area. Concerning some of Nikon's practices, see RGADA, f. 27, d. 558, fol. 18 (petition). On Shorin's business interests in the Nizhnii Novgorod area, see Baron, "Vasilii Shorin."

52. RGADA, f. 1182, bk. 57, fol. 74v; bk. 59, fol. 280v. See, for example, the arrest and exile of a certain Iur'ia Ivanov for harboring thieves who had broken into local churches, in RGADA, f. 396, Arkhiv Oruzheinoi Palaty, d. 42812, Gramota ob otsylke v Sibir' Iur'ia Ivanova z zhenoi i det'mi (March, 1659), esp. fol. 1. Other conflicts arose over the hiding of peasants who had fled from church lands (d. 42892), the ownership of property (d. 43318), or the endowment of local parishes with land and money (d. 43789).

53. RGADA, f. 1182, bk. 57, fols. 93, 173v, 178, 348v; bk. 59, fols. 302, 305; Kapterev, *Patriarkh Nikon i ego protivniki*, pp. 171–73; Torke, *Staatsbedingte Gesellschaft*, pp. 226–27.

54. Cherniavsky, "Old Believers and New Religion," p. 9.

55. Shimko, *Patriarshii kazennyi prikaz*, pp. 139–41. Churches owned by Nikon seemed to have fared worse than others. The census register of 1678 mentions, for example, a church in a village just outside of Moscow that had been "standing without services" for many years. See Kholmogorov, ed., *Istoricheskie materialy o tserkvakh*, 6: 2.

56. Such petitions are found embedded in the tax registers. See Shimko, *Patriarshii kazennyi prikaz*, pp. 142–43. The frequent occurrence of official violence against priests is also demonstrated by the fact that the prison cells of Moscow were filled with priests. See, for example, RGADA, f. 235, Patriarshii kazennyi prikaz, opis' 2, bk. 41, Raskhodnaia kniga 165 goda, fol. 250 (distribution of money to the children of priests who had died in prison). In addition, priests often became the targets of investigation for hiding runaways in their parishes, see SPbFIRI, f. 117, Kollektsiia P. I. Savvaitova, no. 332. In March 1657, priests from the Vologda area were seized and sent to the Banditry Office (*Razboinyi prikaz*). See *ibid.*, no. 435.

57. See, for example, SPbFIRI, f. 117, Kollektsiia P. I. Savvaitova, nos. 319, 324, 419, 437.

58. RGADA, f. 27, d. 558, Spisok s anonimnogo pis'ma . . . o pritesneniiakh dukhovenstvu vo vremia patriarshestva Nikona, fols. 1–33.

59. The author personally knew leading patriarchal officials and was familiar with their corrupt practices (*ibid.*, fols. 11–13, 28, 30). It is likely that he was connected with the patriarchal court for many decades because he spoke very positively of Patriarch Filaret, who died in 1633 (fol. 31). Also, by seventeenth-century standards, he had a remarkable mastery of Church Slavonic (esp. fols. 2–4).

60. *Ibid.*, fols. 24, 27–28.

61. For example, the petition confiscated from Nikita Dobrynin in 1666, in *Materialy*, 4: 1–130.

62. RGADA, f. 27, d. 558, fols. 5, 7–8. See also Nikon's order to issue printed appointment papers (*stavlennye gramoty*), in RGADA, f. 1182, bk. 57, fols. 601, 606 (May, 1658).

63. RGADA, f. 27, d. 558, fols. 11–12.

64. We know only that priests who did in fact manage to obtain their appointment papers also accepted a copy of the revised Service Book. See, for example, RGADA, f. 1182, bk. 57, fol. 446 (October, 1657).

65. Kholmogorovy, eds., *Materialy dlia istorii Vladimirskoi eparkhii*, 1: 18. The tax books covering the Suzdal' eparchy are particularly comprehensive and can be taken as a good example of Nikon's tax policies.

66. *Ibid.*, pp. 103, 138.

67. Priests who worked in parishes belonging to the patriarchal see were sometimes exempt from tax. See, for example, the village of Chiurilovo which belonged to a patriarchal (*patriarshii domovoi*) monastery (*ibid.*, p. 157).

68. See, for example, the *Shield of Faith* which became one of the most important miscellanies of seventeenth-century Old Belief. For a discussion of this text, see Bubnov, *Staroobriadcheskaia kniga*, pp. 117–19, 123–24, 139–41.

69. For more information about Spiridon's *Book*, see Chapter Two.

70. Rumiantseva, *Narodnoe antitserkovnoe dvizhenie*, p. 126. Rumiantseva quotes from an eighteenth-century version of the text housed in the P. M. Stroev Collection at RGB (*ibid.*, p. 121, fn. 23).

71. Billington, *Icon and Axe*, p. 143; "Neglected Figures," pp. 193–95. Billington quotes from an 1824 copy of an eighteenth-century manuscript found in GIM, Sobranie A. I. Khludova, no. 351. He also accepts the ideas expressed in the eighteenth-century Khludov version of Spiridon's *Vita* as historical fact. For a description of the manuscript, see Popov, *Opisanie biblioteki Khludova*, pp. 642–46.

72. RGADA, f. 1182, bk. 57, fol. 73 and Kurdiumov, "Kollektsiia P. I. Savvaitova," pp. 63–70. Cases, charters and other records (nos. 414–61) dating from January 1656 to July 1658 indicate that Vologdans were apparently not concerned with liturgical issues. Several of the texts deal with land and money seized by Nikon and his crony Ivan Kokoshilov (e.g. nos. 443–45).

73. See, for example, RGADA, f. 1182, bk. 57, fols. 91v–92; bk. 59, fol. 557.

74. RGADA, f. 1182, bk. 57, fol. 102v; bk. 59, fols. 286, 295v.

75. Metropolitan Makarii bought two hundred copies of the new Service Book in February of 1656 (RGADA, f. 1182, bk. 57, fol. 73). Novgorodian docu-

ments covering the period from 1652 to 1660 are silent about the liturgical books. See Ianovskii, "Opisanie aktov novgorodskogo Sofiiskogo doma," pp. 22–30.

76. RGADA, f. 163, d. 3, fols. 1–51. Large parts of the *delo* were published in "Sudnye protsessy," pp. 3–13 and Rumiantseva, ed., *Dokumenty prikazov o raskol'nikakh*, pp. 29–58.

77. RGADA, f. 163, d. 3, fol. 13.

78. *Ibid*. See also *BE*, 32 (1895): 654–58.

79. RGADA, f. 163, d. 3, fol. 7. On changes in the *chin vodoosviashcheniia*, see Makarii, *Istoriia russkoi tserkvi*, 12: 200–201.

80. RGADA, f. 163, d. 3, fol. 9.

81. Rumiantseva, *Narodnoe antitserkovnoe dvizhenie*, pp. 133–36, esp. 134.

82. RGADA, f. 163, d. 3, fol. 39. It is, of course, possible that some of Sila's disciples escaped unnoticed. However, even if we allow for this possibility, their number must have been very small. The metropolitan gave an order to search houses and to arrest the relatives of those who went into hiding (*kotorye ukhoroniatsia*). However, there is no indication that any such arrests occurred at this time.

83. "Nowadays [they] cross themselves by putting together the fingers as required. [They] have been doing so ever since the new Service Books were sent by orders of the Great Lord and Holy Nikon, Muscovite Patriarch of All of Great and Little and White Russia. And [they] teach their spiritual children to do the same" (*ibid*., fol. 32).

84. *Ibid*., fol. 37.

85. *Ibid*., fols. 20–22.

86. Sila's religious fervor was very similar. Even after extensive torture, he still insisted that "he feared no one on earth" (*ibid*., fol. 46).

87. Theologians such as P. Tillich, are critical of attempts to dissect the religious experience: "[Faith is] participation in the subject of one's ultimate concern with one's whole being" (Tillich, *Dynamics of Faith*, p. 32).

88. The first books arrived at Rostov in September of 1655. See RGADA, f. 1182, bk. 57, fol. 68.

89. RGADA, f. 163, d. 3, fols. 24, 31–32; "Sudnye protsessy," p. 11.

90. For a more detailed discussion of the connections between the plague and religious dissent in seventeenth-century Russia, see Chapter Six.

91. RGADA, f. 163, d. 2, Rasprosnye i pytochnye rechi raskol'nika [sic] Fedora Shilovtsova, fol. 8.

92. Vozdvizhenskii, *Istoricheskoe obozrenie Riazanskoi ierarkhii*, pp. 118–19.

93. RGADA, f. 153, d. 20, pts. I–X, Delo Posol'skogo prikaza o posylke mitropolita Nikona v Solovetskii monastyr'. Parts of this case have been published in *Sobranie gosudarstvennykh gramot i dogovorov*, vol. 3, nos. 147, 149–154.

94. Tolstoi, *Drevnie sviatyni Rostova*, pp. 29–30, 77.

95. "When they brought Metropolitan Filipp, God admitted the soul of Metropolitan Varlaam and took him to Heaven because you were cheating with the [relics]. This is why God took his soul away from you swindlers (*plutniki*)" (RGADA, f. 163, d. 3, fol. 8; "Sudnye protsessy," p. 5).

96. " . . . And he wants to continue crossing himself as Metropolitan Varlaam and his spiritual father taught him before. . . . " (RGADA, f. 163, d. 3, fol. 15).

Fedor and Aleksei also named Varlaam as the source of their beliefs: " . . . [They] want to] hold their fingers . . . as Metropolitan Varlaam taught them" (*ibid.*, fol. 21). If we can believe information about Sila that circulated among eighteenth-century Old Believers, Varlaam had been his protector and educator. See Koz-hanchikov, ed., *Opisanie sochinenii napisannykh raskol'nikami*, 1: 153. A pamphlet held in possession for some time by the illiterate Sila (*u nego tetrad' davno*) may have been given to him by Varlaam (fol. 30). That pamphlet bore the title *Skazanie o vere* and was probably an excerpt from the *Kniga o vere*, a book that strongly influenced the thinking of Muscovite hierarchs during the late 1640s. See Niess, *Kirche in Russland*.

97. Traditionally several deacons and priests would recite a number of differ-ent litanies and psalms simultaneously or "in many voices" (*mnogoglasno*) which usually resulted in quite chaotic performances. Patriarch Iosif insisted that each litany and psalm had to be recited separately and "in one voice" (*edinoglasno*). See von Gardner, *Gesang der russisch-orthodoxen Kirche*; Rogov, *Muzykal'naia estetika*; Hannick, "Der einstimmige Russische Kirchengesang."

98. "If people of church rank disregard the singing and recitation of the lit-urgy, or if they fail to sing and recite in one voice, you should report them to me in Rostov, my son. We have orders to send these [people] into exile under strict guard . . . " (Belokurov, "Deianie sobora 1649 goda," p. 46, fn. 25).

99. It also did not seem to make any difference to Sila that Varlaam had par-ticipated in the elevation of Nikon to the metropolitan see of Novgorod. See RGADA, f. 153, opis' 1, d. 16, Nastol'naia gramota mitropolita Nikona, fol. 4.

100. "You are not pastors, but wolves and robbers. You have fallen in love with opulent meals and your teachings are deceitful and degenerate. The relics of Metropolitan Filipp did not produce any miracles after you gave the order to pray to him on our rosaries. You lied to us promising that God would have mercy on us when we prayed to St. Filipp and St. Ignatii of Rostov. But you, Metropolitan Iona, did not bring real relics but merely a puppet (*kuklu*)" (RGADA, f. 163, d. 3, fol. 6; "Sudnye protsessy," p. 4). In Sila's religious world, Filipp was the reincarna-tion of the fifteenth-century Metropolitan Isidor who had accepted the Catholic faith at the Council of Florence. Sila was convinced that Filipp had brought along "the heretical papal belief" (RGADA, f. 163, d. 3, fol. 12).

101. Bushkovitch, *Religion and Society*, pp. 89–99.

102. Golubinskii, *Istoriia kanonizatsii sviatykh*, pp. 418–21.

103. Sila accused Iona of many other things. For example, he was convinced that Iona had paid substantial bribes to become metropolitan. He also resented the fact that Iona, previously the archimandrite of the local Bogoiavlenskii Monastery, had replaced his former loyalty to Varlaam with allegiance to Patriarch Nikon whom Sila considered a "big shot" (*bol'shoi shish*). Iona's successor at the monastery closely collaborated with episcopal investigators. See RGADA, f. 163, d. 3, fols. 7–10; "Sudnye protsessy," p. 5; Tolstoi, *Drevnie sviatyni Rostova*, p. 77.

104. "He could not say what exactly had been left out or changed. Instead he said many things, showing that he did not have any knowledge of books" (RGADA, f. 163, d. 3, fol. 12). For similar statements, see *ibid.*, fols. 15–16.

105. "How can he claim to know such a serious matter? That is the task of pas-tors in the church. Nothing that existed previously in the church has been changed,

let alone corrected. Those articles to which he referred when he spoke about books ... were shown to him and explained. ... " (*ibid.*, fol. 16). Sila had acquired some rudimentary knowledge of the liturgy from his parish priest, who had read to him from the Horologion (*chasovnik*) (fol. 15).

106. Gibbenet, *Istoricheskoe issledovanie dela patriarkha Nikona*, 2: 497–504.

107. Tikhomirov, *Klassovaia bor'ba*, p. 250; GIM, Sobranie Sinodal'noi biblioteki, no. 1071; Protas'eva, "Stolbtsy Sinodal'nogo sobraniia," p. 286.

108. P. S. Smirnov, *Vnutrennie voprosy*, pp. CIII, CXX.

109. On Nikon's friendship with Stefan, see Syrtsev, *Vozmushchenie solovetskikh monakhov*, p. 76.

110. *Prilozheniia*, pp. 1–33, esp. 25–26. It is noteworthy that these grievances received the Kremlin's attention only one year after Nikon's abdication.

111. *Materialy*, 4: 175; Titov, *Suzdal'skaia ierarkhiia*, pp. 77–78.

112. A. A. Titov points out that Iosif was absent from the 1656 Church Council. See *ibid.*, p. 78. See also the list of signatories at the 1656 Church Council in *Materialy*, 1: 9, fn. 1 and RGADA, f. 1182, bk. 57, fol. 73v (February, 1656).

113. *Prilozheniia*, p. 36.

114. *Ibid.*, pp. 3–92. The original *svitki* and *stolbtsy* are found in the Collection of the Synodal Library (*ibid.*, pp. IX–X).

115. For a short survey of all complaints, see *ibid.*, pp. 64–70.

116. *Ibid.*, pp. 46, 90.

117. *Ibid.*, p. 48. The Lamb of God (*agnets Bozhii*) is a piece of bread that is taken from the host during the transubstantiation ceremony for special consecration. During the seventeenth century, priests took such pieces to sick parishioners who could not attend Mass. Among other things, Stefan had attempted to restrict the frequency of its use. This regulation was probably not part of Nikon's reform agenda, but the result of Stefan's arbitrariness. See efforts of Stefan to extricate himself from the accusations at the 1660 Church Council (p. 65). The Lamb of God was discussed at the 1666 Church Council, in *DAI*, 5: 463–64. For more information, see *PPBES*, 1: 57–58.

118. "Tipikon," *PPBES*, 2: 2159.

119. *Prilozheniia*, pp. 56–57.

120. *Ibid.*, p. 56. Stefan defended his behavior by claiming that he had acted on Nikon's orders. See *ibid.*, pp. 68–69.

121. Suzdal' clerics did not mind participating in services conducted according to the new Service Book. One of them stated the following: "Archbishop Stefan said the divine liturgy according to the tradition of the Holy Apostles and Fathers using the new Service Books. ... And he [the cleric] fulfilled those parts in the service which corresponded to his priestly rank and his abilities. ... " (*ibid.*, p. 89).

122. *Ibid.*, p. 49. The abbot apparently did not want to say Mass with clerics whom he disliked.

123. *Ibid.* A priest wearing only a stole (*epitrakhel'*) is considered to be only half-dressed since he is supposed to wear an additional outer vestment, the so-called *felon*, during Mass.

124. " ... He treated them to wine, beer and mead, sweet liqueur (*romaneia*) and Rhine wine every day" (*ibid.*, p. 50). On Stefan's failure to enforce basic rules of fasting, see *ibid.*, pp. 49, 59.

125. These clerics represented the full spectrum of ecclesiastical offices in the diocese of Suzdal': archimandrites (9), abbots (4), abbesses (3), archpriests (7), monks and nuns (420), priests and deacons (148), subdeacons and choral singers (40).

126. *Ibid.*, pp. 46, 50–51, 53, 59.

127. *Ibid.*, p. 46.

128. *Ibid.*, p. 53.

129. The best documented example is the refusal of the archimandrites and elders of the Solovki Monastery to pray for the tsar and his family. See, for example, *Materialy*, 3: 53.

130. This custom dates back to Kievan times. See Goetz, *Kirchenrechtliche Denkmäler*, pp. 213–14.

131. Ogloblin, "Obozrenie Sibirskogo prikaza," *Chteniia*, 1895, bk. 2, pt. 4, pp. 197, 368.

132. *Prilozheniia*, pp. 7, 47.

133. *DAI*, 5: 475.

134. *Prilozheniia*, pp. 46, 59. In the Vologda eparchy, icons were apparently also confiscated. However, there is no indication that such measures led to a revolt against the archbishop. See lists of icons (*rospisi ikonam*) belonging to local parish churches (dated August/September, 1653 and February, 1656), in Kurdiumov, "Kollektsiia P. I. Savvaitova," pp. 51–52, 63.

135. *Prilozheniia*, pp. 61–63, 66–68.

136. *Ibid.*, pp. 55–56.

137. *Ibid.*, p. 68.

138. I found only one comparable case. In 1656 Abbot Iona Apraksin, who had just been appointed, remodelled the altars in the main church of the Spaso-Prilutskii Monastery outside Vologda. It is, of course, possible that Stefan was merely overzealous in executing Nikon's policy of replacing traditional altar cloths (*antiminsy*). See Savvaitov, *Opisanie Spaso-Prilutskogo monastyria*, p. 17; Makarii, *Istoriia russkoi tserkvi*, 12: 173–74.

139. See, for example, *Prilozheniia*, pp. 12–13.

140. "[The nuns] said: we know that he gave the order to cover the grave of [our] patron saint (*chudotvoritsa*) of the Rizpolozhenskii Monastery with wooden boards (*zametat' doskami*)" (*ibid.*, p. 56). The bishop claimed in return that this interference with the sacred space of the patron saint had been only a temporary measure (*dlia radi prokhodu s perenosom*).

141. *Ibid.*, pp. 14–15; "Delo ob otmezhivanii po chelobit'nym suzdal'skikh posadskikh liudei patriarshikh, monastyrskikh i votchinnykh zemel'," in Tokmakov, *Opisanie Pokrovskogo devich'ego monastyria*, appendix, pp. 25–71, esp. 69.

142. *Prilozheniia*, p. 67.

143. *Ibid.*, p. 52. A *guba* was a criminal judicial district headed by an elected elder.

144. *Ibid.*, pp. 49–50. Stefan insisted that he had spoken out of ignorance and should be excused (p. 66).

145. On Stefan's triumphant return, see Titov, *Suzdal'skaia ierarkhiia*, p. 81.

146. For more information about Dobrynin, see Chapter Two.

147. Most importantly, see Denisov, *Vinograd rossiiskii*, preface. See also Liubopytnyi, "Katalog starovercheskoi tserkvi," p. 4, 49.

148. See, for example, Fedor Ivanov's letter from Pustoozero to his son Maksim, in *Materialy*, 6: 90–261, esp. 197–99, 235–36; Bubnov, *Staroobriadcheskaia kniga*, pp. 355–57. Ivanov's emphasis on the crucial importance of the 1650s in the formation of Old Belief may have prepared the way for later myths about the legendary Old Believer Church Council of 1656, over which the archpriests allegedly presided. See P. S. Smirnov, *Vnutrennie voprosy*, p. 050; Liubopytnyi, "Katalog staroverckheskoi tserkvi," p. 4.

149. *Materialy*, 6: 65–66, 181, 265–66; 7: 237–39.

150. One of the first of these miscellanies was the so-called *Pustoozerskii sbornik*. The editors identified Avvakum's mission with the "cause of God" (*delo Bozhie*). See Demkova, ed., *Pustoozerskii sbornik*, pp. 11, 138, 162–63, 252–54. For good introductions into the manuscript transmission of the archpriest's work, see Malyshev, "Bibliografiia sochinenii protopopa Avvakuma"; idem, "Sochineniia protopopa Avvakuma."

151. See, for example, his *Book of Conversations* (*Kniga besed*) and *Book of Commentaries* (*Kniga tolkovanii*), in *Pamiatniki istorii staroobriadchestva*, cols. 241–575. Seseikina, "Kniga besed protopopa Avvakuma"; Bubnov, *Staroobriadcheskaia kniga*, pp. 267–81; Demkova, *Zhitie protopopa Avvakuma*, pp. 3–11.

152. See, for example, the monk Avraamii's dedication and preface to the *Shield of Faith*, in *Materialy*, 7: 8, 10–11. See also various post-1666 writings by Ivanov and Avvakum, in *ibid.*, 6: 65, 81–88; Borozdin, *Avvakum* (1898), appendix, p. 33.

153. Borozdin, *Avvakum* (1900), appendix, pp. 7–8.

154. Borozdin, *Avvakum* (1898), pp. IV–VI, 1, 11; P. I. Mel'nikov, "Avvakum Petrovich," in A. A. Kraevskii, ed., *Entsiklopedicheskii slovar, sostavlennyi russkimi uchenymi i literatorami*, 1 (1863): 153; Serman, "Protopop Avvakum"; Malyshev, "K 275–letiiu so dnia smerti protopopa Avvakuma"; idem, "Zametka o rukopisnykh spiskakh 'Zhitiia'," pp. 388–91; idem, "Neizvestnye materialy o protopope Avvakume," p. 404; idem, "Bibliografiia sochinenii protopopa Avvakuma," pp. 443–44.

155. Cherniavsky, "Old Believers and New Religion," pp. 12, 16; Pascal, *Avvakum*, p. XVII.

156. Pokrovskii, *Antifeodal'nyi protest*, p. 24; Borozdin, *Avvakum* (1898), p. IV; Malyshev, "Avvakum suivant les traditions de Pustozersk," "Gde byl sozhzhen protopop Avvakum?," "Ust'-tsilemskoe predanie o protopope Avvakume."

157. A cult of Avvakum appears to have been developed after his execution in Pustoozero in April 1682. Crucial components of this cult were the fabrication of icons showing the martyred archpriest, and the copying of his *Vita*. However, the cult appears to have become popular only during later centuries when the site of Avvakum's exile and execution attracted numerous pilgrims. The late onset of the cult probably explains why only three copies of Avvakum's *Vita* exist in seventeenth-century manuscripts. Of the more than forty other known manuscripts (not including several excerpts of varying lengths), all survive in eighteenth- or nineteenth-century copies (I have not counted twentieth-century copies). See Malyshev, "Tri neizvestnykh sochineniia protopopa Avvakuma," "Zametka o rukopisnykh spiskakh 'Zhitiia'," "Protopop Awwakum w edycjach staroobrzędowcow"; Demkova, *Zhitie protopopa Avvakuma*, pp. 13–17, 25–27, 42–45.

158. *Pamiatniki*, p. 176.

159. In the *Book against the Cross-Rejecting Heresy* (*Kniga na krestobornuiu eres'*) one finds the following statement: "When the evil leader was patriarch, they began to kill the true Orthodox faith. They gave the order to make the sign of the cross with three fingers and to bow in church only from the waist during the fasting period. I and my fathers and brothers immediately began to denounce him as a heretic and the precursor of the Antichrist. In response he tortured us and sent us all into exile. . . . " (*Materialy*, 5: 262).

160. Protas'eva, "Stolbtsy Sinodal'nogo sobraniia," p. 281; Robinson, ed., *Zhizneopisaniia*, p. 232; *Materialy*, 1: 24.

161. RGB, Sobranie G. M. Prianishnikova, no. 61, fol. 11; Malyshev, "Neizvestnye materialy o protopope Avvakume," p. 392.

162. Malyshev, "Neizvestnye materialy o protopope Avvakume," pp. 386, 388, 392; Robinson, ed., *Zhizneopisaniia*, p. 145; Pascal, *Avvakum*, pp. 184–85; Nikolaevskii, "Moskovskii pechatnyi dvor," *Khristianskoe chtenie*, 1891, no. 1: 150–51.

163. Borozdin, *Avvakum* (1898), p. 1; Esipov, ed., *Raskol'nicheskie dela*, 1: 119.

164. Robinson, ed., *Zhizneopisaniia*, pp. 144, 223, 260, 263; Pascal, *Avvakum*, pp. 201–2; Heller, *Die Moskauer Eiferer*, pp. 36–40; Kapterev, *Patriarkh Nikon i ego protivniki*, p. 118.

165. Pascal, *Avvakum*, pp. 190–98; RGADA, f. 1182, bk. 50, Kniga prikhodnaia. Prodazha i bezdenezhnyi otpusk [knig], fol. 326v (1651–52). The name of Avvakum occurs also in conjunction with a certain "unemployed priest Lazar' " (*besmesnyi pop Lazar'*)—probably the Old Believer priest who stayed with Neronov and Avvakum at the Kazan' Cathedral (*ibid.*, fols. 355r–v). Avvakum may have bought the books for Neronov, who was a frequent purchaser of liturgical books during this period (*ibid.*, fols. 260v, 521v, 539v, 636v). There is evidence that Avvakum found refuge in the home of Neronov during this period, see RGB, Sobranie G. M. Prianishnikova, no. 61, fol. 12.

166. *Materialy*, 1: 20–26. It appears that the letter was never noticed or copied by later Old Believers. Indeed, Avvakum himself apparently did not refer back to it. The letter is extremely valuable because it was written much sooner after the events it describes than later Old Believer texts, which have come down to us in several manuscript versions. See Demkova, *Pustoozerskii sbornik*, p. 256.

167. *Materialy*, 1: 28–29.

168. *Ibid.*, p. 29.

169. *Materialy*, 8: 31–32; Borozdin, *Avvakum* (1898), pp. 245–46.

170. See, for example, Baron, ed., *Travels of Olearius*, p. 265 and *Delo*, p. 351. The contents of this sermon can also be inferred from some references in Avvakum's only surviving letter from 1653. Here he calls the patriarch "a wild boar" (*vepr'*) and "a wild monk" (*divii inok*), comparing him and his associates to "swine" (*svini*) without a sense of piety (*blagochestie*). See *Materialy*, 1: 24.

171. Cf. notes 175 and 176 of this chapter.

172. Nikon's generous giving of alms was not only observed by Avvakum. Cf. *Izvestie o zhitii Nikona patriarkha*, pp. 49–50; Brilliantov, *Patriarkh Nikon*, p. 60; *Delo*, p. 351. For other evidence on the popularity of Nikon among ordinary Muscovites, see Chapter Two.

173. *Materialy*, 1: 21, 30.

174. "I am now in my fourth week of being chained by my neck to a chair. They have pity on me and allow me to attend church services. [All of this began when] the priests at the Kazan' Cathedral refused to allow me into their church; they removed me by force from a side altar, saying that they were following the orders of their archdeacon. And I, the sinner, remembered the expulsion of the great St. Chrysostomos and gathered with my brethren in God in the drying room (*sushilo*) of your home for a vigil. This happened on the first Sunday after your arrest and I read to them from the *Life of Chrysostomos. . . .* " (*Materialy*, 1: 20–22).

175. See a charter issued by the Siberian Office dating from September 16, 1653, in Sapozhnikov, "Samosozhzhenie v russkom raskole," p. 7, fn. 2.

176. During the 1670s, Avvakum recalled the early days of his activities and admonished his followers to act like "zealots." See, for example, Borozdin, *Avvakum* (1898), appendix, pp. 15, 65–70.

177. For example, one of Nikon's first official acts was to fire large numbers of priests in the Nizhnii Novgorod area and to replace them with his own appointees. See Pascal, *Avvakum*, p. 195 and Chapter Five.

178. Pascal, *Avvakum*, pp. 226–29.

179. *Ibid.*, p. 202; Mazunin, *Povest' o boiaryne Morozovoi*, p. 95.

180. P. S. Smirnov, *Vnutrennie voprosy*, pp. CXV, 226; *Materialy*, 8: 89–92; Denisov, *Vinograd rossiiskii*, chap. 2.

181. Vvedenskii, "Kostromskii protopop Daniil," p. 846.

182. *Ibid.*

183. *Ibid.*, p. 848.

184. Denisov, *Vinograd rossiiskii*, chap. 3; P. S. Smirnov, *Vnutrennie voprosy*, pp. LVIII, 212, 050.

185. Cf. "Rospis' spornykh rechei protopopa Ivan Neronova." A short description of this manuscript [GIM, Sobranie A. S. Uvarova, no. 494 (131)], which dates from the early eighteenth century, can be found in *Pravoslavnyi sobesednik*, 1869, no. 1: 239. The text was never copied by later Old Believers. According to information surviving in the archive of the Riazan' eparchy, Loggin was officially defrocked on September 1, 1653. See Ieronim, *Riazanskie dostopamiatnosti*, p. 71.

186. "Rospis' spornykh rechei protopopa Ivan Neronova," pp. 41–44.

187. The fact that this quarrel set the scene for Loggin's arrest by Nikon is corroborated by a petition that Neronov submitted to the Church Council of 1666. See *Materialy*, 1: 224–40, esp. 234–35. See also a report by one of Loggin's parishioners, in Vozdvizhenskii, *Istoricheskoe obozrenie Riazanskoi ierarkhii*, p. 101.

188. Vozdvizhenskii, *Istoricheskoe obozrenie Riazanskoi ierarkhii*, p. 103.

189. Baron, ed., *Travels of Olearius*, pp. 251, 284.

190. Neronov's letters survive apparently only in three manuscript *sborniki*. See GIM, Sobranie A. S. Uvarova, no. 494 (131) and RGB, Sobranie Rogozhskogo kladbishcha, no. 667, fols. 336–93; GA Chernigov [Chernigov State Archive], Sobranie Chernigovskoi dukhovnoi seminarii [Collection of the Chernigov Spiritual Seminary], no. 108. I thank N. Iu. Bubnov and N. S. Demkova for sharing this information with me. The only complete copy of Neronov's *Vita* survives in an early eighteenth-century manuscript that belonged to the Ukrainian churchman Dmytryi Tuptalo [Rostovskii]. Subbotin's edition is based on this manuscript that still has Tuptalo's handwritten comments in the margins. See RGADA, f. 381,

Biblioteka Moskovskoi Sinodal'noi tipografii, op. 1, d. 420, fols. 150–77; "Zhitie Neronova"; Klipunovskii, "Ivan Neronov." For a more detailed discussion of these manuscripts, see Michels, "O deiatel'nosti Ivana Neronova."

191. Robinson, ed., *Zhizneopisaniia*, p. 146.

192. "Zhitie Neronova," pp. 254–55, 263–65.

193. *Ibid.*, pp. 272–73, 286–87, 296–98; *Materialy*, 1: 51–69, 78–83.

194. All of these letters have been published in *Materialy*, 1: 34–123. See also Borozdin, *Avvakum* (1898), appendix, no. 1 (Neronov's correspondence with the Pleshcheev brothers).

195. *Materialy*, 1: 54–59, 61–62, 72, 100–103.

196. *Ibid.*, pp. 36–39, 75–77; "Zhitie Neronova," pp. 273–75. On the *edinoglasie* reform, see note 97 of this chapter.

197. *Materialy*, 1: 45, 53, 73–77. N. F. Kapterev wrote extensively about the reformers around Stefan Vonifat'ev in *Patriarkh Nikon i ego protivniki* and "Tserkovno-reformatsionnoe dvizhenie."

198. Kapterev, *Patriarkh Nikon i tsar' Aleksei Mikhailovich*, 1: 1–105; Heller, *Die Moskauer Eiferer*, pp. 67–78.

199. *Materialy*, 1: 36, 44.

200. *Ibid.*, pp. 47–48.

201. *Ibid.*, pp. 67–68.

202. *Ibid.*, pp. 45–50. The petition is mentioned in Avvakum's letter from 1653. See *ibid.*, p. 24.

203. He was accused of breaking into a church and stealing a sacred gift that had been left in front of the icon of the Kazan' Mother of God by the tsar's wife. See *ibid.*, p. 46.

204. *Ibid.*, pp. 32, 49.

205. Neronov was keenly aware of this and accused Nikon of surrounding himself with questionable individuals: "Until now you have called protodeacon Grigorii and the others who are now your advisors in the *Krestovaia* 'enemies of God' and 'destroyers of the Divine Law.' But now they appear with you in council and are your friends" (*ibid.*, pp. 46–47).

206. An editor of the account was puzzled by Olearius' remark since it contradicts the dominant view of Russian historiography in which Neronov appears as a victim of his opposition against the liturgical reforms. See Baron, ed., *Travels of Olearius*, p. 258, fn. 50.

207. "Zhitie Neronova," p. 282.

208. "Zapiski zhizni Neronova." This text survives in a *sbornik* of the A. S. Uvarov Collection, in GIM, Sobranie A. S. Uvarova, no. 494 (131). A short description is found in Leonid, *Opisanie sobraniia grafa A. S. Uvarova*, 1: 579–80. On the apparently only copy of the full version of Neronov's *Vita*, see note 190 of this chapter.

209. "Zapiski zhizni Neronova," pp. 147–48, 156; "Rospis' knig i pisem," p. 338, no. 80.

210. "Zapiski zhizni Neronova," pp. 147, 154, 159, 161.

211. For example, Nikon would receive Neronov at the Kremlin with other Moscow archpriests. See *ibid.*, pp. 156–57; "Zhitie Neronova," pp. 285–86; RGADA, f. 235, opis' 2, bk. 38, fol. 531v; bk. 43, fol. 236v.

212. *Materialy*, 1: 195–98, 228; "Zhitie Neronova," pp. 280, 287.

213. Pascal, *Avvakum*, pp. 226, 228–43; Borozdin, *Avvakum* (1898), pp. 66–87.

214. RGADA, f. 214, Sibirskii prikaz, d. 400; Ogloblin, "Obozrenie Sibir-skogo prikaza," *Chteniia*, 1900, bk. 3, pt. 3, pp. 52, 85, 179, 264; Pascal, *Avvakum*, pp. 238, 241–43; *Pamiatniki istorii staroobriadchestva*, cols. 561–64.

215. Borozdin, *Avvakum* (1900), appendix, pp. 116–18; Nikol'skii, "Sibirskaia ssylka Avvakuma," pp. 144–57. Peter Hauptmann also observed Avvakum's failure to propagate the cause of Old Belief during his exile to Siberia, in Hauptmann, *Altrussischer Glaube*, pp. 68–70. On Avvakum's teachings about the Antichrist, see P. S. Smirnov, *Vnutrennie voprosy*, pp. 9–15.

216. *Materialy*, 1: 104; Vvedenskii, "Kostromskii protopop Daniil," p. 846. Daniil's closest ally in Kostroma was the cathedral priest Pavel. See *ibid.*, p. 849.

217. *Materialy*, 1: 25, 94, 105–6.

218. *Ibid.*, pp. 24, 30–33. During the early 1650s Avvakum's brothers appear to have enjoyed the tacit support of the tsar's wife. See Robinson, ed., *Zhizneopisaniia*, p. 148.

219. Robinson, ed., *Zhizneopisaniia*, pp. 148, 238–39; *Pamiatniki istorii staro-obriadchestva*, cols. 561–64; Nikol'skii, "Sibirskaia ssylka Avvakuma," pp. 145–49, 162, 164–66.

220. "Zhitie Neronova," pp. 246–47.

221. *Materialy*, 1: 114–16.

222. *Ibid.*, pp. 117–18.

223. "Zhitie Neronova," pp. 256–60, 270–71. On the few reform-oriented cler-gymen in Nizhnii Novgorod, see Rozhdestvenskii, ed., "K istorii bor'by s tserkovnymi bezporiadkami," pp. 1–18; Pascal, *Avvakum*, pp. 52–53.

224. "Zhitie Neronova," pp. 260–62. On Neronov's great frustrations with popular hostility against his reform efforts, see his 1636 petition to Patriarch Ioasaf in Rozhdestvenskii, ed., "K istorii bor'by s tserkovnymi bezporiadkami," pp. 18–31. The archpriest speaks about a popular revolt (*miatezh*) against the church.

225. Avvakum's brother Koz'ma probably strengthened the Nizhnii Novgorod community by his extended stay in the Volga town during the Moscow pestilence of 1654. See *Materialy*, 1: 359–60; "Zhitie Neronova," p. 278; Pascal, *Avvakum*, p. 73; Filatov, "Ivan Neronov," p. 322.

226. *Materialy*, 1: 26–34; "Zhitie Neronova," pp. 276–77, 279–80.

227. *Materialy*, 1: 32, 44–45; Pascal, *Avvakum*, pp. 172, 213.

228. In these letters dating from 1653 or 1654 the brothers Ivan, Savin, Grigorii and Andrei Pleshcheev identified themselves as Neronov's "spiritual children." See Borozdin, *Avvakum* (1898), pp. 128–32, 152, 156; Borozdin, *Avvakum* (1900), appendix, pp. 1–6.

229. "Otvet Avvakuma Andreiu Pleshcheevu," in Borozdin, *Avvakum* (1900), appendix, pp. 6–11; *Materialy*, 1: 157.

230. *Materialy*, 1: 26.

231. *Ibid.*, 1: 32–33, 369; Zabelin, *Materialy dlia istorii goroda Moskvy*, 1: 449 (listing Gerasim Avvakumov as parish priest of the St. Dmitrii of Saloniki Church near the Tver' Gates from 1656 to 1669).

232. "Zapiski zhizni Neronova," pp. 143, 145–46, 166.

233. "Zhitie Neronova," pp. 300–302; Svirelin, "Svedeniia o zhizni arkhi-mandrita Grigoriia Neronova," pp. 44–45.

234. "Zhitie Neronova," pp. 299, 301.

235. Similar observations can be made about Neronov's popularity in the vicinity of the Ignat'eva Hermitage where he often resided during the 1650s. Many peasants came to him during crises, such as famines, to receive poor relief, food, and seeds for their fields. In ordinary times, however, Neronov found himself confronted by indifference, if not hostility. For example, in 1658 parish priests from nearby villages vehemently refused to say Mass for the Ignat'eva monks. See "Zapiski zhizni Neronova," p. 163; "Zhitie Neronova," pp. 287–88.

236. One might remember the remarkable career of the Old Believer Afanasii, who became archbishop of Kholmogory and one of the most important figures of the late seventeenth-century Russian church. Afanasii was, in common with Avvakum, a protégé of Archbishop Simeon of Tobol'sk. See Veriuzhskii, *Afanasii kholmogorskii*, pp. 11–13; P. S. Smirnov, *Vnutrennie voprosy*, pp. 020–030.

237. Peter Hauptmann made a similar observation in *Altrussischer Glaube*, pp. 115–17.

Chapter Two

1. Only two letters, dating from 1662 and 1666, made brief references to the liturgical reforms. In one other letter, dated June 1658, Nikon threatened to punish Ukrainian monks living in the Iverskii Monastery for using liturgical books from Ukraine and White Russia instead of his own newly issued books. He was, however, unsuccessful in disciplining the monks: the library of the Iverskii Monastery contained more Ukrainian and White Russian liturgical books dating from the first half of the seventeenth century (nos. 2–25) than books issued by the Muscovite patriarchs (nos. 26–43). See Kapterev, *Patriarkh Nikon i tsar' Aleksei Mikhailovich*, 1: 250, 253, 257; *Akty Iverskogo monastyria*, cols. 54–62, 333–34; *Materialy*, 6: 150. For Nikon's largely unexplored post-1666 correspondence, see RGADA, f. 27, d. 273, pts. I–IV, Perepiska o prebyvanii i soderzhanii patriarkha Nikona v Ferapontove monastyre s 1667–75 goda (now part of d. 140); *Pamiatniki*, pp. 93–104, 105–16; Nikolaevskii, "Zhizn' patriarkha Nikona."

2. *Delo*, p. 109.

3. See, for example, his letter to the monks of a Novgorodian monastery asking for information about Nikon, in *Akty Iverskogo monastyria*, col. 427. Cf. Dobroklonskii, *Rukovodstvo*, 3: 111.

4. "Sudnye protsessy," pp. 7, 11; Viktorov, *Obozrenie patriarshei riznitsy*, pp. 28–29; *Delo*, pp. 12, 15–16.

5. About Almaz Ivanov, see *Delo*, pp. 121–22, 127, 137–47, 178–210, etc. About Aleksei Nikitich Trubetskoi, see *ibid.*, pp. 19–29, 54, 62, 64, etc.

6. RGADA, f. 27, d. 192, Delo po zhalobe na pritesneniia i obidy ot arkhimandrita Troitskogo Sergieva monastyria Ioasafa, fols. 1–178. Many folios are in poor condition and difficult to read. On the dating of the case, see *ibid.*, fols. 116–19.

7. On Ioasaf's role as patriarch, see Dobroklonskii, *Rukovodstvo*, 3: 118. Pitirim succeeded in becoming patriarch only after Ioasaf's death in 1672. For interesting information about this ambitious churchman, see Popov, "Materialy dlia istorii patriarkha Pitirima."

8. Mel'nikov, *Istoricheskie ocherki popovshchiny*, p. 23. It is likely that Mel'nikov came to this assumption after reading Denisov's *Vineyard* and possibly the *Vita* of the Old Believer Kirill.

9. RGADA, f. 1182, bk. 57, fols. 73, 200, 210v. The assumption that Makarii rejected the new books is also contradicted by the fact that the Solovki monks received the new books by order of the Novgorod metropolitan. See *Materialy*, 3: 3–5.

10. RGADA, f. 1182, bk. 57, fols. 68 (Rostov), 71v (Kolomna, Pskov), 73 (Riazan'), 73v (Suzdal', Tver'), etc.

11. RGADA, f. 27, d. 192, fols. 59, 64, 115, 163, 170, 172. This is confirmed by the purchase of fifty new Service Books in September 1655, see RGADA, f. 1182, bk. 57, fol. 68.

12. These priests were apparently visitors from outside the monastery. See RGADA, f. 27, d. 192, fols. 52, 64.

13. *Ibid.*, fols. 23–24, 88, 105, 157, 159, 164. Averkii also attacked monks wearing new Greek cowls (*klobuki*) and called them "Jews and Muslims" (fol. 24).

14. *Ibid.*, fol. 115. Cf. fols. 98, 178. Vavila denounced the monks as "criminals, heretics, Muslims, and precursors of the Antichrist" (fol. 23). The priest Tikhon was Vavila's main accuser. His name appears frequently among the signatures under petitions and interrogation protocols (fols. 26v, 97v, 98v, 111v, 147).

15. " . . . And those brethren who endorsed the petition with their signatures[. . . .]After disciplining them for going public (*dlia svoei oglaski*) they dispersed them to remote subsidiary monasteries for investigation. They spared only some senile monks in the hospital tract who had to pay them about forty or fifty rubles. [Senile] monks who did not pay them off to avoid exile were sent away[. . . .]" (*ibid.*, fol. 148). Cf. fols. 96, 105, 116, 159, 163.

16. "He [seized] homesteads, buildings, and rooms [. . .] and everything that belongs to peasant households. He also [took timber] from the monastery's forest that was cut and stored for a construction project of the tsar. . . . " (*ibid.*, fol. 95). This complaint was raised by fifty-nine monks.

17. The monks in charge of the grainery and the workshop testified that Ioasaf's nephews confiscated carts and foodstuffs. They took bribes and imposed "all conceivable violence" by beating and torturing peasants. See *ibid.*, fols. 106–9, 125.

18. " . . . He beats [us] personally inside and outside his cell" (*ibid.*, fol. 58). Cf. fols. 17, 68, 111, 133.

19. See the interrogation of the elder Andronik: " . . . We got drunk, had great fights[. . .]and while drinking rode across the field and ruined the horses. But I did not take a bribe of nine rubles from the sworn officials (*tseloval'niki*) of three districts. . . . " (*ibid.*, fol. 122). All the elders had separate households (*dvory*) and there is some indication that members of their families lived with them. Makarii Siltsov, for example, was living with his son. See *ibid.*, fol. 110.

20. "They ruin the hinterlands of the Troitsa Monastery[. . . .]Riding on horseback over the lands they beat, torture, and take bribes from the peasants, forcing their wives to go to bed with them. They falsely denounce us, your pious believers, your servants, servicemen and peasants to the archimandrite and provoke all kinds of fights. . . . The archimandrite never gives us our rights in any respect,

but instead completely condones their criminal behavior (*vo vsiakom ikh vorovstve zastupaet*)" (*ibid.*, fol. 125). Cf. fol. 114.

21. *Ibid.*, fols. 15, 28–31, 56.

22. *Materialy*, 3: 10.

23. On significant literary contacts between these monasteries, see Shashkov, "Sochineniia Maksima Greka," pp. 46, 58–61. I thank N. N. Pokrovskii for making this dissertation available to me.

24. *Materialy*, 3: 8.

25. *Ibid.*, pp. 10–11.

26. *Ibid.*, pp. 13–14.

27. *Ibid.*, pp. 21–22.

28. During the early 1650s the monastery and its hinterlands had been regular customers of the patriarchal printing press; the archimandrite and also simple priests and servants acquired liturgical books. See RGADA, f. 1182, bk. 50, fols. 245v, 297, 346, 532, 572v, 598. The Anzera Hermitage, known for its close ties with Patriarch Nikon, had also been a regular purchaser of liturgical books during the early 1650s. These purchases were apparently discontinued a few years later (*ibid.*, fols. 298v, 322v, 520v).

29. For more detail, see Michels "The Solovki Uprising."

30. RGADA, f. 27, d. 190, Delo o podmetnom pis'me, fols. 1–6; d. 195, Delo o nepristoinykh rechakh sviashchennika tserkvi vvedeniia Bogoroditsy Terentiia, fols. 1–60. The protocols of this investigation survive in poor condition. Some pages exist only in fragments, some portions are illegible (e.g. fols. 8–14).

31. Gibbenet, *Istoricheskoe issledovanie dela patriarkha Nikona*, 2: 606. On Pavel of Kolomna, see the second section of Chapter Two.

32. "Slukhi o tom, budto privezeny v Moskvu, dlia prodazhi, knigi o zhitii patriarkha Nikona," in Gibbenet, *Istoricheskoe issledovanie dela patriarkha Nikona*, 2: 653–54.

33. For an early example see the "Poem about Patriarch Nikon", in Malyshev, *Drevnerusskie rukopisi Pushkinskogo Doma*, pp. 189–91.

34. Terentii's accusation against Pitirim was also at odds with other statements of Old Believers such as Neronov and Aleksandr. Both were strongly opposed to Nikon's excommunication of Pitirim and called for Nikon's immediate removal. See a letter by Aleksandr dated July 1662 in RGB, Sobranie Rogozhskogo kladbishcha, no. 667, fols. 191–99v. A similar text by Neronov was published in *Materialy*, 1: 179–92.

35. RGADA, f. 27, d. 195, fols. 35, 42, 57.

36. *Ibid.*, fol. 56.

37. *Ibid.*, fols. 17, 23–24.

38. *Ibid.*, fol. 55.

39. *Ibid.*, fol. 42.

40. *Ibid.*, fol. 23. On the other dinner guests, see *ibid.*, fols. 21, 24.

41. *Ibid.*, fols. 17, 33.

42. *Ibid.*, fol. 54.

43. *Ibid.*, fol. 28.

44. Terentii probably also had the sympathy, if not support, of his host Ivan Moshchintsev and the priest Semen, Moshchintsev's spiritual father. Semen was an

exception among the dinner guests because he actually had the know-how to participate in the controversy. He spoke, for example, about the singing of the hallelujah in church services (*ibid.*, fol. 32).

45. Bogdanov served in the *Razboinyi prikaz* for more than twenty years, until 1657, when he was promoted to the rank of *d'iak*. Bogdanov's participation in the described confrontation apparently led to his transfer to a distant post in the Dvina area. See Veselovskii, *D'iaki i pod'iachie*, pp. 54–55; Buganov, *Moskovskoe vosstanie 1662 goda*.

46. As had other employees of the *Patriarshii prikaz*, Savva lost his position after Nikon's abdication in July 1658. In February 1660, he worked as a simple servant at the patriarchal court (*rabotnishko patriarsh*). See *Delo*, p. 46. Savva's bad fortune changed, in all likelihood, soon after he testified in support of Pitirim in the controversy over whether Nikon should be excommunicated if he ever returned to the patriarchal throne. See *Delo*, pp. 30–31, 36, 46, 70. When Pitirim was transferred to Novgorod a few years later, Savva again appeared in our sources, this time as "a former clerk" (*byvshii pod'iak*). He hated Pitirim so much for withdrawing his protection that he called him a "damned heretic" (*prokliatyi eretik*), in *Materialy*, 1: 480.

47. RGADA, f. 27, d. 190, fol. 6.

48. RGADA, f. 27, d. 195, fol. 40.

49. *Ibid.*, fols. 37, 40.

50. RGADA, f. 27, d. 161, Ob otpravlenii pod nachal v Kozheozerskii monastyr' popa Nikona, fols. 1–5. The Nadeseva Hermitage is not listed in the standard works on Russian monasteries; it was apparently too insignificant to attract attention. See, for example, Vodarskii, "Tserkovnye organizatsii."

51. RGADA, f. 27, d. 161, fol. 1.

52. *Ibid.*, fol. 2.

53. See, for example, the handing out of free copies of the new Service Book to hermits from the Vologda and Novgorod districts who, like Nikon, were apparently unable to pay money, in RGADA, f. 1182, bk. 57, fols. 616, 620.

54. On January 15, 1657, for example, the priest Ivan from the village of Isupovo paid one ruble ten altyn to take home the first edition of the Service Book. Two days later, the priest Fedor from the village of Krasnoe paid the same sum (*ibid.*, fol. 70r–v). Other priests from both village and town parishes followed their example (*ibid.*, fols. 92v, 173v, 208v, 209v, 211v, 235v, 286, etc.).

55. *Ibid.*, fol. 463. Cf. the unexplored archival holdings of the Ipat'evskii Monastery in SPbFIRI, f. 12, Kollektsiia P. M. Stroeva as described in Andreev, ed., *Putevoditel'*, p. 143.

56. P. S. Smirnov, *Vnutrennie voprosy*, pp. XXXII–XXXV.

57. Kutepov, *Sekty khlystov i skoptsov*, pp. 41–43; also Grass, *Die Gottesleute oder Chlüsten*, pp. 7–16.

58. "And with his boldness their master of ceremonies (*ustavshchik*) E[v]fim[ii] ruins [the books] more than anyone else. He understands very little of theology" (Kozhanchikov, ed., *Tri chelobitnye*, p. 30). On Evfimii and the correction of books, see Borozdin, *Avvakum* (1900), pp. 50, 136. That Savvatii greatly underestimated Evfimii's learning is demonstrated in Florovsky, "Chudovskii inok Evfimii."

59. Kozhanchikov, ed., *Tri chelobitnye*, pp. 34–35, 51, 54. Savvatii's criticism of

those in charge of the revision process resulted in accusations that he was grammatically inept. The men whom he denounced as ignoramuses and "upstarts" (*ibid.*, p. 27) saw to it that he was exiled to the Kirillov Monastery. According to Veselovskii, the expulsion occurred in November 1659. See Veselovskii, *D'iaki i pod'iachie*, p. 87.

60. See, for example, the famous *Fifth Petition* of the Solovki monks, which became a standard component of Old Believer miscellanies, in *Materialy*, 3: 213–76; Bubnov, ed., *Sochineniia pisatelei-staroobriadtsev*, pp. 5, 33, 35–36, 41, 44, 50, 57, 86, 114, etc.

61. *Pamiatniki*, p. 178.

62. Documentary information does not demonstrate any ties between Savvatii and Old Believers. Still, Bubnov's assumption that Savvatii's petition was known to the Old Believers Nikita Dobrynin, Avraamii, and Fedor Ivanov remains very interesting. Only in-depth textual comparisons of these Old Believers' writings with Savvatii's petition will yield conclusive evidence. See Bubnov, *Staroobriadcheskaia kniga*, pp. 328, 333, 342–43, 349.

63. There is no evidence that Savvatii's petition was copied at Pustoozero and Vyg. The origins of two nineteenth-century manuscripts (GIM, Sobranie A. I. Khludova, appendix, no. 58 and RGB, Sobranie N. P. Rumiantseva, no. 375) remain to be investigated. See Druzhinin, *Pisaniia staroobriadtsev*, p. 243.

64. Kozhanchikov, ed., *Tri chelobitnye*, pp. 24–25.

65. "Oh Christ, you have been seated on the throne together with the Father and the Holy Spirit" (*ibid.*, p. 23).

66. See, for example, Tschernykh, *Historische Grammatik*, p. 222. Savvatii may, in fact, have known Greek. See his reference to the beauty of the Greek language and the citation of the Greek lexeme *dori* (*kopiia*) in Kozhanchikov, ed., *Tri chelobitnye*, pp. 35–36, 48.

67. *Ibid.*, pp. 23–24.

68. ". . . I did not know the written traditions of the Law" (*ibid.*, p. 30).

69. "I did not know a learned man who was familiar with the traditions of the Law" (*ibid.*).

70. See, for example, the replacement of an instrumental singular by a genitive plural in the prayer passage "*vsiako daianie blago i vsiak dar sovershen, skhodiai ot tebia Ottsa svetov (*svetom)*" (*ibid.*).

71. "The years of our life began like a spider web" vs. "the years of our life had been woven like a spider web" (*ibid.*, p. 33). *Doronosima* has no meaning while *daronosima* is an adjective denoting the holy gifts offered during the liturgy (*ibid.*, p. 47).

72. See especially Belokurov, *Silvestr Medvedev*.

73. Kozhanchikov, ed., *Tri chelobitnye*, p. 13.

74. D. E. Kozhanchikov falsely identified Savvatii with the editor Savvatii. Cf. Sheptaev, ed., "Stikhi spravshchika Savvatiia." On Savvatii's true identity, see Veselovskii, *D'iaki i pod'iachie*, pp. 86–87; Kozhanchikov, ed., *Tri chelobitnye*, p. 13; Popov, comp., "Perepiska d'iaka Tret'iaka Vasil'eva," p. 17.

75. Kudriavtsev, "Izdatel'skaia deiatel'nost' Posol'skogo prikaza"; GIM, Sobranie Sinodal'noi biblioteki, no. 307, fols. 134–36, 189–91; Popov, comp., "Perepiska d'iaka Tret'iaka Vasil'eva," pp. 1–2; Keenan, "Semen Shakhovskoi."

76. Tret'iak's correspondence with Shakhovskoi and other personages—among them Simeon of Tobol'sk, who later became very influential at the patriarchal printing press—has been published in Popov, comp., "Perepiska d'iaka Tret'iaka Vasil'eva," pp. 5–29, esp. 5.

77. Kozhanchikov, ed., *Tri chelobitnye*, pp. 1–55. The publication is apparently based on the only surviving seventeenth-century manuscript in GIM, Sobranie A. S. Uvarova, no. 497 (102), which has been described in Leonid, *Opisanie sobraniia grafa A. S. Uvarova*, 1: 581.

78. On Neronov's quarrels with the archbishops of Rostov and Volodga, which began in November 1664, see *Materialy*, 1: 192–98, 201–13. Avvakum's brief visit to Moscow before his renewed exile to Mezen' is documented in Pascal, *Avvakum*, chap. X.

79. On Nikanor and Feoktist, see the discussion below. Cf. Fedor Ivanov's admission that he had used the new books, in *Materialy*, 1: 400.

80. Remnants of Aleksandr's own works are found in a manuscript that dates from the early 1660s. Later Old Believer miscellanies simply omitted works by Aleksandr, or failed to mention him as the author. See RGB, Sobranie Rogozhskogo kladbishcha, no. 667, fols. 191–99v, 303–16, 430–37v; *Materialy*, 7: 112–50. Old Belief censorship applied also to Aleksandr's most important collaborator, Abbot Feoktist. His letters survived only in the original manuscript copies confiscated by church investigators. Only the so-called *Molebnoe pisanie* and possibly a few other remnants of Feoktist's comprehensive work, have entered Old Believer manuscripts. See GIM, Sobranie Sinodal'noi biblioteki, no. 641, fols. 58–60; Bubnov, ed., *Sochineniia pisatelei-staroobriadtsev*, p. 102; Druzhinin, *Pisaniia staroobriadtsev*, p. 281; *Materialy*, 1: 344. See also the discussions of Nikita Dobrynin and Fedor Trofimov in this chapter.

81. Vereshchagin, "Iz istorii Viatskoi eparkhii," pp. 3–5; Pascal, *Avvakum*, p. 171.

82. The contacts between Neronov and Aleksandr at the Spaso-Kamennyi Monastery outside Volodga are documented in a letter "by a certain strange monk" (*inoka nekoego stranna*) to Archpriest Stefan Vonifat'ev, in *Materialy*, 1: 109–19 (dated July 13, 1654).

83. Vereshchagin, "Iz istorii Viatskoi eparkhii," pp. 9–10.

84. "Rospis' knig i pisem," pp. 334, 337, nos. 56, 79. Unfortunately, none of the texts seems to have survived.

85. *Pamiatniki*, p. 175. Fedor Ivanov refers to Pavel's removal by Nikon (*Materialy*, 6: 196, 284) and mentions him as the predecessor of Aleksandr (*ibid.*, p. 256). He falsely maintains that Pavel did not sign the synodal act of 1654 (p. 196).

86. P. S. Smirnov, *Vnutrennie voprosy*, p. 049; Denisov, *Vinograd rossiiskii*, fols. 14–16, esp. 14. Denisov not only begins his historical account with Pavel's life, but he also calls him "the leader of that good army" (*nachal'nik onogo dobrogo voinstva*).

87. Cf. Belokurov, ed., "Skazaniia o Pavle kolomenskom"; BAN, Sobranie V. G. Druzhinina, no. 1101, Istoricheskoe opisanie pervogo sobora blagochestivykh i revnostnykh muzhei.

88. Subbotin, ed., *Deianie moskovskogo sobora 1654 goda*, p. 6 (author's introduction), fol. 21 (facsimile text); GIM, Sobranie Sinodal'noi biblioteki, no. 379.

89. *Zhitie Ilariona mitropolita suzdal'skogo*, pp. 4–5, 12; "Zhitie Neronova," p. 256; "Rospis' knig i pisem," p. 331, no. 41.

90. Pavel was appointed on October 17, 1652 to replace Bishop Rafail, who had ruled over the bishopric for several decades. Rafail's dismissal came shortly after his investigation of popular revolts at Pskov and Novgorod that had seriously challenged Nikon's authority. Apparently, Rafail's reports did not please Nikon. See Stroev, *Spiski ierarkhov*, col. 1031; Tikhomirov, *Klassovaia bor'ba*, pp. 120–27; 269–75, 362; Pokrovskii, *Russkie eparkhii*, 1: 206, 215–17.

91. RGADA, f. 210, Belgorodskii stol, d. 351, fols. 249–52, Otluchenie ot tserkvi voevody Daniila Karpova kolomenskim episkopom Pavlom; *Opisanie MGAMIU*, 12: 413.

92. Belokurov, ed., "Skazaniia o Pavle kolomenskom"; P. S. Smirnov, *Vnutrennie voprosy*, pp. 048–051.

93. The murder of Bishop Pavel was discussed in the proceedings of the 1666 Church Council. See *Delo*, p. 450.

94. RGADA, f. 235, opis' 2, bk. 42, Prikhodnaia kniga 165 goda, fols. 272–333; Nikolaevskii, *Patriarshaia oblast'*, pp. 11–12.

95. RGADA, f. 235, opis' 2, bk. 49, Prikhodnaia kniga 167 goda, fols. 294–313; Shimko, *Patriarshii kazennyi prikaz*, pp. 117–18, 130.

96. *Materialy*, 1: 9–14, esp. 9. The manuscript of the acts of this church council, which took place in October 1657 (despite Subbotin's uncertainty about the year), can be found in GIM, Sobranie Sinodal'noi biblioteki, no. 30.

97. Pokrovskii, *Russkie eparkhii*, 1: 290; *Istoricheskie svedeniia ob eparkhiiakh*, p. 12.

98. Vodarskii, "Tserkovnye organizatsii," p. 78. The eparchy was downgraded to the rank of bishopric in 1718, and finally abolished at the end of the eighteenth century. See Pokrovskii, *Russkie eparkhii*, 1: 206, 215–17; *Istoricheskie svedeniia ob eparkhiiakh*, p. 12.

99. On the wealth of the Kolomna episcopal palace, see *Puteshestvie antiokhiiskogo patriarkha Makariia*, 2: 149–51. The Predtechenskii Monastery, where Aleksandr was housed at Viatka, had few lands and barely enough income to sustain the bishop and his household. In January 1659, Aleksandr complained to the Patriarch's Office that he had been deceived: according to the land registers of the monastery, he should have direct control over at least ninety-two homesteads (*dvory*); in reality, however, only twenty homesteads belonged to the monastery. See "Akty po delu Ust'-vymskoi desiatiny," pp. 66–67; "Otkaznye knigi v Viatskii arkhiereiskii dom," pp. 56–57.

100. Cited from Pokrovskii, *Russkie eparkhii*, 1: 247.

101. *Materialy*, 1: 311–12. See also another letter by Feoktist to the Morozov family in which he gave further details about the poverty of the bishop and his diocese (*ibid.*, p. 318).

102. This development is documented in letters written between 1658 and 1664, in "Akty po delu Ust'-vymskoi desiatiny"; *Materialy*, 7: 120, 148; *Trudy Viatskoi arkhivnoi kommissii*, 1907, pt. 2, sect. 2, pp. 87–89.

103. Suvorov, ed., "Spor vologodskikh arkhiepiskopov," *Vologodskie gubernskie vedomosti*, 1864, no. 8: 1.

104. An earlier letter of Aleksandr dating from February 23, 1659, laments the reduced number of income-producing churches and shrines (*ibid.*, no. 9: 1). For further information on the miserable financial situation of Aleksandr, see Nikolaevskii, *Patriarshaia oblast'*, pp. 26–29.

105. Pokrovskii, *Russkie eparkhii*, 1: 125; Golubtsov, "Chinovniki Uspenskogo sobora," pp. 255, 260, 262, 266.

106. RGADA, f. 1182, bk. 57, fols. 71v, 204v; S. A. Belokurov, *Sil'vestr Medvedev*, pp. 28–29. Aleksandr acted according to church policy: during these same years Iona of Rostov bought two hundred Service Books, Markell of Vologda one hundred and fifty, and Filaret of Suzdal' one hundred. See RGADA, f. 1182, bk. 57, fols. 68, 73, 200, 209.

107. RGADA, f. 1182, bk. 59, fols. 285v, 293v, 295. Filaret of Smolensk bought sixteen Psalters, and Ilarion of Riazan' twenty. See RGADA, f. 1182, bk. 59, fols. 235, 299.

108. Viktorov, *Opisanie starinnykh dvortsovykh prikazov*, 2: 574.

109. *Materialy*, 8: 131–36.

110. Pascal, *Avvakum*, p. 307. See also a manuscript allegedly compiled by Aleksandr and Feoktist, in GIM, Sobranie Sinodal'noi biblioteki, no. V, fols. 70–174.

111. "Rospis' knig i pisem," pp. 325, 336.

112. *Materialy*, 1: 322; "Rospis' knig i pisem." Parts of this library had been personally assembled by Aleksandr. But since the bishop was busy with other matters, he had entrusted the task of supervising the library to Feoktist who "followed Bishop Aleksandr's advice" (*sovet priemlia ot Aleksandr episkopa*). See *Materialy*, 1: 343.

113. Aleksandr used the monastic name by which Neronov became known after his withdrawal to the Ignat'eva Hermitage.

114. "Rospis' knig i pisem," pp. 324, 326, 328–32, 334–36.

115. *Ibid.*, pp. 324–25, 327–29. These texts are very similar in content to texts compiled in the *Kirillova kniga* and *Litovskii prosvetitel'*. Hans Peter Niess has demonstrated that such texts were crucial for the formation of an Old Believer ideology, in *Kirche in Russland*, pp. 9, 15, 32–40, 142–47, 162–73. See also Lilov, *O tak nazyvaemoi Kirillovoi knige*.

116. "Rospis' knig i pisem," p. 334; "Zapiski zhizni Neronova," p. 143.

117. "Rospis' knig i pisem," p. 331; Stroev, *Spiski ierarkhov*, col. 943.

118. "Rospis' knig i pisem," pp. 324–25, 327, 334–37, nos. 7, 25, 54, 60, 71, 75. There are indications that Aleksandr also knew about works by Superior Efrem Potemkin, who was Spiridon Potemkin's brother. However, these works are not mentioned in the inventory. See *Materialy*, 1: 343; Michels, "Efrem Potemkin."

119. An anonymous treatise on the sign of the cross and an undated letter by Avvakum to the archimandrite reached Alexander's library from Solovki. See "Rospis' knig i pisem," p. 326, no. 22; p. 338, no. 86. Nikanor also was probably the writer of the famous *Fifth Petition*, one of the earliest indictments of the new liturgies—a tract that was to become a canonical text for the Old Belief. See Bubnov, "Skazanie . . . o novykh knigakh."

120. Between September 1661 and July 1663 Aleksandr was also seen in other Kremlin churches. See Belokurov, comp., "Dneval'nye zapiski Prikaza tainykh del," pp. 104, 110, 112, 124, 136, 184.

121. *Drevnie akty Viatskogo kraia*, p. 188.

122. On the Kolomna affair in official church proceedings during this period, see *DAI*, 5: 480; Gibbenet, *Istoricheskoe issledovanie dela patriarkha Nikona*, 2: 532; *Delo*, p. 450.

123. RNB, Solovetskoe sobranie, no. 20/1479, no. 193, O naznachenii v arkhimandrita solovetskogo startsa Nikanora, fol. 393. This charter contradicts the interpretations of Pascal, *Avvakum*, p. 216 (Nikanor was Vonifat'ev's candidate) and Savich, *Solovetskaia votchina*, p. 263 (Nikanor was elected by the Solovki monks).

124. Cf. the series of charters sent by Nikon to Il'ia between 1649 and 1652, in RNB, Solovetskoe sobranie, no. 20/1479, nos. 81–101, esp. 85, 87.

125. RGADA, f. 27, d. 364, pt. 3, fol. 123, Velikogo gosudaria vosem' gramot k Savvinskomu arkhimandritu Nikanoru.

126. Pisarev, *Domashnyi byt patriarkhov*, pp. 242–43, fns. 2–3.

127. RGADA, f. 1182, bk. 57, fols. 43, 194.

128. Savich, *Solovetskaia votchina*, p. 264; Belokurov, "Biblioteka i arkhiv Solovetskogo monastyria," no. 2665; RNB, Solovetskoe sobranie, no. 19/1478, no. 86, Gramota o vysylke v Moskvu startsa Iony byvshego riznichego sviateishago Nikona patriarkha (1659). A Scandinavian diplomatic source suggests that Nikon himself was about to be exiled to Solovki, see Ellersiek, "Russia under Aleksei Mikhailovich and Fiodor Alekseevich," p. 287, fn. 99.

129. Bubnov, ed., *Sochineniia pisatelei-staroobriadtsev*, pp. 18–23. Bubnov dates the first version of this text from the end of 1666, only a few months before the first—the short (*kratkaia*)—redaction of the *Fifth Petition* was composed. I think that Bubnov's date should be considered a *terminus ante quem*. The work that led to the so-called *Sobranie . . . protiv novykh knig* was based on the careful comparison of many liturgical books. The project probably began several years before 1666, coinciding with similar projects undertaken by Bishop Aleksandr. See Bubnov, "Skazanie . . . o novykh knigakh," pp. 114, 132; "Rabota drevnerusskikh knizhnikov," pp. 41–43.

130. Grigorii, *Istoricheskoe opisanie moskovskogo Zlatoustovskogo monastyria*, p. 7.

131. RGADA, f. 1182, bk. 57, fol. 62; "Opisanie sela Pavlovskogo Suzdal'skogo uezda." See also *Vladimirskie gubernskie vedomosti*, 1872, no. 49.

132. Billington, "Neglected Figures," p. 193; Borozdin, *Avvakum* (1900), p. 97; "Zapiski zhizni Neronova," pp. 152–53, 158.

133. RGADA, f. 1182, bk. 57, fols. 193 (August 1656), 445v (October 1657).

134. *Dokumenty*, p. 53; "Rospis' knig i pisem," p. 327, no. 25.

135. "Rospis' knig i pisem," p. 324, no. 7; p. 327, no. 25; Bubnov, "Spiridon Potemkin," esp. pp. 346, 351. For different datings of Spiridon's *Book*, see Borozdin, *Avvakum* (1898), p. 105; (1900), p. 97; Bubnov, ed., *Sochineniia pisatelei-staroobriadtsev*, pp. 13–15; Druzhinin, *Pisaniia staroobriadtsev*, pp. 231, 233.

136. The work of Fedor Ivanov contains so many panegyrical references to Spiridon that one wonders about the originality of Ivanov's work. Only a careful comparison of Ivanov's writings with those of Spiridon can provide greater clarity. Considering the significant similarities between works by Ivanov and Avvakum, one wonders to what degree Spiridon was responsible for creating Avvakum's idiom of Old Belief. See *Materialy*, 1: 400–401; 6: 78–79, 230–32; Ponyrko, "D'iakon Fedor—soavtor Avvakuma."

137. See, for example, Bubnov, "Spiridon Potemkin," p. 347. Bubnov lists forty-five manuscripts, four of which date from the second half of the seventeenth, or from the early part of the eighteenth, century. See *ibid.*, pp. 355–60.

138. Cited from *ibid.*, p. 347. Old Believer texts contain numerous anti-Judaic topoi, but to this day no historian has explored Old Believer attitudes toward Jews. See also Spiridon's *Povest' o bogomer'skikh zhidov* in an unpublished collection of his works, in IRLI, Mezen'skii fond, no. 123.

139. Cited from Bubnov, "Spiridon Potemkin," pp. 347–48. On the reception of Spiridon's work by later generations of Old Believers, see Bubnov, *Staroobriadcheskaia kniga*, pp. 134–38.

140. RNB, Osnovnoe sobranie, Q. I. 486, fols. 188v–200; GIM, Sobranie A. I. Khludova, no. 351, fols. 38–42, Otvet Avvakuma Andreiu Pleshcheevu; Borozdin, *Avvakum* (1900), pp. 116–17 and appendix, pp. 6–11, esp. 6; "Materialy dlia istorii russkogo raskola," pp. 591–98.

141. Billington, "Neglected Figures," pp. 193–95; GIM, Sobranie A. I. Khludova, no. 351, fol. 141, Zhitie Spiridona Potemkina; Popov, *Opisanie biblioteki Khludova*, pp. 645–46.

142. "Rospis' knig i pisem," pp. 324, 326; *Materialy*, 1: 398–99; "O slozhenii perst," in *Pamiatniki istorii staroobriadchestva*, cols. 693–700; Robinson, ed., *Zhizneopisaniia*, p. 232.

143. "Rospis' knig i pisem," p. 335, no. 60; Demkova, "Iz istorii rannei staroobriadcheskoi literatury," pp. 385–89; Kurdriavtsev, ed., "Sbornik XVII veka," esp. pp. 180–212. After his renewed exile to Mezen' Avvakum stayed in contact with Feoktist, the caretaker of Aleksandr's library. See "Rospis' knig i pisem," p. 335, no. 59.

144. Its author, Avvakum's student Avraamii, told interrogators that he had received numerous writings from Feoktist, in *Materialy*, 7: 388. On the composition of the *Shield*, see Bubnov, *Staroobriadcheskaia kniga*, pp. 336–43 and "Knigotvorchestvo," pp. 33–34, 37. For a discussion of the *Shield*'s ideology and other works by Avraamii that drew on this compilation, see Crummey, "The Works of Avraamii," pp. 127–38, esp. 128.

145. *Materialy*, 1: 344–50; 7: 53–63.

146. Denisov, *Vinograd rossiiskii*, chap. 5. See also the massive circulation of Fedor Ivanov's work during the eighteenth and nineteenth centuries, in Druzhinin, *Pisaniia staroobriadtsev*, pp. 272–80.

147. *Materialy*, 1: 397–99.

148. *Ibid.*, pp. 404–5, 424.

149. *Materialy*, 6: 1–45. It is likely that these texts had been hidden by Ivanov's wife, Kseniia, who—after his exile to Pustoozero—helped him disseminate his writings to Moscow residents. See *Pamiatniki*, p. 53.

150. Bubnov, "Knigotvorchestvo," p. 32 and *Staroobriadcheskaia kniga*, pp. 60–68, 239–44.

151. Avraamii's *Shield* emphasizes that Ivanov preached at least once to a large audience. See *Materialy*, 1: 421.

152. *Materialy*, 1: 397, 401, 406; 6: 60–78 (Letter to Ivan Avvakumovich); *Pamiatniki*, p. 69; Mazunin, *Povest' o boiaryne Morozovoi*, pp. 9–13, 67–68, 70. On Abbot Sergei's contradictory behavior, see Rumiantseva, *Narodnoe antitserkovnoe dvizhenie*, p. 209, fn. 28 and Chapter Four.

153. "Rospis' knig i pisem," p. 335; *Materialy*, 1: 399.

154. *Materialy*, 1: 228–29, 407–8. For more information about Neronov's

conflict with the archbishop of Vologda, see Michels, "The First Old Believers," pp. 499–501.

155. Bubnov, "Knigotvorchestvo," p. 29 and *Staroobriadcheskaia kniga*, pp. 109, 123, 380.

156. *Materialy*, 5: 196, 214–17, 263; 8: 101–2.

157. *Materialy*, 1: 405; 6: 237–39; Robinson, ed., *Zhizneopisaniia*, p. 269. It appears that Ivanov's parents died in the pestilence of 1654 and that he became a client of Boyar Nikita Ivanovich Odoevskii (1601–89). Since Odoevskii was one of the most powerful men in Muscovy, he could easily have secured a position for Ivanov at the Kremlin. On Odoevskii's contacts with the "zealots-of-piety," see Heller, *Die Moskauer Eiferer*, pp. 42–46.

158. *Materialy*, 1: 342–43; "Rospis' knig i pisem," pp. 332, 338, nos. 45, 81.

159. *Materialy*, 1: 471–79; Kozlovskii, "F. M. Rtishchev"; *Delo*, pp. 290, 317–18.

160. *Materialy*, 1: 474.

161. *Ibid.*

162. *Ibid.*, p. 473.

163. *Ibid.*, p. 477. This innovation, which called for one consecration ceremony instead of the two traditional ones, was criticized even by supporters of the liturgical reforms such as Paisii Ligarides. It is therefore not surprising that the Church Council of 1667 abolished this change. See Makarii, *Istoriia russkoi tserkvi*, 12: 199–201; Kapterev, *Patriarkh Nikon i tsar' Aleksei Mikhailovich*, 1: 512.

164. F. M. Rtishchev was in possession of a tract about the consecration of holy water which had been coauthored by Dionisii, and it is probably no coincidence that Irodion addressed a letter to the boyar. The text is found in RNB, Osnovnoe sobranie, F. I. 244; Kozlovskii, "F. M. Rtishchev," p. 80. Dionisii's activities at the patriarchal printing press have left numerous traces. See Stroev, *Opisanie staropechatnykh knig Tolstogo*, pp. 295–99; Kapterev, *Kharakter otnoshenii Rossii k pravoslavnomu vostoku*, pp. 217–19.

165. *Materialy*, 5: 136–40; *Pamiatniki istorii staroobriadchestva*, cols. 751–52.

166. Subbotin found this passage so outrageous that he did not publish it. See *Materialy*, 5: 137. The full text can be found in *Pamiatniki istorii staroobriadchestva*, col. 751.

167. Interestingly enough, Avvakum did not condone Irodion's behavior: "Irodion tells these wrongdoings to his friends and laughs with them. Lord, when such a spiritual matter occurs one should keep silent. Instead one must inform the hierarchs so that the church [building] is consecrated and faithful people attending services in it are not defiled" (*Materialy*, 5: 139).

168. Dionisii was an ambitious man on the rise. He replaced Arsenii the Greek as chief of the patriarchal printing press and reached the zenith of his power during the 1666 Church Council. See Kapterev, *Patriarkh Nikon i tsar' Aleksei Mikhailovich*, 2: 370–87 and Varakin, *Ispravlenie knig*, pp. 35–37.

169. Irodion then taught his parishioners the three-finger sign of the cross. See *Materialy*, 1: 483.

170. See especially Fedor Ivanov's letter to Maksim which was written during the late 1670s and widely disseminated during subsequent centuries. See *Materialy*, 6: 246; Druzhinin, *Pisaniia staroobriadtsev*, pp. 274–75.

171. *Materialy*, 4: 175–76.

172. Rumiantsev, *Nikita Dobrynin*, 1: 93, 101, 144–45.

173. *Prilozheniia*, p. 22.

174. *Ibid.*, pp. 8–9.

175. *Ibid.*, p. 9.

176. "He took the ancient frame from the miracle-working icon of the Mother of God . . . and stripped it of panagias, golden crosses, and cassocks set in precious pearls and stones . . . From another Marian icon, which had been given as a donation, he took two panagias to wear himself. In addition, he took three golden panagias with precious stones from two local icons and wore them from time to time. And when he did this, he said that the Mother of God did not walk around in gold and precious stones" (*ibid.*, p. 40).

177. *Ibid.*, p. 41.

178. *Materialy*, 1: 376–80.

179. Rumiantsev, *Nikita Dobrynin*, 1: 11–18, esp. 13.

180. *Materialy*, 4: IX, 3, 66, 114, 135, 144, 146, 157, 166, etc. The anti-Jewish topoi in Dobrynin's work suggest the influence of Spiridon Potemkin's work since these topoi appear to be of less significance in other Old Believer writings. Both Dobrynin's and Spiridon's works are in need of further study.

181. Large portions of Dobrynin's so-called long petition recall the first polemic works commissioned by Aleksandr of Viatka during the late 1650s. There is a significant emphasis on maintaining the purity of prayer texts and a tendency to substantially excerpt from both old and new liturgical books. See *Materialy*, 4: 11–15, 18–24, 147–48, 152–55, etc.

182. *Prilozheniia*, pp. 4, 108–12.

183. Titov, *Suzdal'skaia ierarkhiia*, p. 81; *Prilozheniia*, p. 112.

184. *Prilozheniia*, pp. 108–9.

185. *Ibid.*, pp. 109–10; RGADA, f. 210, Moskovskii stol, d. 365, fols. 152–57.

186. *Prilozheniia*, p. 108, fn. 1.

187. Titov, *Suzdal'skaia ierarkhiia*, p. 81; *Materialy*, 4: 170.

188. Titov, *Suzdal'skaia ierarkhiia*, p. 81.

189. *Materialy*, 4: VII–XVIII, 1–178; Ligarides, "Oproverzhenie chelobitnoi popa Nikity." I suggested elsewhere that Dobrynin was quite popular among Suzdalians as long as he helped them articulate their own grievances against the archbishop. However, hardly anyone was interested in Dobrynin's liturgical ideas, and Dobrynin apparently refrained from making them an issue in his early petitions to the Kremlin. See Michels, "Nikita Konstantinovich Dobrynin," esp. pp. 28–29.

190. *Materialy*, 1: 380–81; 2: 63; Rumiantsev, *Nikita Dobrynin*, 1: 12, 15, 35–39, 144–52.

191. *Materialy*, 6: 233–34.

192. "Rospis' knig i pisem," p. 332, no. 45.

193. "Pod'iaka Fedora Trofimova dve zapiski," p. 287.

194. *Ibid.*, p. 288.

195. See particularly his reference to *rimskii kostel* (*ibid.*, p. 291).

196. Kokoshilov was in charge of arresting and interrogating suspects. Cf. RGADA, f. 396, Arkhiv Oruzheinoi Palaty, d. 42637, O prisylke v patriarshii rozriad privodnogo cheloveka Karpa Grigor'eva, esp. fol. 3. For further information, see Shimko, *Patriarshii kazennyi prikaz*, pp. 13, 15–16, 19, esp. fns. 70, 90 and Pascal, *Avvakum*, p. 100.

197. "Pod'iaka Fedora Trofimova dve zapiski," p. 285.

198. See complaints against Kokoshilov dating from 1661, in RGADA, f. 141, opis' 3, g. 1661, d. 120, Chelobitnaia patriarshikh detei boiarskikh na patriarshego d'iaka Ivana Kokoshilova, chto on v desiatiny dlia zboru ikh ne posylaet, a posylaet plemiannika svoego dlia obogashcheniia; d. 121, Ochnaia stavka Ivana Vladykina s d'iakom Ivanom Kokoshilovym v prisylke na patriarsh dvor bez gosudareva ukazu plemiannika svoego. In 1661 Kokoshilov was still a leading investigator at the *Patriarshii prikaz.* See RGADA, f. 396, d. 43009.

199. "Rospis' knig i pisem," p. 332 and *Materialy,* 4: XXIX. The text is part of a fifteen-page scroll that contains also a *Molenie vsego osviashchennogo sobora k velikomu gosudariu, chtob patriarshim prikaznym osviashchennogo chinu ne sudit'.*

200. On the bishops of Siberia, see Butsinskii, *Sibirskie arkhiepiskopy,* pp. 8–10, 34–40, 59–64.

201. "Pod'iaka Fedora Trofimova dve zapiski," pp. 293–94. Trofimov also describes how Gruzdev and the Siberian bishops had enriched themselves during the year 1662 when they exchanged inflated copper money for silver coins (*ibid.*). On the secular aspirations of other church leaders, cf. *ibid.,* pp. 294–96.

202. Trofimov participated in the new church services which the patriarch celebrated in the Uspenskii Cathedral. He shared the fate of other former clients of Nikon's such as the deacon of the Uspenskii Cathedral, Vasilii Ivanov, and the patriarchal cantor, Ivan. See *Delo,* pp. 36, 46–47, 70; *Materialy,* 4: 287; Pascal, *Avvakum,* p. 278.

203. "Rospis' knig i pisem," pp. 331, 337, 339; *Materialy,* 1: 339–40, 342–43, 402; P. S. Smirnov, *Vnutrennie voprosy,* pp. LVI–LVII.

204. "Rospis' knig i pisem," pp. 331, 333.

205. *Materialy,* 1: 32; 4: XXIV–XXV; Pascal, *Avvakum,* p. 278.

206. Among the anonymous texts in Aleksandr's library that address themes familiar from Lazar's known writings, see "Rospis' knig i pisem," p. 325, no. 14; p. 328, nos. 31–32; pp. 336–37, nos. 60, 63, 70, 77. Compare these texts to *Materialy,* 4: 179–220. For the place of Lazar's work in Old Belief's literary history, see Bubnov, *Staroobriadcheskaia kniga,* pp. 231–33, 236–38, 244–47.

207. The relationship between this founding archive and other archives of seventeenth-century Old Belief—most importantly, the archive of the Solovki monks—remains to be investigated. On this question, see Demkova, "Old Belief's Founder-Fathers."

208. This lack of any real authority on the part of the "Pustoozero prisoners," foremost among them Archpriest Avvakum, has also been observed in Hauptmann, *Altrussischer Glaube,* pp. 115–17. For comparison, see the tremendous coercive power invested in eighteenth- and nineteenth-century Old Believer "patriarchs" such as Andrei Denisov and Il'ia Kovylin ["In the church he is the patriarch and in the world the secular sovereign (*vladyka mira*)"], in P. S. Smirnov, *Istoriia russkogo raskola,* pp. 99–100, 105–6.

209. Rumiantsev, *Nikita Dobrynin,* 1: 160, 162, 171, 177.

210. *Materialy,* 1: 351–52, 385–93, 440–44; 2: 7, 9–11.

211. *Materialy,* 1: 416–17, 419–20, 425–26. On Lazar's heroism before the 1666 Church Council, see *Materialy,* 2: 23–24, 27–29; 6: 244–45.

212. They were joined by the learned monk Epifanii who played a crucial role

in the writing of Avvakum's *Vita*. See Robinson, ed., *Zhizneopisaniia*, pp. 54–58; Zenkovsky, "Der Mönch Epifanii."

213. A good survey of the Pustoozero texts is found in Bubnov, "Rukopisnoe nasledie pustozerskikh uznikov."

214. On the mysterious disappearance of writings by Nikita Dobrynin, see Rumiantsev, *Nikita Dobrynin*, 1: 28–29. A few of Dobrynin's and Trofimov's writings have survived in their autographs in the Synodal Collection (GIM). See Druzhinin, *Pisaniia staroobriadtsev*, pp. 213, 257–58.

215. The most blatant example is the silence about Ivan Neronov. His *Vita* is absent from the *Vinograd rossiiskii*, and there are only short references to him in Avvakum's *Vita* and a letter by Fedor Ivanov. See *Pamiatniki istorii staro-obriadchestva*, p. 16; *Materialy*, 6: 197–98.

216. "Otryvok iz dela o pis'makh protopopa Avvakuma i startsa Avraamiia," in *Pamiatniki*, pp. 52–53, 315–17.

217. Avvakum's *Vita*, probably the most important text of early Old Belief, demonstrates that the social dissemination of Pustoozero texts was very limited before 1700. Out of thirty-seven copies known to V. I. Malyshev, the eminent Avvakum scholar, only two date from the seventeenth century. N. S. Demkova recently added nine more manuscripts, one of which could be dated to the years following Avvakum's execution in 1682. One additional manuscript dates from the turn of the century. See Malyshev, "Zametka o rukopisnykh spiskakh 'Zhitiia' protopopa Avvakuma," esp. pp. 379–80; Demkova, *Zhitie protopopa Avvakuma*, pp. 13–16, 42–45, 49–50. On the limited number of surviving manuscript copies of other texts produced at Pustoozero, see Bubnov, *Staroobriadcheskaia kniga*, pp. 264–67.

218. Crummey introduced the useful concept of "sacred canon," in his "Old Belief as Popular Religion," p. 707.

219. Demkova, "Old Belief's Founder-Fathers," p. 7; Druzhinin, "Slovesnye nauki," esp. pp. 227–29; Iukhimenko, "Vinograd rossiiskii"; Karmanova, "Legendarnye predaniia v Vygovskoi agiografii"; Ponyrko, "Kirillo-Epifanievskii zhitiinyi tsikl."

220. Malyshev, "Istoriia ikonnogo izobrazheniia protopopa Avvakuma," "Novye materialy o protopope Avvakume." In 1723, for example, the Posad dweller Timofei Trifonovich stated to an investigator that he and his circle of friends "honored the writings" and "good memory" of Archimandrite Spiridon Potemkin. See Esipov, ed., *Raskol'nich'i dela XVIII stoletiia*, 2: 27.

221. See, for example, Samuil Vymorkov, the son of a sacristan who preached against the new rites in the Tambov region during the early 1720s. Samuil was an autodidact who had studied the Bible and apocalyptic texts such as the well-known *Kirillova kniga*. See Semevskii, *Slovo i delo 1700–1725*, pp. 125–85.

222. Interestingly enough, none of the early eighteenth-century "Old Believ-ers" discussed by M. Cherniavsky made references to Old Believer texts. Rather, they had formed their own opinions and written their own texts. See Cherniavsky, "Old Believers and New Religion," pp. 24–37. On early eighteenth-century dis-enters and Old Believer libraries, cf. Luppov, *Kniga v Rossii*, pp. 264–76; Barsov, "Opisanie rukopisei i knig v Vygoleksinskoi biblioteke."

Chapter Three

1. See, for example, Cherniavsky, "Old Believers and New Religion," pp. 7–8; Kliuchevsky, *A Course in Russian History*, p. 329; Pokrovskii, *Antifeodal'nyi protest*, p. 390; Robinson, ed., *Zhizneopisaniia*, p. 43; Robinson, *Bor'ba idei*, p. 196.

2. P. S. Smirnov, "Literatura i oblicheniia staroobriadcheskogo raskola," *Istoriia russkogo raskola*; Zhuravlev, *Polnoe istoricheskoe izvestie o raskol'nikakh*, esp. p. 57. Zhuravlev's influential work had gone through six printings by the end of the nineteenth century.

3. A survey and summary of some important anti-Raskol texts is found in Chistiakov, "Istoricheskoe rassmotrenie."

4. Crummey, "Interpretations of the Old Belief," p. 4. V. S. Rumiantseva distinguished between "Old Belief" (*staroverie*) and "early sectarianism" (*ranne-sektantstvo*) as two directions (*napravleniia*) within "the Raskol Movement" (*raskolnicheskoe dvizhenie*). However, she also observed that the sectarians never developed an identity distinct of Old Belief ("*rannesektantstvo razvivalos' ... pod formoi staroveriia*") and argued that Old Believers like Avvakum and Spiridon Potemkin were the principal "leaders," "publicists," and "prophets" of the Raskol. See Rumiantseva, *Narodnoe antitserkovnoe dvizhenie*, pp. 219–22.

5. See, for example, Robinson, *Bor'ba idei*, pp. 194–246.

6. "Okruzhnoe poslanie rostovskogo mitropolita Iony."

7. *Ibid.*, pp. 174, 176.

8. *Ibid.*, p. 174.

9. On the other hand, those obeying the bishop and submitting to "correction" (*ispravlenie*) were glorified as "men of God," "messengers of God," "bearers of God" (*bogonosnye muzhi*), "bearers of Christ's name" (*khristoimenitye*), etc. (*ibid.*, pp. 172–77).

10. Vozdvizhenskii, *Istoricheskoe obozrenie Riazanskoi ierarkhii*, p. 106.

11. *Ibid.*, p. 109.

12. Vvedenskii, "Missionerskaia deiatel'nost' riazanskogo arkhiepiskopa Misaila"; Vozdizhenskii, *Istoricheskoe obozrenie Riazanskoi ierarkhii*, p. 126.

13. Vozdvizhenskii, *Istoricheskoe obozrenie Riazanskoi ierarkhii*, pp. 87–97, esp. 94.

14. Kapterev, *Patriarkh Nikon i tsar' Aleksei Mikhailovich*, 1: 1–19.

15. The next usage apparently dates from 1660, when Metropolitan Iona of Rostov instructed the priests of his diocese to identify schismatics in their parishes. A schismatic was anyone who failed to attend Mass, or who kept others from doing so: "A memorandum has been sent to you concerning the schismatics and corrupters of the church (*tserkovnye razvratniki*) who do not attend church services and prevent Orthodox Christians from going to church.... Write to Rostov about these schismatics ... who fail to obey you priests and deacons and continue to stay away from church services ... who do not go to their spiritual fathers for confession and don't receive the Body and Blood of the Lord in communion...." [NA IIALI KNTs, Kollektsiia drevnikh aktov, razriad 1, opis' 2, d. 86, Spisok s gramoty iz Rostova (October 18, 1660), fol. 1]. To my knowledge this is the only surviving copy of this interesting text.

16. For example, when an angry mob attacked Nikon for protecting a rich merchant during the Novgorod uprising in 1650, he denounced the population of Novgorod for "crime" (*vorovstvo*), "lawlessness" (*bezchinie*), and the creation of "trouble" (*smuta*). See Tikhomirov, *Klassovaia bor'ba*, pp. 334–35, 340–42. A concern with the outbreak of a schism is also absent from the letters Nikon wrote during the 1650s and early 1660s. Cf. "Gramoty ot Nikona patriarkha k Nikite Alekseevichu Siuzinu" and "Vypiski iz pisem patriarkha Nikona k tsariu Alekseiu Mikhailovichu." Nikon, who is often viewed as the creator of the Russian Schism, did not perceive those who opposed him as supporters of a schism. The idea originated among Nikon's opponents, and it is therefore not surprising that Nikon himself was on occasion accused of schism (*raskol*) by other hierarchs. Cf. a letter by Bishop Kallist of Polotsk in RGADA, f. 153, d. 41, fols. 1–4, Gramota polotskogo i vitebskogo episkopa Kallista ... o nedeistvitel'nosti kliatvy nalozhennoi patriarkhom Nikonom na Pitirima mitropolita (April 22, 1662).

17. See Zernova, *Knigi kirillovskoi pechati*, pp. 80–81; NB MGU, Sobranie knig kirillicheskoi pechati, no. 512; Pozdeeva, ed., *Katalog knig kirillicheskoi pechati*, p. 212. I thank I. V. Pozdeeva for calling my attention to this text.

18. See, for example, the references to "schismatic slanders" (*navety skhizmaticheskie*) and "schismatic delusions" (*prelesti skhizmaticheskie*), in NB MGU, Sobranie knig kirillicheskoi pechati, no. 512, fols. 22, 28.

19. *Ibid.*, fols. 9, 21, 28, 29, etc.

20. *Ibid.*, fol. 9.

21. *Ibid.*, fols. 28, 40–41.

22. *Ibid.*, fols. 53, 55, 64.

23. The *Pouchenie velikogo gospodina sviateishago Iosifa patriarkha moskovskogo i vseia velikiia Rusi arkhiereom i sviashchennoinokam i mirskim iereom, vsemu sviashchennomu chinu* had originally been printed in Moscow in 1642 as part of a *sbornik* containing other sermons of the patriarch and subsequently became part of numerous Old Believer text compilations. See Zernova, *Knigi kirillovskoi pechati*, p. 57, no. 165. The original version of the text is reproduced in a nineteenth-century miscellany, in IIFIF SO, Sobranie rukopisei, no. 14/77, Sbornik staroobriadcheskii, fols. 2–40. I thank N. N. Pokrovskii for kindly allowing me to use this miscellany.

24. IIFIF SO, no. 14/77, fols. 10v, 11, 16v.

25. *Ibid.*, fols. 4v, 17, 20v.

26. Vozdvizhenskii, *Istoricheskoe obozrenie Riazanskoi ierarkhii*, pp. 99, 106.

27. It is curious, however, that he did not apply the term to Sila Bogdanov and his circle (see Chapter One). In a letter to Nikon he called these dissenters "corrupters of the church" (*tserkovnye razvratniki*). See Barsov, "Sudnye protsessy," p. 3.

28. "Chelobitnaia Avraamiia startsa," p. 25; Druzhinin, *Pisaniia staroobriadtsev*, pp. 31–33.

29. See, for example, writings by Nikita Dobrynin and Lazar', in *Materialy* 4: 81, 104, 205.

30. Cited from Makarii, *Istoriia russkogo raskola*, pp. 148–49.

31. In addition to the works discussed below, cf. a treatise by the Greek hierarch Dionisii in Kapterev, *Patriarkh Nikon i tsar' Aleksei Mikhailovich*, vol. 2, appendix, no. 11, pp. XIV–XL; Kapterev, "Sochinenie protiv raskola greka

Dionisiia"; GIM, Sobranie Sinodal'noi biblioteki, no. 372.

32. *Materialy*, 9: 7–8. For the text of Nikita's petition, see *Materialy*, 4: 1–130.

33. *Ibid.*, 4: XII.

34. RGB, Sobranie Moskovskoi Dukhovnoi Akademii, no. 68; *Materialy*, 9: 11. In western-Russian texts, that is, Russian texts written in the Polish-Lithuanian Commonwealth, the term *raskol* appears to have signified adherence to the Union of Brest. It is likely that Polotskii, who came from the Commonwealth, was familiar with this rhetoric. See, for example, the following letter written in 1658 from Vilnius to the Muscovite tsar: " . . . Uniates have begun to arrive [here]. They desire to celebrate Mass according to their own custom in order to generate schisms (*uchinit' raskoly*) among residents of the Orthodox Christian faith and Greek law. . . . " (*AI*, 4: 261).

35. NB MGU, Sobranie knig kirillicheskoi pechati, no. 564, Simeon Polotskii. Zhezl pravleniia, fol. 17; Pozdeeva, ed., *Katalog knig kirillicheskoi pechati*, p. 231. For more information about the *Zhezl* and its function in the fight against *raskol*, see Chistiakov, "Istoricheskoe rassmotrenie," pp. 93–103.

36. This particular reference was added by Polotskii to the first rough version of the acts (*deianiia*). This editorial procedure indicates how Polotskii applied concepts from another cultural sphere to events in Russia. See *Materialy*, 2: 59, fn. 2.

37. Kapterev, *Patriarch Nikon i tsar' Aleksei Mikhailovich*, 2: 31–33.

38. RGIA, f. 834, Rukopisi Sv. Sinoda, opis' 5, no. 38, fols. 1–7, Rospis' knigam vziatym s pechatnogo dvora v Novgorodskoi eparkhii dlia tserkvei i monastyrei (1668).

39. RNB, Sobranie M. P. Pogodina, no. 1560, fols. 82–87v, Slovo uchitel'noe Ioanna sviashchennika ot Bozhestvennogo pisaniia, esp. fol. 86v.

40. See especially Iurkevich, "Pop Lazar' raskolouchitel'."

41. NB MGU, Sobranie knig kirillicheskoi pechati, no. 564, fol. 1v.

42. "Vozzvanie patriarkha Ioasafa i vsego osviashchennogo sobora k tsariu Alekseiu Mikhailovichu," in Kapterev, *Patriarkh Nikon i tsar' Aleksei Mikhailovich*, vol. 2, appendix, no. 10, pp. XIX–XX. This edition is based on GIM, Sobranie Sinodal'noi biblioteki, no. 130, fols. 192–93.

43. "Vsenarodnoe vozzvanie patriarkha Ioasafa," in Kapterev, *Patriarkh Nikon i tsar' Aleksei Mikhailovich*, vol. 2, appendix, no. 9, pp. XV–XIX, esp. XVII. The published text is based on GIM, Sobranie Sinodal'noi biblioteki, no. 130, fols. 203v-6.

44. A good survey of polemic works against *raskol* written under Ioakim can be found in P. Smirnov, *Patriarkh Ioakim moskovskii*, pp. 40, 101–7. See also RNB, Osnovnoe sobranie, O. I. 209, fols. 13–181v, Brozda dukhovnaia; RGADA, f. 381, opis' 1, no. 359, Uveshchatel'naia gramota patriarkha Ioakima ko vsem pravoslavnym o khranenii sebia ot raskol'nicheskikh lzheuchitelei.

45. Veriuzhskii, *Afanasii kholmogorskii*, pp. 84, 605; *Uvet dukhovnyi*, fols. 54r–v, 55, 65v, 88v–89. On the *Uvet* and its use by local hierarchs in their fight against *raskol*, see Chistiakov, "Istoricheskoe rassmotrenie," pp. 103–10.

46. *Uvet dukhovnyi*, fols. 3r–v, 13v, 83v, 86.

47. *Dokumenty*, pp. 124–28.

48. *Materialy*, 2: 5, fn. 1. The list bore the title "rough draft list of schismatics" (*vypiska chernaia raskol'nikov*).

49. Reproduced in Sapozhnikov, "Samosozhzhenie v russkom raskole," p. 6.

50. The religious affairs of the frontier town Simbirsk, founded in 1648 to subdue Nogai Tartars, were beyond the control of the church and very similar to those of Nizhnii Novgorod and environs. On the Mikifor case, see "Zapisnye knigi Tainogo prikaza," *RIB* 21 (1907): 1149–50; Zapozhnikov, ed., *Pis'ma vostochnykh ierarkhov*, pp. 11–14.

51. RGADA, f. 163, d. 3, fol. 33; "Sudnye protsessy," p. 12.

52. See, for example, RGADA, f. 210, Prikaznyi stol, d. 16, fols. 514–20, Obvinenie riazanskogo arkhiepiskopskogo syna boiarskogo . . . v proiznesenii neprigozhikh slov pro patriarkha Filareta (1626–1630). Cf. *ibid.*, d. 14, fols. 138–47 and d. 33, fols. 425–27.

53. RGADA, f. 27, d. 161, fol. 2.

54. RGADA, f. 27, d. 195, fol. 5.

55. See, for example, the acts of the 1666 Church Council, in *DAI*, 5: 463, 469. For more information, see Chapter Six.

56. See, for example, the daily use of the sign of the cross and the erection of large wooden crosses along the roads (especially in the Russian north). These symbols were used even by people who did not attend churches. See Baron, *Travels of Olearius*, p. 252 (on crossing in front of icons); Rushinskii, comp., "Religioznyi byt," p. 166; Veriuzhskii, *Afanasii kholmogorskii*, pp. 96, 354, 357 (on old crosses in the remote hinterlands of the Russian north).

57. RNB, Solovetskoe sobranie, no. 20/1479, Sobranie gramot, no. 156, Gramota o ponuzhdenii vo vsekh votchinakh prikhozhan k ispovedi i k prichastiiu, fols. 330–31.

58. RGIA, f. 834, Rukopisi Sv. Sinoda, opis' 2, no. 1850, Skazki i imennye ispovednye rospisi, fol. 6. On the twenty-four old Novgorodian parish districts called *pogosty*, see Bogoslovskii, *Zemskoe samoupravlenie*, vol. 1, appendix, no. I, pp. 3–8; Papkov, "Pogosty."

59. Suffice it here to refer to a curious polemic work written in 1696 against the schism by Afanasii Liubimov, the first bishop of the newly founded Kholmogory eparchy. The archbishop identified the drunkenness, moral laxness, and unruliness of local clerics and laymen as among the principal roots of the schism in his diocese. See RNB, Solovetskoe sobranie, d. 665/723, Okruzhnoe pouchitel'noe poslanie po eparkhii . . . protivu raskol'nikov, fols. 6v, 10, 14, 21v-22v.

60. RGADA, f. 27, d. 562, Gramota patriarkha antiokhiiskogo Makariia tsariu Alekseiu Mikhailovichu o postavlenii v Nizhnii Novgorod arkhiereia, fols. 1–6, esp. 2.

61. *Ibid.*, fol. 6.

62. Makarii, *Istoriia Nizhegorodskoi ierarkhii*, pp. 1–9.

63. RGADA, f. 163, d. 4, Chelobitnaia nizhegorodskogo mitropolita Filareta ob ukaze voevodam prinimat' k rozysku i gradskomu sudu raskol'nikov, fols. 1–5. The text has been published in part in "Sudnye protsessy," pp. 13–14.

64. "Nakaz ob osvidetel'stvovanii tserkvei"; "Perepisnye knigi chasoven'."

65. See in particular the measures against *raskol* taken by Archbishop Afanasii of Kholmogory. For example, in February 1702 Afanasii gave orders not only to fight the drunkenness and illiteracy of parish priests, but also to enforce use of the new liturgical books. See "Nakaz nashchet 'gramotnosti' sviashchennikov." In particular, officials were " . . . to look at and describe the church books according to

which [these] priest[s] say Mass: during which years were these books issued and which editions are they?" (*Arkhangel'skie gubernskie vedomosti*, 1869, no. 2: 2).

66. RGADA, f. 27, d. 306, O samozhigateliakh krest'ianakh Nizhegorodskogo uezda, fols. 1–5.

67. Gasitskii, ed., *Nizhegorodskii letopisets*, p. 76.

68. RGADA, f. 27, d. 303, Predosterezhenie pravoslavnykh ot ukloneniia v raskol, fols. 1v–4v.

69. It appears that parish priests began to use the term more systematically during the 1680s only after they had been asked to identify schismatics in confessional lists. Also important was the concomitant distribution of the previously mentioned *Uvet dukhovnyi* to the local clergy. See RGIA, f. 834, opis' 2, nos. 1849–54, Statements by parish priests and confessional lists (1690s); Veriuzhskii, *Afanasii kholmogorskii*, pp. 84, 120–25.

70. "Sledstvennoe delo o kazakakh-raskol'nikakh," in Druzhinin, *Raskol na Donu*, pp. 245–61, esp. 250.

71. "Akty raskola na Donu," p. 141.

72. *Pamiatniki*, p. 29.

73. See, for example, Avvakum's polemics against self-proclaimed peasant preachers discussed in P. S. Smirnov, *Vnutrennie voprosy*, pp. 41–42. Cf. Abbot Ilarion's attitudes towards peasant schismatics living in the vicinity of his hermitage in Chapter Four. Ilarion's close relations with Neronov and Bishop Pavel demonstrate that he was an Old Believer—or at least shared many of Old Belief's ideals. See *Zhitie Ilariona mitropolita suzdal'skogo*, pp. 4–5, 12; "Zhitie Neronova," p. 256; Georgievskii, *Florishcheva pustyn'*, p. 23.

74. Efrosin, "Otrazitel'noe pisanie," pp. 9–10, 49, 62.

75. Cf. A. Denisov, *Vitiistvennaia beseda, uveshchaiushchaia vsiu koleblia-shchuiusia Pomorskuiu Tserkov', ispolnennaia ubezhdeniia, iasnosti i zhivogo chuvstva, chto priniatie na sebia zvaniia, po nasiliu mira, imeni Raskol'nika, sviatosti Pravoslavnoi very ne narushaet* cited in Liubopytnyi, "Katalog starovercheskoi tserkvi," p. 6, no. 33.

76. Cited after Dmitrevskii, *Raskol-staroobriadchestva*, p. 72. On Tuptalo's polemic work, see Chistiakov, "Istoricheskoe rassmotrenie," pp. 127–40.

Chapter Four

1. Shchapov, *Russkii raskol*, pp. 200–16, esp. 208.

2. Smolitsch, *Russisches Mönchtum*, pp. 357–82, esp. 374.

3. Almost none of these communities are mentioned in the comprehensive lists of seventeenth-century Russian monasteries and hermitages recently published by the demographer A. E. Vodarskii, based on newly discovered census data from the years 1661 and 1678. Other relevant information may still be found in the voluminous, but little-explored files of the Petrine College of Economics. Cf. Vodarskii, "Tserkovnye organizatsii," esp. pp. 78–96; Vodarskii, ed., *Vladeniia russkoi tserkvi*, pp. 9–102. On the holdings of RGADA, f. 281, Gramoty Kollegii ekonomii, see Vodarskii's commentaries and footnotes, in Vodarskii, *ibid.*, pp. 103–29, 132.

4. Smolitsch, *Russisches Mönchtum*, pp. 191–92 and Vodarskii, ed., *Vladeniia russkoi tserkvi*, p. 134.

5. El'chaninov, ed., *Pistsovaia kniga*, pp. 30–31.

6. "Pistsovaia kniga Aleksandrovoi slobody," *Vladimirskie gubernskie vedomosti*, 1854, no. 19: 147.

7. Suvorov, "Vozdvizhenskii muzheskii monastyr'"; "Monastyri byvshie vo gorode Pereiaslavle."

8. Titov, *Gorod Liubim*, pp. 55–58.

9. This happened after the abbot had sent the following complaint to Moscow: "... They stopped living according to the monastic rule: they drink alcohol and leave the monastery to see their sisters, daughters, and numerous local traders, and they have begun to work for their own profit. And when he, their superior, told them about it ... the monks assembled their families and those village traders who were in agreement with them and began to do nasty things (*pakosti*) to him. ..." (*Ibid.*, pp. 33–34).

10. This information was originally gathered by M. Ia. Diev and has been summarized in P. S. Smirnov, *Vnutrennie voprosy*, pp. XXXIII–XXXIV.

11. See, for example, *Dokumenty*, p. 87.

12. *Prilozheniia*, pp. 17–20.

13. *Dokumenty*, p. 134.

14. RGADA, f. 153, opis'; Makarii, *Istoriia russkoi tserkvi*, 12: 268–69; Lipinskii, *Opisanie sobraniia dokumentov*, p. 3; Vodarskii, ed., *Vladeniia russkoi tserkvi*, pp. 123–24.

15. A. V. Smirnov, comp., *Materialy dlia istorii Vladimirskoi gubernii*, 1: 44–59. For similar data about the "ascription" (*pripisanie*) of small monasteries to larger monastic institutions, see Veriuzhskii, *Afanasii kholmogorskii*, chap. 7.

16. See, for example, Krylov, "Ob uprazdnennykh monastyriakh Rostovsko-iaroslavskoi pastvy"; "Monastyri byvshie vo Vladimirskoi gubernii"; Leonid, ed., "Tserkovno-istoricheskoe opisanie uprazdnennykh monastyrei."

17. Vodarskii, ed., *Vladeniia russkoi tserkvi*, p. 80; *Dokumenty*, pp. 51, 67, 79–80, 91–93; Stroev, *Spiski ierarkhov*, cols. 716, 723.

18. Cf. Makarii, ed., *Pamiatniki Nizhegorodskoi gubernii*, pp. 411, 436. Makarii cites inventories (*opisi*) from the first half of the seventeenth and the second half of the eighteenth century. A collective petition from 1660 to B. I. Morozov mentions eighteen monks by name, in RGADA, f. 396, d. 42835, fol. 210. This Avraamii is not to be confused with the Old Believer Avraamii. See P. S. Smirnov, *Vnutrennie voprosy*, pp. IX, fn. 12.

19. RGADA, f. 396, d. 42835, fols. 1–213, Chelobitnye i otpiski o raznykh delakh boiarinu B. I. Morozovu, kasaiushchiesia do votchin i krest'ian ego; d. 42849, fols. 1–11, Delo po chelobit'iu boiarina B. I. Morozova Nizhegorodskogo uezda Kazanskogo monastyria na stroitelia Avraamiia v peregorodke k monastyriu ulitsy ot sela ego Lyskova.

20. RGADA, f. 396, d. 42835, fol. 109; d. 42849, fols. 1, 11.

21. RGADA, f. 396, d. 42835, fol. 38; d. 42849, fol. 3.

22. RGADA, f. 396, d. 42849, fols. 4, 10. Cf. documents illustrating some of Kalitin's activities, in *DAI*, 5: 339; 6: 79–81, 83, 239–41, 336 (1668–74); 8: 101; 10: 79 (1678–84); 12: 293 (October 1685).

23. RGADA, f. 396, d. 42835, fol. 210r-v.

24. See, for example, Morozov's instructions from November 1652 to appoint

only literate priests who could actually read liturgical books, in RGADA, f. 396, d. 42297, Otpiski i pamiati o raznykh delakh, kasaiushchikhsia do votchin i krest'ian boiarina B. I. Morozova, fols. 171–72. On Morozov and the "zealots-of-piety," see Heller, *Die Moskauer Eiferer*, pp. 30–43.

25. RGADA, f. 27, d. 68, Sobornoe ulozhenie patriarkha Iosifa kasatel'no podtverzhdeniia belomu dukhovenstvu (1651), fols. 7-10; f. 396, d. 42297, fol. 138.

26. This is illustrated by the fact that even in 1666, church services at the monastery were considerably shorter than, for example, in Moscow because they were sung in many voices (*mnogoglasno*). See *Materialy*, 1: 463.

27. *Ibid.*, 1: 459.

28. In particular, he denounced the Greek spelling of the Apostle Paul's name in the new Service Book. See *Materialy*, 1: 461–63.

29. A letter by the Greek Patriarch Makarii, who stayed at the Zheltovodskii Monastery during the late 1660s, implies that the peasants of Lyskovo were among the most dangerous schismatics of the Nizhnii Novgorod area. See RGADA, f. 27, d. 562, fols. 2, 4.

30. Makarii, ed., *Pamiatniki Nizhegorodskoi gubernii*, pp. 424, 436.

31. Vodarskii, ed., *Vladeniia russkoi tserkvi*, p. 39; Makarii, ed., *Pamiatniki Nizhegorodskoi gubernii*, p. 424.

32. Titov, *Troitskii Zheltovodskii monastyr'*, pp. 38–41.

33. *Ibid.*, p. 24. This attack must have been shocking to the church because many leading clerics of the seventeenth century had connections with the Zheltovodskii Monastery: its archimandrites were assigned to the bishoprics of Riazan', Kazan', and Kolomna during the second half of the seventeenth century; the former archbishop of Siberia, Simeon of Tobol'sk, played a vital role at the monastery after 1664. Most importantly, Patriarch Nikon and Archpriest Avvakum, who both came from the vicinity of Lyskovo, had connections with the monastery and seem to have assimilated its religious rigor. See *ibid.*, pp. 25–27, 31–32 and Pascal, *Avvakum*, pp. 94–95.

34. Makarii, ed., "Opisnaia kniga," esp. p. 145.

35. *Materialy*, 1: 460–61.

36. The nuns owned thirteen old books and only three new ones. See Makarii, ed., "Opisnaia kniga", p. 148.

37. About the availability of *pistsovye knigi*, which would contain such information, see Vodarskii, ed., *Vladeniia russkoi tserkvi*, p. 105.

38. Makarii, ed., "Opisnaia Kniga," pp. 140–56.

39. P. S. Smirnov, *Vnutrennie voprosy*, p. 27.

40. Many relatives from Kurmysh, the topographic name of the area of Nikon's origin, visited and stayed with Nikon when he lived at the Ferapontov Monastery. See *Delo*, p. 345.

41. *Materialy*, 1: 459.

42. Makarii, ed., *Pamiatniki Nizhegorodskoi gubernii*, p. 437. It is likely that Avraamii escaped and founded another monastic community in the area. On the activities of one Avraamii who fits our Avraamii's personality profile, see Dmitrii, *Rozysk o Brynskoi vere*, pp. 606–8.

43. *Dokumenty*, pp. 50–52, 56, 58, 60–62, 71–72.

44. Dobronravov, "Blagoveshchenskii muzhskoi monastyr'," pp. 5, 171, 174.

45. *Pamiatniki*, p. 329; *Dokumenty*, pp. 50–51.

46. " . . . The abbot and the archpriest give orders (*veliat*) not to go to confession to priests who say Mass according to the new Service Books" (*Pamiatniki*, p. 329).

47. By contrast, there were only forty-two monks at the Blagoveshchenskii Monastery. See Dobronravov, "Blagoveshchenskii muzhskoi monastyr'," p. 10; *Dokumenty*, p. 51; *Pamiatniki*, pp. 329, 332.

48. RGADA, f. 27, d. 258, Delo rozysknoe o raskol'nikakh, pt. IV, fols. 1–89. Merkurii denied any involvement, but officials kept him under heavy guard as a crucial suspect. See *ibid.*, fols. 42–43; *Dokumenty*, p. 73.

49. RGADA, f. 27, d. 258, pt. IV, fol. 10. For the testimonies of the priests, see *ibid.*, fols. 11, 18, 26.

50. Dobronravov, "Blagoveshchenskii muzhskoi monastyr'," pp. 15, 114, 178–93, esp. 193; Stroev, *Spiski ierarkhov*, col. 688.

51. *PSPVI*, 4: 161.

52. This is suggested by the following evidence: the Shuia community had traditionally been in touch with the schismatic Pokrovskii Monastery of Ivanovo; a monk from Shuia was one of the founders of a new schismatic community in the forests of Nizhnii Novgorod during the 1680s; the Shuia district was the target of a *raskol* investigation in 1666. See Borisov, *Opisanie goroda Shui*, pp. 280–81; Kurnosyi, "Istoriia o begstvuiushchem sviashchenstve," p. 185; *Pamiatniki*, pp. 333–34; *Dokumenty*, pp. 77, 84.

53. Denisov, *Pravoslavnye monastyri*, pp. 103–4 and Vodarskii, ed., *Vladeniia russkoi tserkvi*, p. 57.

54. Borisov, *Opisanie goroda Shui*, appendix, no. 95, p. 441. The German traveler Peter Petrejus observed that Muscovites often went home naked after losing their clothes, boots, and hats in taverns. See his "Historien und Bericht von Muschkow," p. 309.

55. The local population stood firmly behind the abbot. See Borisov, *Opisanie goroda Shui*, pp. 125, 450.

56. Borisov, *Opisanie goroda Shui*, p. 57, fn. 1; "Razboi i razboiniki okolo goroda Shuii."

57. Borisov, *Opisanie goroda Shui*, p. 21; "Pennaia pamiat' za ubiistvo."

58. "Dvoinoi oklad i zapisannye raskol'niki," in *PSPVI*, 4: 258; Borisov, *Opisanie goroda Shui*, pp. 44, 48, 102.

59. Stepanovskii, *Vologodskaia starina*, p. 271; Mordvinov, ed., *Zhitiia sviatykh ugodnikov*, pp. 13–14, 98–99. The census of 1678 lists three small monasteries in Tot'ma and environs: the Nikolaevskaia Babozerskaia Pustyn' (sixteen *dvory*), the Sumorin Monastery (nine *dvory*), and the Uspenskaia Negrenskaia Pustyn' (five *dvory*). See Vodarskii, ed., *Vladeniia russkoi tserkvi*, p. 81.

60. *DAI*, vol. 5, no. 53, pp. 311–13.

61. *Ibid.*, no. 94, pp. 425–27.

62. Breshchinskii, ed., "Zhitie Korniliia," pp. 67–68.

63. *Ibid.*, pp. 73, 101; Crummey, *Old Believers and Antichrist*, pp. 33–35, 62, 64.

64. Dmitrevskii, *Raskol-staroobriadchestva*, p. 27.

65. Svirelin, "Svedeniia o zhizni arkhimandrita Grigoriia Neronova," pp. 44–45.

66. Bubnov, ed., *Sochineniia pisatelei-staroobriadtsev*, pp. 28–30.

67. In Moscow, Feodosii was wanted as one of the principal teachers of Feodosiia Morozova. See *Pamiatniki*, p. 52.

68. SPbFIRI, f. 117, d. 1097, Gramota moskovskogo patriarkha Ioakima . . . o doprose igumena Pavlova monastyria Iosifa, fol. 2.

69. During the late nineteenth century the manuscript belonged to the historian of Vologda, N. I. Suvorov, who allowed Subbotin to inspect it. Its current whereabouts are unknown. See *Materialy*, 1: 305–7.

70. Stroev, *Spiski ierarkhov*, col. 477; Alekseev, "Istoriia o begstvuiushchem sviashchenstve," p. 54.

71. I rely here on information gathered in Skvortsov, *Ocherki tverskogo raskola*, pp. 13–14.

72. Stroev, *Spiski ierarkhov*, col. 644; Feofilakt, "Oblichenie raskol'nicheskoi nepravdy," fol. 2 as quoted in Skvortsov, *Ocherki tverskogo raskola*, p. 14. A brief discussion of this curious work is found in P. S. Smirnov, *Vnutrennie voprosy*, pp. 055–056.

73. According to a report by Voevoda Ivan Volynskii, Iov lived with about twenty monks and thirty novices on the Chira River. An eyewitness noted that Iov's followers were recruited from both sexes and all ages and that they lived together in one community. See Druzhinin, *Raskol na Donu*, p. 72, fn. 26.

74. *Ibid.*, p. 192.

75. Skvortsov, *Ocherki tverskogo raskola*, p. 17.

76. "Akty raskola na Donu," p. 168; P. S. Smirnov, *Vnutrennie voprosy*, p. XXIII, fn. 37.

77. Pascal, *Avvakum*, p. 315; Makarii, ed., *Pamiatniki Nizhegorodskoi gubernii*, p. 423.

78. Arkhangelov, *Sredi raskol'nikov i sektantov Povolzh'ia*, p. 66.

79. RGADA, f. 125, opis' 1, g. 1674, d. 30, Stolp solovetskii i sumskii, fols. 1–4.

80. Among them, for example, were the Zelenaia, Mavrinskaia, and Savateinskaia hermitages. See RNB, Solovetskoe sobranie, no. 20/1479, nos. 140, 145, 151, Gramoty mitropolita novgorodskogo Korniliia.

81. See, for example, Kozhanchikov, ed., *Istoriia Vygovskoi pustyni*, pp. 68, 85, 95–96, 118–19, etc.

82. These monasteries included the Iur'egor'skaia, Shevenskaia, Kenozerskaia, Kurzhenskaia, Muromskaia, and other hermitages. See RNB, Osnovnoe sobranie, Q.I. 1062, Zhitie inoka Kirilla, fols. 65v, 73v–74, 95v, 117r–v.

83. RGADA, f. 27, d. 614, Izvet startsa Serapiona tsariu Alekseiu Mikhailovichu na viaznikovskikh pustynnikov, fol. 2; *Pamiatniki*, p. 80.

84. *Ibid.* Mikhailo may have been in charge of the second most prestigious parish church in Ivanovo, the Krestodvizhenskaia Church. If so, he would have been the elected *popovskaia starosta*—a position with considerable influence in the area. See Borisov, *Opisanie goroda Shui*, pp. 149–50.

85. *Pamiatniki*, pp. 69, 324.

86. Another important monastic figure who received Old Believer recognition was the nun Melaniia from a hermitage not far from the town of Belev. She had a strong influence on Feodosiia Morozova, and Avvakum addressed one of his letters to her. See *Pamiatniki*, p. 312 and Rumiantseva, *Narodnoe antitserkovnoe dvizhenie*, p. 210, fn. 51.

87. *Poslaniia Ignatiia tobol'skogo*, fols. 115–20, esp. 115.

88. *Ibid.*, fols. 117–18.

89. In the West, the combination of free love and infanticide occurred primarily in the stereotype of the witches' sabbath. Cf. Cohn, *Europe's Inner Demons*.

90. I follow here the distinction between small and large monasteries that was suggested by Ia. E. Vodarskii in his doctoral dissertation. See Vodarskii, "Naselenie Rossii v kontse XVII–XVIII vv.", p. 29.

91. RGADA, f. 27, d. 161, fols. 3–5. On Avvakum's imprisonment at the monastery, see *Pamiatniki*, p. 176.

92. See, for example, RGADA, f. 1182, bk. 57, fol. 618v (books given to Bogolep L'vov); bk. 59, fol. 188v.

93. *Materialy*, 1: 464–67, esp. 466.

94. Kononov, *Sud'by Kozheozerskoi pustyni*, pp. 13–15.

95. *Materialy*, 1: 464–65.

96. Kononov, *Sud'by Kozheozerskoi pustyni*, p. 15.

97. *Ibid.*, pp. 13–14; *Materialy*, 1: 465.

98. The charter, which ordered the restoration of priest Nikon's mental health (*umom istselet'*), was explicitly addressed to Bogolep L'vov and not to the abbot of the monastery. See RGADA, f. 27, d. 161, fol. 2.

99. Kononov, *Sud'by Kozheozerskoi pustyni*, p. 15; *Materialy*, 1: 464–65.

100. "He began to torture Panteleiko to find out about the money missing from his cell. He kindled a flat iron in the baking oven and was about to lay hands on [his victim]; Panteleiko, however, was so horrified by the prospect of being burnt with the iron that he stabbed himself in the stomach with a knife" (*Materialy*, 1: 465).

101. Stroev, *Spiski ierarkhov*, cols. 36–37.

102. *DAI*, 5: 458; *Materialy*, 2: 12.

103. One of Bogolep's associates, monk Iosaf, threatened to beat the new abbot, who had to barricade himself in his cell for several days. See *Materialy*, 1: 465.

104. See, for example, *Pamiatniki*, pp. 144, 361.

105. "He drinks and revels continuously and hardly goes to church. Instead, he brews many beers, keeps young children in his cell, and violates them with criminal fornication (*voruet bludnym vorovstvom*). . . . " (SPbFIRI, f. 117, d. 424, Delo . . . po obvineniiu igumenom Kornil'eva monastyria . . . startsa Andreiana i ego sovetnikov v vorovstve i bezchinstvakh, fol. 4).

106. *Opisanie svitkov*, 1: 10.

107. Vodarskii, "Tserkovnye organizatsii", p. 87; Denisov, *Pravoslavnye monastyri*, pp. 593–94; Stroev, *Spiski ierarkhov*, col. 94.

108. The archimandrites of this monastery played a crucial role in the eradication of dissent. For example, Makarii, who was very likely responsible for removing Dosifei in 1670, disciplined dissenting monks at the Solovki Monastery. Makarii's successor, Barsonofii, participated in the Church Council of 1677 that condemned the pilgrimages of dissenters to the relics of a princess from Tver'. Cf. Denisov, *Pravoslavnye monastyri*, pp. 590–93; *Istoriko-statisticheskoe opisanie Tikhvinskogo Bogoroditskogo monastyria*, pp. 120–21; *Pamiatniki*, p. 336; Dosifei, *Geograficheskoe,*

istoricheskoe i statisticheskoe opisanie Solovetskogo monastyria, 1: 164–65; Golubinskii, *Istoriia kanonizatsii sviatykh*, pp. 162–68.

109. GPNTB SO, Sobranie M. N. Tikhomirova, no. 158, Sbornik staro-obriadcheskii, fols. 409–11v; Tikhomirov, *Opisanie Tikhomirovskogo sobraniia rukopisei*, p. 62; Denisov, *Spisok monastyrei*, p. 611.

110. See, for example, a charter by Metropolitan Makarii from early 1661, in *AI*, 4: 296–99; GPNTB SO, Sobranie M. N. Tikhomirova, no. 158, fols. 409v–10.

111. Kurdiumov, "Akty P. M. Stroeva," pp. 314–15, nos. 24–25, 28.

112. According to records in the archive of the Bogoroditskii Monastery, the Besednyi Monastery ceased to be listed as an "ascribed monastery" (*pripisnyi monastyr'*) in 1663. To make up for this loss another monastic institution, the Nikolaevskii Mostizhskii Monastery, was taken over by the archimandrites during the same year. See *Istoriko-statisticheskoe opisanie Tikhvinskogo Bogoroditskogo monastyria*, pp. 130–31.

113. Vodarskii, "Tserkovnye organizatsii", p. 87. For a listing of small monas-teries and hermitages that were subjected to the control of the Bogoroditskii Monastery during the seventeenth and early eighteenth centuries, see *Istoriko-statisticheskoe opisanie Tikhvinskogo Bogoroditskogo monastyria*, pp. 130–35.

114. Serbina, *Tikhvinskii posad v XVI–XVIII vv.*, pp. 377–79.

115. Pavlovskii, comp., *Putevoditel' po monastyriam i sviatym mestam Rossiiskoi imperii*, p. 464; Vodarskii, "Tserkovnye organizatsii," p. 87. Neither my own research nor the cited studies by P. S. Smirnov and Ia. L. Barskov have produced any evidence of liturgical dissent in and around Tikhvin during the 1670s.

116. P. S. Smirnov, *Vnutrennie voprosy*, pp. LXXIV–LXXV; *Materialy*, 4: 299; "Raskol v Olonetskoi eparkhii."

117. Druzhinin claimed that Dosifei also made his way to the Don River where he supposedly founded several alternative monastic communities. See Druzhinin, *Raskol na Donu*, pp. 73–77. Barskov asserted that Dosifei was an Old Believer and responsible for making Avvakum's sponsor, Feodosiia Morozova, a nun (*Pamiatniki*, p. 310). It is, of course, possible that our Dosifei and the two other Dosifeis were one and the same. However, we need a more careful assessment of the sources in order to establish the identities of these various Dosifeis. For exam-ple, there is a remarkable contrast between testimonies of our Dosifei's northern Russian followers Efrosin and Sergei, on which I rely here, and sources such as the Old Belief *sinodiki* and Ivan Alekseev's *Istoriia o begstvuiushchem sviashchenstve*. According to Efrosin and Sergei, their patron Dosifei spent most of his life at the Troitsa Monastery outside Olonets. For other illuminating facts about the identity of Dosifei, see P. S. Smirnov, *Vnutrennie voprosy*, p. XXIV, fn. 38.

118. Denisov, *Spisok monastyrei*, pp. 606–9. The monastery owned 484 households in 1678. See Vodarskii, "Tserkovnye organizatsii," p. 79.

119. RGADA, f. 27, d. 140, Gramoty iz dela o patriarkhe Nikone, pt. I, no. XXXVI, fols. 182, 187–88; *Pamiatniki*, pp. 93–104, esp. 93, 99. Excerpts from other letters can be found in Nikolaevskii, "Zhizn' patriarkha Nikona."

120. Varlaam, comp., "O prebyvanii patriarkha Nikona v zatochenii," pp. 133, 136–39.

121. *Ibid.*, pp. 136, 161; Nikolaevskii, "Zhizn' patriarkha Nikona," pp. 93, 98–99, 106, 380.

122. Varlaam, comp., "O prebyvanii patriarkha Nikona v zatochenii," p. 163. By contrast, Ioakim's charter spoke of Nikon as a simple monk (*monakh*).

123. Abbot Afanasii insisted that he had referred to Nikon only as the "most holy former (*byvshii*) patriarch," but his testimony was contradicted by other monks who admitted that they and local peasants had called Nikon the "most holy patriarch" (*ibid.*, pp. 163–65). For Old Believer texts that denounced Nikon as the Antichrist or its precursor, see P. S. Smirnov, *Vnutrennie voprosy*, pp. 20–29.

124. *Delo*, pp. 348–51, 370, 372.

125. Varlaam, comp., "O prebyvanii patriarkha Nikona v zatochenii," p. 164; *Akty Iverskago monastyria*, cols. 276–77.

126. ". . . The musketeers and servants of the monastery beat with clubs and whips all who make Nikon angry. . . . The clubs they use always lie ready under guard next to Nikon's cell" (*Delo*, p. 345).

127. *Ibid.*, pp. 355, 359–60.

128. See, for example, the exile of the monks Antonii and Trifilii, in *Pamiatniki*, pp. 301, 317.

129. *Delo*, p. 362.

130. One should consider that almost all liturgical books owned by Nikon at the Ferapontov Monastery were confiscated in 1676 (*ibid.*, pp. 386–88). After his confinement at the Kirillov Monastery, Nikon was given a limited number of newly printed books by order of the archimandrite of the Chudov Monastery (*ibid.*, p. 404).

131. RGADA, f. 1182, bk. 57, fols. 5, 23 (1655), 69v (1656), 94v (1657), fol. 462 (1658), 682r–v (1660); bk. 59, fols. 561, 570 (1660).

132. RGADA, f. 1182, bk. 57, fols. 81v, 176v, 178v, 350v (Pomor'e); *ibid.*, fols. 4, 8, 21v, 93v, 99v (Kholmogory).

133. See, for example, the so-called *Fifth Petition*, in Bubnov, ed., *Sochineniia pisatelei staroobriadtsev*, pp. 113, 156–57. For a more detailed analysis of the revolt and its relationship to Old Belief, see Michels, "Solovki Uprising."

134. *Pamiatniki*, pp. 116–22; *Materialy*, 3: 297–98, 323–45; RGADA, f. 125, opis' 1, g. 1669–70, d. 5, Stolp solovetskii i sumskii, fols. 95–96; Barsov, ed., "Akty solovetskogo bunta," pp. 64–65.

135. *Materialy*, 3: 327. One escapee remarked: "These criminals made a written contract with each other and all signed underneath. . . . " (*Pamiatniki*, pp. 116–17).

136. RGADA, f. 125, opis' 1, g. 1669–70, d. 5, fol. 6. On the use of new liturgical books by Solovki monks and priests, see *ibid.*, g. 1674, d. 19, fols. 3, 7 and f. 1182, bk. 65, fol. 182v; Michels, "Solovki Uprising," p. 6.

137. RNB, Solovetskoe sobranie, no. 18/1477, Sobranie gramot, no. 197 (Gramota o blagochinii monastyrskom), no. 325; no. 20/1479, Kopii s patriarshikh i arkhiereiskikh gramot, no. 161, Gramota o nevvedenii v monastyre novykh obychaev (Febr. 9, 1621); Dosifei, *Opisanie Solovetskogo monastyria*, 3: 208–9.

138. RNB, Solovetskoe sobranie, no. 18/1477, no. 35, Tri gramoty o prisylke startsa Iosifa Pleshcheeva; no. 44, Gramota o smirenii buntuiushchikh monakhov.

139. See, for example, his anger about monk Matvei: "He spreads lies about us on every occasion and calls us the enemy of the Solovki Monastery" (*ibid.*, no. 89, fol. 215).

140. RNB, Solovetskoe sobranie, no. 18/1477, opis'; NA IIALI KNTs,

Kollektsiia drevnikh aktov, razriad 1, opis' 3, d. 20, Kniga raskhodnaia Shueretskiia volosti 1676 goda, fols. 5v, 7v.

141. RNB, Solovetskoe sobranie, no. 19/1478, no. 10, Gramota o prisylke pod nachal Fedora Godunova (1646), no. 35; *Materialy*, 3: 105; Belokurov, "Biblioteka i arkhiv," pp. 8–9.

142. RNB, Solovetskoe sobranie, no. 18/1477, no. 282, Gramota o prisylke byvshago suzdal'skogo arkhiepiskopa Iosifa (1635); no. 19/1478, no. 115, Gramota o prisylke mitropolita Makariia (1666).

143. Savich, *Solovetskaia votchina*, p. 264; *Materialy*, 3: 84–88.

144. Belokurov, "Biblioteka i arkhiv," pp. 8–9.

145. Dosifei, *Opisanie Solovetskogo monastyria*, 3: 219.

146. Belokurov, "Biblioteka i arkhiv," p. 8.

147. *Materialy*, 3: 101.

148. *Ibid.*, pp. 82, 87–88. A treatise attributed to Firsov attacks the new liturgical books. Despite his rhetoric, however, Firsov was very ambivalent about the new books and there is evidence that he temporarily supported their use at Solovki. See *ibid.*, pp. 108, 111. See also Nikol'skii, ed., *Sochineniia Gerasima Firsova*, pp. 145–224.

149. *Materialy*, 3: 145, 327. On Nikanor's renunciation of Old Belief, see *ibid.*, p. 200.

150. *Materialy*, 3: 417; RNB, Solovetskoe sobranie, no. 20/1479, no. 122; Dosifei, *Opisanie Solovetskogo monastyria*, 1: 164–65.

151. *Materialy*, 3: 88–89. See the glorification of Gennadii by eighteenth-century Old Believers by contrast, in RNB, Osnovnoe sobranie, O. XVII. 48, fols. 163–81v, Kratkoe skazanie o revnosti i podvizekh inoka Gennadiia.

152. Molchanov, "Bunt solovetskikh monakhov"; P. S. Smirnov, *Vnutrennie voprosy*, p. XIV; "Vygoretskii letopisets," esp. p. 795; Denisov, *Istoriia o otsekh solovetskikh*; Esipov, ed., *Raskol'nich'i dela*, vol. 2, appendix, no. 1, pp. 1–55.

153. Nikolaevskii, "Zhizn' patriarkha Nikona," p. 676.

154. Andreev, ed., *Putevoditel'*, p. 135.

155. *Materialy*, 1: 426–31; Arkhangelov, *Sredi raskol'nikov i sektantov Povolzh'ia*, p. 6; "Istoriia o vere i chelobitnaia o strel'tsakh."

156. *Pamiatniki*, p. 352; RGADA, f. 125, opis' 1, g. 1669–70, d. 5, fols. 245–46. Cf. the sending of *raskol'niki* from Viazniki to the archimandrite of the Spaso-Evfimiev Monastery in Suzdal', who oversaw their distribution to loyal monasteries in the area, in RGADA, f. 27, d. 258, pt. V, fols. 79–80.

157. *Dokumenty*, pp. 159, 169–72, 185–87; Druzhinin, *Raskol na Donu*, p. 83.

158. For another remote monastery in the town of Kargopol' that most likely became schismatic, see Breshchinskii, ed., "Zhitie Korniliia," p. 90; RGADA, f. 125, opis' 1, g. 1669–70, d. 5, fol. 206; Denisov, *Spisok monastyrei*, p. 616.

159. *AAE*, 4: 490. For data on the Nizhnii Novgorod region, cf. RGADA, f. 141, opis' 3, g. 1656, d. 11, Delo po chelobit'iu staritsy Marfy na nizhegorodskogo pristava (monk Lavrentii and his niece Marfa); f. 184, opis' 1, d. 1421, Patriarkh Nikon, fol. 40 (monk seeking refuge with a Protestant pastor).

160. *AAE*, 3: 428.

161. Kharlampovich, *Malorossiiskoe vliianie*, pp. 112–13.

162. Smolitsch, *Russisches Mönchtum*, pp. 273–77; Dobroklonskii, *Rukovodstvo*, 3: 239–45.

163. D. N. Smirnov, *Ocherki zhizni i byta nizhegorodtsev*, pp. 71–72; *AAE*, 3: 240–42; *Opisanie aktov sobraniia grafa A. S. Uvarova*, pp. 168–69, no. 147; *Akty Kholmogorskoi i Ustiuzhskoi eparkhii*, pt. 2, no. 142.

164. *AAE*, vol. 4, nos. 325, 328; Kurdiumov, "Akty P. M. Stroeva," p. 223, nos. 378, 381; Dobroklonskii, *Rukovodstvo*, 3: 244–45. Cf. the violent monks whom Patriarch Nikon forced to leave the Khutynskii Monastery in Novgorod, in SPbFIRI, f. 171, Novgorodskii Sofiiskii dom, pereplet III, no. 98, fols. 276–78, Podlinnaia gramota patriarkha Nikona ... o smirenii startsev i sluzhek Khutynskogo monastyria (1654).

165. "Perepis' vologodskikh starits," *Vologodskie eparkhial'nye vedomosti*, 1865, no. 1: 54–56; *Opisanie svitkov*, 4: 32.

166. In August 1649, for example, Metropolitan Nikon forbade the monks of the Solovki Monastery "to feed feminine-looking children or keep them in their cells." See RNB, Solovetskoe sobranie, no. 20/1479, no. 85, fols. 199, 202.

167. See, for example, friends of Archpriest Avvakum who were appointed abbots, abbesses, and archimandrites during the 1640s and early 1650s, in P. S. Smirnov, *Vnutrennie voprosy*, p. LVIII, fn. 85.

168. See, for example, the exile of monks in 1647 to the Kirillov Monastery for "indecent words" about the tsar, in *Chteniia*, 1885, bk. 4, smes', pp. 2–3. See also Kurdiumov, "Akty P. M. Stroeva," pp. 223, 227, nos. 377, 400; *Akty Kholmogorskoi i Ustiuzhskoi eparkhii*, pt. 2, nos. 170–71.

169. RGADA, f. 210, Moskovskii stol, d. 421, fol. 1028a, Zaderzhanie raskol'nika.

170. RGADA, f. 27, d. 258, pt. I, fols. 20–21.

171. *Ibid.*, fols. 19, 25, 29.

172. RGADA, f. 210, Belgorodskii stol, d. 768, Rozysk bezhavshego iz Kozheozerskogo monastyria startsa Ieva, nazyvaiushchii sebia lozhno Saltykovym, fols. 242–43, 247–50.

173. Iev apparently tried to distance himself from this episode after his arrest. See RGADA, f. 125, opis' 1, g. 1669–70, d. 5, fols. 6–8, esp. 8.

174. RGADA, f. 210, Belgorodskii stol, d. 768, fol. 265.

175. Quoted from Shchapov, *Russkii raskol*, p. 221.

176. GPNTB SO, Sobranie M. N. Tikhomirova, no. 348, Vozglashenie uveshchatel'noe Ioakima patriarkha, fols. 30r-v, 31r-v, esp. 31r.

177. SPbFIRI, f. 117, d. 966, Delo o syske skryvshogosia monakha Dorofeia, fols. 1–7.

178. *Prilozheniia*, pp. 97–98. Ilarion and Dorofei were probably very similar to the schismatic monks Feodosii, Iosif, and Pafnutii, who enjoyed great prestige among the Cossack warriors of the southern steppe. Cf. "Akty raskola na Donu," pp. 128, 132.

179. Monks had also participated in a similar revolt twenty years earlier, see Buganov, ed., *Vosstanie 1662 goda v Moskve*, pp. 261–63.

180. RGADA, f. 141, opis' 2, g. 1648, dd. 93–95, 98; *Opisanie MGAMIU*, 12: 332; Pokrovskii, *Russkie eparchii*, 1: 522, fn.3.

181. Nikolaevskii, "Zhizn' patriarkha Nikona", p. 76. One of these monks "stabbed a boyar's son to death with his own hands" (*Delo*, p. 347). On the nun Alena, see Kartsov, *Religioznyi raskol*, 1: 93–94.

182. For Avvakum's view of monastic discipline and piety see, for example, his *Moral Instruction* (*nravouchenie*), in Borozdin, *Avvakum* (1900), appendix, no. 31. See also his letters to some nuns *ibid.*, nos. 5–6.

183. German was the student of Nektarii, the former archbishop of Siberia, who had retired to the Tver' Monastery. On the disciplinary measures taken by these idealist reformers, see Uspenskii, *Istoricheskoe opisanie Nilovoi Stolobenskoi pustyni*, pp. 92–93, 168–69. Information about German's letter is found in Skvortsov, *Ocherki tverskogo raskola*, p. 21 and Shchapov, *Russkii raskol*, p. 212.

184. RGADA, f. 210, Moskovkii stol, d. 398, fols. 139–53, Arest beglogo startsa Kirillova Beloozerskogo monastyria.

185. Ilarion was probably shorn a monk in 1652 by Bishop Pavel of Kolomna and soon afterward became abbot of the hermitage. During the 1890s, the library of the hermitage still held a Service Book donated by Vonifat'ev in 1653. See Georgievskii, *Florishcheva pustyn'*, pp. 23, 290.

186. RGADA, f. 210, Moskovskii stol, d. 398, fols. 139–41.

187. RGADA, f. 27, d. 259, Rozysk o monakhakh, monakhinakh i bel'tsakh, fols. 37–39.

188. RGADA, f. 210, Moskovskii stol, d. 398, fol. 141. On the use of bears in divination and trained acts, see Zguta, *Russian Minstrels*, pp. 8–9, 48, 54, 60, 64, 111–12.

189. Rozhdestvenskii, ed., "Chelobitnaia nizhegorodskikh popov," pp. 18–31.

190. *Ibid.*, p. 26. The described event took place during Rogation Week, which is the sixth week after Easter. However, such mockeries of monasteries were by no means limited to this time of year. Cf. Kapterev, *Patriarkh Nikon i ego protivniki*, p. 172.

191. Rozhdestvenskii, ed., "Chelobitnaia Nizhegorodskikh popov," p. 23.

192. RGADA, f. 27, d. 306, O samozhigateliakh krest'ianakh Nizhegorodskogo kraia, fols. 1–13, esp. 4–5.

193. *Ibid.*, fols. 12–13.

194. RGADA, f. 27, d. 258, pt. IV, fol. 121; *Dokumenty*, pp. 108–9. Unfortunately, a part of the number is illegible.

195. *Dokumenty*, p. 130. Evpraksiia's teachings can, in part, be reconstructed from information gathered by the Secret Chancellery. For example, she preached against basic social institutions sanctified by the church, such as marriage and infant baptism (*ibid.*, p. 136). She also advocated extreme forms of fasting and self-castigation including total abstention from food (p. 58). Cf. other female prophets, in Huber, *Women and Authority*; reviewed in *Church History* 56, no. 2 (1987): 257–58; Livanov, "Prorochitsa raskol'nitsa Ustina Nikiforovna."

196. Stroev, *Spiski ierarkhov*, col. 308; *Pamiatniki*, p. 332.

197. *Dokumenty*, p. 129.

198. " . . . And these monks do not live in monasteries. Instead, they live in forests and villages rushing from hole to hole like poisonous snakes" (*Dokumenty*, p. 130). About Evpraksiia's disciples, the runaway nuns Ekaterina and Maremiana, see *ibid.*, p. 135.

199. *Dokumenty*, pp. 77–78, 87. Church investigators assumed that Vavila and Leonid had absorbed the teachings of the preacher Kapiton. Such contacts may have existed, even though Kapiton's role remains obscure and Vavila explicitly

denied having been taught by him (*ibid.*, pp. 77, 88). It is more likely that the nun Evpraksiia was their teacher. The church considered her just as dangerous as Kapiton (pp. 65, 94, 101, 129), and Vavila and Leonid apparently knew her well (pp. 52, 81).

200. See, for example, *ibid.*, pp. 80, 83.

201. Vavila grew up in a village of the Riazan' district, but left home in the early 1650s to join a small rural hermitage (*ibid.*, pp. 57, 80). Leonid was a peasant from the Suzdal' district and became a monk in 1656 (pp. 82–83). The origins of Evpraksiia are obscure. We can only establish that she lived among peasants or in small cells not far from peasant villages (pp. 129, 131–32).

202. Efrosin, "Otrazitel'noe pisanie," pp. 48, 83.

203. "Dopolnenie k stat'e o pustyniakh." The unnamed author speculates that the monastic cells' proximity to ancient gravesites might indicate the local survival of pagan traditions. See also "Kurgany vo Vladimirskoi gubernii."

204. Vozdvizhenskii, *Istoricheskoe obozrenie Riazanskoi ierarkhii*, pp. 166–68.

205. RGADA, f. 159, Novgorodskii prikaz, opis' 3, d. 450, fols. 145–49, Delo o raskol'nikakh v Viatskom krae, esp. fol. 147.

206. RGADA, f. 27, d. 258, pt. V, fols. 48, 50–54; *Dokumenty*, pp. 109–12.

207. RGADA, f. 27, d. 258, pt. V, fols. 48, 51; *Dokumenty*, pp. 110–12. For more information about the connections between plague and religious despair, see Chapter Six.

208. RGADA, f. 184, opis' 2, d. 156, Zagolovki arkhivnykh dokumentov za 1594–1651, fols. 13–14, 25. Included, for example, is a letter written by monk Innokentii Korsakov informing his son about the murder of a close relative.

209. "Zhitie Neronova," p. 283; *Materialy*, 1: 306; A. V. Smirnov, comp., *Materialy dlia istorii Vladimirskoi gubernii*, 3: 10.

210. See, for example, a petition from 1670 by the widow Anna Vasil'eva requesting permission to build a monastic cell, in RGADA, f. 396, d. 43581. See a similar petition by the noble woman Anastasiia, in SPbFIRI, f. 117, d. 425, fols. 1–2.

211. RGADA, f. 27, d. 259, fol. 12; *Dokumenty*, pp. 97–98 (widow Melaniia); Kozhanchikov, ed., *Istoriia Vygovskoi pustyni*, p. 360 (widow Sofiia); "Sudnye protsessy," p. 38 (widow Fevronitsa).

212. See, for example, the arrest of pregnant widows—among them the widow of a deceased priest—in Galich during the 1670s for fornication (*bludnoe delo*), in RGADA, f. 210, Prikaznyi stol, d. 447, fols. 13–14. See also the exile of a widow and her daughter from Moscow to Nizhnii Novgorod during the 1640s, in RGADA, f. 396, d. 41896, fols. 1–2. We also need to consider the poverty of many widows, indicating that most widows could not afford to pay the donations (*vklady*) required to join regular monastic communities. See, for example, petitions written in the 1650s in the name of impoverished Posad widows requesting support (*zhalovan'e*), in RGADA, f. 396, dd. 42667–68.

213. RGADA, f. 396, d. 42424, fols. 1–2.

214. I do not claim that joining religious communities was the most important escape from hardship or social isolation. In a review of a publication on slavery (*kholopstvo*) by R. Hellie, C. Goehrke points out that many unattached women entered noble households to achieve some basic form of social security, in *JGO*, N.S. 35, no. 3 (1987): 414–15. Not all widows, spinsters, and divorcees were so

lucky. Many eked out a living as beggars, and schismatic communities seem to have had a particular attraction for these outcasts.

215. RGADA, f. 210, Prikaznyi stol, d. 799, fols. 23–57, Rassprosnye rechi trekh raskol'nits (1680–81).

216. *Pamiatniki*, pp. 296–304, 306–12; *Materialy*, 2: 103; Barsov, ed., *Novye materialy*, p. 155; Mazunin, *Povest' o boiaryne Morozovoi*, pp. 92–109, 208–15. Both Morozova and Potemkina identified themselves as Old Believers. This is not surprising since Morozova was the widow of Avvakum's boyar patron Gleb I. Morozov, and Potemkina the mother of the Old Believer Spiridon Potemkin.

217. The protection offered to schismatics by aristocratic widows recalls better-known Western parallels. See, for example, Queen Sancia of Naples who used her wealth and influence to aid outlawed heretics. See review of Kirshner, *Women of the Medieval World*, in *Church History* 56, no. 2 (1987): 243.

218. RGADA, f. 27, d. 258, pt. II, fol. 2; *Pamiatniki*, pp. 73, 78. Avdo'tia Vasil'evna was the widow of Prince Semen Romanovich Pozharskii, who had been a member of the Boyar Duma from 1646 until his death in June 1659. Cf. Crummey, *Aristocrats*, p. 187; RGADA, f. 27, d. 258, pt. IV, fols. 134; pt. V, fol. 69; *Dokumenty*, 105, 107.

219. RGADA, f. 159, opis' 1, d. 1395, fol. 32 (widow Tat'iana, mother of nobleman Fedor Dirin); fols. 25, 86v (widow Afrosinia, aunt of nobleman Dmitrii Khvostov). See, for example, the fate of the Polish *szlachta* woman Evfimiia during the 1660s, in Tokmakov, *Opisanie Pokrovskogo devich'ego monastyria*, appendix, pp. 22–25.

220. RGADA, f. 27, d. 258, pt. V, fols. 19–20; *Dokumenty*, p. 92. For similar statements, cf. *ibid.*, fols. 4, 16 and p. 99.

221. RGADA, f. 27, d. 258, pt. V, fols. 1, 5, 15, 46; d. 259, fols. 11–13, 18–19; *Dokumenty*, pp. 93, 95–96, 113.

222. For example, most of the nineteen nuns who joined the previously mentioned Kazan' monk Porfirii had dressed themselves in monastic habit (*chernoe plat'e na sebia nakladyvali sami soboiu*). See RGADA, f. 159, opis' 3, d. 450, fol. 148; f. 27, d. 258, pt. IV, fol. 85; *Dokumenty*, pp. 104–6.

223. Vozdvizhenskii, *Istoricheskoe obozrenie Riazanskoi ierarkhii*, p. 84; *Dokumenty*, p. 19.

224. Veselovskii, comp., *Dokumenty o postroike Pustoozerskoi tiur'my*, p. 25. Krasulin's radicalism was clearly not in response to the new liturgies. He apparently had come into conflict with the government for refusing to swear the oath of allegiance to the tsar (*ibid.*, pp. 23–24).

225. *AI*, 5: 113.

226. *Opisanie svitkov*, 1: 6.

227. SPbFIRI, f. 117, d. 930, Otpiska beloozerskogo voevody . . . o posylke . . . razstrigi Nikol'skogo monastyria, staritsy Kilikii (July, 1670), fols. 1–4.

228. van Klenk, *Voyagie van den heere Koenraad van Klenk*, p. 37.

229. Pisarev, *Domashnii byt patriarkhov*, appendix, pp. 125, 249.

230. RGADA, f. 396, d. 42467, fols. 1–2, Gramota ot tsaritsy Marii Il'ininy; d. 42472, fols. 1–31, Doprosy raznogo zvaniia liudei, vziatykh na zastavakh.

231. For example, the Uspenskii Monastery in Vladimir had sixty-four nuns sharing forty-five cells. In addition, six dislocated nuns were living with them temporarily. See Tikhonravov, *Kniaginin Uspenskii devichii monastyr'*, pp. 103–4.

232. See, for example, the measures taken by the metropolitan of Riazan', in Vozdvizhenskii, *Istoricheskoe obozrenie Riazanskoi ierarkhii*, pp. 134–35.

233. *AI*, 5: 113. The council of 1682 established a direct connection between *raskol* and the absence of proper ecclesiastical controls. See Vinogradskii, *Tserkovnyi sobor*, pp. 79–92.

234. "Donesenie Pitirimovo o raskol'shchikakh."

235. For more information about Pitirim, see P. S. Smirnov, *Istoriia russkogo raskola*, pp. 183–86.

236. RGADA, f. 163, d. 4, Delo po chelobit'iu Filareta mitropolita (1672). The metropolitans of Novgorod were faced with a similar dilemma. See RGB, Sobranie biblioteki Obshchestva istorii i drevnostei rossiiskikh, no. 103, Kniga obraztsovaia novgorodskogo arkhiereiskogo doma s 1651 po 1697 god, fols. 1–146v. A description of this interesting *sbornik* is found in Stroev, *Biblioteka Imperatorskogo OIDR*, pp. 37–40.

237. *AI*, 5: 113.

238. Quoted from Shchapov, *Russkii raskol*, p. 213.

239. See, for example, the peasant Zakharii Stefanov from a remote Pomor'e village who convinced his father, mother, and sisters to withdraw into a monastic cell in the forest, in Kozhanchikov, ed., *Istoriia Vygovskoi pustyni*, p. 100–101. See also the activities of wandering preachers such as Pimen and Vitalii in Karelia, in *ibid.*, pp. 27–34; Breshchinskii, ed., "Zhitie Korniliia," p. 93. The fabric of northern monastic life is evident in the *Vita* of the monk Epifanii, who was accused of schism at the 1666 Church Council. See Robinson, ed., *Zhizneopisaniia*, pp. 179–202.

240. See, for example, the activities of the monk Iosif alias Ivan Kazanets, in Sapozhnikov, "Samosozhzhenie v russkom raskole," pp. 14–17.

241. Numerous examples can be found in Druzhinin, *Raskol na Donu*. See, in particular, the example of unattached monks and nuns attracted by the preacher Iov (*ibid.*, pp. 71–72). Another typical example is provided by the monk Tikhon who had fled from Kazan' with his sister, the nun Evdokiia. They were captured while wandering from one steppe settlement to another (p. 84).

242. Lileev, ed., *Novye materialy*, esp. pp. 34–38; Lileev, *Iz istorii razkola*, esp. pp. 269–74.

243. See, for example, Andrei Denisov's letters to his community (*pravouchitel'nye poslaniia*) emphasizing the reading of liturgical books, prayer, and unquestioning submission to the precepts of the community elders (*sobornyi sovet*). See Liubopytnyi, "Katalog starovercheskoi tserkvi," nos. 21, 23, 88, 90.

244. Typical in this regard is a letter, allegedly written in the first years of the eighteenth century, which described life in an isolated hermitage in glowing terms. See Mel'nikov, *Istoricheskie ocherki popovshchiny*, p. 48.

245. The story of *Bol'shoi Kitezh* exists in popular variations for the areas of Nizhnii Novgorod, Arhkangel'sk, and Gorodets. See *ibid.*, pp. 46–47.

246. One of them was about the peasant monk Mark, who wandered all the way to Japan (*Opon'skoe tsarstvo*) in search of paradise. See *ibid.*, pp. 40–42.

Chapter Five

1. *DAI*, 5: 459. See also the following passage: "They have developed a disdain for the newly printed books that appeared under Patriarch Nikon as well as after his departure, and [they] fail to praise God according to these books. . . . " (*ibid.*).

2. *Ibid.*, p. 460.

3. See especially the 1674 Church Council, which dealt with the persistence of old liturgical vestments among the parish clergy, in Pokrovskii, *Russkie eparkhii*, 1: 296.

4. *AI*, 5: 114.

5. See, for example, the instructions cited in *DAI*, 5: 462, 472.

6. *Ibid.*, pp. 460–64.

7. Protas'eva, "Stolbtsy Sinodal'nogo sobraniia," p. 296.

8. For more information on this particular liturgical reform, see Chapter One. For a recent discussion, see Heller, *Die Moskauer Eiferer*, pp. 102–14.

9. The following reason was given to justify the cancellation of the reform: "There was great uproar (*velikaia molva*) in Moscow, and Orthodox Christians of all ranks stayed away from churches because the liturgical chants had become too long and burdensome for them" (RGADA, f. 27, d. 48, Deianie moskovskogo tserkovnogo sobora 1649 goda, fol. 3). A published version is found in Belokurov, "Deianie moskovskogo sobora 1649 goda," p. 36.

10. RGADA, f. 27, d. 68, fols. 1–3, Deianie moskovskogo sobora 1651 goda. See also Belokurov, "Deianie moskovskogo sobora 1649 goda," pp. 48–49.

11. *Ibid.*

12. *AAE*, 4: 493.

13. For examples of such letters of ordination, see Pascal, *Avvakum*, pp. 100, 104, 195, 365 and GIM, Sobranie Sinodal'noi biblioteki, no. 424, Zapis' stavlennykh gramot 1645–66 gg.

14. The Patriarch's Office distributed alms to the children of priests who had perished in prison, see RGADA, f. 235, opis' 2, bk. 41, fol. 250 (January, 1657).

15. See, for example, the *Uveshchanie o blagochinnom stoianii v tserkvi s oblicheniem bezchinstvuiushchikh* written under Patriarch Ioasaf, in Evgenii, *Slovar' istoricheskii*, 1: 297. See also RGADA, f. 381, Biblioteka Sinodal'noi tipografii, opis' 1, no. 422, Izveshchenie chudes, byvshikh v . . . Moskve o slozhenii trekh pervykh perstov. Also of interest is a *Pouchenie sviatitel'skoe k novopostavlennomu popu* dating from the end of the seventeenth century, in *Zapiski Otdela rukopisei GBL* 43 (1982): 92.

16. BAN, Sobranie V. G. Druzhinina, no. 1091, Prisiaga Ioakima patriarkha khotiashchim vzyti na stepen' sviashchenstva . . . izdana pechatnaia v Moskve 1679 goda. Interestingly enough, the same text can also be found in a nineteenth-century compilation of Old Believer texts, in *Zapiski Otdela rukopisei GBL* 45 (1986): 101.

17. BAN, Sobranie V. G. Druzhinina, no. 1091, fol. 3.

18. Piskarev, *Drevnie gramoty Riazanskogo kraia*, pp. 127–33.

19. *Ibid.*, pp. 84–86.

20. *Opisanie Solotchinskogo arkhiva*, p. 3, no. 13.

21. RGADA, f. 1433, Muromskii mitropolichii dvor, opis' 1, d. 3.

22. *Opisanie Solotchinskogo arkhiva*, p. 3, no. 10.

23. No cases involving *raskol* were recorded during the last two decades of the seventeenth century. Cf. RGADA, f. 1433, opis' 1; *Opisanie Solotchinskogo arkhiva*; Piskarev, *Drevnie gramoty Riazanskogo kraia*; Vozdvizhenskii, *Istoricheskoe obozrenie Riazanskoi ierarkhii*.

24. *Opisanie svitkov*, 3: 36–37.

25. SPbFIRI, f. 117, no. 1177, Skazka sviashchennika Sergeia (March, 1677), fols. 1r–v.

26. *Opisanie svitkov*, 3: 35.

27. Other priests serving in the Vologda eparchy were accused of beating peasants, hiding taxes, or using violence to enrich themselves. See *Opisanie svitkov*, 1: 22–23; 2: 16, 38; 3: 7.

28. SPbFIRI, f. 117, no. 650, Delo ob izbienii syshchika beloozertsa Druzhiny Chernova po naucheniiu sviashchennikov (March–October, 1665), fols. 1–6.

29. See, for example, SPbFIRI, f. 117, no. 465, Delo po obvineniiu Blagoveshchenskogo tserkovnogo starosty Fedora Lapotnika v samovolnoi prodazhe pechatnogo sluzhebnika i v khishcheniiakh iz tserkvi (October, 1658), esp. fol. 2.

30. See, for example, petitions requesting the reissue of papers lost to fire, thieves, and mice, in SPbFIRI, f. 117, nos. 1518, 1555, 1649, 1652.

31. See, for example, the high concentration of such petitions during the years immediately following the 1666 Church Council, in SPbFIRI, f. 117, nos. 829–30, 846, 852, 855, 859, 861–2, 864–5.

32. SPbFIRI, f. 117, no. 868, Chelobitnaia prikhozhan Georgievskoi tserkvi ob ostavlenii u nikh sviashchennika Fedora Kharitonova (March, 1670), fol. 1.

33. *Ibid.*, fol. 1v.

34. Dokuchaev-Baskov, *Tserkovno-prikhodskaia zhizn'*, pp. 13, 15.

35. Ianovskii, "Opisanie aktov novgorodskogo Sofiiskogo doma," pp. 55, 65, 68–69, 76.

36. RGIA, f. 834, Rukopisi Sv. Sinoda, opis' 2, nos. 1849–54, Skazki i imennye ispovednye rospisi.

37. Cited from Kapterev, *Patriarkh Nikon i tsar' Aleksei Mikhailovich*, 1: 510.

38. See the brief description of relevant archival documents in Naster, "Kratkii obzor dokumental'nykh materialov," pp. 308–9.

39. The explanation is simply that we have more comprehensive archival information for this eparchy than for others.

40. "Akty i materialy v kholmogorskom sobore," pp. 25–26; Veriuzhskii, *Afanasii kholmogorskii*, pp. 370–71. I have found that other eparchies did not invest as much time and effort in confiscating old liturgical books.

41. Such petitions are cited in Veriuzhskii, *Afanasii kholmogorskii*, pp. 196, 200–201.

42. See, for example, orders given in December 1687 to Aleksei, the cathedral priest of Kholmogory, to test priests in their knowledge of the Mass and other ceremonies. Candidates not found acceptable by Aleksei had to undergo further training. See "Nakaz ob osvidetel'stvovanii tserkvei."

43. One of these candidates was the village priest Ivan: "The priest Ivan does not know how to conduct the divine liturgy and baptizes infants without myrrh

and oil. . . . " (*Arkhangel'skie gubernskie vedomosti*, 1869, no. 2: 2). One might also mention the case of priest Ivanov from the distant Mezen' district on the White Sea littoral. Ivanov was granted episcopal permission to leave Kholmogory before his education had been completed. The reason cited was that the impending spring thaw would have considerably delayed his return to his home parish. However, Ivanov was given his ordination papers only on condition that he submit himself to the guidance of an experienced local priest. See Veriuzhskii, *Afanasii kholmogorskii*, p. 203, fn. 36. For other cases illustrating the effort to educate priests in the fundamentals of the liturgy, see *ibid.*, pp. 202–9.

44. *Akty Kholmogorskoi i Ustiuzhskoi eparkhii*, 2: 484–89, no. 201.

45. Veriuzhskii, *Afanasii kholmogorskii*, p. 374.

46. Golubtsov, *Chinovniki kholmogorskogo sobora*, p. IX.

47. *Pamiatniki*, p. 125.

48. "Gramota o privedenii monastyria s votchinami k krestnomu tselovaniiu (June 16, 1647)," in Dosifei, *Opisanie Solovetskogo monastyria*, 3: 139–43; Michels, "Solovki Uprising," pp. 11–14.

49. *Pamiatniki*, pp. 132–33.

50. RGADA, f. 210, Moskovskii stol, d. 421, Begstvo popa i d'iachka posle vvedeniia bogosluzheniia po ispravlennym knigam, fol. 41.

51. *Ibid.*, fols. 42–43, esp. 43.

52. For information about the participation of the priests Semen, Matvei, and Grigorii from Kem' in the Solovki revolt, see RGADA, f. 125, opis' 1, g. 1669–70, d. 5, fols. 154, 172.

53. *Pamiatniki*, p. 131.

54. RGADA, f. 125, opis' 1, g. 1669–70, d. 5, fol. 330. For similar examples, see *ibid.*, fols. 332, 416 and *Pamiatniki*, pp. 356–57.

55. NA IIALI KNTs, Kollektsiia drevnikh aktov, razriad 1, opis' 3, no. 25, Kniga Shueretskoi volosti . . . protornaia, komu skol'ko za chto placheno mirskikh deneg (1673), fols. 2v, 9v, 25v.

56. *RIB*, 38: 373.

57. See, for example, NA IIALI KNTs, Kollektsiia drevnikh aktov, razriad 1, opis' 2, nos. 10/3, 22, 68.

58. RNB, Solovetskoe sobranie, no. 20/1479, nos. 126, 154, 156–57; Dosifei, *Opisanie Solovetskogo monastyria*, 3: 226–27.

59. Cf. memoranda dating from June 1671 and August 1672, in *AAE*, 4: 235–36, 241–43. On this region, see "Vaga", in *BE*, 5: 332 and "Verkhovazhskii posad," in *BE*, 6: 78. On the Solovki parishes, cf. Makarii, "Khristianstvo v predelakh Arkhangel'skoi eparkhii," pp. 36–37; Veriuzhskii, *Afanasii kholmogorskii*, p. 329.

60. " . . . And on the Lord's holidays and . . . on Sundays . . . the white priests and deacons fail to chant liturgical prayers due to their laziness. Accordingly, there is no divine service performed in the holy churches of God" (*AAE*, 4: 241). On the failure to use the new liturgical books, the memorandum observed the following: "In the holy churches of God there is much corruption (*neispravlenie*) because they don't chant and recite in one voice. And [they say Mass] according to the old printed books and not according to the newly revised ones" (*ibid.*).

61. In addition, printed and handwritten copies of John Chrysostomos' *Book on the Priesthood* (*Kniga o sviashchenstve*) were distributed to all parishes, apparently

with the aim of infusing a basic sense of priestly mission into the minds of these parish priests (*AAE*, 4: 236). The *Book* was issued by the patriarchal printing press in August 1664. See Zernova, *Knigi kirillovskoi pechati*, p. 94, no. 308.

62. The parishes of the Pskov eparchy may have been an exception to this rule. In 1685, Metropolitan Markell wrote in great alarm to the tsar that he was powerless to impose his will over local parishes. Peasants refused to accept priests who were not drunkards and troublemakers (*bezchinniki*), and they also were "all in favor of the church schism" (*vse dlia raskola tserkovnogo*). See *AI*, 5: 200–201.

63. RGADA, f. 210, Prikaznyi stol, d. 901, Nanesenie v sele Fedueve raskol'nikami poboev zakazchiku-stroiteliu Troiskogo monastyria Rafailu, fols. 148–51. Some documents from this investigation have been printed or paraphrased, in Sapozhnikov, "Samosozhzhenie v russkom raskole," pp. 23–26.

64. Sapozhnikov, "Samosozhzhenie v russkom raskole," p. 25.

65. *Ibid.*

66. *Ibid.*, pp. 23–25. A petition dated April 29, 1683 was signed by the brothers Ivan, Peter, Vladimir, and Vasilii Dolgorukov.

67. *Ibid.*, pp. 8, 27; Dmitrii, *Rozysk o Brynskoi vere*, p. 585.

68. During the 1680s, Prokopii was arrested on the Don River and interrogated. See "Akty raskola na Donu," p. 203 and Druzhinin, *Raskol na Donu*, pp. 82–83. For information about the priest Semen from the Poshekhon'e district, see P. S. Smirnov, *Vnutrennie voprosy*, p. XXXV, fn. 47.

69. SPbFIRI, f. 117, no. 1873, Delo po izvetnoi chelobitnoi na sviashchennikov Ivana Polikarpova i syna ego Nikifora; Kurdiumov, "Kollektsiia P. I. Savvaitova," p. 283.

70. SPbFIRI, f. 171, Novgorodskii Sofiiskii dom, pereplet V, no. 241, fols. 227–31, Otpis' popa Ivanishcha Ivanova (November, 1679); Ianovskii, "Opisanie aktov novgorodskogo Sofiiskogo doma," p. 48.

71. The records of the Vologda diocesan archive illustrate such conflicts in considerable detail, including *Opisanie svitkov*, 1: 1, 6, 13–15, 22–24; 2: 7, 9, 16, 38. See, for example, a petition by the parishioners of priest Vasil': "He burned down the altar with the altar cloth and gospel book to look for hidden money (*kladovye den'gi*). Finally, he and his cronies took 900 rubles from underneath the church building. . . . " (*ibid.*, 1: 23–24). Shortly afterward, Vasil' stabbed a peasant to death in a drunken stupor.

72. RGADA, f. 27, d. 258, pt. I, fols. 6, 10, 14; *Dokumenty*, pp. 124–25, 127.

73. RGADA, f.27, d. 258, pt. I, fols. 11–12; *Dokumenty*, pp. 125–26.

74. Dmitrii was captured in late October 1666. He denied his past behavior, claiming he had always wanted to say Mass according to the new books. He insisted that the peasants had forced him to use the old books, and he even identified the worst schismatics in his parish by name. However, the repeated failure to seize Dmitrii, his attempt to hide, and his loud protests against the new books suggest he made up the story. See RGADA, f. 27, d. 258, pt. I, fols. 14–16; *Dokumenty*, pp. 126–28.

75. RGADA, f. 210, Prikaznyi stol, d. 447, fols. 1–310, Sysknoe delo pro zloupotrebleniia galitskogo voevody P. F. Rakhmaninova.

76. *Ibid.*, fols. 9–10v.

77. See, for example, *ibid.*, fols. 1–6. Ivan Fedorovich Lyzlov, a patriarchal

boyar who headed the Patriarch's Office during the 1670s, later became a *dumnyi dvorianin* at the court of Patriarch Ioakim and was apparently also appointed to the Boyar Duma in the Kremlin. On the careers of both officials, see *DAI*, 6: 193–94; 10: 79; Crummey, *Aristocrats*, pp. 58, 97–98, 100–101, 206, etc.; Torke, *Staatsbedingte Gesellschaft*, pp. 81–86.

78. "He seized [them] and sent bailiffs without an order from the Most Holy Patriarch Ioakim. . . . " (RGADA, f. 210, Prikaznyi stol, d. 447, fol. 257).

79. *Ibid.*, fol. 11.

80. *Ibid.*, fol. 147.

81. *Ibid.*, fol. 150.

82. See, for example, *ibid.*, fols. 73, 138, 140, 249.

83. Evdokim's brother, the deacon Tikhon, was married to the daughter of Archpriest Feofilakt. His sister was the spouse of the *zemskii starosta*, Lazar' Korovin. The clerk Ivan Savinov was Evdokim's brother-in-law. See *ibid.*, fols. 37, 39.

84. *Ibid.*, fols. 29–32. Unfortunately, the alleged remarks are not specified in the documents. All we know is that the voevoda apparently spoke about the power of the Holy Spirit to change human nature (*estestvo chelovecheskoe*). See *ibid.*, fols. 32, 35.

85. *Ibid.*, fol. 181.

86. *Ibid.*, fols. 213, 221.

87. Rakhmaninov stubbornly denied the accusation, claiming that Evdokim "incites (*nagovarivaet*) many people against [him]" (fol. 33).

88. Rakhmaninov confronted many of the parish priests directly during their interrogations. On such occasions the voevoda made every effort to convince the Muscovite emissaries that he had been framed, and that the real issue was the use of the old liturgies. For example, he repeatedly accused the priests of covering up Evdokim's schismatic behavior (*ibid.*, fols. 236–37, 243, 251), and asserted that he had become the victim of a conspiracy (fol. 213).

89. Iushkov, *Ocherki*, p. 43; Conybeare, *Russian Dissenters*, pp. 69–70.

90. See, for example, *Opisanie svitkov*, 1: 23–24; 2: 9, 16, 38; 3: 7; 4: 54, etc.

91. RGADA, f. 27, d. 259, fols. 29–31; Stroev, *Spiski ierarkhov*, cols. 1031–32.

92. RGADA, f. 27, d. 259, fols. 29–30; Nikolaevskii, "Cherty eparkhial'nogo upravleniia."

93. RGADA, f. 27, d. 259, fols. 30–31.

94. *DAI*, 5: 489.

95. *Ibid.*, p. 460.

96. *AI*, 5: 114.

97. See, for example, RGADA, f. 27, d. 558, fols. 1–33, Spisok s anonimnogo pis'ma; Shchapov, *Russkii raskol*, pp. 63, 387, 389; *DAI*, 12: 352–54.

98. *DAI*, 5: 460. The 1674 Church Council specifically addressed the problem of widowed priests. See Kapterev, *Tsar' i moskovskie sobory*, p. 37.

99. *RIB*, 38: 373; RGADA, f. 210, Prikaznyi stol, d. 91, fols. 293–302, Sysk ob eretichestve vdovogo popa Kondratiia (1634–35). For a similar case, see *ibid.*, fols. 23–25 and *Opisanie MGAMIU*, 15: 110.

100. Cf. the efforts of Novgorod church authorities to capture defrocked priests, in RGADA, f. 210, Novgorodskii stol, d. 83, fols. 75–83, Poimka razstrig

(1632–44) and *Opisanie MGAMIU*, 12: 24; d. 150, fols. 731–40, Ssylka razstrigi popa na vechnoe zhitie za vorovstvo i volshebstvo; d. 210, fols. 161–63, 284–93, 356–57, Ssylka kostromskogo razstrizhennago popa (1689–90); *Opisanie MGAMIU*, 12: 49, 88.

101. RGADA, f. 27, d. 614, fol. 4; *Dokumenty*, p. 136.

102. P. S. Smirnov, *Vnutrennie voprosy*, p. XXXII.

103. RGADA, f. 163, d. 7a, fol. 48.

104. For more information on such families, see Chapter Six.

105. "Chelobitnaia vologodskomu arkhiepiskopu Gavriilu," esp. p. 2.

106. *Ibid.*, p. 2.

107. GA Vologda, f. 1260, Sobranie N. I. i I. N. Suvorovykh, opis' 4, d. 55, fols. 1–5, Delo o vologodskikh raskol'nikakh.

108. V. Veriuzhskii found this case among surviving records of the Antoniev-Siiskii Monastery. See Veriuzhskii, *Afanasii kholmogorskii*, pp. 79–80, esp. fn. 40.

109. *Ibid.*, p. 79, fn. 37.

110. GA Vologda, f. 1260, opis' 4, d. 55, fol. 2.

111. "K istorii raskola"; *Pamiatniki*, p. 326.

112. *Pamiatniki*, pp. 51–52, 314–15; Mel'nikov, *Istoricheskie ocherki popovshchiny*, pp. 64–66; Meletii, *Drevnie gramoty*, p. 39.

113. Druzhinin, *Raskol na Donu*, pp. 46–47, 58–59.

114. "Akty raskola na Donu," p. 215.

115. Pokrovskii, *Russkie eparkhii*, 1: 374–84; Druzhinin, *Raskol na Donu*, pp. 219–20.

116. Druzhinin, *Raskol na Donu*, p. 85, fn. 82.

117. "Akty raskola na Donu," pp. 138–39; Druzhinin, *Raskol na Donu*, pp. 85–86.

118. "Akty raskola na Donu," pp. 182–83.

119. Druzhinin, *Raskol na Donu*, pp. 141–42, 146, 251, 295, 298.

120. See, for example, priests such as Ivan Alfimov, Antonii, Ermil, and Tarasii (*ibid.*, pp. 88, 91–92, 273, 299).

121. Buganov, ed., *Vosstanie 1662 goda v Moskve*, pp. 10, 17, 26, 32; nos. 250–52. The priest Filaret from Rostov wrote a pamphlet in support of the revolt at Kolomenskoe, in RGADA, f. 396, d. 43354, Sudnoe delo (August, 1666), fols. 10–14. A charter by the tsar dated October 1670 announced the capture and execution of a priest who had disseminated seditious letters (*vorovskie pis'ma*) among peasant insurgents of the Nizhnii Novgorod eparchy. See A. V. Smirnov, comp., *Materialy dlia istorii Vladimirskoi gubernii*, 3: 291.

122. I am relying here on sources cited in Sapozhnikov, "Samosozhzhenie v russkom raskole," p. 28.

123. This attack is not to be confused with other attacks against the same monastery by local peasants that occurred a few years later. For more information, see Chapter Six.

124. The information cited here has been summarized in Barsov, "Paleostrov," pp. 49–51.

125. Whether this fire was caused by a religious frenzy or by the exchange of gunfire cannot be reconstructed on the basis of existing evidence. There is no doubt that at least some of the insurgents, possibly under Ignatii's leadership, had locked themselves in the church building which then went up in flames (*AI*, 5: 253).

The interpretation of a nineteenth-century historian that about 2,700 (sic) peasants committed a mass suicide may have to be reconsidered in light of the cited evidence. See Sapozhnikov, "Samosozhzhenie v russkom raskole," p. 29.

126. Later Old Believer sources glorified Ignatii as a martyr of the "old belief" (*staraia vera*). See Kozhanchikov, ed., *Istoriia Vygovskoi pustyni*, pp. 37–48. On the documented escape of Ignatii's associates, see *AI*, 5: 253–55.

127. Avvakum and his student Avraamii called on their followers to have pity on the "Nikonians" and to pray for their conversion, in *Materialy*, 5: 241; 7: 77; P. S. Smirnov, *Vnutrennie voprosy*, pp. 83–85.

128. Cf. the activities of another fugitive priest on Lake Onega, in Efrosin, *Otrazitel'noe pisanie*, p. 31; RNB, Osnovnoe sobranie, O. XVII. 48, Skazanie ob inoke Gennadie, fol. 168v.

129. P. Smirnov, *Ioakim patriarkh moskovskii*, p. 90.

130. *Poslaniia Ignatiia tobol'skogo*, pp. 147–52; *Uvet dukhovnyi*, fols. 42v-43; "Zapiski Matveeva," pp. 38–39; "Zapiski Krekshina," pp. 41–42; "Zapiski Medvedeva," pp. 18–23.

131. *Prilozheniia*, p. 152; "Zapiski Matveeva," p. 40; "Zapiski Krekshina," pp. 43–44; "Zapiski Medvedeva," pp. 24–26; Veriuzhskii, *Afanasii kholmogorskii*, pp. 40–41.

132. *Prilozheniia*, p. 153.

133. Prugavin, *Bibliografiia staroobriadchestva*, no. 280.

134. On the dissemination of this text in the eparchies of Vologda and Viatka, see *Opisanie svitkov*, 4: 15. Similar texts were distributed by the archbishop of Kholmogory in October 1682. See Veriuzhskii, *Afanasii kholmogorskii*, p. 84, fn. 51.

135. *PSVPI*, 4: 161–63.

136. "Posledovateli ucheniia ob Antikhriste," pp. 12–13.

137. A new diaspora church served by diaspora priests did, in fact, emerge during the eighteenth century. The best discussion of this church is found in Mel'nikov, *Istoricheskie ocherki popovshchiny*. Unfortunately, Mel'nikov did not provide much information about the seventeenth-century prehistory of this church.

Chapter Six

1. This also applies to social groups such as the boyar elite and the musketeers (*strel'tsy*) not discussed in this chapter. An excellent example of boyar spirituality is found in the correspondence between Evdokiia Urusova and her children, in Vysotskii, ed., "Perepiska kniagini Urusovoi"; RGADA, f. 210, Bezglasnyi stol, d. 26. See also the case of the military man Kondratii Ostrepov, who was disciplined for staying away from church and praying in his home, in *DAI*, 10: 466–67. Since evidence about these social groups is very limited, I focus here on craftsmen, merchants, and peasants.

2. See, for example, a decree by Metropolitan Makarii of Novgorod from June 1656 that called on the population of his diocese to attend church services and to have children baptized inside the Orthodox Church, in *AAE*, 4: 497. For similar acts, see *ibid.*, no. 19 and *AI*, vol. 5, no. 156. Other such sources have been identified and summarized in Dobroklonskii, *Rukovodstvo*, 3: 232–34.

3. The text is summarized in Kapterev, *Patriarkh Nikon i tsar' Aleksei Mikhailovich*, 1: 8–10. The memorandum is largely based on an earlier patriarchal memorandum from 1636.

4. *Polnoe sobranie zakonov*, vol. 1 (1830), no. 47, p. 246. For similar texts, which were sent to the hinterlands of Novgorod, Kostroma, and other cities, see RGADA, f. 210, Novgorodskii stol, d. 96, Mery k izkoreneniiu bezchiniia vo vremia posta i suevernykh obychaev, fols. 1–13, 251–54, 316.

5. *DAI*, 5: 461–62.

6. Many such *rospisi* have survived from the 1680s and 1690s, in RGIA, f. 834, Rukopisi Sv. Sinoda, opis' 2, nos. 1849–54, Skazki i imennye ispovednye rospisi.

7. *Akty Kholmogorskoi i Ustiuzhskoi eparkhii*, 2: 475–77.

8. *AI*, 5: 262–64. See also two memoranda sent to parishes in the hinterlands of the Spaso-Prilutskii Monastery which have survived in the archive of the Holy Synod, in RGIA, f. 834, opis' 5, no. 193, Pamiat' o nakazanii monastyrskikh krest'ian za neispolnenie tserkovnykh obriadov; no. 210, Pamiat' o prikazanii vsem krest'ianam . . . byt' v voskresenii na liturgii.

9. This can also be documented by a case involving the landowner Ivan Sytin and Patriarch Nikon. Each side accused the other of inciting peasants to fight over harvests and fishing rights, demonstrating that hatred of the patriarch resulted primarily from violence and economic exploitation. See "Chelobitnaia Ivana Sytina na krest'ian patriarkha Nikona." One is reminded of the Novgorod revolt of 1650 during which Nikon was severely beaten for giving protection to corrupt food merchants. See Tikhomirov, *Klassovaia bor'ba*, pp. 334–43. Cf. also a complaint by a Novgorodian miller about the confiscation of his mill, in Ianovskii, "Opisanie aktov novgorodskogo Sofiiskogo doma," p. 23.

10. Cf. Ianovskii, "Opisanie aktov novgorodskogo Sofiiskogo doma." The outstanding feature of these petitions was that they were written collectively. On collective petitions and their historical origins, see Torke, *Staatsbedingte Gesellschaft*, pp. 89–118. By contrast, Old Believer petitions were compiled by isolated individuals such as the priest Dobrynin and Archpriest Avvakum.

11. See, for instance, Bogoslovskii, ed., "Zemskie chelobitnye v drevnei Rossii"; P. P. Smirnov, "Chelobitnye dvorian i detei boiarskikh." On petitions written by town dwellers, see P. P. Smirnov, *Posadskie liudi*, vol. 2; on peasant petitions, cf. *dokumenty pomestno-votchinnykh fondov otdel'nykh uezdov* in SPbFIRI and described in Andreev, ed., *Putevoditel'*, pp. 243–49. Religious issues were remarkably absent from all the petitions kept in these files. Cf. also the *Dela Sarskoi i Podonskoi mitropolii*, in Viktorov, *Sobranie rukopisei I. D. Beliaeva*, pp. 96, 98; Lebedev, *Sobranie aktov I. D. Beliaeva*, p. 87 and the petitions in the archive of the Uspenskii Cathedral, in Protas'eva, "Stolbtsy Sinodal'nogo sobraniia," pp. 289–91, nos. 1444, 1838; Usp. 32. They ask for protection from violence, or for the lowering of taxes and other economic burdens (e.g. nos. 1764–65, 1796). Other petitions address conflicts arising from regulations on second or third marriages. See Protaseva, *ibid.*, p. 297.

12. See, for example, Ianovskii, "Opisanie aktov novgorodskogo Sofiiskogo doma," p. 35.

13. Vodarskii, "Tserkovnye organizatsii," pp. 78–79.

14. Tikhomirov, *Klassovaia bor'ba*, p. 406; Veselovskii, *Feodal'noe zemlevladenie*, p. 443.

15. See, for example, "Akty cherepovetskogo Voskresenskogo monastyria," nos. 1753–56 and Viktorov, *Sobranie rukopisei I. D. Beliaeva*, pp. 96–97. These documents demonstrate that conflicts between monastic clergy and peasants frequently concerned the distribution of land, money, and cattle. Patriarchal instructions to the abbot focused on the disciplining of unruly peasants and other secular matters.

16. P. P. Smirnov, *Posadskie liudi*, 2: 33–34.

17. Klibanov's notable work concentrates, however, on urban prophets at the beginning of the eighteenth century. See, for example, Klibanov, "K kharakteristike novykh iavlenii v russkoi obshchestvennoi mysli."

18. See, for example, the conclusion drawn by one of the best-informed studies, in Ankudinova, "Sotsial'nyi sostav pervykh raskol'nikov," p. 68.

19. *Materialy*, 1: 455.

20. *Ibid.*, pp. 402–3. Ivanov mentioned the following Moscow residents: Dmitrii Kiprianov, Iakov Vasil'ev, and Iakov Stoianov. Dmitrii Kiprianov, who traded in bread (*kalachnik*), is otherwise known as the recipient of a letter by Avvakum, in *Materialy*, 5: 231.

21. On Avvakum's preaching, see *Materialy*, 1: 199. The Old Believer Lazar' preached in the town of Romanov and appears to have had some impact on local merchants. See *Pamiatniki*, pp. 53–67. A manuscript belonging to Stefan Vonifat'ev suggests that Old Belief preachers may have had a special interest in addressing the religious and social needs of merchants, in Kapterev, *Patriarch Nikon i ego protivniki*, p. 104, fn. 4.

22. *Materialy*, 1: 481.

23. *Ibid.*, p. 483. The case dates from August 30, 1664, exactly one day after Avvakum had been sent to the prison colony of Mezen', and contains a curious and otherwise unconfirmed piece of information: the priests, who admonished their parishioners to use the new books, had allegedly been bribed by former Patriarch Nikon. On the dating of Avvakum's renewed exile from Moscow, see *Pamiatniki istorii staroobriadchestva*, p. XV.

24. *Materialy*, 1: 232; "Zhitie Neronova," p. 290.

25. The new stone church at the monastery was erected by Vologda masons and architects, and Neronov saw to it that they were generously remunerated. See "Zhitie Neronova," p. 281. For more information on Neronov's victimization by the local bishop, see Michels, "The First Old Believers," pp. 499–502.

26. See, for example, Avvakum's letters to Moscow, in *Materialy* 5: 231–39; P. S. Smirnov, *Vnutrennie voprosy*, pp. V–VII, 157–59.

27. GIM, Sobranie Sinodal'noi biblioteki, no. 1629, fols. 1–7. As the original archival *delo* was not accessible to me, I have relied on the excerpts and summaries in P. S. Smirnov, *Vnutrennie voprosy*, pp. 099–100 and Rumiantseva, *Narodnoe antitserkovnoe dvizhenie*, pp. 202–3.

28. See, for example, the horrible devastation recorded in "Akty o morovom povetrii," pp. 474–75.

29. Cited in P. S. Smirnov, *Vnutrennie voprosy*, p. 0100, based on an excerpt from GIM, Sobranie Sinodal'noi biblioteki, no. 1630, which was unfortunately not available to me.

30. Ozment, *Mysticism and dissent*, pp. 137–67, 228–30.

31. See an excerpt from the investigation of three Moscow priests, in Borozdin, *Avvakum* (1898), p. 10. The original manuscript of the case is found in RGADA, f. 27, d. 68, fols. 4–10, Rassledovanie o sviashchennikakh nesoglashavshikhsia na vvedenie [edinoglasnogo peniia].

32. RGADA, f. 210, Novgorodskii stol, d. 150, fols. 358–68; *Opisanie MGAMIU*, 12: 49.

33. Belokurov, *Materialy dlia russkoi istorii*, pp. 228–44.

34. RGB, Muzeinoe sobranie, no. 2776, *Rozysknoe delo* against Quirin Kuhlmann and the German pastor Kondrat Nordermann. The text is described in Kudriavtsev, *Muzeinoe sobranie rukopisei*, p. 362. See also Tschizewskij, *Aus zwei Welten*, pp. 231–52; Billington, *Icon and Axe*, pp. 171–74; Kuhlmann, *Ausgewählte Dichtungen, Der Kühlpsalter, Himmlische Liebes-Küsse*.

35. Salomies, *Der Hallesche Pietismus*, pp. 20–33; Tschizewskij, "Jakob Boehme und Russland"; Billington, *Icon and Axe*, p. 171–72.

36. The records of the actual investigation have been lost, but we are fortunate to have information about the case from a priest who wrote a short polemic against the heretic. See RNB, Sobranie M. P. Pogodina, no. 1560, fols. 82v–87, Slovo uchitel'noe Ioanna sviashchennika ot Bozhestvennogo pisaniia, esp. fol. 82v. Short excerpts are cited in P. S. Smirnov, *Vnutrennie voprosy*, p. CXX, fn. 237; for a description of this *sbornik*, see Bychkov, *Opisanie rukopisei Imperatorskoi publichnoi biblioteki*, pp. 188–211, esp. 209–10.

37. RNB, Sobranie M. P. Pogodina, no. 1560, fols. 81r–v, 82, Spisok s podmetnoi povesti pis'ma ruki Isidora Kriuchk[ov]a. The text has been published in part in Barsov, ed., *Novye materialy*, pp. 156–57.

38. RNB, Sobranie M. P. Pogodina, no. 1560, fol. 82.

39. *Ibid.*, fol. 81.

40. Quoted from Rovinskii, *Podrobnyi slovar'*, cols. 227–31. Cf. a patriarchal order from 1674–75 prohibiting the sale of "German" woodcuts, in *AAE*, vol. 4, no. 200.

41. According to Patriarch Ioakim's edict, such broadsheets and pamphlets were confiscated by church officials. But even Rovinskii, usually well informed, did not know if such texts have survived from the seventeenth century. We do know the archival locations for similar eighteenth-century materials. See Rovinskii, *Podrobnyi slovar'*, cols. 231–32.

42. Druzhinin, *Raskol na Donu*, appendix, no. 4, pp. 271–72.

43. *Ibid.*, p. 272. For a discussion of the *Theologia Deutsch*, see Ozment, *Mysticism and dissent*, pp. 14–60.

44. "According to God's creation, we are all brothers. Whoever wants to preach in public (*izveshchatisia*) from the Scriptures is welcome to do so. No matter where they are from, we will [regard] them without flattery and pride because God is [our] father and calls upon everyone. . . . " (Druzhinin, *Raskol na Donu*, p. 272).

45. *Ibid.*, p. 271. On contacts between Ukrainian and southern Russian merchants during these years, see also the testimony of the schismatic Koz'ma Kosoi (*ibid.*, p. 274). For general information on southern business connections with Ukrainian town dwellers, see Aksakov, *Issledovanie o torgovle na ukrainskikh iarmarkakh*.

46. "They preach and write that the last day and the world's end and trans-

formation are imminent. [All of this] and Our Lord Jesus Christ's Second Coming will occur in this and that year and month. . . . However, the years about which they prophesized went by, and their false prophesy did not come true" (quoted from P. S. Smirnov, *Vnutrennie voprosy*, p. 45).

47. "Akty raskola na Donu," pp. 132–34.

48. *Ibid.*, p. 133

49. *Ibid.* We apparently only have a short letter in Koz'ma's hand. See Druzhinin, *Raskol na Donu*, p. 276.

50. "Akty raskola na Donu," p. 133.

51. Druzhinin, *Raskol na Donu*, pp. 277, 279–81.

52. " . . . He concludes this from many [passages in the] Scriptures and from clear arguments in the Books of the Prophets" (*ibid.*, p. 277).

53. On Thomas Müntzer, see Moeller, *Deutschland im Zeitalter der Reformation*, pp. 98–100; Ozment, *Mysticism and dissent*, pp. 61–97.

54. Druzhinin, *Raskol na Donu*, pp. 279, 281.

55. *Ibid.*, pp. 96, 267, 269–70, 274, 282.

56. *Ibid.*, pp. 273, 276.

57. RGADA, f. 210, Prikaznyi stol, d. 218, fols. 7–8; *Opisanie MGAMIU*, 15: 257.

58. RGADA, f. 1433, opis' 1, dd. 21, 50, Gramoty o raskol'nike Semene Konstantinove Smol'ianove.

59. *Dokumenty*, p. 86; *Pamiatniki*, pp. 29, 71; RGADA, f. 27, d. 303, fols. 1–4v, Predosterezhenie pravoslavnykh ot ukloneniia v raskol, esp. fol. 1v; Rumiantseva, ed., *Dokumenty prikazov o raskol'nikakh*, p. 99. The voluminous archive of the Vologda eparchy does not contain a single accusation of schism against a local town dweller. However, we know that at least one trader was a buyer of old liturgical books. Also, one man was strongly suspected of being a religious dissenter because, despite repeated admonishment, he failed to come to church services. See SPbFIRI, f. 117, no. 465, fol. 2; no. 1790.

60. RGADA, f. 159, opis' 3, d. 450, fol. 144.

61. RGADA, f. 210, Moskovskii stol, d. 641, Obvinenie [Romanovtsev] v prinadlezhnosti k raskolu i sysk po obvineniiu voevody Ivana Grimkova v zloupotrebleniiakh, fols. 176–78.

62. Iosif was arrested in connection with the investigation of a defrocked monk (*rostriga*), Gerasim, who apparently had been hiding in his home. See "Pamiat' Sysknogo prikaza." We know that other schismatics stayed temporarily with inhabitants of the *Basmannaia sloboda*. See, for example, "Sudnye protsessy," p. 32.

63. Ankudinova, "Sotsial'nyi sostav," p. 60; "Zhitie Neronova," pp. 270–71; Pascal, *Avvakum*, p. 72; RGADA, f. 27, d. 303, fol. 1v.; Rumiantseva, ed., *Dokumenty prikazov o raskol'nikakh*, p. 99.

64. See, for example, the *Skazanie o obrashchenii raskol'nikov zavolzhskikh* cited in P. S. Smirnov, *Vnutrennie voprosy*, p. XXVIII.

65. On the Posad dweller Gerasim Telitsin, who distributed suspicious religious pamphlets, see *Pamiatniki*, p. 135. For information about other schismatics interrogated or executed at Kholmogory, see Veriuzhskii, *Afanasii kholmogorskii*, pp. 72–99.

66. Cf. Shchapov, *Russkii raskol*, p. 226 and Ankudinova, "Sotsial'nyi sostav," p. 61, fn. 8.

67. Shchapov, *Russkii raskol*, p. 241.

68. Shchapov postulated that trade routes extending along the Northern Dvina and Sukhona rivers were very important for the dissemination of dissent. However, it remains unclear what historical evidence formed the basis for this assessment. See *ibid.*, p. 256.

69. "Sudnye protsessy," pp. 17–18.

70. *DAI*, 12: 105–6.

71. *Ibid.*, p. 103.

72. "Sudnye protsessy," pp. 32–34.

73. *AI*, 4: 366–67; 5: 200–201; "Delo o proiznesenii nepristoinykh slov"; Protas'eva, "Stolbtsy Sinodal'nogo sobraniia," p. 289.

74. "Sudnye protsessy," pp. 16–17. Kuz'min, for example, expressed the fervent conviction that Tsar Mikhail had been no other than the incarnation of the Archangel Michael on earth.

75. "Please, my Lord, . . . defend me against these opponents of the holy church. . . . If Semen [Gavrilov] and Ivan [Dement'ev] are not disciplined and punished for this in Great Novgorod . . . it will be completely impossible to control other acts of opposition against the church. . . . I have no one in Great Novgorod who could help me except you (*pomoshchi sebe krome tebia ne imeiu*)" (RGADA, f. 159, opis' 1, d. 1395, fol. 111).

76. RGADA, f. 159, opis' 1, d. 1395, Sysk o raskol'nikakh v gorode Novgorode, fols. 298–303; Rumiantseva, *Narodnoe antitserkovnoe dvizhenie*, appendix, no. 12, pp. 232–33. Although one can discern later contacts with Old Believers (e.g., Avvakum's wife), Dement'ev's ideas and activities had much more in common with those of the other urban radicals discussed here.

77. RGADA, f. 159, opis' 3, d. 1945, Prodolzhenie sysknogo dela o raskol'nikakh v Novgorode, fol. 24.

78. On Dement'ev's wealth, see Shchapov, *Russkii raskol*, p. 238. On his contacts with Prince Ivan Khovanskii, who was then voevoda of Novgorod, see RGADA, f. 159, opis' 1, d. 1395, fols. 306–7; Rumiantseva, *Narodnoe antitserkovnoe dvizhenie*, appendix, no. 12, p. 234.

79. See, for example, RGADA, f. 159, opis' 3, d. 1945, fols. 23–27.

80. RGADA, f. 159, opis' 1, d. 1395, fols. 143–45; Rumiantseva, *Narodnoe antitserkovnoe dvizhenie*, appendix, nos. 7, 12, pp. 228–29, 234.

81. RGADA, f. 159, opis' 1, d. 1395, fols. 93, 96, 109, 306; Rumiantseva, *Narodnoe antitserkovnoe dvizhenie*, appendix, nos. 6, 12, pp. 227–28, 234.

82. See, for example, Gavrilov's report that he had once been shipwrecked on Lake Ladoga en route to Sweden. See RGADA, f. 159, opis' 1, d. 1395, fols. 111, 142.

83. *Ibid.*, fols. 314–15, 317. Rukavichnik lived in the Merchant Quarter of Novgorod and seems to have distributed hosts to town residents.

84. *Ibid.*, fol. 222.

85. *Delo*, p. 217. For basic information on the peculiarities of Pskovian and Novgorodian religion during the preceding centuries, see Billington, *Icon and Axe*, pp. 79–84.

86. See, for example, Borozdin, *Avvakum* (1900), appendix, no. 14, pp. 34–38.

87. For relevant information, see Hill, *World Upside Down*, pp. 41–45; Ginzburg, *Cheese and Worms*; Leff, *Heresy in the later Middle Ages*.

88. Kartsov, *Religioznyi raskol*, 1: 76–101. Ankudinova refers to both the Stepan Razin rebellion and the Kolomenskoe uprising, in Ankudinova, "Sotsial'nyi sostav," pp. 67–68. Rumiantseva's stated goal is to identify the main centers of *raskol* before and after the Razin rebellion, in Rumiantseva, *Narodnoe antitserkovnoe dvizhenie*, pp. 5–7, 219–22.

89. RGADA, f. 163, d. 12, Delo ob olonetskom raskol'nike Tereshke Artem'eve, fols. 1–9; "Sudnye protsessy," pp. 35–40.

90. RGADA, f. 163, d. 12, fols. 3–5; "Sudnye protsessy," pp. 36–37.

91. RGADA, f. 163, d. 12, fols. 5–6; "Sudnye protsessy," pp. 37–38. Why the priest was abducted remains a mystery. Possibly the kidnappers needed him for basic religious services such as burials or baptisms. It is also conceivable that they wanted to punish him.

92. RGADA, f. 163, d. 12, fols. 6–7; "Sudnye protsessy," pp. 37–38.

93. RGADA, f. 163, d. 12, fols. 7–8; "Sudnye protsessy," pp. 38–39.

94. For good introductions to seventeenth-century Onega society, see Cherniakova, "Naselenie Olonetskogo kraia" and Miuller, *Ocherki*, pp. 13–19, 80–86, 117–19, 132–36.

95. See, for example, Starostina, "Volneniia krest'ian Tolvuiskogo pogosta," "Shueretskaia volost' v XVI-XVII vv."

96. Starostina, "Mirskaia chelobitnaia zaonezhskikh pogostov." I thank T. V. Starostina for calling my attention to this important text.

97. *Ibid.*, p. 125. Lands belonging to the church were highly concentrated in the north. See, for example, the census records of 1678, in Gorchakov, *Monastyrskii prikaz*, appendix, no. 43, pp. 140–46. On the predominance of patriarchal lands in some northern regions, see Gorchakov, *O zemel'nykh vladeniiakh*, appendix, no. 15, p. 99. On the incorporation of northern peasant lands into Nikon's new monasteries, see *DAI*, 5: 481–82.

98. Starostina, "Mirskaia chelobitnaia zaonezhskikh pogostov," p. 110. A *pogost* was a northern peasant settlement with a church and a market place which served as the commercial, administrative, and religious center for surrounding villages.

99. See Chapter Five, pp. 184–85.

100. Barsov, "Paleostrov," pp. 50–51. We have some information about Iakov Evstav'ev Vtorogo, Emel'ian's relative. Originally from Shunga, Vtorogo had moved to Povenets where he served for many years as head of the customs house (*tamozhennyi golova*). During the 1670s he was identified as one of the main rebel leaders on Lake Onega. It is likely that the Vtorogo clan got involved in the revolt because peasants had appealed to them for help. See Starostina, "Mirskaia chelobitnaia zaonezhskikh pogostov," p. 111.

101. "Sudnye protsessy," p. 30.

102. "Sudnoe delo o razorenii Paleostrovskogo monastyria," *Olonetskie gubernskie vedomosti*, 1849, no. 8, pt. II, col. 4. I thank I. A. Cherniakova of the Institute of History in Petrozavodsk for making a copy of this rare text available to me.

103. I have relied here on Barsov, "Paleostrov," p. 35. On local tensions with other monasteries, see Miuller, ed., *Kareliia*, pp. 215–18, 266–67, 319–20, 348–49; Michels, "Violent Old Belief," pp. 225–26.

104. "Sudnoe delo o razorenii Paleostrovskogo monastyria," *Olonetskie gubernskie vedomosti*, 1849, no. 12, pt. IV, col. 3.

105. *Ibid.*

106. *Ibid.*, cols. 3–4.

107. "Sudnoe delo o razorenii Paleostrovskogo monastyria," *Olonetskie gubernskie vedomosti*, 1849, nos. 10–11, pt. III, col. 3; no. 12, pt. IV, col. 3.

108. When he was about to be drowned, for example, the priest Mark was addressed in the following way: "Priest, why do you [give] reports and testimonies (*skazki*) against us?" ("Sudnoe delo o razorenii Paleostrovskogo monastyria," *Olonetskie gubernskie vedomosti*, 1849, no. 12, pt. IV, col. 3).

109. At least one of them was actually murdered: " . . . I]n the Petrovskii and Chelmuzhskii Pogost . . . the [parish] church has been standing in ruins and without services for seven years because of the schismatics. These brigands and church schismatics killed the former priest. . . . " ("Sudnoe delo o razorenii Paleostrovskogo monastyria," *Olonetskie gubernskie vedomosti*, 1849, no. 8, pt. II, col. 5).

110. *Ibid.*, no. 12, pt. IV, col. 5.

111. Cf. *ibid.*, cols. 2–3. As one eyewitness put it, "they ride from village to village and stay in Shunga Pogost during the trade fair. There they walk around, carefully armed with guns, and beat those who are not in agreement with them. Honorable people (*priamye liudi*) dare not speak with them or denounce them because they fear being beaten and murdered" (*ibid.*, col. 4).

112. Tikhomirov, *Klassovaia bor'ba*, p. 403; RGADA, f. 210, Prikaznyi stol, d. 22, fols. 409–11, 413–16; *Opisanie MGAMIU*, 15: 39; Andreev, ed., *Putevoditel'*, pp. 133, 156; "Akty cherepovetskogo Voskresenskogo monastyria," pp. 72–74, 77, 80; Lebedev, *Sobranie aktov I. D. Beliaeva*, pp. 87–88.

113. *Drevnie akty Viatskogo kraia*, pp. 192–201.

114. " . . . And peasants who did not participate in this revolt (*bunt*) were shackled, bound, brutally tortured, and beaten to death. . . . These rebels were our judges for a long time . . . and tried all kinds of matters with arbitrariness. They punished us as they pleased . . . and they put guards (*karauly*) with guns and skis on the roads" (*ibid.*, p. 194).

115. *Ibid.*, pp. 195–96. Apparently the church building was converted into a place for hoarding weapons: " . . . They also stored such large piles of clubs and pickets in the refectory of the Church of the Archangel Michael. . . . " (p. 194).

116. Sapozhnikov, "Samosozhzhenie v russkom raskole," p. 30; Syrtsev, *Samosozhigatel'stvo*, pp. 18–19.

117. "Akty raskola v Sibiri," pt. 2, pp. 14–17.

118. *Ibid.*, pp. 14, 16.

119. *Ibid.*, p. 16.

120. *Ibid.*, pp. 15–16. For example, orders were given to kidnap the monks from the Reshetnikov farm. It was apparently thought that the separation of peasants from monks would help to defuse the situation (*ibid.*, p. 16).

121. For more information on schismatic clerics and peasant revolt, see Michels, "Violent Old Belief," pp. 219–23; "Akty raskola v Sibiri," pt. 1, pp. 214–22; Sapozhnikov, "Samosozhzhenie v russkom raskole," pp. 11–17.

122. See, for example, the activities of Ivan Ul'iakhin and his men who greatly

frightened the monks of the Krestnyi Monastery outside of Kargopol', in RGADA, f. 159, opis' 1, d. 1945, fols. 160–96; f. 163, d. 7a, fols. 12–13, 25, 41. See also the activities of schismatic brigands in the area along the Vaga River, in Veriuzhskii, *Afanasii kholmogorskii*, pp. 80–82. On Siberia, see the observations of Dmytryi Tuptalo about how schismatic preachers coerced their followers to commit suicide, in Dmitrii, *Rozysk o Brynskoi vere*, pp. 580–84.

123. See Sapozhnikov, "Samosozhzhenie v russkom raskole," pp. 8–37.

124. *Ibid.*, pp. 19, 29, 32, 34–36. D. I. Sapozhnikov refers to two cases in the district of Olonets, one possible case on Kizhi Island, and the Pudozh suicides discussed below. An investigation that escaped Sapozhnikov is found in RGADA, f. 163, d. 7a, fols. 23–38, Sysk raskol'nikov v Olonetskom uezde po izvetu . . . popov (January–July, 1684).

125. "Delo o pudozhskikh raskol'nikakh," esp. p. 389.

126. See also the following statement by women and children who escaped from a similar incident in a place called Dory outside of Kargopol': " . . . And in Dory [we] lived against [our] will (*ponevole*): wives with their husbands, and children with their fathers" (RGADA, f. 163, 7a, fol. 43).

127. The peasants had stacked huge quantities of explosives in their compound. See "Akty raskola v Sibiri," pt. 2, p. 22.

128. *Ibid.*, p. 20.

129. "Akty raskola v Sibiri," pt. 1, p. 224.

130. "Akty raskola v Sibiri," pt. 2, p. 11.

131. " . . . We heard from beggars that the people who lived in that house were giving alms" (RGADA, f. 163, d. 7a, fol. 35).

132. Cf. RGADA, f. 163, d. 11, Donesenie ustiuzhskogo voevody . . . o samosozhzheniiakh raskol'nikov v raznykh volostiakh Ustiuzhskogo uezda; f. 27, d. 306, O samozhigateliakh krest'ianakh Nizhegorodskogo kraia.

133. The case attracted considerable attention in Novgorod because several monks were suspected of helping the brothers. See RGADA, f. 163, d. 7a, fols. 63–75, Delo o pobege raskol'nikov zakliuchennykh v Oshevenskom i Spasskom monastyriakh.

134. *Ibid.*, fol. 66.

135. RGADA, f. 210, Prikaznyi stol, d. 433, Zaderzhanie startsa Trofima po obvineniiu v raskole, fols. 207–8; Rumiantseva, ed., *Dokumenty prikazov o raskol'nikakh*, pp. 75–77.

136. RGADA, f. 210, Belgorodskii stol, d. 820, fols. 1–10, Delo o tserkovnom miatezhnike monakhe Dosifee.

137. RGADA, f. 159, opis' 3, d. 563, fols. 93–97, Otpiska arzamasskogo voevody o rasprostranenii raskol'nicheskogo ucheniia; "Nakaz . . . dlia poimki bezhavshogo iz Moskvy raskol'nika Savel'ia Greshnogo (October 30, 1683)," *DAI*, 10: 444–45.

138. See, for example, the curious case of the peasant Zakharii Iakovlev from the Kolomna area. In February 1670 Iakovlev returned to his native village after having made a pilgrimage to discover that his wife and children had been exiled to Kholmogory for "opposition against the church" (*tserkovnaia protivnost'*). See Veselovskii, comp., *Dokumenty o postroike Pustoozerskoi tiur'my*, pp. 21–22. The flight of a schismatic family from the village of Rabotka in the district of Nizhnii Novgorod was apparently so noteworthy that it was recorded in the census book

(*perepisnaia kniga*) of 1674. See Peretiatkovich, *Povol'zhe*, p. 281. Cf. *Akty Kholmogorskoi i Ustiuzhskoi eparkhii*, 1: 687–90, 1178–88.

139. See, for example, RGADA, f. 27, d. 258, pt. III, fols. 21–30; *Dokumenty*, pp. 162–67.

140. RGADA, f. 27, d. 258, pt. III, fols. 7–12; *Dokumenty*, pp. 187–91.

141. RGADA, f. 27, d. 258, pt. III, fols. 10, 12; *Dokumenty*, pp. 187, 191.

142. RGADA, f. 27, d. 258, pt. III, fols. 7–8; *Dokumenty*, pp. 189–90.

143. RGADA, f. 27, d. 258, pt. II, fols. 68–70, 86–97, 105, 109–12; pt. III, fol. 1; *Dokumenty*, pp. 169–78.

144. RGADA, f. 27, d. 258, pt. II, fol. 90; *Dokumenty*, p. 176.

145. RGADA, f. 27, d. 258, pt. II, fols. 58–65; *Dokumenty*, pp. 178–81.

146. RGADA, f. 27, d. 258, pt. III, fols. 1–3; *Dokumenty*, pp. 185–87.

147. See, for example, the records in the archive of the powerful Spaso-Prilutskii Monastery, in Naster, "Kratkii obzor dokumental'nykh materialov," pp. 304–5.

148. RGADA, f. 27, d. 258, pt. II, fols. 2, 96; *Dokumenty*, pp. 177, 185–87; SPbFIRI, f. 117, d. 424, Delo po obvineniiu igumenom Kornil'eva monastyria startsa Andreiana i ego sovetnikov v vorovstve (August-September, 1656), fols. 1–20.

149. See, for example, the shocking death statistics in "Itogi morovogo povetriia"; "Akty o morovom povetrii," pp. 508–11.

150. Belokurov, ed., "Skazanie o postroenii obydennogo khrama v Vologde," pp. III–X; *Akty Kholmogorskoi i Ustiuzhskoi eparkhii*, 1: 111–13.

151. RGADA, f. 27, d. 258, pt. V, fols. 48, 54–55; d. 259, f. 27, fols. 48, 51; *Dokumenty*, pp. 111–12.

152. Calvi, *Histories of a Plague Year*, pp. 227–41; Cipolla, *Faith, Reason, and Plague*, pp. 1, 41–74; Biraben, *Les hommes et la peste*, 2: 62–83; Hoeniger, *Der Schwarze Tod*, pp. 13–14, 104–25.

153. Gottfried, *Black Death*, p. 81; Biraben, *Les hommes et la peste*, 2: 83 ("piété individuelle"); Hoeniger, *Der Schwarze Tod*, p. 67 ("Reinigung der Seele").

154. Calvi, *Histories of a Plague Year*, p. 251; Duby, ed., *Revelations*, pp. 510–13, 528–33.

155. Rushinskii, comp., "Religioznyi byt," p. 92; Kapterev, *Kharakter otnoshenii Rossii k pravoslavnomu vostoku*, pp. 60–62.

156. *Akty Kholmogorskii i Ustiuzhskoi eparkhii*, 3: 359, 419–20, 425, 451; Ogloblin, "Mangazeiskii chudotvorets Vasilii."

157. See, for example, Solov'ev, *Opisanie iaroslavskogo obydennogo khrama*, pp. 85–86, 167–83; Suvorov, "Opisanie Spasoobydennoi tserkvi"; Savvaitov, *Opisanie vologodskogo Dukhova monastyria*, p. 47.

158. Belokurov, ed., "Skazanie o postroenii odydennogo khrama v Vologde," pp. 14–15.

159. *Ibid.*, pp. 15–17. This religious intensity, which was indeed very pleasing to local churchmen, was followed by a rapid decline of interest in church matters. During the 1670s and 1680s, Vologda hierarchs again pointed to the general failure of peasants to attend church services. Cf. RGIA, f. 834, opis' 5, nos. 193, 210.

160. Cf. Dohar, *The Black Death*, pp. 142–44. Dohar observes that the impact of Lollard preachers on the population at large was minimal, confirming my own findings.

161. For contrast, cf. the many cases involving "fornication" (*blud*) that can be found in the inventories of the Russian State Archive of Ancient Acts, in RGADA, f. 141, opis' 3, g. 1657, dd. 58–59, 137; g. 1660, d. 5; g. 1662, d. 119; f. 210, Novgorodskii stol, d. 244, fols. 319–21 (1697–98); d. 318, fols. 226–45 (1682–83) as described in *Opisanie MGAMIU*, 12: 104–5, 135.

162. Ogloblin, ed., "Bytovye cherty XVII veka," *Russkaia starina* 81 (1894): 225.

163. RGADA, f. 159, opis' 1, d. 2226, fols. 1–15, Sudnyi spisok ... po sledstvennomu delu ssyl'noi moskovskoi raskol'nitsy Mavry Grigor'evoi; Rumiantseva, ed., *Dokumenty prikazov o raskol'nikakh*, pp. 87–97.

164. Belokurov, ed., "Dela Nikona."

165. *Ibid.*, pp. 90, 94–95.

166. *Ibid.*, pp. 90, 95–97, 99. In this context, cf. Duby's discussion of Elizabeth of Schönau, in his *Revelations*, p. 516.

167. Ogloblin, ed., "Bytovye cherty XVII veka," *Russkaia starina* 81 (1894): 223–24. On the widespread Western perception that religious solitude was a sign of insanity, see Duby, ed., *Revelations*, p. 510.

168. Rumiantseva, *Narodnoe antitserkovnoe dvizhenie*, p. 188.

Conclusion

1. Denisov, *Vinograd rossiiskii*, fol. 6.

2. Eleonskaia, *Russkaia publitsistika*, pp. 80–81; P. S. Smirnov, *Vnutrennie voprosy*, pp. 6–9.

3. See, for example, Kliuchevsky, *A Course in Russian History*, pp. 327, 329–30; Cherniavsky, "Old Believers and New Religion," pp. 7–8; Robinson, ed., *Zhizneopisaniia*, p. 43; idem, *Bor'ba idei*, p. 196.

4. Zenkovsky, "Old Believer Avvakum," p. 1.

5. Crummey, "The Works of Avraamii," pp. 124, 138.

6. One might compare these urban brotherhoods to Ukrainian *bratstva* that became adamant defenders of "true Orthodoxy" against the incursion of Polish Catholicism following the Union of Brest (1596). However, unlike Old Believer congregations, Ukrainian brotherhoods had their own printing presses; this fact helps to explain why, at least in the short run, they were more influential. See Isaievych, *Bratstva*; idem, *Pershodrukar' Ivan Fedorov*.

7. Consider, for example, the mass circulation of Martin Luther's writings throughout Germany only a few years after he had posted the Wittenberg Theses. Cf. Kuczynski, *Thesaurus libellarum*, which lists ca. three thousand different printed pamphlets propagating the message of the Reformation during Luther's lifetime. One German scholar made the following observation underscoring the significance of the printing press: "[Pamphlets were] ... quickly printed and reprinted by printing shops, put up for sale (*feilgeboten*) in book guides, and read or recited in schools, universities, taverns, and market places" (Laube, ed., *Flugschriften*, p. 12). Cf. also Balzer, *Bürgerliche Reformationspropaganda*.

8. On the limited dissemination of even the most important Old Believer texts during the second half of the seventeenth century, see Chapters One and Two.

9. One could also cite the anger and condescension with which Old Believers attacked their contemporaries for not obeying them. See Avvakum's commentaries on popular violence, drunkenness, fornication, crypto-Lutherans, and "Frankish" books, in Borozdin, *Avvakum* (1900), appendix, pp. 16–17, 20, 24–25; *Materialy*, 5: 335.

10. For a good introduction to Western dissent, see Russell, *Religious Dissent.*

11. Hill, *World Upside Down*, pp. 17, 87–106.

12. On such demands in the proclamations of the German peasantry, see Blickle, *Communal Reformation*, pp. 26, 199.

13. Delumeau, *Catholicism between Luther and Voltaire*, chaps. 3–4.

14. See, for example, Grundmann, *Religiöse Bewegungen*, pp. 38–50.

15. See, for example, Morris, *Papal Monarchy*, pp. 339–57.

16. See, for example, Grundmann, *Religiöse Bewegungen*, pp. 170–203.

17. Hobsbawm, *Primitive rebels*, pp. 1–29.

18. See, for example, Freeze, *Russian Levites*, pp. 3–4, 48–51.

19. Lupinin, *Religious Revolt*, p. 13.

20. Nikolaevskii, *Patriarshaia oblast'*, pp. 33–34.

21. RGADA, f. 153, d. 61, Kontsepty piatnadtsati predlozhenii uchinennykh ot tsaria . . . patriarkhu . . . o ustroenii eparkhii; Vinogradskii, *Tserkovnyi sobor*, pp. 8–10.

22. Druzhinin, "Slovesnye nauki," esp. pp. 227–29; Ponyrko, "Uchebniki ritoriki."

23. For more information on this transformation process, see Malyshev, "Istoriia ikonnogo izobrazheniia protopopa Avvakuma"; Bobkov, "Neizvestnoe izobrazhenie protopopa Avvakuma"; Zenkovsky, "Ideological World of the Denisov Brothers"; Crummey, "Interpreting the Fate of Old Believer Communities"; idem, *Old Believers and Antichrist*, pp. 58–100; Barsov, *Brat'ia Denisovy*; Druzhinin, *Pomorskie paleografy*; Lileev, *Iz istorii raskola.*

Archival Documents and Manuscripts

Biblioteka Rossiiskoi Akademii nauk (BAN) [Library of the Russian Academy of Sciences], Manuscript Division, St. Petersburg:

BAN, Sobranie V. G. Druzhinina [Collection of V. G. Druzhinin], nos. 1091, 1101.

Gosudarstvennaia publichnaia nauchno-technicheskaia biblioteka Sibirskogo otdeleniia Rossiiskoi Akademii nauk (GPNTB SO) [The State Scientific and Technical Public Library of the Siberian Division of the Russian Academy of Sciences], Manuscript Division, Novosibirsk:

GPNTB SO, Sobranie M. N. Tikhomirova [Collection of M. N. Tikhomirov], nos. 158, 348.

Gosudarstvennyi arkhiv Vologodskoi oblasti (GA Vologda) [State Archive of the Vologda Region], Vologda:

GA Vologda, f. 1260, Sobranie N. I. i I. N. Suvorovykh [Collection of N. I. and I. N. Suvorov], opis' 4, d. 55.

Gosudarstvennyi istoricheskii muzei (GIM) [State Historical Museum], Manuscript Division, Moscow:

GIM, Sobranie A. I. Khludova, no. 351; appendix, no. 58.

GIM, Sobranie Sinodal'noi biblioteki [Collection of the Synodal Library], nos. V, 30, 93, 130, 307, 372, 379, 424, 641, 1071, 1629–30.

GIM, Sobranie A. S. Uvarova [Collection of A. S. Uvarov], nos. 494 (131), 497 (102).

Institut iazyka, literatury i istorii Karel'skogo nauchnogo tsentra Rossiiskoi Akademii nauk. Nauchnyi arkhiv (NA IIALI KNTs) [Institute of Language, Literature and History of the Karelian Research Center of the Russian Academy of Sciences. Research Archive], Petrozavodsk:

NA IIALI KNTs, Kollektsiia drevnikh aktov [Collection of Ancient Acts], razriad 1:

opis' 2, nos. 10/3, 22, 68, 86.

opis' 3, nos. 20, 25.

Institut istorii, filologii i filosofii Sibirskogo otdeleniia Rossiiskoi Akademii nauk (IIFIF SO) [Institute of History, Philology, and Philosophy of the Siberian Division of the Russian Academy of Sciences], Novosibirsk:

IIFIF SO, Sobranie rukopisei [Collection of Manuscripts], no. 14/77.

Institut russkoi literatury (Pushkinskii Dom) Rossiiskoi Akademii nauk (IRLI) [Institute of Russian Literature (Pushkin House) of the Russian Academy of Sciences], Manuscript Division, St. Petersburg:

IRLI, Mezen'skii fond [Mezen' Fond], no. 123.

Nauchnaia biblioteka Moskovskogo gosudarstvennogo universiteta (NB MGU) [Research Library of Moscow State University], Manuscript Division, Moscow:

NB MGU, Sobranie knig kirillicheskoi pechati XV–XVII vv. [Collection of Printed Cyrillic Books], nos. 512, 514, 564.

Rossiiskaia gosudarstvennaia biblioteka (RGB) [Russian State Library], Manuscript Division, Moscow:

RGB, Muzeinoe sobranie [Museum Collection], no. 2776.

RGB, Sobranie biblioteki Obshchestva istorii i drevnostei rossiiskikh [Collection of the Library of the Society of Russian History and Antiquities], no. 103.

RGB, Sobranie Moskovskoi Dukhovnoi Akademii [Collection of the Moscow Spiritual Academy], no. 68.

RGB, Sobranie G. M. Prianishnikova [Collection of G. M. Prianishnikov], no. 61.

RGB, Sobranie Rogozhskogo kladbishcha [Collection of the Rogozhskoe Cemetery], no. 667.

RGB, Sobranie N. P. Rumiantseva [Collection of N. P. Rumiantsev], no. 375.

Rossiiskaia natsional'naia biblioteka (RNB) [Russian National Library], Manuscript Division, St. Petersburg:

RNB, Osnovnoe sobranie [Basic Collection]:

   F. I. 244.

   O. I. 209, O. XVII. 48.

   Q. I. 486, Q. I. 1062.

RNB, Sobranie M. P. Pogodina [Collection of M. P. Pogodin], no. 1560.

RNB, Solovetskoe sobranie [Collection of the Solovki Monastery], nos. 18–20/1477–79, 665/723.

Rossiiskii gosudarstvennyi arkhiv drevnikh aktov (RGADA) [Russian State Archive of Ancient Acts], Moscow:

RGADA, f. 27, Tainyi prikaz [Secret Chancellery], dd. 48, 68, 89, 140, 161, 190, 192, 195, 203, 258, pts. I–VI, 259, 273, pts. I–IV, 303, 306, 558, 562, 614.

RGADA, f. 125, Monastyrskii prikaz [Monastery Office], opis' 1, g. 1669–70, d. 5; g. 1674, dd. 19, 30.

RGADA, f. 141, Prikaznye dela starykh del [Chancellery Affairs of Ancient Years]:

opis' 2, g. 1648, dd. 93–95, 98.

opis' 3, g. 1654, d. 62; g. 1656, d. 11; g. 1657, dd. 58–59, 69, 137; g. 1660, d. 5; g. 1661, dd. 120–21; g. 1662, d. 119.

RGADA, f. 153, Dukhovnye rossiiskie dela [Russian Spiritual Affairs], dd. 16, 20, pts. I–X, 31, 37, 41, 48, 61.

RGADA, f. 159, Novgorodskii prikaz [Novgorod Office]:

opis' 1, dd. 1395, 2226.

opis' 3, dd. 450, 563, 1945.

RGADA, f. 163, Raskol'nicheskie dela [Schismatic Affairs], dd. 2–4, 7a, 11–12.

RGADA, f. 184, Arkhiv S. A. Belokurova [Archive of S. A. Belokurov]:

opis' 1, dd. 172, 1421.

opis' 2, d. 156.

RGADA, f. 210, Razriadnyi prikaz [Service Chancellery]:

Belgorodskii stol [Belgorod Desk], dd. 351, 768, 820, 1202.

Besglasnyi stol [Nameless Desk], d. 26.

Moskovskii stol [Moscow Desk], dd. 365, 398, 421, 641.

Novgorodskii stol [Novgorod Desk], dd. 83, 96, 150, 210, 244, 318.

Prikaznyi stol [Chancellery Desk], dd. 14, 16, 22, 33, 91, 218, 298, 416, 433, 447, 799, 901.

Vladimirskii stol [Vladimir Desk], d. 60.

RGADA, f. 214, Sibirskii prikaz [Siberian Office], dd. 23, 400.

RGADA, f. 235, Patriarshii kazennyi prikaz [Patriarchal Treasury Office], opis' 2, bks. 41–43, 49.

RGADA, f. 381, Biblioteka Sinodal'noi tipografii [Library of the Synodal Typography], opis' 1, nos. 359, 420, 422.

RGADA, f. 396, Arkhiv Oruzheinoi Palaty [Archive of the Armory], dd. 41896, 42297, 42424, 42467, 42472, 42667–68, 42812, 42835, 42849, 42892, 43009, 43318, 43354, 43581, 43789.

RGADA, f. 1182, Prikaz knigopechatnogo dela [Patriarchal Printing Press], bks. 50, 57, 59.

RGADA, f. 1201, Solovetskii monastyr' [Archive of the Solovki Monastery], dd. 69, 80, 83.

RGADA, f. 1433, Muromskii mitropolichii dvor [Court of Metropolitan See of Riazan' at Murom], opis' 1, dd. 3, 21, 50.

Rossiiskii gosudarstvennyi istoricheskii arkhiv (RGIA) [Russian State Historical Archive], St. Petersburg:

RGIA, f. 834, Rukopisi Sv. Sinoda [Manuscripts of the Holy Synod]:

opis' 2, nos. 1849–54.

opis' 5, nos. 38, 193, 210.

Sankt-Peterburgskii filial Instituta rossiiskoi istorii Rossiiskoi Akademii nauk (SPbFIRI) [St. Petersburg Branch of the Institute of Russian History of the Russian Academy of Sciences], St. Petersburg:

> SPbFIRI, f. 117, Kollektsiia P. I. Savvaitova [Collection of P. I. Savvaitov], nos. 319, 324, 332, 419, 424–25, 435, 437, 465, 650, 661, 829–30, 846, 852, 855, 859, 861–62, 864–65, 868, 930, 966, 1097, 1177, 1518, 1555, 1649, 1652, 1790, 1873.

> SPbFIRI, f. 171, Sobranie Sofiiskogo arkhiereiskogo doma [Collection of the House of St. Sophia at Novgorod], pereplet III, no. 98; pereplet V, no. 241.

Published Primary and Secondary Sources

Aksakov, I. S. *Issledovanie o torgovle na ukrainskikh iarmarkakh*. St. Petersburg, 1858.

"Akty cherepovetskogo Voskresenskogo monastyria." In Titov, *Opisanie slaviano-russkikh rukopisei*, 6: 67–86.

"Akty i materialy, sobrannye v kholmogorskom Spaso-Preobrazhenskom sobore." *Trudy Arkhangel'skogo statisticheskogo komiteta za 1865 god*, pp. 1–96.

Akty istoricheskie, sobrannye i izdannye Arkheograficheskoiu kommissieiu (AI). 5 vols. St. Petersburg, 1841–1842.

Akty Iverskogo Sviatoozerskogo monastyria (1582–1706). Ed. Archimandrite Leonid. Vol. 5 of *RIB*. St. Petersburg, 1878.

Akty Kholmogorskoi i Ustiuzhskoi eparkhii. 3 pts. Vols. 12, 14 and 25 of *RIB*. St. Petersburg, 1890–1908.

"Akty o morovom povetrii." *DAI*, 3: 442–521.

"Akty, otnosiashchiesia k istorii donskikh kazakov i k raskolu na Donu." *DAI*, 12: 122–283.

"Akty, otnosiashchiesia k raskolu v Sibiri." 2 pts. *DAI*, 8: 214–26; 10: 8–23.

"Akty po delu o prisoedinenii k Viatskoi eparkhii Ust'-vymskoi desiatiny." *Trudy Viatskoi arkhivnoi kommissii*, 1908, pt. 2, sect. 2, pp. 61–78.

Akty, sobrannye v bibliotekakh i arkhivakh Rossiiskoi imperii Arkheograficheskoiu ekspeditsieiu Imperatorskoi Akademii nauk (AAE). 4 vols. St. Petersburg, 1836.

Alekseev, I. "Istoriia o begstvuiushchem sviashchenstve." In *Letopisi russkoi literatury i drevnosti*. Ed. N. S. Tikhonravov, 4 (1862), pt. 3, pp. 53–69.

Andreev, A. I. et al., eds. *Putevoditel' po arkhivu Leningradskogo otdeleniia Instituta istorii*. Moscow-Leningrad, 1958.

Andreev, V. V. *Raskol i ego znachenie v narodnoi russkoi istorii.* St. Petersburg, 1870.

Ankudinova, L. E. "Sotsial'nyi sostav pervykh raskol'nikov." *Vestnik Leningradskogo universiteta. Seriia istorii, iazyka i literatury* 14 (1956): 54–68.

——. "Obshchestvennye politicheskie vzgliady pervykh raskol'nikov i narodnye massy." *Uchenye zapiski Leningradskogo universiteta* 270 (1959): 60–82.

Arkhangelov, S. A. *Sredi raskol'nikov i sektantov Povolzh'ia. Istoriko-bytovye ocherki raskola i sektantstva v Nizhegorodskom krae.* St. Petersburg, 1899.

Balzer, B. *Bürgerliche Reformationspropaganda: die Flugschriften des Hans Sachs in den Jahren 1523–1525.* Stuttgart, 1973.

Baron, S. H. "Vasilii Shorin: Seventeenth-century Russian merchant extraordinary." *Canadian-American Slavic Studies* 6, no. 4 (Winter, 1972): 503–48.

Barskov, Ia. L., ed. *Pamiatniki pervykh let russkogo staroobriadchestva (Pamiatniki).* St. Petersburg, 1912.

Barsov, E. V. "Paleostrov, ego sud'ba i znachenie v Obonezhskom krae." *Chteniia,* 1868, bk. 1, smes', pp. 19–222.

——. "Opisanie rukopisei i knig, khraniashchikhsia v Vygoleksinskoi biblioteke." *LZAK* 6 (1872–1875): 1–85.

——, ed. "Sudnye protsessy XVII–XVIII vekov po delam tserkvi." *Chteniia,* 1883, bk. 3, pt. 5, pp. 1–42.

——, ed. "Akty, otnosiashchiesia k istorii solovetskogo bunta." *Chteniia,* 1883, bk. 4, smes', pp. 1–92.

——, ed. *Novye materialy dlia istorii staroobriadchestva XVII–XVIII vekov.* Moscow, 1890.

Barsov, N. I. *Brat'ia Andrei i Semen Denisovy.* Moscow, 1866.

Barsukov, N. A. *Solovetskoe vosstanie (1668–1676 gg.).* Petrozavodsk, 1954.

Batalden, St., ed. *Seeking God. The Recovery of Religious Identity in Orthodox Russia, Ukraine and Georgia.* DeKalb/Ill, 1993.

Belokurov, S. A. *Sil'vestr Medvedev ob ispravlenii bogosluzhebnykh knig pri patriarkhakh Nikone i Ioakime.* Moscow, 1885.

——, ed. "Dela sviateishogo Nikona patriarkha pache zhe reshchi chudesa vrachebnaia." *Chteniia,* 1887, bk. 1, smes', pp. 81–114.

——. *Materialy dlia russkoi istorii.* Moscow, 1888.

——. "Biblioteka i arkhiv Solovetskogo monastyria posle osady (1676 goda)." In idem, *Materialy dlia russkoi istorii,* pp. 1–87.

——, ed. "Skazanie o postroenii obydennogo khrama v Vologde 'vo izbavlenie ot smertonosnyia iazvy'." *Chteniia,* 1893, bk. 3, pt. 2, pp. III–X, 11–21.

——. "Deianie moskovskogo sobora 1649 goda." In idem, *Iz dukhovnoi zhizni moskovskogo obshchestva XVII veka.* Moscow, 1902, pp. 31–52.

———, ed. "Skazaniia o Pavle episkope kolomenskom." *Chteniia*, 1905, bk. 2, smes', pp. 31–52.

———, comp. "Dneval'nye zapiski Prikaza tainykh del 7165–7183 gg." *Chteniia*, 1908, bk. 1, pt. 1, pp. I–X, 1–224; bk. 2, pt. 1, pp. 225–346.

Benz, E. *Ecclesia spiritualis: Kirchenidee und Geschichtstheologie der franziskanischen Reformation*. Stuttgart, 1964.

Bibliograficheskii ukazatel' literatury po issledovaniiu pravoslaviia, staroobriadchestva i sektantstva v sovetskoi istoricheskoi nauke. Moscow, 1974.

Billington, J. H. *The Icon and the Axe. An Interpretive History of Russian Culture*. New York, 1970.

———. "Neglected Figures and Features in the Rise of the Raskol." *Russia and Orthodoxy. Essays in honor of Georges Florovsky*. Vol. 2 (The Hague, 1975), pp. 189–206.

Biraben, J. N. *Les hommes et la peste en France et dans les pays européens et méditerranéens*. 2 Vols. Paris, 1975–76. Vols. 35–36 of *Civilisations et sociétés*.

Blickle, P. *Die Revolution von 1525*. Munich, 1975.

———. *Communal Reformation. The Quest for Salvation in Sixteenth-Century Germany*. New Jersey-London, 1992.

Bobkov, E. A. "Neizvestnoe izobrazhenie protopopa Avvakuma nachala XIX veka." *TODRL* 28 (1974): 420–21.

Bogoslovskii, M. M. *Zemskoe samoupravlenie na russkom severe v XVII veke*. 2 vols. Moscow, 1909–1912.

———, ed. "Zemskie chelobitnye v drevnei Rossii (Iz istorii zemskogo samoupravleniia na severe v XVII veke)." *Bogoslovskii vestnik*, 1911, no. 1: 133–50; no. 2: 215–41; no. 3: 403–19; no. 4: 685–96.

Borisov, V. A. *Opisanie goroda Shui i ego okrestnostei, s prilozheniem starinnykh aktov*. Moscow, 1851.

Borozdin, A. K. *Protopop Avvakum. Ocherk iz istorii umstvennoi zhizni russkogo obshchestva v XVII veke*. Vol. 47 of *Zapiski istoriko-filologicheskogo fakul'teta Imperatorskogo St. Peterburgskogo universiteta*. St. Petersburg, 1898. Revised Edition. St. Petersburg, 1900.

Brady, Th. "Social History." In Ozment, St., ed. *Reformation Europe: A Guide to Research*. St. Louis, 1982, pp. 161–81.

Breshchinskii, D. N., ed. "Zhitie Korniliia Vygovskogo pakhomievskoi redaktsii." In Panchenko, A. M., ed. *Drevnerusskaia knizhnost' po materialam Pushkinskogo Doma: sbornik nauchnykh trudov*. Leningrad, 1985, pp. 62–107.

Brilliantov, I. *Patriarkh Nikon v zatochenii na Beleozere. Istoricheskii ocherk*. St. Petersburg, 1899.

Brokgauz, F. A.; Efron, I. A., eds. *Entsiklopedicheskii slovar' (BE)*. 41 vols. St. Petersburg, 1890–1904.

Bubnov, N. Iu. "Rukopisnoe nasledie pustozerskikh uznikov (1667–1682 gg.)." In *Knigotorgovoe i bibliotechnoe delo v Rossii v XVII-pervoi polovine XIX v.*. Leningrad, 1981, pp. 69–84.

——. "Knigotvorchestvo moskovskikh staroobriadtsev XVII v." In *Russkie knigi i biblioteki v XVI-pervoi polovine XIX veka*. Leningrad, 1983, pp. 23–37.

——, ed. *Sochineniia pisatelei-staroobriadtsev XVII veka*. Vol. 7, pt. 1 of *Opisanie Rukopisnogo otdela Biblioteki Akademii nauk SSSR*. Leningrad, 1984.

——. "Spiridon Potemkin i ego 'Kniga'." *TODRL* 40 (1985): 345–63.

——. "Rabota drevnerusskikh knizhnikov v monastyrskoi biblioteke (Istochniki solovetskogo 'Skazaniia . . . o novykh knigakh' 1667 g.)." In *Kniga i ee rasprostranenie v Rossii v XVI-XVIII vv. Sbornik trudov*. Leningrad, 1985, pp. 37–58.

——. "'Skazanie . . . o novykh knigakh' (1667) - istochnik p'iatoi solovetskoi chelobitnoi." In *Materialy i soobshcheniia po fondam Otdela rukopisnoi i redkoi knigi Biblioteki Akademii nauk SSSR*, 1986, pp. 112–33.

——. *Staroobriadcheskaia kniga v Rossii vo vtoroi polovine XVII veka*. St. Petersburg, 1995.

Buganov, V. I. *Moskovskoe vosstanie 1662 goda*. Moscow, 1960.

——, ed. *Vosstanie 1662 goda v Moskve. Sbornik dokumentov*. Moscow, 1964.

Bushkovitch, P. *Religion and Society in Russia. The Sixteenth and Seventeenth Centuries*. Oxford, 1992.

Butsinskii, P. N. *Sibirskie arkhiepiskopi Makarii, Nektarii, Gerasim*. Kharkov, 1891.

Bychkov, A. F. *Opisanie tserkovno-slavianskikh i russkikh rukopisei Imperatorskoi publichnoi biblioteki*. St. Petersburg, 1882.

Calvi, G. *Histories of a Plague Year. The Social and the Imaginary in Baroque Florence*. Berkeley-Los Angeles-Oxford, 1989.

"Chelobitnaia Avraamiia startsa." *LZAK* 6 (1877), pt. 2, pp. 1–129.

"Chelobitnaia Ivana Konstantinova syna Sytina na krest'ian sviateishago patriarkha Nikona." *Zapiski Otdeleniia russkoi i slavianskoi arkheologii*, 2: 530–81.

"Chelobitnaia vologodskomu arkhiepiskopu Gavriilu odnogo sviashchennika Vologodskogo uezda na nekotorykh svoikh prikhozhan-raskol'nikov 1691 goda." *Vologodskie gubernskie vedomosti*, 1864, no. 4: 1–2.

Cherniakova, I. A. "Naselenie Olonetskogo kraia v XVII veke (po pistsovym i perepisnym knigam)." In *Voprosy istorii evropeiskogo severa*. Petrozavodsk, 1988, pp. 115–33.

Cherniavsky, M. "The Old Believers and the New Religion." *Slavic Review* 25 (March, 1966), no. 1: 1–39.

Chernov, V. A. "Na kakom iazyke pisal Avvakum?" *TODRL* 42 (1989): 369–73.

Chistiakov, M. "Istoricheskoe rassmotrenie deiatel'nosti pravoslavnogo russkogo dukhovenstva v otnoshenii k raskolu ot ego vozniknoveniia do uchrezhdeniia Sv. Sinoda." *Pravoslavnoe obozrenie*, 1888, bk. 2: 65–210.

Chistov, K. V. *Russkie narodnye sotsial'no-utopicheskie legendy.* Moscow, 1967.

Chrysostomus, J. "Die 'Pomorskie Otvety' als Denkmal der Anschauungen des russischen Altgläubigentums gegen Ende des 1. Viertels des XVIII. Jahrhunderts." *Orientalia Christiana Analecta* 148 (1957): I–XVIX, 1–209.

Chteniia v Imperatorskom Obshchestve istorii i drevnostei rossiiskikh pri Moskovskom universitete (Chteniia). 264 vols. Moscow, 1845–1918.

Chumicheva, V. "Stranitsy istorii solovetskogo vosstaniia (1666–1676)." *Istoriia SSSR*, 1990, no. 1: 167–75.

Cipolla, C. M. *Faith, Reason, and the Plague in Seventeenth-Century Tuscany.* Ithaca/N.Y., 1979.

Cohn, N. *Europe's Inner Demons. An Enquiry Inspired by the Great Witch-Hunt.* New York, 1975.

Conybeare, F. C. *Russian Dissenters.* Vol. 10 of *Harvard Theological Studies.* Cambridge/Mass., 1921.

Crummey, R. O. *The Old Believers and the World of Antichrist: The Vyg Community and the Russian State, 1694–1855.* Madison-Milwaukee-London, 1970.

———. *Aristocrats and Servitors. The Boyar Elite in Russia, 1613–1689.* Princeton, 1983.

———. "Religious Radicalism in Seventeenth-Century Russia: Reexamining the Kapiton Movement. " *Forschungen zur Osteuropäischen Geschichte* 46 (1992): 171–85.

———. "Interpreting the Fate of Old Believer Communities in the Eighteenth and Nineteenth Centuries." In Batalden, ed. *Seeking God*, pp. 144–59.

———. "Old Belief as Popular Religion: New Approaches." *Slavic Review* 52, no. 4 (Winter, 1993): 700–12.

———. "The Origins of the Old Believers' Cultural Systems: The Works of Avraamii." *Forschungen zur Osteuropäischen Geschichte* 50 (1994): 121–38.

———. "Past and Present Interpretations of Old Belief." In Nichols, R. and Michels, G., eds. *Russia's Dissident Old Believers* (forthcoming).

Daugny, J. "Les Raskol'niks: Les protestants de l'orthodoxie." *Nouvelle Revue* (Paris, 1910), ser. 3, vol. 15, pp. 483–92.

Delo o patriarkhe Nikone. Izdanie Arkheograficheskoi kommissii po dokumentam moskovskoi Sinodal'noi (byvshei Patriarshei) biblioteki (Delo). St. Petersburg, 1897.

"Delo o proiznesenii nepristoinykh slov pskovskimi strel'tsami." *Sbornik Moskovskogo arkhiva Ministerstva iustitsii,* vol. 6 (Moscow, 1914), pp. 191–99.

"Delo o pudozhskikh raskol'nikakh." *AI*, 5: 378–94.

Delumeau, J. *Catholicism between Luther and Voltaire: a new view of the Counter-Reformation.* London-Philadelphia, 1977.

Demkova, N. S. *Zhitie protopopa Avvakuma. Tvorcheskaia istoriia proizvedeniia.* Leningrad, 1974.

———. "Iz rannei istorii staroobriadcheskoi literatury." *TODRL* 28 (1974): 385–92.

———, ed. *Pustoozerskii sbornik. Avtografy sochinenii Avvakuma i Epifaniia.* Leningrad, 1975.

———. "Texts of the Old Belief's Founder-Fathers." In Nichols, R. and Michels, G., eds. *Russia's Dissident Old Believers* (forthcoming).

Denisov, L. I. *Pravoslavnye monastyri Rossiiskoi imperii. Polnyi spisok.* Moscow, 1908.

Denisov, S. *Istoriia o otsekh i stradal'tsakh solovetskikh.* St. Petersburg, 1905.

———. *Vinograd rossiiskii ili opisanie postradavshikh v Rossii za drevletserkovnoe blagochestie.* Moscow, 1906.

Dmitrevskii, V. I. *Raskol-staroobriadchestva v Rostovsko-iaroslavskom krae pered vremenem sv. Dmitriia, mitropolita rostovskogo.* Iaroslavl', 1909.

Dmitrii, Metropolitan of Rostov, *Rozysk o raskol'nicheskoi Brynskoi vere, o uchenii ikh, o delakh ikh i iz"iavlenie iako vera ikh neprava, uchenie ikh dushevredno, i dela ikh ne bogougodny.* Moscow, 1824.

Dobroklonskii, A. *Rukovodstvo po istorii russkoi tserkvi.* Vol. 3, *Patriarshii period 1589–1700 god.* Moscow, 1889.

Dobronravov, V. G. "Blagoveshchenskii muzhskoi monastyr' v gorode Viaznikakh: istoriko-statisticheskoe opisanie." *Trudy Vladimirskoi arkhivnoi kommissii* 9 (1907): 1–197.

Dohar, W. J. *The Black Death and Pastoral Leadership. The Diocese of Hereford in the Fourteenth Century.* Philadelphia, 1995.

Dokuchaev-Baskov, K. A. *Tserkovno-prikhodskaia zhizn' v gorode Kargopole v XVI–XIX vekakh.* Moscow, 1900.

"Donesenie Pitirimovo o raskol'shchikakh." *Chteniia,* 1860, bk. 4, smes', pp. 281–82.

"Dopolnenie k stat'e o pustyniakh Vladimirskoi gubernii." *Vladimirskie gubernskie vedomosti,* 1854, no. 36: 279–80.

Dopolneniia k aktam istoricheskim, sobrannye i izdannye Arkheograficheskoiu kommissieiu (DAI). 12 vols. St. Petersburg, 1846–1872.

Dosifei, Archimandrite. *Geograficheskoe, istoricheskoe i statisticheskoe opisanie Solovetskogo monastyria.* 3 vols. Moscow, 1853.

Drevnie akty, otnosiashchiesia k istorii Viatskogo kraia. Viatka, 1881.

Droblenkova, N. F., comp. "Spisok pechatnykh rabot V. I. Malysheva za predshestvuiushchie gody (1940–1971)." In *Rukopisnoe nasledie Drevnei Rusi: Po materialam Pushkinskogo Doma.* Leningrad, 1972, pp. 406–21.

———, comp. "Spisok pechatnykh rabot V. I. Malysheva (prodolzhenie)." In Panchenko, A. M., ed. *Drevnerusskaia knizhnost' po materialam Pushkinskogo Doma. Sbornik nauchnykh trudov.* Leningrad, 1985, pp. 340–45.

Druzhinin, V. G. *Raskol na Donu v kontse XVII veka.* St. Petersburg, 1889. Reprint. Vol. 234 of *Slavistic Printings and Reprintings.* Ed. C. H. van Schooneveld. The Hague-Paris, 1969.

———. "Slovesnye nauki v Vygovskoi pomorskoi pustyni." *Zhurnal Ministerstva Narodnogo Prosveshcheniia* N. S. 33 (1911), no. 6: 225–48.

———. *Pisaniia russkikh staroobriadtsev. Perechen' spiskov, sostavlennyi po pechatnym opisaniiam rukopisnykh sobranii.* St. Petersburg, 1912.

———. *Pomorskie paleografy nachala XVIII stoletiia.* St. Petersburg, 1921.

Duby, G., ed. *Revelations of the Medieval World.* Vol. 2 of *A History of Private Life.* Cambridge-London, 1988.

Efrosin, Monk. "Otrazitel'noe pisanie o novoizobretennom puti samoubiist-vennykh smertei (1691)." *Pamiatniki drevnei pis'mennosti* 108 (1895): 1–107.

El'chaninov, I. N., ed. *Pistsovaia kniga dvortsovoi Lovetskoi rybnoi slobody 1674, 1675 i 1676 gg.* Vol. 2 of *Trudy Rybinskogo otdeleniia Iaroslavskogo estestvenno-istoricheskogo obshchestva.* Iaroslavl', 1918.

Eleonskaia, A. S. *Russkaia publitsistika vtoroi poloviny XVII veka.* Moscow, 1978.

Ellersiek, H. "Russia under Aleksei Mikhailovich and Fiodor Alekseevich, 1645–1682: The Scandinavian Sources." Ph.D. diss., Los Angeles, 1955.

Esipov, G. V., ed. *Raskol'nich'i dela XVIII stoletiia, izvlechennye iz del Preobra-zhenskogo prikaza i Tainoi rozysknykh del Kantseliarii.* 2 vols. St. Petersburg, 1863.

Evgenii, Metropolitan. *Slovar' istoricheskii o byvshikh v Rossii pisateliakh dukhovnogo china greko-rossiiskoi tserkvi.* 2 vols. St. Petersburg, 1827.

Feofilakt, Archbishop. "Oblichenie raskol'nicheskoi nepravdy." Tver', 1745.

Filatov, I. F. "Ivan Neronov. Pora stanovleniia." *TODRL* 48 (1993): 319–22.

Florovskii, A. "Chudovskii inok Evfimii: Odin iz poslednikh pobornikov 'grecheskogo ucheniia' v Moskve v kontse XVII veka." *Slavia,* 1949, nos. 1–2.

Freeze, G. *The Russian Levites. Parish Clergy in the Eighteenth Century.* Cambridge/Mass., 1977.

Gasitskii, A. S., ed. *Nizhegorodskii letopisets.* Nizhnii-Novgorod, 1886.

Georgievskii, V. T. *Florishcheva pustyn'. Istoriko-arkheologicheskoe opisanie.* Viazniki, 1896.

Gibbenet, N. A. *Istoricheskoe issledovanie dela patriarkha Nikona.* 2 vols. St. Petersburg, 1884.

Ginzburg, C. *The Cheese and the Worms. The Cosmos of a Sixteenth-Century Miller.* Baltimore, 1980. Reprint. New York, 1983.

———. *Night Battles. Witchcraft and Agrarian Cults in the Sixteenth and Seventeenth Centuries*. New York, 1985.

Goetz, L. K. *Kirchenrechtliche und kulturgeschichtliche Denkmäler Altrusslands*. Stuttgart, 1905.

Golubinskii, E. E. *Istoriia kanonizatsii sviatykh v russkoi tserkvi*. Moscow, 1903.

———. *K nashei polemike s staroobriadtsami*. Moscow, 1905.

Golubtsov, A. P. *Chinovniki kholmogorskogo Preobrazhenskogo sobora*. Moscow, 1903.

———. "Chinovniki moskovskogo Uspenskogo sobora." *Chteniia*, 1907, bk. 4, pt. 1, pp. 1–312; 1908, bk. 2, pt. 1, pp. I–LIV.

Gorchakov, M. I. *Monastyrskii prikaz (1649–1725). Opyt istoriko-iuridicheskogo issledovaniia*. St. Petersburg, 1868.

———. *O zemel'nykh vladeniiakh vserossiiskikh mitropolitov, patriarkhov i sv. Sinoda (988–1738)*. St. Petersburg, 1871.

Gottfried, R. *The Black Death. Natural and Human Disaster in Medieval Europe*. New York, 1985.

"Gramoty ot Nikona patriarkha k Nikite Alekseevichu Siuzinu." *Zapiski Otdeleniia russkoi i slavianskoi arkheologii*, 2: 581–91.

Grass, K. K. *Die Gottesleute oder Chlüsten*. Vol. 1 of *Die russischen Sekten*. Leipzig, 1907.

Grigorii, A. *Istoricheskoe opisanie moskovskogo Zlatoustovskogo monastyria*. Moscow, 1871.

Grundmann, H. *Religiöse Bewegungen im Mittelalter*. Hildesheim-Olms, 1961.

Gur'ianova, N. S. *Krest'ianskii antimonarkhicheskii protest v staroobriadcheskoi eskhatologicheskoi literature perioda pozdnego feodalizma*. Novosibirsk, 1988.

Hammann, K. *Ecclesia spiritualis: Luthers Kirchenverständnis in den Kontroversen mit Augustin von Alveldt und Ambrosius Catharinus*. Göttingen, 1898.

Hannick, Ch. "Der einstimmige Russische Kirchengesang in der Auffassung der Altgläubigen und der Orthodoxen Kirche." In *Sprache, Kultur und Geschichte der Altgläubigen*, pp. 46–64.

Hauptmann, P. *Altrussischer Glaube. Der Kampf des Protopopen Avvakum gegen die Kirchenreformen des 17. Jahrhunderts*. Göttingen, 1963.

Heller, W. "Die Geschichte der russischen Altgläubigen und ihre Bedeutung. Ein Forschungsbericht." *Kirche im Osten* 31 (1988): 137–69.

———. *Die Moskauer "Eiferer für die Frömmigkeit" zwischen Staat und Kirche (1642–1652)*. Wiesbaden, 1988.

Hennigsen, G., ed. *The Inquisition in Early Modern Europe: Studies on Sources and Methods*. New York, 1986.

Hill, Ch. *The World Upside Down. Radical Ideas During the English Revolution.* Reprint. New York, 1985.

Hobsbawm, E. J. *Primitive rebels. Studies in archaic forms of social movements in the 19th and 20th centuries.* New York, 1965.

Hoeniger, R. *Der Schwarze Tod in Deutschland. Ein Beitrag zur Geschichte des 14. Jahrhunderts.* Wiesbaden, 1973.

Hösch, E. *Orthodoxie und Häresie im alten Russland.* Wiesbaden, 1975.

Huber, E. C. *Women and the Authority of Inspiration.* Lanham/Md., 1985.

Ianovskii, P. "Opisanie aktov novgorodskogo Sofiiskogo doma." *LZAK* 14 (1902): 3–146.

Ieronim, Archimandrite. *Riazanskie dostopamiatnosti.* Riazan', 1889.

Isaievych, Ia. D. *Bratstva ta ikh rol' v rozvytku ukrains'koi kul'tury XVI–XVIII st..* Kyiv, 1966.

———. *Pershodrukar' Ivan Fedorov i vynyknennia drukarstva na Ukraini.* L'viv, 1975.

Istoricheskie svedeniia ob eparkhiiakh v Rossii s utverzhdeniia pravoslavnogo khristianstva v Rossii do nashego vremeni. Moscow, 1881.

"Istoriia o vere i chelobitnaia o strel'tsakh Savvy Romanova." In *Letopisi russkoi literatury i drevnosti.* Ed. N. S. Tikhonravov, 5 (1863), pt. 2, pp. 111–48.

Istoriko-statisticheskoe opisanie pervoklassnogo Tikhvinskogo Bogoroditskogo bol'shogo muzheskogo monastyria, sostoiashchogo Novgorodskoi eparkhii v gorode Tikhvine. St. Petersburg, 1859.

"Itogi morovogo povetriia v Moskve v 1654 godu." *Chteniia,* 1892, bk. 4, smes', pp. 25–26.

Iukhimenko, E. M. "'Vinograd rossiiskii' Semena Denisova. Tekstologicheskii analiz." In Likhachev, D. S., ed. *Drevnerusskaia literatura. Istochnikovedenie. Sbornik nauchnykh trudov.* Leningrad, 1984, pp. 249–66.

Iurkevich, M. "Pop Lazar' raskolouchitel'." *Kishinevskie eparkhial'nye vedomosti,* 1874, no. 21: 791–801.

Iushkov, S. V. *Ocherki iz istorii prikhodskoi zhizni na severe Rossii v XV–XVII vv..* St. Petersburg, 1913.

Izvestie o rozhdenii i vospitanii i o zhitii sviateishogo Nikona patriarkha moskovskogo i vseia Rossii, napisannoe klirikom ego Ioannom Shusherinym. Moscow, 1871.

Jedin, H. *Probleme der Kirchenspaltung im 16. Jahrhundert.* Regensburg, 1970.

Kablits, I. I. *Russkie dissidenty-starovery i dukhovnye khristiane.* St. Petersburg, 1881.

Kämpfer, F. "Verhöre über das Entfernen von Ikonen aus den Kirchen." In Hauptmann, P., ed. *Unser ganzes Leben Christus unserm Gott überantworten. Studien zur ostkirchlichen Spiritualität.* Göttingen, 1982, pp. 295–302.

Kalugin, V. V. "'Psy' i 'zaitsy' (Ivan Groznyi i protopop Avvakum)." In *Staroobriad-chestvo v Rossii*, pp. 44–63.

Kapterev, N. F. *Svetskie arkhiereiskie chinovniki v drevnei Rossii*. Moscow, 1874.

———. *Kharakter otnoshenii Rossii k pravoslavnomu vostoku v XVI i XVII stoletiiakh*. Moscow, 1885. 2nd edition. Sergiev Posad, 1914.

———. *Patriarkh Nikon i ego protivniki v dele ispravleniia tserkovnykh obriadov*. Moscow, 1887.

———. "Sochinenie protiv raskola Iverskogo arkhimandrita greka Dionisiia." *Pravoslavnoe obozrenie*, 1887, no. 7: 1–70.

———. *Tsar' i tserkovnye moskovskie sobory XVI i XVII stoletii*. Moscow, 1906.

———. "Tserkovno-reformatsionnoe dvizhenie vo vremia patriarshestva Iosifa i ego glavnye predstaviteli." *Bogoslovskii vestnik*, 1908, bk. 1, pp. 309–505.

———. *Patriarkh Nikon i tsar' Aleksei Mikhailovich*. 2 vols. Sergiev Posad, 1909–12.

Karlovich, V. M. *Istoricheskie issledovaniia sluzhashchie k opravdaniiam staroobriadtsev*. Vol. 1 (Moscow, 1881). Vols. 2–3 (Chernovtsy, 1883–1886).

Karmanova, O. Ia. "Legendarnye predaniia v Vygovskoi agiografii nachala XVIII veka." In *Vygovskaia pomorskaia pustyn' i ee znachenie v istorii russkoi kul'tury. Tezisy dokladov mezhdunarodnoi nauchnoi konferentsii*. Petrozavodsk, 1994, pp. 37–39.

Karpov, P. *Sistematicheskii ukazatel' statei po . . . bogosloviiu, pomeshchennykh v zhur-nalakh: Khristianskoe chtenie, Pravoslavnoe obozrenie, Chtenie v Obshchestve liubitelei dukhovnogo prosveshcheniia, Pravoslavnyi sobesednik, Strannik, Vera i razum, Dushepoleznoe chtenie*. St. Petersburg, 1888.

Kartsov, V. G. *Religioznyi raskol kak forma antifeodal'nogo protesta v istorii Rossii*. 2 vols. Kalinin, 1971.

Kazakova, N. A. and Ia. S. Lur'e, *Antifeodal'nye ereticheskie dvizheniia na Rusi XIV-nachala XVI veka*. Moscow, 1955.

Keenan, E. L. "Semen Shakhovskoi and the Condition of Orthodoxy." *Harvard Ukrainian Studies* 12–13 (1988–1989): 795–815.

Kharlampovich, K. V. *Malorossiiskoe vliianie na velikorusskuiu tserkovnuiu zhizn'*. Vol. 119 of *Slavistic Printings and Reprintings*. Kazan', 1914. Reprint. The Hague/Paris, 1968.

Kholmogorov, V. I., ed. *Istoricheskie materialy o tserkvakh i selakh XVI–XVIII stoletii*. 11 vols. Moscow, 1882–1911.

Kholmogorovy, V. I. and G. I., eds. *Materialy dlia istorii Vladimirskoi eparkhii*. 4 vols. Vladimir, 1894–1896.

Kirshner, J. *Women of the Medieval World*. Oxford, 1985.

"K istorii raskola." *Russkaia starina* 43 (December, 1912): 674–75.

Klibanov, A. I. *Narodnaia sotsial'naia utopiia*. Moscow, 1962.

———. "K kharakteristike novykh iavlenii v russkoi obshchestvennoi mysli vtoroi poloviny XVII-nachala XVIII vv." *Istoriia SSSR*, 1963, no. 6: 85–103.

———. "Protopop Avvakum i apostol Pavel." In *Staroobriadchestvo v Rossii*, pp. 12–43.

Klipunovskii, F. "Ivan Neronov." *Universitetskie izvestiia* 7 (Kiev, 1886), no. 2: 1–40.

Kliuchevsky, V. O. *A Course in Russian History. The Seventeenth Century.* New York-London, 1994.

Knie, F. *Die Russisch-Schismatische Kirche; ihre Lehre und ihr Cult.* Graz, 1894.

Kononov, A. *Sud'by Kozheozerskoi Bogoiavlenskoi pustyni Arkhangel'skoi eparkhii.* St. Petersburg, 1894.

Kotkov, S. I., ed. *Moskovskaia rech' v nachal'nyi period stanovleniia russkogo natsional'nogo iazyka.* Moscow, 1974.

Kozhanchikov, D. E., ed. *Opisanie nekotorykh sochinenii napisannykh russkimi raskol'nikami v pol'zu raskola [=Zapiski Aleksandra B(rovskogo)].* 2 vols. St. Petersburg, 1861.

———, ed. *Istoriia Vygovskoi staroobriadcheskoi pustyni (izdana po rukopisi Ivana Filipova).* St. Petersburg, 1862.

———, ed. *Tri chelobitnye spravshchika Savvatiia, Savvy Romanova i monakhov Solovetskogo monastyria.* St. Petersburg, 1862.

Kozlov, O. F. "Delo Nikona." *Voprosy istorii*, 1976, no. 1: 102–14.

Kozlovskii, I. P. "F. M. Rtishchev: Istoriko-biograficheskoe issledovanie." *Universitetskie izvestiia* 46 (Kiev, 1906), no. 1: 1–52; no. 2: 53–100.

Kraft, E. *Moskaus griechisches Jahrhundert. Russisch-griechische Beziehungen und metabyzantinischer Einfluss 1619–1694.* Stuttgart, 1995.

Krylov, A. "Ob uprazdnennykh monastyriakh rostovsko-iaroslavskoi pastvy." *Iaroslavskie eparkhial'nye vedomosti*, 1860, pp. 39–51.

Kuczynski, A. *Thesaurus libellarum historiam reformationis illustrantium.* Nieuwkoop, 1969.

Kudriavtsev, I. M. *Muzeinoe sobranie rukopisei.* Moscow, 1961.

———. "Izdatel'skaia deiatel'nost' Posol'skogo prikaza." *Kniga: Issledovaniia i materialy*, 8 (1963): 179–244.

———, ed. "Sbornik XVII v. s podpisiami protopopa Avvakuma i drugikh pustoozerskikh uznikov." *Zapiski Otdela rukopisei GBL* 23 (1972): 148–212.

Kuhlmann, Q. *Ausgewählte Dichtungen.* Comp. O. Weitbrecht. Potsdam, 1923.

———. *Der Kühlpsalter.* Vols. 3–4 of *Neudrucke deutscher Literaturwerke. Neue Serie.* Ed. R. L. Beare. Tübingen, 1971.

———. *Himmlische Liebes-Küsse.* Vol. 23 of *Deutsche Neudrucke. Reihe Barock.* Ed. B. Biehl-Werner. Tübingen, 1971.

Kurdiumov, M. G. "Opisanie aktov, khraniashchikhsia v arkhive Imperatorskoi Arkheograficheskoi kommissii. Akty P. M. Stroeva." *LZAK* 17 (1906): 256–411; 19 (1908): 155–339.

——. "Opisanie aktov, khraniashchikhsia v arkhive Imperatorskoi Arkheograficheskoi kommissii. Kollektsiia P. I. Savvaitova." *LZAK* 27 (1915): 1–433.

"Kurgany vo Vladimirskoi gubernii." *Vladimirskie gubernskie vedomosti*, 1856, no. 27: 209–12.

Kurnosyi, I. "Istoriia o begstvuiushchem sviashchenstve." In Esipov, ed. *Raskol'nich'i dela XVIII veka*, 2: 179–89.

Kutepov, K. *Sekty khlystov i skoptsov*. Kazan', 1882.

Laube, A., ed. *Flugschriften der Bauernkriegszeit*. Berlin, 1975.

Lea, H. C. *The Inquisition in the Middle Ages*. New York, 1961.

Lebedev, D. P. *Sobranie istoriko-iuridicheskikh aktov I. D. Beliaeva*. Moscow, 1881.

Leff, G. *Heresy in the later Middle Ages: the relation of heterodoxy to dissent*. 2 vols. Manchester-New York, 1967.

Le Goff, J., ed. *Hérésies et sociétés dans l'Europe pré-industrielle, 11e-18e siècles*. Vol. 10 of *Civilisations et Sociétés*. Paris, 1968.

Leonid, Archimandrite. *Sistematicheskoe opisanie slaviano-rossiiskikh rukopisei sobraniia grafa A. S. Uvarova*. Moscow, 1893–94.

Leonid, Monk, ed. "Tserkovno-istoricheskoe opisanie uprazdnennykh monastyrei, nakhodivshikhsia v predelakh Kaluzhskoi eparkhii." *Chteniia*, 1863, bk. 1, pt. 1, pp. 1–170.

Le Roy Ladurie, E. *Montaillou. The Promised Land of Error*. New York, 1979.

Letopis' zaniatii Imperatorskoi Arkheograficheskoi kommissii (LZAK). 35 vols. St. Petersburg, 1862–1928.

Levitskii, N. "Neskol'ko dannykh kasatel'no nekotorykh sochinenii pervykh raskolouchitelei ob antikhriste." *Khristianskoe chtenie*, 1890, bk. 2, pp. 695–738.

Liberzon, I. Z. "Deiatel'nost' Arkheograficheskoi kommissii po spaseniiu arkhiva Solovetskogo monastyria." *Vspomogatel'nye istoricheskie distsipliny* 8 (1987): 325–32.

Ligarides, P. "Oproverzhenie chelobitnoi popa Nikity." In *Materialy*, 9: 6–265.

Lileev, M. I. *Opisanie rukopisei, khraniashchikhsia v biblioteke Chernigovskoi dukhovnoi seminarii*. St. Petersburg, 1880.

——, ed. *Novye materialy dlia istorii raskola na Vetke i v Starodub'e XVII–XVIII vv.* Kiev, 1893.

——. *Iz istorii raskola na Vetke i v Starodub'e XVII–XVIII vv.*. Kiev, 1895.

Lilov, A. I. *O tak nazyvaemoi Kirillovoi knige. Bibliograficheskoe izlozhenie v otnoshenii k glagolemomu staroobriadchestvu*. Kazan', 1858.

Lipinskii, M. A. *Opisanie sobraniia dokumentov, prinadlezhashchikhsia Rostovskomu muzeiu tserkovnykh drevnostei*. Iaroslavl', 1886.

Liubarskii, P., comp. "Liubopytnoe izvestie o Viatskoi eparkhii i o byvshikh v nei arkhiereiakh s nachala i ponyne." *Chteniia* 7 (1848), smes', pp. 47–64.

Liubopytnyi, P. "Katalog ili biblioteka staroverchheskoi tserkvi." *Chteniia*, 1863, bk. 1, pt. 2, pp. 1–66.

Livanov, F. "Prorochitsa raskol'nitsa Ustina Nikiforovna." *Otechestvennye zapiski*, 1865, no. 8: 556–604; no. 9: 1–62.

Lupinin, N. *Religious Revolt in the XVIIth Century: The Schism of the Russian Church*. Princeton, 1984.

Luppov, S. P. *Kniga v Rossii v pervoi chetverti XVIII veka*. Leningrad, 1973.

Makarii, Archbishop. "Khristianstvo v predelakh Arkhangel'skoi eparkhii." *Chteniia*, 1878, bk. 3, pp. 1–86.

Makarii, Archimandrite, ed. "Opisnaia kniga tserkvei Kniagininskogo uezda 1672 goda." *Zapiski Otdeleniia russkoi i slavianskoi arkheologii*, 1: 140–56.

———. *Istoriia Nizhegorodskoi ierarkhii, soderzhashchaia v sebe skazanie o nizhegorodskikh ierarkhakh s 1672 do 1850 goda*. St. Petersburg, 1857.

———, ed. *Pamiatniki tserkovnykh drevnostei Nizhegorodskoi gubernii*. St. Petersburg, 1857.

Makarii, Metropolitan. *Istoriia russkogo raskola izvestnogo pod imenem staroobriadchestva*. St. Petersburg, 1855.

———. *Istoriia russkoi tserkvi*. 12 vols. St. Petersburg, 1866–1883. Reprint. Düsseldorf, 1968–1969.

———. *Patriarkh Nikon v dele ispravleniia tserkovnykh knig i obriadov*. Moscow, 1881.

Maksimov, S. *Rasskazy iz istorii staroobriadchestva*. St. Petersburg, 1861.

Malyshev, V. I. "Ust'-tsilemskoe predanie o protopope Avvakume." *TODRL* 6 (1948): 372–75.

———. "Tri neizvestnykh sochineniia protopopa Avvakuma i novye dokumenty o nem." *Doklady i soobshcheniia Filologicheskogo instituta Leningradskogo gosudarstvennogo universiteta imeni A. A. Zhdanova* 3 (1951): 255–66.

———. "Zametka o rukopisnykh spiskakh 'Zhitiia' protopopa Avvakuma (materialy dlia bibliografii)." *TODRL* 8 (1951): 379–91.

———. "Neizvestnye i maloizvestnye materialy o protopope Avvakume." *TODRL* 9 (1953): 387–404.

———. "Bibliografiia sochinenii protopopa Avvakuma i literatury o nem 1917–1953 godov." *TODRL* 10 (1954): 435–46.

———. "K 275-letiiu so dnia smerti protopopa Avvakuma." *Izvestiia Otdeleniia literatury i iazyka Akademii nauk SSSR*, 1958, no. 1: 88–90.

———. *Ust'-tsilemskie rukopisnye sborniki XVI–XX vv.*. Syktyvkar, 1960.

———. "Avvakum suivant les traditions de Pustozersk." In *Mélanges Pierre Pascal. Recueil d'articles offert à M. Pierre Pascal par ses disciples et ses amis.* Vol. XXXVIII of *Revue des Études Slaves.* Paris, 1961, pp. 135–41.

———. "Gde byl sozhzhen protopop Avvakum?" *Russkie novosti*, no. 898 (Febr. 2, 1962): 3.

———. "Protopop Awwakum w edycjach staroobrzędowcow nadbałtyckich w latach dwudziestych i trzydziestych XX wieku." *Slavia Orientalis* 2 (1962): 215–21.

———. *Drevnerusskie rukopisi Pushkinskogo Doma (obzor fondov).* Moscow-Leningrad, 1965.

———. "Novye materialy o protopope Avvakume." *TODRL* 21 (1965): 334–45.

———. "Istoriia ikonnogo izobrazheniia protopopa Avvakuma." *TODRL* 22 (1966): 382–401.

———. "Sochineniia protopopa Avvakuma v drevlekhranilishche Pushkinskogo Doma AN SSSR." *TODRL* 29 (1974): 331–38.

Masanov, I. F. *Bibliografiia Vladimirskoi gubernii.* Vladimir, 1905.

"Materialy dlia istorii russkogo raskola." *Pravoslavnyi sobesednik*, 1858, no. 2: 586–98.

Mazunin, A. I. *Povest' o boiaryne Morozovoi.* Leningrad, 1979.

Meletii, Archimandrite. *Drevnie tserkovnye gramoty vostochno-sibirskogo kraia (1653–1726).* Kazan', 1875.

Mel'gunov, S. P. *Religiozno-obshchestvennye dvizheniia XVII–XVIII vv..* Moscow, 1922.

Mel'nikov, P. *Istoricheskie ocherki popovshchiny.* Moscow, 1864.

Meyendorff, P. *Russia, Ritual and Reform: The Liturgical Reforms of Nikon in the 17th Century.* New York, 1991.

Michels, G. "The Solovki Uprising: Religion and Revolt in Northern Russia." *The Russian Review* 51 (1992), no. 2: 1–15.

———. "The Violent Old Belief: An examination of religious dissent on the Karelian frontier." *Russian History/Histoire Russe* 19, nos. 1–4 (1992): 203–29.

———. "The Puzzle of the Early Old Belief: A Look at New Information about Seventeenth-Century Russian Dissent." *Modern Greek Studies Yearbook* 9 (1993): 467–78.

———. "The First Old Believers in Tradition and Historical Reality." *Jahrbücher für die Geschichte Osteuropas* 41 (1993), no. 4: 481–508.

———. "O deiatel'nosti Ivana Neronova v pervye gody Nikonovskoi reformy." In Pokrovskii, N. N., ed. *Russkoe obshchestvo, literatura pozdnego feodalizma: sbornik nauchnykh trudov.* Vol. 17 of *Arkheografiia i istochnikovedenie v Sibiri.* Novosibirsk, 1996, pp. 23–36.

———. "The Place of Nikita Konstantinovich Dobrynin in the History of Early Old Belief." *Revue des Études Slaves* LXIX, nos. 1–2 (1997): 21–31.

———. "Efrem Potemkin." In *The Modern Encyclopedia of Religions in Russia and the Soviet Union* (forthcoming).

Miliukov, P. *History of Russia*. 2 vols. New York, 1968.

Miuller, R. B. *Ocherki po istorii Karelii XVI–XVII vv.* Petrozavodsk, 1947.

———, ed. *Kareliia v XVII veke. Sbornik dokumentov.* Petrozavodsk, 1948.

Moeller, B. *Deutschland im Zeitalter der Reformation.* Göttingen, 1981.

Molchanov, A. "Bunt solovetskikh monakhov i ego znachenie dlia raskola voobshche i v chastnosti dlia raskola pomorskogo." *Pamiatnaia knizhka Arkhangel'skoi gubernii na 1909 god*, pp. 1–38.

"Monastyri byvshie vo gorode Pereiaslavle." *Vladimirskie gubernskie vedomosti*, 1854, no. 30: 233–34.

"Monastyri byvshie vo Vladimirskoi gubernii." *Vladimirskie gubernskie vedomosti*, 1854, no. 32: 249–51.

Moore, R. I. *The Origins of European Dissent.* Oxford, 1985.

Mordvinov, V., comp. *Zhitiia sviatykh ugodnikov Bozhiikh, v predelakh Vologodskoi eparkhii pochivaiushchikh.* Moscow, 1879.

Morris, C. *The Papal Monarchy. The Western Church from 1050 to 1250.* Oxford, 1989.

"Nakaz nashchet sobraniia svedenii 'gramotnosti' sviashchennikov Vazheskogo uezda i ikh synovei." *Arkhangel'skie gubernskie vedomosti*, 1869, no. 7: 2.

"Nakaz ob osvidetel'stvovanii tserkvei i ob ispytanii sviashchennikov v znanii sviashchennosluzheniia (December, 1687)." *Arkhangel'skie gubernskie vedomosti*, 1869, no. 5: 2.

Naster, G. M. "Kratkii obzor dokumental'nykh materialov XVII–XVIII vv. iz byvshego arkhiva Sinoda." *Arkheograficheskii ezhegodnik za 1959 god*, pp. 303–10.

Nechaev, V. V. "Raskol'nicheskaia kontora 1725–1764." In *Opisanie MGAMIU*, vol 7 (Moscow, 1890), pt. 2, 1–63.

"Neprigozhie rechi Kipriana metropolita novgorodskogo." *Chteniia*, 1896, bk. 1, pt. 1, pp. 1–28.

Neubauer, H. *Car und Selbstherrscher. Beiträge zur Geschichte der Autokratie in Russland.* Wiesbaden, 1964.

Nichols, R. and Michels, G., eds., *Russia's Dissident Old Believers* (forthcoming).

Niess, H. P. *Kirche in Russland zwischen Tradition und Glaube? Eine Untersuchung der Kirillova kniga und der Kniga o vere aus der 1. Hälfte des 17. Jahrhunderts.* Göttingen, 1977.

Nikolaev, A. V. *Sistematicheskii parallel'nyi ukazatel' po vsem dukhovnym zhurnalam i eparkhial'nym vedomostiam s 1-go goda ikh izdaniia do 1871.* Voronezh, 1871.

Nikolaevskii, P. F. "Zhizn' patriarkha Nikona v ssylke i zakliuchenii posle osuzhdeniia ego na moskovskom sobore 1666 goda." *Khristianskoe chtenie*, 1886, nos. 1–6: 45–110, 378–428, 663–86.

——. *Patriarshaia oblast' i russkie eparkhii v XVII veke.* St. Petersburg, 1888.

——. "Moskovskii pechatnyi dvor pri patriarkhe Nikone." *Khristianskoe chtenie*, 1890, nos. 1–2: 114–41, 434–67; 1891, no. 1: 147–86; no. 2: 151–86.

——. "Cherty eparkhial'nogo upravleniia XVII veka po sledstvennomu delu o kolomenskom arkhiepiskope Iosife." *Khristianskoe chtenie*, 1904, nos. 1–2: 45–63, 238–65.

Nikol'skii, N., ed. "Sochineniia solovetskogo inoka Gerasima Firsova po neizdannym tekstam (K istorii severno-russkoi literatury XVII veka)." *Pamiatniki drevnei pis'mennosti i iskusstva* 188 (1916): I–XLIII, 1–233.

Nikol'skii, V. K. "Sibirskaia ssylka protopopa Avvakuma." *Uchenye zapiski (Institut istorii)* 2 (1927): 137–67.

Nolte, H. H. "Die Reaktion auf die spätpetrinische Altgläubigenunterdrückung." *Kirche im Osten* 19 (1976): 11–28.

Novikov, N. N. "Moskovskie i drugie starinnye prikazy." In Vol. 20 of *Drevniaia rossiiskaia vivliofika*. Moscow, 1791, pp. 277–421.

"Novoe raskol'nicheskoe uchenie. Po povodu raskol'nicheskogo sochineniia." *Khristianskoe chtenie*, 1887, bk. 1, pp. 406–14.

Oakley, F. *The Western Church in the Later Middle Ages.* Ithaca-London, 1988.

Ogloblin, N. N. "Mangazeiskii chudotvorets Vasilii." *Chteniia*, 1890, bk. 1, pt. 2, pp. 3–8.

——, ed. "Bytovye cherty XVII veka." *Russkaia starina* 73 (1892): 449–58, 675–82; 74 (1892): 681–94; 76 (1892): 165–82; 81 (1894): 223–36.

——. "Obozrenie stolbtsov i knig Sibirskogo prikaza (1592–1773)." *Chteniia*, 1895, bk. 2, pt. 4, pp. 1–422; 1898, bk. 1, pt. 3, pp. 1–162; 1900, bk. 3, pt. 3, pp. 1–394; 1902, bk. 1, pt. 3, pp. 1–288.

Ogurtsev, N. G. *Opyt mestnoi bibliografii. Iaroslavskii krai.* Iaroslavl', 1924.

"Okruzhnoe poslanie rostovskogo mitropolita Iony pri vstuplenii ego v pastvu." *AI*, 4: 172–77.

Oparina, T.A. "Prosvetitel' litovskii-neizvestnyi pamiatnik ideologicheskoi bor'by XVII veka." In Romodanovskaia, E. K., ed. *Literatura i klassovaia bor'ba epokhi pozdnego feodalizma v Rossii.* Vol. 7 of *Arkheografiia i istochnikovedenie v Sibiri.* Novosibirsk, 1987, pp. 43–57.

Opisanie aktov sobraniia grafa A. S. Uvarova. Akty istoricheskie opisannye I. M. Kataevym i A. K. Kabanovym. Moscow, 1905.

Opisanie del arkhiva Solotchinskogo monastyria. Vol. 1 of *Opisi del Riazanskogo istoricheskogo arkhiva.* Riazan', 1889.

Opisanie dokumentov i bumag, khraniashchikhsia v Moskovskom arkhive Ministerstva iustitsii (Opisanie MGAMIU). 21 vols. Moscow, 1869–1921.

"Opisanie sela Pavlovskogo Suzdal'skogo uezda." *Vladimirskie gubernskie vedomosti,* 1875, no. 7: 1.

"Otkaznye knigi v Viatskii arkhiereiskii dom na Kotel'nicheskii Predtechenskii monastyr' i Bobinskii stan 7166 goda." *Trudy Viatskoi arkhivnoi kommissii,* 1908, pt. 2, sect. 2, pp. 1–60.

Ozment, St. *Mysticism and dissent; religious ideology and social protest in the sixteenth century.* New York, 1973.

"Pamiat' Sysknogo prikaza v Oruzheinyi prikaz ob otpiske . . . Bronnoi slobody dvora, prinadlezhavshego raskol'niku . . . Os'ke Savel'niku." *Chteniia* 5 (1848), smes', pp. 71–72.

Pamiatniki istorii staroobriadchestva XVII veka. Vol. 39 of *RIB.* Leningrad, 1927.

Papkov, A. A. "Pogosty v znachenii pravitel'stvennykh okrugov i sel'skikh prikhodov v severnoi Rossii." *Russkii arkhiv* 257 (Nov. 1898): 55–85; 258 (Dec. 1898): 13–29.

Pascal, P. *Avvakum et les débuts du raskol. La crise religieuse au XVIIe siècle en Russie.* Paris, 1938.

——. "Po sledam protopopa Avvakuma v SSSR." *Russkie zapiski. Ezhemesiachnyi zhurnal* 17 (1939): 122–40.

Pavlovskii, A. A., comp. *Vseobshchii illiustrirovannyi putevoditel' po monastyriam i sviatym mestam Rossiiskoi imperii i sviatoi gory Afonu.* Nizhnii Novgorod, 1907.

"Pennaia pamiat' za ubiistvo (October 30, 1665)." *Chteniia* 5 (1848), smes', p. 144.

"Perepisnye knigi chasoven' v Vazhskom uezde i v Ust'ianskikh sokhakh." In *Akty Kholmogorskoi i Ustiuzhskoi eparkhii,* 2: 347–762.

Peretiatkovich, G. *Povol'zhe v XVII i nachale XVIII vv..* Odessa, 1882.

Peters, E., ed. *Heresy and Authority in Medieval Europe.* Philadelphia, 1980.

Petrejus, P. "Historien und Bericht von dem Grossfürstenthumb Muschkow mit dero schönen fruchtbaren Provincien und Herrschaften." In *Rerum Rossicarum scriptores exteri a collegio archeografico editi (=Skazaniia inostrannykh pisatelei o Rossii, izdannye Arkheograficheskoiu kommissieiu).* Vol. 1 (St. Petersburg, 1851), pp. 139–382.

Pisarev, N. *Domashnii byt russkikh patriarkhov.* Kazan', 1904.

Piskarev, I. *Drevnie gramoty i akty Riazanskogo kraia.* St. Petersburg, 1854.

"Pistsovaia kniga Aleksandrovoi slobody 1677 goda." *Vladimirskie gubernskie vedomosti,* 1854, nos. 17–20.

"Pod'iaka Fedora Trofimova dve zapiski o vinakh patriarkha Nikona i nekotorykh blizkikh emu lits." In *Materialy,* 4: 285–98.

Pokrovskii, I. M. *Russkie eparkhii v XVI–XIX vv.; ikh otkrytie, sostav i predely.* 2 vols. Kazan', 1897–1913.

Pokrovskii, N. N. *Antifeodal'nyi protest uralo-sibirskikh krest'ian-staroobriadtsev v XVIII v.*. Novosibirsk, 1974.

Polnoe sobranie postanovlenii i razporiazhenii po vedomosti pravoslavnogo ispovedaniia (PSPVI). 10 vols. St. Petersburg, 1869–1916.

Polnoe sobranie zakonov Rossiiskoi imperii. 45 vols. St. Petersburg, 1830–43.

Polnyi pravoslavnyi bogoslovskii entsiklopedicheskii slovar' (PPBES). 2 vols. St. Petersburg, 1913. Reprint. London, 1971.

Ponyrko, N. V. "Kirillo-Epifanievskii zhitiinyi tsikl i zhitiinaia traditsiia v Vygovskoi staroobriadcheskoi literature." *TODRL* 29 (1974): 154–69.

———. "D'iakon Fedor—soavtor Avvakum." *TODRL* 31 (1976): 362–65.

———. "Uchebniki ritoriki na Vygu." *TODRL* 36 (1982): 154–62.

Popov, A. N., comp. "Perepiska d'iaka Tret'iaka Vasil'eva." *Vremennik Moskovskogo Obshchestva istorii i drevnostei rossiiskikh* 9 (1851), smes', pp. 1–29.

———. *Opisanie rukopisei i katalog knig tserkovnoi pechati biblioteki A. I. Khludova.* Moscow, 1872.

Popov, M. G., ed. "Materialy dlia istorii patriarkha moskovskogo Pitirima." *Khristianskoe chtenie*, 1890, no. 2: 489–523.

Poslaniia blazhennogo Ignatiia mitropolita sibirskogo i tobol'skogo. Kazan', 1857.

"Posledovateli ucheniia ob Antikhriste: Varlaam Levin." In Esipov, ed. *Raskol'nich'i dela XVIII veka*, 1: 8–59.

"Povest' o rozhdenii, vospitanii, i o zhitii i konchine Nikona." *Izvestiia Otdeleniia russkogo iazyka i slovesnosti Akademii nauk* 5 (1900), no. 1: 177–89.

Pozdeeva, I. V. "Zapisi na staropechatnykh knigakh kirillovskogo shrifta kak istoricheskii istochnik." *Fedorovskie chteniia za 1976*, pp. 39–54.

———. Et al., eds. *Katalog knig kirillicheskoi pechati XV–XVII vv., nakhodiashchikhsia v nauchnoi biblioteke Moskovskogo universiteta.* Moscow, 1980.

———. "Drevnerusskoe nasledie v istorii traditsionnoi knizhnoi kul'tury russkogo staroobriadchestva." In *Sprache, Kultur und Geschichte der Altgläubigen*, pp. 224–63.

Protas'eva, T. N. "Stolbtsy Sinodal'nogo sobraniia." *Arkheograficheskii ezhegodnik za 1959 god*, pp. 279–97.

Prugavin, A. S. *Bibliografiia staroobriadchestva i ego razvetvlenii.* Vol. 1 of *Raskolsektanstvo; materialy dlia izucheniia religiozno-bytovykh dvizhenii russkogo naroda.* Moscow, 1887.

Puteshestvie antiokhiiskogo patriarkha Makariia v Rossiiu v polovine XVII veka, opisannoe ego synom arkhidiakonom Pavlom Aleppskim. Transl. and ed. G. Murkos. 5 pts. Moscow, 1896–1900.

"Raskol v Olonetskoi eparkhii." *Olonetskie eparkhial'nye vedomosti*, 1898, no. 1: 11–13.

"Razboi i razboiniki okolo goroda Shui v XVII stoletii." *Drevniaia i novaia Rossiia*, 1881, no. 1: 205–8.

Riasanovsky, N. V. *A History of Russia*. Oxford, 1977.

Robinson, A. N. "Tvorchestvo Avvakuma i obshchestvennye dvizheniia v kontse XVII veka." *TODRL* 18 (1962): 149–75.

———, ed. *Zhizneopisaniia Avvakuma i Epifaniia*. Moscow, 1963.

———. *Bor'ba idei v russkoi literature XVII veka*. Moscow, 1974.

Rogov, A. I. "Narodnye massy i religioznye dvizheniia v Rossii vo vtoroi polovine XVII veka." *Voprosy istorii*, 1973, no. 3: 32–43

———. *Muzykal'naia estetika Rossii XI–XVIII vv*. Moscow, 1973.

"Rospis' knig i pisem, vziatykh pri obyske u igumena Feoktista na Viatke." In *Materialy*, 1: 323–39.

"Rospis' spornykh rechei protopopa Ivan Neronova s patriarkhom Nikonom." In *Materialy*, 1: 41–51.

Rovinskii, D. A. *Podrobnyi slovar' russkikh graviur XVI–XIX vv*. St. Petersburg, 1895.

Rozhdestvenskii, N. V., ed. "K istorii bor'by s tserkovnymi bezporiadkami . . . v russkom bytu XVII veka (Chelobitnaia nizhegorodskikh sviashchennikov 1636 goda)." *Chteniia*, 1902, bk. 2, smes', pp. 1–31.

Rumiantsev, I. I. *Nikita Konstantinovich Dobrynin ("Pustosviat"). Istoriko-kriticheskii ocherk (K istorii bor'by pravoslaviia s staroobriadchestvom v XVII veke)*. 2 vols. Sergiev Posad, 1917.

Rumiantseva, V. S. *Narodnoe antitserkovnoe dvizhenie v Rossii v XVII veke*. Moscow, 1986.

———, ed. *Narodnoe antitserkovnoe dvizhenie v Rossii XVII veka. Dokumenty Prikaza tainykh del o raskol'nikakh 1665–1667 gg. (Dokumenty)*. Moscow, 1986.

———, ed. *Dokumenty Razriadnogo, Posol'skogo, Novgorodskogo i Tainogo prikazov o raskol'nikakh v gorodakh Rossii. 1654–1684 gg.*. Moscow, 1991.

Rushinskii, L., comp. "Religioznyi byt russkikh po svedeniiam inostrannykh pisatelei XVI i XVII vekov." *Chteniia*, 1871, bk. 3, pt. 1, pp. 1–337.

Russell, J. B. *Religious Dissent in the Middle Ages*. New York, 1971.

Russkaia istoricheskaia biblioteka (RIB). 39 vols. St. Petersburg-Moscow, 1872–1927.

Sakharov, F. K. *Literatura istorii i oblicheniia russkogo raskola. Bibliograficheskii ukazatel' knig, broshiur i statei o raskole*. 3 vols. Tambov-St. Petersburg, 1887–1900.

———, ed. *Khronologicheskaia opis' del o raskole, khraniashchikhsia v arkhivakh gubernskogo goroda Vladimira (1720–1855)*. Vladimir, 1905.

Sakharov, I. P., ed. *Zapiski russkikh liudei: sobytiia vremen Petra Velikogo*. St. Petersburg, 1841. Reprinted and introduced by H. Torke. Vol. 27 of *Russian Memoir Series*. Newtonville/Mass., 1980.

Salomies, I. *Der Hallesche Pietismus in Russland zur Zeit Peters des Grossen*. Helsinki, 1936.

Sapozhnikov, D. I. "Samosozhzhenie v russkom raskole so vtoroi poloviny XVII veka do kontsa XVIII veka. Istoricheskii ocherk po arkhivnym dokumentam." *Chteniia*, 1891, bk. 3, pt. 4, pp. 3–171.

Sarafanova, N. S. "Proizvedeniia drevnerusskoi pis'mennosti v sochineniiakh Avvakuma." *TODRL* 18 (1962), pp. 329–40.

Savich, A. A. *Solovetskaia votchina XV–XVII*. Perm', 1927.

Savva, Archimandrite. *Ukazatel' Moskovskoi patriarshei riznitsy i biblioteki*. Moscow, 1858.

Savvaitov, P. I. *Opisanie vologodskogo Spasokammenogo Dukhova monastyria*. St. Petersburg, 1860.

———. *Opisanie vologodskogo Spaso-Prilutskogo monastyria*. Vologda, 1884.

Semevskii, M. I. *Slovo i delo 1700–1725. Tainaia kantseliariia pri Petre Velikom*. St. Petersburg, 1885.

Serbina, K. H. *Ocherki iz sotsial'no-ekonomicheskoi istorii russkogo goroda. Tikhvinskii posad v XVI–XVIII vv*. Moscow-Leningrad, 1951. Reprint. The Hague-Paris, 1970.

Serman, I. Z. "Protopop Avvakum v tvorchestve N. S. Leskova." *TODRL* 14: 404–7.

Seseikina, I. V. "'Kniga besed' protopopa Avvakuma kak pamiatnik polemicheskoi literatury XVII veka." Cand. thesis. St. Petersburg, 1991.

Shashkov, A. T. "Sochineniia Maksima Greka v staroobriadcheskoi rukopisnoi traditsii i ideologicheskaia bor'ba v Rossii vo vtoroi polovine XVII-pervoi polovine XVIII vv." Cand. thesis. Sverdlovsk, 1982.

Shchapov, A. P. *Russkii raskol staroobriadchestva, rassmatrivaemyi v sviazi s vnutrennim sostoianiem russkoi tserkvi i grazhdanstvennosti v XVII veke i v pervoi polovine XVIII veka. Opyt istoricheskogo issledovaniia o prichinakh proiskhozhdeniia i rasprostraneniia russkogo raskola*. Kazan', 1859.

———. *Zemstvo i raskol*. St. Petersburg, 1862.

Sheptaev, L. S., ed. "Stikhi spravshchika Savvatiia." *TODRL* 21 (1965): 5–28.

Shimko, I. I. *Patriarshii kazennyi prikaz. Ego vneshniaia istoriia, ustroistvo i deiatel'nost'*. Moscow, 1894.

Shul'gin, V. S. " 'Kapitonovshchina' i ee mesto v raskole XVII v." *Istoriia SSSR*, 1969, no. 4: 130–39.

Shvedova, O. I. "Ukazatel' 'Trudov' gubernskikh uchenykh arkhivnykh kommissii i otdelnykh ikh izdanii." *Arkheograficheskii ezhegodnik za 1957*, pp. 377–433.

Skvortsov, D. I. *Ocherki tverskogo raskola i sektanstva*. Moscow, 1895.

Smirnov, A. V. *Ukazatel' soderzhaniia neoffitsial'noi chasti "Vladimirskikh gubernskikh vedomostei" s 1838 po 1900, vkliuchaiushchaia i "Vladimirskie eparkhial'nye vedomosti" s 1865 po 1900*. Vladimir, 1902.

———, comp. *Materialy dlia istorii Vladimirskoi gubernii*. 3 vols. Vladimir, 1901–4.

Smirnov, D. N. *Ocherki zhizni i byta nizhegorodtsev XVII-XVIII vekov*. Gor'kii, 1978.

Smirnov, P. *Patriarkh Ioakim moskovskii*. Moscow, 1881.

Smirnov, P. P. "Chelobitnye dvorian i detei boiarskikh vsekh gorodov vo pervoi polovine XVII veka." *Chteniia*, 1915, bk. 3, pt. 1, pp. 1–70.

———. *Posadskie liudi i klassovaia bor'ba do serediny XVII veka*. 2 vols. Moscow-Leningrad, 1948.

Smirnov, P. S. *Istoriia russkogo raskola staroobriadchestva*. St. Petersburg, 1895.

———. *Vnutrennie voprosy v raskole v XVII veke*. St. Petersburg, 1898.

———. "Literatura i oblicheniia staroobriadcheskogo raskola v XIX veka." *Khristianskoe chtenie*, 1906, bk. 1, pp. 46–64, 604–30; bk. 2, 530–52.

———. *Iz istorii raskola pervoi poloviny XVIII veka*. St. Petersburg, 1908.

———. *Spory i razdeleniia v russkom raskole v pervoi chetverti XVIII veka*. St. Petersburg, 1909.

Smolitsch, I. *Russisches Mönchtum. Entstehung, Entwicklung und Wesen 988–1917*. Vols. 11–12 of *Das Östliche Christentum*. Würzburg, 1953.

———. *Geschichte der Russischen Kirche 1700–1917*. Vol. 1 (Leiden, 1964). Vol. 2 (Berlin, 1991). Ed. G. Freeze. In Vol. 45 of *Forschungen zur Osteuropäischen Geschichte*.

Sobranie gosudarstvennykh gramot i dogovorov. 5 vols. Moscow, 1813–94.

Solov'ev, I. *Opisanie iaroslavskogo Spaso-Proboinskogo obydennogo khrama*. Iaroslavl', 1869.

Sprache, Kultur und Geschichte der Altgläubigen. Akten des Heidelberger Symposions vom 28. bis 30. April 1986. Ed. B. Panzer. Heidelberg, 1988.

Staroobriadchestvo v Rossii (XVII–XVIII vv.). Sbornik nauchnykh trudov. Ed. E. M. Iukhimenko. Moscow, 1994.

Starostina, T. V. "Mirskaia chelobitnaia zaonezhskikh pogostov 1677 g." *Voprosy istorii*, 1961, no. 1: 107–27.

———. "Volneniia krest'ian Tolvuiskogo pogosta v XVII v." *Voprosy istorii*, 1961, no. 1: 128–45.

——. "Shueretskaia volost' v XVI–XVII vv." In *Krest'ianstvo i klassovaia bor'ba v feodal'noi Rossii. Sbornik statei pamiati Ivana Ivanovicha Smirnova.* Leningrad, 1967, pp. 195–208.

Steinke, K. "Eine Dokumentation der Altgläubigen zum Zweifingerkreuz. Bemerkungen zur Handschrift Nr. 17 im Slawischen Institut an der Universität Heidelberg." *Kirche im Osten* 32 (1989): 73–108.

Stepanovskii, I. K. *Vologodskaia starina. Istoriko-arkheologicheskii sbornik.* Vologda, 1890.

Stroev, P. M. *Obstoiatel'noe opisanie staropechatnykh knig slavianskikh i rossiiskikh, nakhodiashchikhsia v biblioteke grafa F. A. Tolstogo.* Moscow, 1829.

——. *Biblioteka Imperatorskogo Obshchestva istorii i drevnostei rossiiskikh.* Moscow, 1845.

——. *Spiski ierarkhov i nastoiatelei monastyrei rossiiskoi tserkvi.* St. Petersburg, 1877.

Subbotin, N. I., ed. *Deianie moskovskogo sobora 1654 goda o knizhnom ispravlenii.* Moscow, 1873.

——, ed. *Materialy dlia istorii raskola za pervoe vremia ego sushchestvovaniia (Materialy).* 9 vols. Moscow, 1875–1894.

"Sudnoe delo o razorenii Paleostrovskogo monastyria." *Olonetskie gubernskie vedomosti,* 1849, nos. 8–14, pts. I–IV.

Sullivan, J. "Manuscript Copies of Simeon Denisov's 'The Russian Vineyard'." *The Slavonic and East European Review* 58 (April, 1980), no. 2: 182–94.

——. "Staroobriadcheskaia rukopisnaia traditsiia. 'Vinograd rossiiskii' Semena Denisova." In *Sprache, Kultur und Geschichte der Altgläubigen,* pp. 313–30.

Suvorov, N. I., ed. "Spor vologodskikh arkhiepiskopov Markella i Simona s pervymi dvumia episkopami viatskimi Aleksandrom i Ionoiu ob Ust'-vymskoi desiatine (1659–1676)." *Vologodskie gubernskie vedomosti,* 1864, nos. 8–9, 11–12.

——. "Vozdvizhenskii muzheskii monastyr' byvshii v gorode Vologde." *Vologodskie eparkhial'nye vedomosti,* 1866, no. 18: 696–700.

——. "Opisanie Spasoobydennoi vsegradskoi, chto v Vologde, tserkvi." *Vologodskie eparkhial'nye vedomosti,* 1879, nos. 16–17.

——. *Opisanie sobraniia svitkov, nakhodiashchikhsia v Vologodskom eparkhial'nom drevnekhranilishche (Opisanie svitkov).* 13 vols. Vologda, 1899–1917.

Svirelin, A. I. "Svedeniia o zhizni arkhimandrita pereiaslavskogo Danilova monastyria Grigoriia Neronova." *Trudy Vladimirskoi uchenoi arkhivnoi kommissii* 6 (1904): 1–47.

Syrtsev, I. Ia. *Samosozhigatel'stvo sibirskikh staroobriadtsev v XVII i XVIII stoletiiakh.* Tobol'sk, 1888.

——. *Vozmushchenie solovetskikh monakhov-staroobriadtsev v XVII veke.* Kostroma, 1888.

Tel'charov, A. D. "Fond Vladimirskoi uchenoi arkhivnoi kommissii." *Arkheograficheskii ezhegodnik za 1985*, pp. 229–33.

The Travels of Olearius in Seventeenth-Century Russia. Transl. and ed. S. H. Baron. Stanford, 1967.

Tikhomirov, M. N. *Opisanie Tikhomirovskogo sobraniia rukopisei*. Moscow, 1968.

———. *Klassovaia bor'ba v Rossii v XVII v.*. Moscow, 1969.

Tikhonravov, K. N. *Kniaginin Uspenskii devichii monastyr' vo Vladimire Kliaz'menskom*. Sect. 2, pt. 8 of *Vladimirskii istoriko-statisticheskii sbornik (=Pamiatnaia knizhka Vladimirskoi gubernii na 1862 god)*. Vladimir, 1869.

Tillich, P. *Dynamics of Faith*. New York, 1957.

Titov A. A. *Troitskii Zheltovodskii monastyr' starogo Makariia*. Moscow, 1887.

———. *Gorod Liubim i uprazdnennye obiteli v Liubime i ego uezde*. Moscow, 1890.

———. *Suzdal'skaia ierarkhiia*. Vol. 4 of *Materialy dlia istorii russkoi tserkvi*. Moscow, 1892.

———. "*Iaroslavskie eparkhial'nye vedomosti*." *Neoffitsial'naia chast'. Spisok i ukazatel' statei, pomeshchennykh v "Vedomostiakh" za vse vremia ikh sushchestvovaniia. 1860–1892 gg.*. Sergiev Posad, 1893.

———. *Opisanie slaviano-russkikh rukopisei, nakhodiashchikhsia v sobranii A. A. Titova*. 6 vols. Moscow, 1900–1913.

Tokmakov, I. F. *Istoricheskoe i arkheologicheskoe opisanie Pokrovskogo devich'ego monastyria v gorode Suzdale*. Moscow, 1889.

Tolstoi, M. V. *Drevnie sviatyni Rostova Velikogo*. Moscow, 1847.

Torke, H. J. *Die staatsbedingte Gesellschaft im Moskauer Reich: Zar und Zemlja in der altrussischen Herrschaftsverfassung 1613–1689*. Leiden, 1974.

Trudy Otdela drevnerusskoi literatury Akademii nauk SSSR (TODRL). 50 vols. Leningrad, 1934–.

Tschernykh, P. J. *Historische Grammatik der Russischen Sprache*. Halle, 1977.

Tschizewskij, D. "Jakob Boehme und Russland." *Evangelium und Osten*, vol. 8 (Riga, 1935), pp. 175–83.

———. *Aus zwei Welten. Beiträge zur Geschichte der slawisch-westlichen Beziehungen*. Den Haag, 1956.

Uspenskii, B. A. "The Schism and Cultural Conflict in the Seventeenth Century." In Batalden, ed. *Seeking God*, pp. 106–43.

Uspenskii, V. *Istoricheskoe opisanie Nilovoi Stolobenskoi pustyni Tverskoi eparkhii*. Tver', 1876.

Uspensky, N. "The Collision of Two Theologies in the Revision of Liturgical Books in the Seventeenth Century." In idem, *Evening Worship in the Orthodox Church*. New York, 1985, pp. 191–240.

Uvet dukhovnyi, vo utverzhdenie blagochestivykh liudei, vo uverenie-zhe i obrashchenie k pokaianiiu ot prelesti raskol'nikov sviatoi Tserkvi. Moscow, 1682.

van Klenk, K. *Voyagie van den heere Koenraad van Klenk aen zaarsche majesteit van Moscoviën.* St. Petersburg, 1900.

Varakin, D. S. *Ispravlenie knig v XVII stoletii.* Moscow, 1910.

Varlaam, Arkhimandrite, ed. "O prebyvanii patriarkha Nikona v zatochenii v Ferapontove i Kirillove beloozerskikh monastyriakh po aktam poslednego." *Chteniia*, 1858, bk. 3, pt. 1, pp. 129–68.

Vereshchagin, A. S. "Iz istorii Viatskoi eparkhii. Pervyi episkop viatskii Aleksandr (1658–1674)." *Trudy Viatskoi arkhivnoi kommissii*, 1908, pt. 2, sect. 3, pp. 3–55.

Veriuzhskii, V. *Afanasii arkhiepiskop kholmogorskii, ego zhizn' i trudy v sviazi s istoriei Kholmogorskoi eparkhii za pervye 20 let ee sushchestvovaniia i voobshche russkoi tserkvi v kontse XVII veka.* St. Petersburg, 1908.

Veselovskii, S. B., comp. *Dokumenty o postroike Pustoozerskoi tiur'my, o pope Lazare, Ivane Krasuline i Grigor'e Iakovleve.* Vol. 2 of *Pamiatniki pervykh let russkogo staroobriadchestva.* St. Petersburg, 1914.

———. *Feodal'noe zemlevladenie v severo-vostochnoi Rusi.* Moscow, 1947.

———. *D'iaki i pod'iachie XV–XVII vv.* Moscow, 1975.

Viktorov, A. E. *Slaviano-russkie rukopisi V. M. Undol'skogo, opisannye samim sostav-itelem i byvshim vladel'tsem sobraniia.* Moscow, 1870.

———. *Obozrenie starinnykh opisei patriarshei riznitsy.* Moscow, 1875.

———. *Opisanie zapisnykh knig i bumag starinnykh dvortsovykh prikazov 1584–1725 gg..* 2 vols. Moscow, 1877–1883.

———. *Sobranie rukopisei I. D. Beliaeva.* Moscow, 1881.

Vinogradov, V. V. "K izucheniiu stilia protopopa Avvakuma, printsipov ego slovoupotrebleniia." *TODRL* 14 (1958): 371–79.

Vinogradskii, N. *Tserkovnyi sobor v Moskve 1682 goda. Opyt istoriko-kriticheskogo issledo-vaniia.* Smolensk, 1899.

Vodarskii, Ia. E. "Tserkovnye organizatsii i ikh krepostnye krest'iane vo vtoroi polovine XVII-nachale XVIII veka." In *Istoricheskaia geografiia Rossii XII-nachalo XX veka.* Moscow, 1975, pp. 70–96.

———. "Naselenie Rossii v kontse XVII–XVIII vv." Avtoreferat dissertatsii. Moscow, 1975.

———, ed. *Vladeniia i krepostnye krest'iane russkoi tserkvi v kontse XVII veka.* Moscow, 1988.

von Gardner, J. *Gesang der russisch-orthodoxen Kirche bis zur Mitte des 17. Jahrhun-derts.* Vol. 15 of *Schriften zur Geistesgeschichte des Östlichen Europa.* Wiesbaden, 1983.

Vorob'ev, G. *O moskovskom sobore 1681–82 gg. Opyt istoricheskogo issledovaniia.* St. Petersburg, 1885.

Vozdvizhenskii, T. *Istoricheskoe obozrenie Riazanskoi ierarkhii i vsekh tserkovnykh del seia eparkhii.* Moscow, 1820.

Vvedenskii, S. "Missionerskaia deiatel'nost' riazanskogo arkhiepiskopa Misaila sredi inorodtsev Tambovskogo kraia v 1653–1656 gg." *Bogoslovskii vestnik,* 1910, no. 19: 527–51.

———. "Kostromskii protopop Daniil." *Bogoslovskii vestnik,* 1913, no. 4: 844–54.

"Vygoretskii letopisets." *Bratskoe slovo,* 1888, no. 10: 793–815.

"Vypiski iz pisem patriarkha Nikona k tsariu Alekseiu Mikhailovichu v ego gosudarevy pokhody." *Zapiski Otdeleniia russkoi i slavianskoi arkheologii,* 2: 591–93.

Vysotskii, N. G., ed. "Perepiska kniagini E. P. Urusovoi s svoimi det'mi." *Starina i novizna* 20 (1916): 3–37.

Wachendorf, J. "Regionalismus, Raskol und Volk als Hauptprobleme der Russischen Geschichte bei A. P. Shchapov." Inaug. diss., Cologne, 1964.

Ware, T. *The Russian Orthodox Church.* London, 1993.

Zabelin, I. E. *Materialy dlia istorii, arkheologii i statistiki goroda Moskvy.* 2 vols. Moscow, 1884–1891.

"Zapiski Andreia Artamonovicha grafa Matveeva." In Sakharov, ed. *Zapiski russkikh liudei,* pp. 1–94.

"Zapiski novgorodskogo dvorianina Petra Nikiforovicha Krekshina." In Sakharov, ed. *Zapiski russkikh liudei,* pp. 1–128.

Zapiski Otdela rukopisei GBL. 50 vols. Moscow, 1938–.

Zapiski Otdeleniia russkoi i slavianskoi arkheologii Imperatorskogo russkogo arkheologicheskogo obshchestva. 13 vols. St. Petersburg, 1851–1918.

"Zapiski Sil'vestra Medvedeva." In Sakharov, ed. *Zapiski russkikh liudei,* pp. 1–62.

"Zapiski zhizni Neronova." In *Materialy,* 1: 134–66.

Zapozhnikov, D., ed. *Pis'ma vostochnykh ierarkhov.* Simbirsk, 1898.

Zdravosmyslov, K. Ia. *Arkhiv i biblioteka Sviateishogo Sinoda i konsistorskie arkhivy.* St. Petersburg, 1906.

Zenkovsky, S. A. "Der Mönch Epifanii und die Entstehung der altrussischen Autobiographie." *Welt der Slawen* 1 (1956): 276–92.

———. "The Old Believer Avvakum: His Role in Russian Literature." *Indiana Slavic Studies* 1 (1956): 1–51.

———. "The Ideological World of the Denisov Brothers." *Harvard Slavic Studies* 3 (1957): 49–66.

———. "The Russian Church Schism: Its Background and Repercussions." *The Russian Review* 16 (1957): 37–58.

———. *Russkoe staroobriadchestvo. Dukhovnye dvizheniia semnadtsatogo veka.* Vol. 21 of *Forum Slavicum.* Ed. D. Tschizewskij. München. 1970.

Zernova, A. S. *Knigi kirillovskoi pechati, izdannye v Moskve v XVI–XVII vekakh.* Moscow, 1958.

Zguta, R. *Russian Minstrels. A History of the Skomorokhi.* Oxford, 1978.

"Zhitie Grigoriia Neronova, sostavlennoe posle ego smerti." In *Materialy,* 1: 243–305.

Zhitie preosviashchenneishogo Ilariona mitropolita suzdal'skogo, byvshogo Florishchevoi pustyni pervogo stroitelia. Kazan', 1868.

Zhivov, V. M. and M. B. Pliukhanova, eds. *Pustoozerskaia proza. Protopop Avvakum, inok Epifanii, pop Lazar', d'iakon Fedor.* Moscow, 1989.

Zhuravlev, A. I. *Polnoe istoricheskoe izvestie o drevnikh strigol'nikakh i novykh raskol'nikakh tak nazyvaemykh staroobriadtsakh.* St. Petersburg, 1890.

Zimin, A. A. *I. S. Peresvetov i ego sovremenniki; ocherki po istorii russkoi obshchestvenno-politicheskoi mysli serediny XVI veka.* Moscow, 1958.

Library of Congress Cataloging-in-Publication Data

Michels, Georg Bernhard.
    At war with the church : religious dissent in seventeenth-century
  Russia / Georg Bernhard Michels.
        p.   cm
    Includes bibliographical references (p.   ) and index.
    ISBN 0-8047-3358-9 (cloth : alk. paper)
    1. Russkaia pravoslavnaia tserkov'--History--17th century.
  2. Dissenters, Religious -- Russia -- History -- 17th century. 3. Russia-
  - Church history -- 17th century.   I. Title.
  BX599.M53   1999
  281.9'47'09032--dc21   98-48248

This book is printed on acid-free, recycled paper.

Original printing 1999
Last figure below indicates year of this printing:

08 07 06 05 04 03 02 01 00 99

Typeset by Harrison Shaffer in 10/13 ITC Galliard.